Pandemic and Narration

Covid-19 Narratives in Latin America

Edited by

Andrea Espinoza Carvajal
University of Exeter

Luis Medina Cordova
University of Birmingham

Series in Politics

Copyright © 2025 by the Authors.

All rights reserved. No part of this publication may be reproduced, stored in a retrieval system, or transmitted in any form or by any means, electronic, mechanical, photocopying, recording, or otherwise, without the prior permission of Vernon Art and Science Inc.

www.vernonpress.com

In the Americas:
Vernon Press
1000 N West Street, Suite 1200
Wilmington, Delaware, 19801
United States

In the rest of the world:
Vernon Press
C/Sancti Espiritu 17,
Malaga, 29006
Spain

Series in Politics

Library of Congress Control Number: 2023950777

ISBN: 979-8-8819-0166-0

Also available: 978-1-64889-821-1 [Hardback]; 979-8-8819-0028-1 [PDF, E-Book]

Product and company names mentioned in this work are the trademarks of their respective owners. While every care has been taken in preparing this work, neither the authors nor Vernon Art and Science Inc. may be held responsible for any loss or damage caused or alleged to be caused directly or indirectly by the information contained in it.

Every effort has been made to trace all copyright holders, but if any have been inadvertently overlooked the publisher will be pleased to include any necessary credits in any subsequent reprint or edition.

Cover design by Vernon Press. Cover image: Melisa Mejía Alarcón, Untitled Artwork 9.

This book is dedicated to our families and friends in Latin America. We thank you for all the videocalls and the love we shared while self-isolating half a world away.

Table of Contents

	List of Acronyms	ix
	About the Authors	xi
	Introduction	xvii
	Andrea Espinoza Carvajal *University of Exeter*	
	Luis Medina Cordova *University of Birmingham*	
Chapter 1	**¿La Vida Volverá?**	1
	Affect in Musicians' Narrations of the Pandemic in Chile	
	Eunice Rojas *Furman University*	
	Daniel Sarkela *University of Florida*	
Chapter 2	**Putting Eggs in One Basket**	17
	Political Discourse and Action During the Covid-19 Vaccination Rollout in Chile	
	Kelly Bauer *George Washington University*	
	Claudio Villalobos Dintrans *Independent Researcher*	
	Pablo Villalobos Dintrans *Millennium Institute for Care Research*	
Chapter 3	**Covid-19, Human Rights and Denialism in Brazil**	41
	How has Former President Jair Bolsonaro Adopted a Denialist Rhetoric to Covid-19, Early Treatment and the Use of Vaccines?	
	Ulisses Terto Neto *Goiás State University, UEG, Brazil*	

Caio Augusto Guimarães de Oliveira
Federal University of Goiás, UFG, Brazil

Luciano Rodrigues Castro
Federal University of Goiás, UFG, Brazil

Ana Paula de Castro Neves
Federal University of Goiás, UFG, Brazil

Chapter 4	**"Monstruos" and "Mujeres Callejeras"**	73

Covid-19, Gender-based Violence and Discourses of Blame in Peru

Saskia Zielińska
King's College London

Chapter 5	**Aborting in Isolation**	91

Testimonial Narratives, Affect and Feminist Political Identities in Covid-19 Argentina

Lea Happ
King's College London

Chapter 6	**When Community Utopias Neutralise Biomedical Morals**	111

The Poetry of Covid-19 in Peru and Chile

Daniel A. Romero Suárez
Pontificia Universidad Católica del Perú

Chapter 7	**Pasajeras**	135

A Lockdown Anthology as Female Solidarity Across Borders

Katie Brown
University of Exeter

Chapter 8	**Nothing is Normal, Everything is Normal**	155

Disruption and Continuity in Guayaquil's Pandemic Experience

Andrea Espinoza Carvajal
University of Exeter

Luis Medina Cordova
University of Birmingham

Chapter 9	**The End of The World**	169
	Decoding the Ideological Framework of Latin American Pandemic Narrative Today	
	Barbara Ann French *Germanna Community College*	
Chapter 10	**Costa Rica Trabaja y Se Cuida**	191
	Oral Historical Reflections on Pandemic Inequities	
	Carmen Coury *Southern Connecticut State University*	
Chapter 11	**The Collective Narratives of Covid-19 in Guatemala**	217
	The State, The Church, The People	
	Trudy Mercadal *Independent Researcher*	
	Index	245

List of Acronyms

ANVISA	Health Regulatory Agency, Brazil
CAVEI	Comité Asesor en Vacunas e Inmunizaciones, Chile
CCSS	Caja Costarricense de Seguro Social, Costa Rica
CDA	Critical Discourse Analysis
CEM	Centros de Emergencia Mujer, Peru
COE	Comité de Operaciones de Emergencia, Ecuador
CPC	Confederación de la Producción y del Comercio, Chile
ENDES	Encuesta Demográfica y de Salud Familiar, Peru
FDA	Food and Drug Administration, US
GBV	Gender-Based Violence
ICU	Intensive Care Unit
ILE	Interrupción Legal del Embarazo
IMF	International Monetary Fund
INEC	Instituto Nacional de Estadística y Censos, Ecuador
IVE	Interrupción Voluntaria del Embarazo
LASA	Latin American Studies Association, US
MAGA	Ministry of Agriculture, Guatemala
MEP	Ministerio de Educación, Costa Rica
MIMP	Ministerio de la Mujer y Poblaciones Vulnerables, Peru
Minsal	Ministerio de Salud, Chile
MSP	Ministerio de Salud Pública, Ecuador
NeMLA	Northeast Modern Languages Association, US
PCI	Parliamentary Commission of Inquiry, Brazil

PUC	Pontificia Universidad Católica, Chile
SenRed	Socorristas en Red, Argentina
Seremi	Secretarías Regionales Ministeriales, Chile
STF	Supreme Federal Court, Brazil
UNESCO	United Nations Educational, Scientific and Cultural Organization
UNICEF	United Nations International Children's Emergency Fund
USAID	US Agency for International Development
WHO	World Health Organisation

About the Authors

Andrea Espinoza Carvajal

Andrea Espinoza Carvajal is a postdoctoral fellow at the University of Exeter. She specialises in violence against women in Latin America, particularly in Ecuador and the Andean region. Her work focuses on how women react, adapt, and/or normalise behaviours to survive, endure or disrupt hierarchical and subordinative power structures. Her research follows a feminist and decolonial epistemology and relies on ethnographic and arts-based research methods. She holds an MSc in Latin American Development and a PhD in Gender and Development from King's College London. She has worked as Lecturer in International Relations and Gender Education at King's College London's Department of War Studies. In 2022, she joined the "Connecting Three Worlds: Socialism, Medicine and Global Health After World War II" research team at the University of Exeter.

Luis Medina Cordova

Luis Medina Cordova is Lecturer in Modern Languages at the University of Birmingham. He specialises in contemporary Ecuadorian and Latin American literature. After being awarded a PhD in Latin American Studies by King's College London in 2020, he has held teaching positions at King's College London and the University of Manchester. He joined the University of Birmingham in 2021, the same year in which he received the Association of Hispanists of Great Britain & Ireland Publication Prize. His monograph, *Imagining Ecuador*, published in 2022 by Tamesis Books (Boydell & Brewer), explores contemporary Ecuadorian fiction, its connections with economic phenomena and its impacts on World Literature. His latest research project, funded by the British Academy, focuses on identifying and archiving literary responses to Covid-19 in Spanish-speaking Latin America.

Eunice Rojas

Eunice Rojas is the Herman N. Hipp Professor of Modern Languages and Literatures at Furman University where she also serves as Chair of the Interdisciplinary Minor in Latin American and Latinx Studies. She is the author of *Gringos Get Rich: Anti-Americanism in Chilean Music* and *Spaces of Madness: Insane Asylums in Argentine Narrative*, and she is the co-editor of *Sounds of Resistance: The Role of Music in Multicultural Activism*. She studies contemporary

Latin American, and particularly Southern Cone, literature and music dealing with discourses of political, social, or cultural resistance to oppression.

Daniel Sarkela

Daniel Sarkela is a graduate student at the University of Florida, where he is pursuing concurrent Master's degrees in Latin American studies and classical guitar performance. His research interest is the intersection of music and politics in Latin America, and his thesis is an examination of how indigenous Kichwa music influenced protest songs originating from the 2019 *paro nacional* in Ecuador. Maintaining an active concert career, Daniel incorporates his ethnomusicological studies into his performances

Kelly Bauer

Kelly Bauer is an Associate Professor of Political Science at George Washington University and a member of the Red De Politólogas – #NoSinMujeres. Her research explores identity and development politics in Latin America. She is the author of *Negotiating Autonomy: Mapuche Territorial Demands and Chilean Land Policy*, which analyses how Chilean bureaucrats navigates extending elite and neoliberal governance and citizenship through Indigenous land policy in post-Pinochet Chile. She also researches politics of knowledge, migration politics, and teaching and learning pedagogy.

Claudio Villalobos Dintrans

Claudio Villalobos Dintrans has a BS in Biological Sciences from the Pontificia Universidad Católica de Chile and a PhD in Pharmacology from Wayne State University. He is currently a Health Program Specialist at National Institute of Neurological Disorders and Stroke (NINDS) in the United States National Institutes of Health, after holding positions at PPD/Thermo Fisher Scientific, Nebraska Wesleyan University, University of California Los Angeles, and Universidad de Chile. His research on the neuronal mechanisms of decision-making using rodent models is most recently published in Cell Reports and Frontiers in Neural Circuits, and he also writes about the politics of research funding and diversity in STEM.

Pablo Villalobos Dintrans

Pablo Villalobos Dintrans holds a BA in economics and business, as well as a master's in economics and public policy from the Pontificia Universidad Católica de Chile. He also holds an MA in economics from Boston University and received his doctoral degree in public health (DrPH) from the Harvard T.H. Chan School of Public Health. Currently, he works as a consultant for local and international organizations in areas such as health policy, health financing, health systems, population aging, and long-term care. He is a member of the Millennium Institute for Care Research (MICARE) and the Global Network of Long-Term Care (GNLTC) of the World Health Organization.

Ulisses Terto Neto

Terto Neto is a human rights lawyer and law professor at Goiás State University (UEG, Brazil). He holds a PhD in Law from the University of Aberdeen (Scotland, United Kingdom) and a Master's Degree in Public Policies from the Federal University of Maranhão (UFMA, Brazil). Terto Neto has developed his career in human rights, advising social movements and NGOs. He has published articles on law and human rights defenders, human rights and access to justice and also two books *The Legal Aid Public Policy: The Legal Aid Office in the State of Maranhão as a Political Request of the Popular and Democratic Camp (Juruá, 2010)* and *Protecting Human Rights Defenders in Latin America: A Legal and Socio-Political Analysis of Brazil (Palgrave Macmillan, 2018)*. In recent years, Terto Neto has been involved either as a researcher or as a lawyer in the politics of human rights in Latin America.

Caio Augusto Guimarães de Oliveira

Oliveira holds a Master's Degree in Human Rights from the Interdisciplinary Postgraduate Program in Human Rights (PPGIDH) at the Federal University of Goiás (UFG, Brazil), and a Bachelor's degree in International Relations from the Federal University of Pampa (UNIPAMPA, Brazil).

Luciano Rodrigues Castro

Castro holds a Master's Degree in Human Rights and is currently a PhD applicant in the Interdisciplinary Postgraduate Program in Human Rights (PPGIDH) at the Federal University of Goiás (UFG, Brazil). His work is interdisciplinary, usually in the fields of International Relations, International Law and Social Sciences.

Ana Paula de Castro Neves

Castro Neves holds a Master's Degree in Human Rights and is currently a PhD applicant in the Interdisciplinary Postgraduate Program in Human Rights (PPGIDH) at the Federal University of Goiás (UFG, Brazil).

Saskia Zielińska

Saskia completed her PhD at the Department of International Development at King's College London, where she investigated adolescent pregnancy in Ayacucho,

Peru, using a framework of multi-sided violence. She holds a post-doctoral research fellowship on the AHRC-funded Adolescent Parenthoods in Latin America project, led by Dr Rebecca Ogden at the University of Sheffield, which looks at the experiences of adolescent pregnancy and motherhood in Cuba, Colombia, and Mexico. She also teaches more broadly on political economy and sociology of development at King's College London and the School of Oriental and African Studies (SOAS). She is also a founding member of the editorial collective of the online publication *Feminist Perspectives*. Saskia has an MSc in Development Studies from SOAS and an MPhil in Latin American Studies from the University of Oxford.

Lea Happ

Lea Happ is a doctoral candidate at King's College London, based at the Department of Global Health and Social Medicine. Her doctoral research explores pharmaceutical abortion, feminist activist thought and practices, and constructions of political subjectivities in post-legalisation Argentina. Her work sits at the intersection of feminist political theory, reproductive sociology, and science and technology studies. She is a member of the editorial collective of the online publication *Feminist Perspectives* and holds an MSc in Gender, Development, and Globalisation from the London School of Economics, as well as a BA in Politics and International Relations from the University of Cambridge.

Daniel A. Romero Suárez

Daniel A. Romero Suárez (PhD, Vanderbilt University) is Professor of Literature at the Pontificia Universidad Católica del Perú (PUCP). His current research agenda focuses on the intersections among medicine, literature, and collective memory. Daniel has published articles and book chapters on the characteristics of poetry of disease. His current work also gravitates around terminal language in poetry, eco-fiction in the Southern Cone, and the new possibilities of analysis offered by digital humanities.

Katie Brown

Katie Brown is Senior Lecturer in Latin American Studies at the University of Exeter. She specializes in contemporary Latin American culture, with a particular focus on Venezuela. Her main research interests are the circulation of people (travel, migration and exile) and of texts (publishing, translation and reception). She also researches and teaches about cultural responses to politics in the 20th and 21st century. She is the author of *Writing and the Revolution: Venezuelan Metafiction (2004-2012)* (Liverpool University Press, 2019) and co-editor of *Crude Words: Contemporary Writing from Venezuela* (Ragpicker Press,

2016) and *Escribir afuera: Cuentos de intemperies y querencia*s (Kálathos, 2021). Her translation of *Desde la salvajada* (From Savagery) by Alejandra Banca will be published by Selkies House in 2024.

Barbara Ann French

Barbara French holds a PhD in Hispanic Literature from El Colegio de México. Her research primarily focuses on Vice Regal narrative produced in New Spain during the seventeenth century and how the evolution of literary modules has shaped contemporary prose. After being awarded her PhD in 2019, she received the ACLS/ Mellon Community College Fellowship for her book project "Narrating Hope", which explores the ideological frameworks that shaped the depiction of hope in prose narrative during time of epidemiological outbreak in colonial Mexico. Her current contribution to this volume was also a product of the research conducted for the fellowship.

Carmen Coury

Carmen Coury is an Associate Professor of Latin American History at Southern Connecticut State University, where she teaches courses on Colonial and Modern Latin American history. She earned her PhD in History from Yale University. Her research is guided by the view that nation-building is not an exclusively top-down process, but that national narratives and identities are constantly being negotiated and reinterpreted on the ground. Her first book, *The Saints of Progress: A History of Coffee, Migration, and Costa Rican National Identity*, was published by the University of Alabama Press in 2019. This work narrates the development of the Tarrazú Valley, a historically remote —though internationally celebrated— coffee-growing region in Costa Rica, to grapple with the state-making process from the periphery. In particular, this book deconstructs Costa Rica's exceptionalist mythology, which imagines Costa Rica as a "white", democratic, non-violent, and egalitarian republic.

Trudy Mercadal

Trudy Mercadal holds a BA in International Relations and an MA in Liberal Arts, from Barry University in Florida, as well as a MA in Communications and a PhD in Comparative Studies from Florida Atlantic University. After 20 years of teaching in undergraduate and graduate programs, she moved to Guatemala to work in the field of human rights and international cooperation. Her current research interests are historic memory and violence in post-conflict societies. She also works in a reading comprehension and critical thinking program she developed in Movimiento de Jóvenes de la Calle, an organization for unhoused youth, and as a researcher for Territorios Clínicos de la Memoria, Argentina, on postwar trials and testimony.

Introduction

Andrea Espinoza Carvajal
University of Exeter

Luis Medina Cordova
University of Birmingham

When the Covid-19 pandemic started in early 2020, we —the editors of this volume— were more than 9200 kilometres away from our family homes. As Ecuadorian scholars living and working in the UK, we followed the spread of the virus in Latin America as closely as in the country where we reside. We devoured every bit of information we could find coming from *there*, never forgetting that we were *here* instead. In our minds, *there* meant a familiar world that we could only be told about by our relatives, friends, the news and social media. Their stories, first-hand accounts, reports and updates on how the health crisis unfolded in Ecuador merged with our own pandemic experience in London. Words about isolation, self-distancing, xenophobia, violence, illness and death shaped the world our loved ones inhabited and resonated with us, creating a feeling of companionship and knitting a sense of distanced commonality. We realised that we never understood more clearly or felt so vividly that —as Michel Foucault concluded in reading Jorge Luis Borges— "before the imminence of death, language rushes forth" (54). Our experience suggested that we could tweak Foucault's idea to fit the pandemic context we survived: in the Covid-19 crisis, narrative rushed forth. Foregrounding the role of narrative in the making sense of a devastating health crisis motivates and shapes this volume.

This collection of essays emerges by shedding light on the fact that, as the SARS-CoV-2 virus spread, infecting and killing millions worldwide, everyday life continued to be told across Latin America. That is, it continued to be narrated. Narrating was not only a form of sharing the details of a new experience but also a way of constructing a novel reality. Every story, reflection and description acted as a thread weaving factual, fictional or hybrid versions of an unfolding crisis. And in a world full of uncertainty, narrative also filled the gaps. While pandemics are not new to the history of humanity, Covid-19 affected a hyperconnected world (Medina Cordova, "Microcuentos" 40) where accounts about the virus's origin, symptoms and characteristics could travel faster than the virus itself. For many, first came the story and then came the health crisis.

At the early stages of the pandemic —when there was little knowledge about an effective treatment, a shortage of protective equipment, no vaccines had been developed and it was uncertain how fast a successful one could be produced and distributed— misinformation thrived in social media; misinformation often led to fear and panic, evoking negative emotions, which, in turn, contributed to the spread of the virus (Oyeyemi et al. 455, 459).

By 2020, Latin Americans had no fresh memory of a virus spreading so fast, affecting so many people and causing so many hospitalisations. Some of them may have heard stories about infectious disease epidemics like the Ebola outbreak affecting West Africa (2014-2016) or witnessed Zika spreading in the Americas and the Pacific region (2014-2017). Others may have remembered the pain of the HIV/AIDS epidemic in the 1980s or feared the much more recent Influenza A (H1N1) outbreak in 2009. However, Covid-19 had a different timeline and reach. It took only three months to pass from a "pneumonia of unknown cause" reported in Wuhan in the Hubei Province, China, in December 2019 to the moment when the World Health Organisation (WHO) declared a pandemic in March 2020.

Yet despite its unique nature, the Covid-19 crisis also resonated with crises past. Valero and Zárate argue that learning from previous epidemics like the so-called Spanish flu in 1918, the development of tuberculosis across the twentieth century and cholera in the 1990s contribute to understanding the effects of a health crisis from social, economic and cultural perspectives (2). Greene and Vargha add that by recounting the narratives of past pandemics, historians contribute to comprehending the dynamic of a crisis. Historical narratives provide examples of how pandemics behave, with some of them acting, for example, as "a bag of popcorn popping in the microwave", where the tempo of visible case-events begins slowly, escalates to a frenetic peak, and then recedes to a point where it is eventually contained (Greene and Vargha). Nonetheless, being a fraction of the information circulating on the news cycles and in social media during the pandemic, historical precedents gave little comfort to people searching for certainty in the present. Looking at the past might have offered ideas and expectations about what was happening and what could happen. However, evidence-based discourses had to compete with rumours and conspiracy theories spreading in real time, leaving people overflown with personal and collective, truthful and fictional stories.

We put together *Pandemic and Narration* to help understand what happened in Latin America during the health crisis. However, the reach of our contribution is not limited to the region—we hope to impact the global record of the pandemic by becoming a point of reference for thinking about Covid-19 in a light that deviates from the quantitative approaches that dominated ways of reflecting about the virus. We propose to see narrative as a departing point to have a closer look at the experiences of people enduring their pandemic lives, societies struggling with violence and inequality and political discourses trying to explain the unravelling of the state and its health system. Our focus is on personal and collective stories shared across different media, including the news and political discourses, but also music, poems, short stories and hybrid forms of telling. We consider the Covid-19 crisis a crucial moment when narrative demonstrated its capacity to explain, create and reconcile the realities that unfolded after the arrival of the virus. In a context of lockdown where people could not experience life as before, were threatened by an invisible virus and found themselves constrained by the dearth of information about the nature of the disease it caused, narrative emerged to co-opt people's attention.

Through the voices of those in positions of power, including the former presidents Jair Bolsonaro (Brazil) and Donald Trump (US), denialist narratives influenced policies and social attitudes towards the virus (Cueto et al. 4). Conspiracy theories created xenophobia towards Asian communities (*Covid-19 Fueling Anti-Asian Racism*; Huang et al. 683). People wishing to contribute with messages of hope by calling home a safe space made invisible the horrors of violence against women within households (Al-Ali 336–337; Peterman et al. 15). At the same time, voices protesting inequality and systemic violence emerged to denounce old and new injustices (Donoso et al. 344). Messages of care and solidarity circulated worldwide, shattering cultural and linguistic barriers. Everyday struggles burst into stories to make sense of the new world and share unique experiences defining it.

Making sense of the new reality was a priority for people enduring the health crisis, as disruption was not only located in changes such as the lockdowns or the use of face-covering but in the sense of time itself. Writing shortly after the declaration of Covid-19 as a pandemic, Jordheim et al. argued that coronavirus altered the order of time: "the present moves faster, the past seems further removed, and the future appears completely unpredictable". The best people could do to reorient themselves, the authors suggested, was to counteract the feeling of a world out of sync by creating "new rhythms, new shared times" through gestures like applauding healthcare workers from balconies at collectively agreed times. In this volume, we propose to see individual and shared narratives as elements that vitally contributed to redrawing the world and helped people to sync with the new rhythms of life.

The essays gathered here analyse narrative in literary and non-literary responses to Covid-19 in Latin America. We aim to help build a comprehensive understanding of the experience by exploring narratives produced in different circumstances across the region. Therefore, this volume assembles chapters looking at the news, government reports, political speeches, NGO communications and social media. These resources provide a window into narratives meant to be consumed collectively and whose goals ranged from (dis)informing, persuading, agitating and controlling to calming and reassuring. A different type of narrative production emerged from the arts, as evidenced by other essays also available here. Accounts from literature and music offer more intimate perspectives, sharing personal and reflective views of what happened in countries like Peru or Ecuador, thereby enabling contextually specific understanding of what happened in the world in the time of Covid-19.

Narrative and Affect

The chapters following this introduction broadly coincide on two main standpoints to approach the Covid-19 crisis: on the one hand, understanding narrative as essential to human beings, building on Fisher's "narrative paradigm"; and on the other, acknowledging affect and emotion as powerful elements to relate, communicate and interact during a time of crisis, in line with Gibbs' work on affect theory and the ubiquity of contagion in the contemporary world ("After Affect" 186). On narrative, Fisher reminds us that different root metaphors have been put forth to represent the essential nature of human beings: Homo Faber, Homo Economicus, Homo Politicus and Homo Sociologicus. To that list, he proposes the incorporation of Homo Narrans by arguing that the idea of human beings as storytellers "holds that symbols are created and communicated ultimately as stories meant to give order to human experience and to induce others to dwell in them in order to establish ways of living in common" (63). This paradigm resonates with the manifold ways contributors to this volume engage with narrative as an emerging thread weaving a new type of life. Moreover, Fisher proposes that narrations are "historical as well as situational" (58) and stories or accounts compete to satisfy the demands of narrative probability and narrative fidelity. The demand for stories explaining the world alongside the existence of conflicting accounts was a given in the first months of the Covid-19 pandemic, as the research in this volume shows. Academics, scientists, politicians and the general public consistently tried to draw pictures of what was happening by narrating it.

As mentioned above, in a crisis, narrative rushes forth. Even before people started to explain what living during the Covid-19 pandemic meant, audiences rushed to engage with pandemic fiction. In March 2020, news outlets reported a surge in demand for movies and books about pandemics. Steven Soderbergh's film *Contagion* (2011) became the second-most popular movie on iTunes in the US (Lindahl), and Albert Camus' novel *La Peste* (1947) sold 2,156 times in the UK, almost ten times more than in February 2019 (Willsher). Song and Fergnani explain that in the early stages of the pandemic, artistic productions reflected fears of infectious disease outbreaks and contributed to envisioning where and how they may occur, their consequences and complexities (11). Elements like the plot of the stories having three phases —emergence, transmission and termination— soothed people's unease as they appeared to provide an insight into what was happening in the real world (9).

Affect theory also underpins this project. As much as stories bind us, we similarly understand how fear, anger and hope resonated between individuals and groups in the crisis. Building on Tomkins's work, Gibbs explains that affect is part of a larger cognitive system that does not operate on the command-control principles usually assumed in discussions of cognition but rather as a series of distributed functions, "which include affect, sensory perception and memory" ("Contagious Feelings"). In that sense, Gibbs continues, affect calls forth ideas and attitudes with which it has become associated in the individual's inner world. However, this does not mean that affect is restricted to the individual. After all, Tomkins reminds us that "no affect is an island" (216). Gibbs argues that bodies can catch feelings as easily as they catch fire (or a virus): "affect leaps from one body to another, evoking tenderness, inciting shame, igniting rage, exciting fear — in short, communicable affect can inflame nerves and muscles in a conflagration of every conceivable kind of passion" ("Contagious Feelings"). In this light, affect theory provides a reference framework enabling us, first, to see affect as a drive to action emerging from individuals and communities, and second, to recognise affect's power to bind people and connect them with their surroundings.

During the pandemic, creating a narrative —in an art form, as personal storytelling, as bits of information in the news or as a political instrument— was a form of explaining and understanding events unknown. As native Spanish speakers, we started thinking and discussing what it meant to *vivir la pandemia*, to live through the pandemic; that is, not to be distant observers of an unravelling crisis but to be immersed in what was unfolding. Reflecting on living through the pandemic was an exercise to explore what was changing within us and our surroundings. We noticed that our day-to-day was full of stories we told ourselves in intimate, introspective ways and stories we told others that could be similar or very different from the formers. We bring those stories and the act of telling them to the spotlight. Hence, we focus on narrative, which we understand broadly and interdisciplinarily.

We narrate everything; thus, narrative is everywhere, and we all engage in it. Narrative, Roland Barthes famously argued when discussing its universality, comes in an infinite variety of forms and "it is present at all times, in all places, in all societies; indeed narrative starts with the very history of mankind; there is not, there has never been anywhere, any people without narrative; all classes all human groups, have their stories" (237). Given its presence in almost all human discourse, narrative certainly played a role in what is arguably the biggest story of the twenty-first century (so far, at least): the Covid-19 pandemic, which killed more than six million people in little more than two years and rapidly became a major global challenge.

The gods send disasters to people, Foucault remarked by reflecting on Homer's epics, so that people can tell of them (53). In Latin America, there is so much to be told about Covid-19. People and communities in the region survived and endured death, loss and grief. Yet, at the same time, they gathered strength from solidarity and witnessed the materialisation of continued yet renewed frustrations about social injustice and inequality. This edited collection engages with the narratives of the crisis; narratives created to inform, make sense, give testimony, denounce, manipulate, support or heal. We believe that our intimate and shared realities are constructed by the stories we create, consume, share and interiorise to make our own. After all, as narrative theorists have taught us, "we do not have any mental record of who we are until narrative is present as a kind of armature, giving shape to that record" (Abbott 3). Our very definition as human beings, Peter Brooks argues, "is very much bound up with the stories we tell about our own lives and the world in which we live" (19). Narrative, therefore, becomes our frame and window to explore an uncertain (pandemic) world.

Charles Rosenberg describes epidemics as social phenomenon and points out how they have a dramaturgic form. Epidemics, Rosenberg notes, "start at a moment in time, proceed on a stage limited in space and duration, follow a plot line of increasing and revelatory tension, move to a crisis of individual and collective character" (3). Part of accepting the existence of an epidemic is "the creation of a framework within which its dismaying arbitrariness may be managed. Collective agreement on that explanatory framework may be seen as the inevitable second stage in any epidemic" (5). Negotiating that framework requires creating and sharing stories.

Sharing stories, however, is a double-edged sword. Narrative contributes to making sense of reality, healing and memory-building at individual and collective levels. Nevertheless, it could also be a weapon of disinformation, manipulation and fearmongering. Inquiring into narrative signifies bringing together perspectives that look at many different phenomena unified by a shared focus on what has been said about Covid-19. We mean this in a broad sense. That is, the contributors of this collection build on humanities and the social sciences approaches not only to reflect on how the pandemic has been discussed or represented in stories specifically about it; they also explore how the virus found its way to discourses across all aspects of the life experience of society. Narrative, in this sense, refers to literary creation —fictional and non-fictional— that emerged from Latin America's pandemic reality and, at the same time, refers to the communication of political propaganda, vaccination campaigns, feminist demands and community practices born in this context.

Narratives that go beyond literature and circulated as part of political, economic, health and social discourse caught our contributors' attention because they helped shape frameworks to understand, interact with and question the experience of living through and surviving the pandemic.

This volume's focus on narrative provides an alternative source to reflect on Latin America's Covid-19 experience. Alternative to death tolls, infection rates, weekly cases, vaccination counts and the plethora of statistics that illustrated the gravity of the situation in the build-up to, during and after the peak of the crisis. While they are essential to understanding the situation, numbers only tell part of the story. A comprehensive picture of the pandemic can only be achieved when we engage with the stories created and told around the virus. Health is no stranger to narrative, and neither is Latin America, a region whose nations have historically been constructed in the pages of their literature. Building on Doris Sommer's work on Latin America's national romances, Medina Cordova explains that "during the late 1800s and the first half of the twentieth century, after most of the region gained independence from colonial powers, novels became a way to build national imaginaries for the newly created nations" (*Imagining Ecuador* 7). In the early republican years of Latin American countries, writers were often close to the political powers of the time and, in many cases, they were also politicians themselves, serving as presidents, ambassadors or holders of a myriad of public offices; they were often in a position from where the personal views that their writings reflected could become national projects.

In Latin America, therefore, narrative is crucial for understanding, representing, moulding and constructing reality. Furthermore, as Ángel Rama insightfully explained, the "construction" of the region is not only limited to the intellectual production of the elites, but historically, it is a reflection of context, culture and history pushing for "massive efforts of vast societies to construct their symbolic languages" (4). The narratives from the Covid-19 crisis are not foreign to these efforts to find shared elements to make sense of pain, grief, trauma and hope for a different future.

A Narrative Lens

This volume foregrounds the value of narratives to enrich the understanding of our contemporary experience. Following an interpretivist and qualitative approach, we move away from objective and dispassionate perspectives to fully embrace how experience is subjective, multiple and often contradictory. Patterson and Monroe highlight that narrative requires agency, a viewpoint and an order created by the narrator; in that sense, narrative cannot be voiceless or contextless as "the speakers create the context to be analysed by drawing in what they consider relevant cultural influences" (316). Narrative is thus vital to grasp social crises and their aftermath. In this volume, our contributors highlight how civil society responded to the pandemic but also call attention to how politicians used narrative to manipulate and evade responsibilities. Analysing Covid-19 records is a mechanism for understanding community experiences, politics and policies because:

> Humans not only tell stories to evoke emotion, but we also make arguments based on evidence to support our viewpoints. Through this same narrative construction process, policy actors build stories which they use to inform, influence, and evaluate policies. All policy narratives presumably have some goal of influencing policy outcomes or decisions (Crow and Jones 233).

Not only narratologists, literary and Cultural Studies scholars but also behavioural and cognitive scientists as well as economists, among others, have reflected upon the value of narrative, pointing to its role in providing unique perspectives and contextual insight. Behavioural and cognitive scientists, for example, have studied the relationship between narrative and health for decades, often asking if good stories can make people healthier. In this area, Ramírez-Esparza and Pennebaker have discussed the "appeal" of narrative for psychology and psychotherapy research, arguing that "in our gut, we all 'know' that constructing good stories is emotionally healthy" (218). Although they alert about the need to define what constitutes narrative, discern how it is causally linked to wellbeing and determine its relevance to therapeutic processes both within and between cultures, their principle is that writing stories about emotional upheavals results in improved physical and mental health "at least at the aggregate level" (218). If, as Ramírez-Esparza and Pennebaker posit, linguistic features like using positive emotion words can be healing, how should we regard language choices to describe the SARS-CoV-2 virus? One prominent example, of course, is the war lexicon that public health officials, physicians, politicians and the press relied on for depicting the "fight" against Covid-19 worldwide. The contributors to this volume explore their voices and those of the communities they addressed to reveal what we can learn from their selection of words that cannot be learnt otherwise.

Tropes about the economy were another profoundly influential driver of discourse during the health emergency. And economics, many scholars have demonstrated, can be approached through narrative too. In the 1990s, the New Economic Criticism helped to make visible an "emerging body of literary and cultural criticism founded upon economic paradigms, models and tropes" (Osteen and Woodmansee 2), consciously attempting to bridge disciplines as far apart as literary and economic theory. More recently, Robert J. Shiller has argued in favour of studying "narrative economics", which proposes that stories, particularly those that "go viral", can drive major economic events. Although Shiller's book was originally published in 2019, right before the start of the pandemic, his vocabulary is remarkably similar to that many of us use to talk about coronavirus. With the term "narrative economics", he refers to the "word-of-mouth contagion of ideas in the form of stories" and "the efforts that people make to generate new contagious stories or to make stories more contagious" (xvii). Shiller's point is that some stories, like viruses, can jump from mouth to mouth so notoriously that they become capable of provoking significant impacts on economic behaviour. His original examples of economic narratives, contagious stories that could change how people make economic decisions, include the rise of Bitcoin. Yet the paperback edition of Shiller's book, released in 2020, already identifies the Covid-19 pandemic as a source of narratives that will have economic effects over time. With this book, we hope to contribute to unpacking such narratives in Latin America.

Our work dialogues with scholarship concerned with interrogating language to help elucidate the multi-layered and uneven impacts of Covid-19 on peoples, communities and the world. In this area, a modern linguist like Catherine Boyle explains that "we know from our literary, cultural, linguist and historical research that words like war, conflict, contagion, invasion, fear, sanity and cleansing inhabit the ways in which we articulate our responses —collective and subjective— to moments of crisis" ("Worldmaking in the Time of Covid-19"). Having a clear understanding of these articulations is vital in volatile geopolitical situations like the pandemic, when misunderstanding, xenophobia and violence became global currency in a world where global, however, "does not in any way signify equality in experience" (Boyle, "Poor Connection" 180).

This volume is also in conversation with research analysing how writers and artists provided testimonies and reflections on their Covid-19 experiences while they were living them alongside their audiences. We echo Medina Cordova's call for paying attention to how literary responses to the virus form a body of writing whose analysis "can afford us a unique opportunity for contextually understanding what drove the transformations we are seeing now, as well as the transformations we are yet to witness" ("Narrating a Global Crisis" 111). Some of our contributors interrogate such a body of writing to reveal alternative ways of seeing and understanding the virus and uncover what it can tell us about what comes after once the pandemic is entirely over. In this sense, our work resonates with the ideas put forward by the Pandemic Fictions Research Group, whose members have discussed how the crisis discourse of the pandemic permeated into fictional productions and constituted a new corpus that they named "Corona Fictions". Corona Fictions, the group remarks, "not only distil the importance of human connection, touch, and freedom to move outside, but also indicate the willingness for social change after the lockdown" (Pandemic Fictions Research Group 336).

The essays in this collection reveal social change once the virus is at bay as a theme traversing Covid-19 narratives in Latin America. How the need for social change was narrated during the crisis and how governments and other institutions communicated with the communities that demanded it is within the scope of our inquiry. Therefore, we are also in dialogue with research that examined how governments deployed strategic messages to further their political agendas as the coronavirus outbreak intensified. In this area, Espinoza Carvajal has brought attention to how the Ecuadorian government heavily featured the word "gender" in its campaigns to combat violence against women during lockdowns but failed to support victims of abuse adequately (Espinoza Carvajal 9). The government's words, she argues, amount to very little if the state is unprepared for meaningful intervention. In the essays that follow, in contrast, words are capable of speaking louder than actions. The contributors to this volume demonstrate that narrative played a critical in shaping our experience of the pandemic.

Covid-19 in Latin America

Latin America was one of the regions most affected by the Covid-19 outbreak. It faced an unmatched catastrophic toll—by March 2022, the region reported approximately 15% of cases and 28% of deaths worldwide (Schwalb et al. 409). This is an exceptionally high percentage considering that the region represents only 8.4% of the world population (*Desigual y letal* 6). The situation became more challenging than elsewhere due to lack of social protection, limited health infrastructure and nearly 60% of informal employment, which made social distancing often impossible to respect (*COVID-19 in Latin America and the Caribbean* 2). The rate of contagion, combined with the lack of infrastructure, contributed to the collapse of health systems in Manaus, Brazil (Ribeiro da Silva and Pena 2) and Guayaquil, Ecuador (León Cabrera and Kurmanaev). In these two cities, images of people queuing outside hospitals, unable to find a bed, became a dramatic portrait of the crisis. The pain of people in Manaus, Guayaquil and other communities across the region was memorialised and circulated worldwide through images of overflowing morgues, mass graves and corpses on the streets.

Understanding the experience of Covid-19 as narrated in Latin America contributes to demystifying phrases blasted when the virus started to circulate, like the assumption that people around the world were enduring the same storm. A localised review of the crisis provides more than a reflection; it contributes to understanding the material and practical meaning of enduring a global health crisis. Yet attention to Latin America has been scarce. Anne-

Introduction xxvii

Emanuelle Birn argues that, in this and other pandemics, the region was "viewed by historians, journalists, and policymakers in the Global North as a hapless victim, collaterality, or curiosity —a colourful, almost fictional, afterthought that is derivative of, secondary to, and irrelevant to the main theatre of action" (355). The perspective criticised by Birn ignores the region's historical understanding of pandemics and how health actors have long engaged in destiny-forging actions based on local and regional knowledge, approaches, and exchanges that have enabled varieties of resistance and solidarity in epidemic and endemic times alike (364).

Knowledge emerging from the region contributes to understanding Latin America's experience in relation to other parts of the world and the particularities within its territory, peoples and communities. Across Latin American countries, Marcos Cueto explains, there were different patterns of governmental response. However, three similarities emerged: negligence in the management of resources, a tendency towards disregarding the life of ageing and racialised populations and political use of the pandemic to attack political opposition (Cueto, 00:23:24–54). Considering the impact of the pandemic on people in the region and around the world, understanding Covid-19 from the narratives that emerged from different voices enduring the crisis is a priority of our analysis of the crisis, the study of the region, and the possibility of learning from a unique experience of endurance and survival.

This edited collection brings together multiple perspectives on what happened during the peak of the crisis in Latin America and how it intersected with long-standing problems within the region. Our contributors tell stories of communities in Chile, Argentina, Guatemala, Mexico, Brazil, Peru, Ecuador, Venezuela and Costa Rica. Their analyses remind us that crises are shaped by history and local context but can also resonate with experiences beyond national borders.

The idea for this volume developed from two virtual panels in 2021 as part of the annual conferences of the Northeast Modern Languages Association and the Latin American Studies Association. The conversations in both spaces — which brought together scholars from Ecuador, Peru, Bolivia, the US and the UK— centred around the need to interrogate the multiple ways in which the pandemic was narrated in Latin America, when lockdowns across the globe had the majority of us confined to our homes. Back then, our goal was to foster interdisciplinary dialogues that contributed to understanding the collective and subjective responses to Covid-19 in a region where the health emergency interacted with structural long-standing frailties. Continuing that spirit of the exchange nurtured in 2021, this volume posits that comprehending the global crises gripping Latin America requires paying attention to the stories crafted and circulated in pandemic times. The essays in the upcoming pages do that precisely.

In Chapter 1, Rojas and Sarkela take us to March 2020, when Chile was in its fifth month of demonstrations against systemic inequality, government corruption, police violence and the lingering vestiges of Pinochet's dictatorship (1973–1990). When Covid-19 arrived, none of the other social problems disappeared. Instead, they overlapped with the health crisis. Before the new and uncertain scenario, artists responded with music. Rojas and Sarkela analyse two songs engaging with the musical tradition of the Chilean New Song, resonating with the emotions and memories of the dictatorship past while also engaging with current feelings of contemporary disenchantment and frustration. Contrasting with the narrative of hope and despair presented by musicians, the government crafted another message, one that could fit their political agenda. In the next chapter, Bauer, Claudio and Pablo Villalobos argue that the Piñera administration described the vaccine rollout as technical and apolitical to advance its political agenda in a context of low approval ratings, ongoing protests and upcoming elections. Using a database of quotes from political, medical and public health experts in Chile, the researchers unpack the creation and deployment of a political discourse that positioned the vaccine rollout as one of technical innovation and efficient trade designed to favour the administration's image.

Brazilians also endured the challenging situation of politicians using their power to craft messages favouring only their political agenda. In Chapter 3, Terto Neto, Guimarães de Oliveira, Rodrigues Castro and Castro Neves eloquently ask one straightforward question: why did Jair Bolsonaro adopt a denialist rhetoric about Covid-19, early treatment and the use of vaccines? They build on Critical Discourse Analysis to explain how the former president's and the government's discourses created an agenda to deconstruct democratic institutions and advance a populist extreme right programme. Moreover, they explain that the discursive representation of the pandemic, social distancing and vaccination were strongly linked to political intentions to delegitimise democracy.

The pandemic fed ongoing political tensions and social unrest. It deepened Latin America's inequality and affected already weakened communities, disproportionally impacting vulnerable groups like immigrants, women and indigenous peoples. Immigrants and other minorities faced barriers "in accessing regular health services due to inadequate information, the absence of culturally appropriate care, or insufficient legal provisions" (Bojorquez et al. 1243). For women, access to reproductive health and support in cases of violence deteriorated. In Chapters 4 and 5, Zielińska and Happ discuss women's positions in Peru and Argentina, respectively. Zielińska examines the variety of patriarchal discourses with regard to gender-based violence during the pandemic in Peru, highlighting how the state contributed to victim-blaming narratives. On the other hand, Happ traces the experience of people who had abortions with the support of feminist activists in Argentina during the first months of the outbreak. Analysing the narratives created by those who experienced abortions, her work proposes, offers a chance to trace the construction of feminist identities in challenging contexts like the Covid-19 crisis.

Narrative could also mean support, guidance and hope. Romero's and Brown's contributions (Chapters 6 and 7) show how what was weakened and broken by the pandemic could be restored by literary creation. Romero argues that in Latin America, a region with a long history of economic precarity, poetry helps build a shared sense of belonging to a collective whole. His work remarks that when the spread of the disease overlaps with racism, inequality and other social injustices, it makes visible fractures within society. Still, it is in that scenario that poetry acts as what represents collective identities and moves beyond fragmenting discourses. Brown finds a similar community-building power in her analysis of *Pasajeras: Antología del cautiverio* (2020), a female compilation bringing together poems, essays, diary entries, reflections and images created during lockdown by 60 Venezuelan women scattered around the world. Her chapter explores the significance of various aspects of *Pasajeras*: creating an all-female anthology in a male-dominated literary culture; countering the isolation not just of the lockdown but of Venezuela's ongoing social and economic crisis; and crossing borders between the physical book and the digital. The anthology suggests that, for the participating writers, creating in the middle of a quarantined reality was a form of salvation.

For many, salvation from the virus was directly connected to adapting to the new life precipitated by the pandemic. Limiting human contact, working from home and wearing face-coverings became common behaviours that were soon recognised as staples of the so-called "new normal" we all had to acknowledge and adapt to. The contradictory meanings of the new normal in Ecuador are interrogated in Chapter 8. Espinoza Carvajal and Medina Cordova reflect on the Covid-19 experience of Guayaquil, the economic capital of the Andean country, to contrast official and non-official narratives about what the new normal conditions of living fully meant in Ecuador. They note that while the Ecuadorian government related the new normal with sanitary measures to cut the transmission chain of the virus, cultural responses reminded us of the everyday violence underlying life in Guayaquil before and during the outbreak, which structures normality, be that old or new.

Stories build frames of reference to decode the world. In Latin America, religious myths discussing sin, death and punishment have been present in the way people talk about the effects of the disease. French's contribution (Chapter 9) looks at the influence of historical prose in the constitution of pandemic narratives today, arguing that the ideological frameworks of epidemic forces of divine destruction and capital sin found in early modern Latin American texts persist in contemporary narratives of the crisis. Focusing on media discourses, she offers examples such as a 2020 news article where a Mexican bishop is quoted suggesting that Covid-19 was divine punishment for abortion, euthanasia and sexual diversity. French posits that "early teachings" laid the foundations for future epidemiological narratives and continue to be used as a lens for understanding world events.

The stories we hear about the pandemic transform how we talk about it. In her work about Costa Rica (Chapter 10), Coury refers to interviews to discuss how narratives integrate into how informants described their pandemic experiences. Narrators expressed their thoughts on how the pandemic impacted their jobs, the broader economy, their understanding of government responsibility and their interpersonal relationships. These oral testimonies, the author explains, encompass many pandemic experiences and perspectives and a salient concern all narrators shared about the widening, deep-rooted socio-economic inequities within Costa Rican society and between the Global North and the Global South. In the final chapter, Mercadal zooms in on the pandemic experience of Guatemala, where historical problems of violence, inequality, poverty and corruption made Covid-19's impact catastrophic. Mercadal's work analyses three public narratives —that of a polarised government, the Church's leadership, and community groups—as they emerged through social and news media to reflect on how the citizenry's trust in the government worsened without efficient planning and transparency.

Conclusion

This collection provides a Latin American perspective to reflect on a global crisis. It highlights the importance of situating knowledge and experience in the bounds of time and space. While the pandemic affected the whole world, not everyone experienced the same inequalities or survived the same circumstances. As our contributors explain, the experience of women in Argentina was not the same as the experience of women in Peru, nor the political tensions in Chile were the same as in Costa Rica or Guatemala. However, even within difference, this volume contributes to thinking about resonance; that is, to see a glimpse of similar structural problems and anxieties that affected the region across different cases—thereby, we open the possibility to see communicating vessels with other experiences in the Global South and provide insight on the world from a regional point of view.

The contributors to this volume stress the pre-pandemic structural problems of the countries studied and how historical and political contexts contributed to the worsening of the health crisis. The crisis generated by the pandemic did not start in a vacuum. It affected communities with long-lasting and normalised forms of social injustice. The pandemic stirred up what looked "normal", contributed to the unrest of vulnerable groups and catalysed public discontent with government and states. In this sense, Covid-19 disclosed overlapping inequalities and built over them. Focusing primarily on the crisis' first two years (2020-2022), this collection opens the possibility of exploring what happened during the early stages of the pandemic and questions what is happening in its aftermath, when the days of people dying outside of hospitals have become a memory for most.

This volume shows how communities pleaded for a different future but also lived the disquiet of foreseeing a future where the normal was a continuity of the pre-pandemic time, with the same old social injustice and discontent. We anticipate that narratives of recovery and restoration will overpower those of pain and struggle, and "normality" will bury again some of the inequalities that shape the catastrophic impact of Covid-19 in Latin America. While we attempted to engage with pandemic experiences across Latin America, our contributors can only analyse evidence from a few places. The focus on narrative, nonetheless, allows us to follow the traces of a somewhat shared experience, narrating the local but connecting with the regional and global experience.

Bibliography

Abbott, H. Porter. *The Cambridge Introduction to Narrative*. Cambridge University Press, 2002.

Al-Ali, Nadje. "Covid-19 and Feminism in the Global South: Challenges, Initiatives and Dilemmas". *European Journal of Women's Studies*, vol. 27, no. 4, 2020, pp. 333–347.

Barthes, Roland. "An Introduction to the Structural Analysis of Narrative". *New Literary History*, vol. 6, no. 2, 1975, pp. 237–272.

Birn, Anne-Emanuelle. "How to Have Narrative-flipping History in a Pandemic: Views of/from Latin America". *Centaurus*, vol. 62, 2020, pp. 354–369.

Bojorquez, Ietza, et al. "Migration and Health in Latin America During the COVID-19 Pandemic and Beyond". *The Lancet*, vol. 397, no. 10281, 2021, pp. 1243–1245.

Boyle, Catherine. "Poor Connection: Testimony of a Pandemic". *Conexión Inestable: testimonio de una pandemia. Poor Connection: Testimony of a Pandemic*, edited by Catherine Boyle et al., Universidad de Buenos Aires. Editorial Facultad de Filosofía y Letras, 2022, pp. 173–180.

—. "Worldmaking in the Time of Covid-19". *Language Acts and Worldmaking*, 2020, https://languageacts.org/worldmaking-time-covid-19/.

Brooks, Peter. "The Law as Narrative and Rhetoric". *Law's Stories: Narrative and Rhetoric in the Law*, edited by Peter Brooks and Paul Gewirtz, Yale University Press, 1996, pp. 14–22.

COVID-19 in Latin America and the Caribbean: An overview of government responses to the crisis. OECD, 11 November 2020.

Covid-19 Fueling Anti-Asian Racism and Xenophobia Worldwide. Human Rights Watch, 12 May 2020, https://www.hrw.org/news/2020/05/12/covid-19-fueling-anti-asian-racism-and-xenophobia-worldwide.

Crow, Deserai, and Michael Jones. "Narratives as tools for influencing policy change". *Policy & Politics*, vol. 46, no. 2, 2018, pp. 217–34.

Cueto, Marcos. "Covid-19, Salud Global y América Latina". *Instituto de Estudios Peruanos*, 15 August 2022, https://tiemposdepandemia2022.iep.org.pe

Cueto, Marcos, et al. "The Regulation of Necropolitics: Governmental Responses to COVID-19 in Brazil and India in the First Year of the Pandemic". *SciELO Preprints*, 8 June 2022, https://doi.org/10.1590/SciELOPreprints.4244. Preprint.

Desigual y letal. Amnistía Internacional & CESR, 2022.

Donoso, Sofía, et al. "Is it Worth the Risk? Grievances and Street Protest Participation During the COVID-19 Pandemic in Chile". *Journal of Politics in Latin America*, vol. 14, no. 3, 2022, pp. 338–362.

Espinoza Carvajal, Andrea. "COVID-19 and the Limitations of Official Responses to Gender-Based Violence in Latin America: Evidence from Ecuador". *Bulletin of Latin American Research*, vol. 39, no. S1, 2020, pp. 7–11.

Fisher, Walter R. *Human Communication as Narration: Toward a Philosophy of Reason, Value, and Action*. University of South Carolina Press, 1989.

Foucault, Michel. "Language to Infinity". *Language, Counter-Memory, Practice*, edited by Bouchard, Donald F., Cornell University Press, 1980, pp. 53–67.

Gibbs, Anna. "After Affect. Sympathy, Synchrony, And Mimetic Communication". *The Affect Theory Reader*, edited by Melissa Gregg and Gregory J. Seigworth, Duke University Press, 2010, pp. 186–206.

—. "Contagious Feelings: Pauline Hanson and the Epidemiology of Affect". *Australian Humanities Review*, no. 24, 2001, https://australianhumanitiesreview.org/2001/12/01/contagious-feelings-pauline-hanson-and-the-epidemiology-of-affect/.

Greene, Jeremy, and Dora Vargha. "How Epidemics End". *Boston Review*, 30 June 2020, https://www.bostonreview.net/articles/jeremy-greene-dora-vargha-how-epidemics-end-or-dont/.

Huang, Justin, et al. "The Cost of Anti-Asian Racism During the COVID-19 Pandemic". *Nature Human Behaviour*, vol. 7, 2023, pp. 682–695.

Jordheim, Helge, et al. "Epidemic Times". *Somatosphere*, 2 April 2020, http://somatosphere.net/2020/epidemic-times.html/.

León Cabrera, José María, and Anatoly Kurmanaev. "Ecuador's Death Toll During Outbreak Is Among the Worst in the World". *The New York Times*, 23 April 2020, https://www.nytimes.com/2020/04/23/world/americas/ecuador-deaths-coronavirus.html.

Lindahl, Chris. "Beyond 'Contagion': Interest in Outbreak Movies, Podcasts, and More Surges Across the Internet". *IndieWire*, 17 March 2020, https://www.indiewire.com/features/general/contagion-pandemic-outbreak-movies-coronavirus-1202218477/.

Medina Cordova, Luis. "Microcuentos: Very Short Latin American Fiction in and for Pandemic Times". *Journal of World Literature*, vol. 7, no. 1, 2022, pp. 39–53.

—. *Imagining Ecuador. Crisis, Transnationalism and Contemporary fiction*. Tamesis, 2022.

—. "Narrating a Global Crisis from Guayaquil in Real Time: Early Literary Responses to the COVID-19 Outbreak in Latin America". *Bulletin of Latin American Research*, vol. 39, no. S1, 2020, pp. 108–111.

Osteen, Mark, and Martha Woodmansee. "Taking Account of the New Economic Criticism". *The New Economic Criticism. Studies at the interface of literature and economics*, edited by Martha Woodmansee and Mark Osteen, Routledge, 1999, pp. 2–41.

Oyeyemi, Sunday Oluwafemi, et al. "Ebola, Twitter, and Misinformation: A Dangerous Combination?". *BMJ*, vol. 349, 2014, https://pubmed.ncbi.nlm.nih.gov/25315514/.

Pandemic Fictions Research Group. "From Pandemic to Corona Fictions: Narratives in Times of Crises". *PhiN-Beiheft*, no 24, 2020, https://web.fu-berlin.de/phin/beiheft24/b24t21.pdf

Patterson, Molly, and Kristen Monroe. "Narrative in Political Science". *Annual Review of Political Science*, vol. 1, 1998, pp. 315–331.

Peterman, Amber, et al. "Pandemics and Violence Against Women and Children". *CGD Working Paper*, no. 528, 2020, https://www.cgdev.org/publication/pandemics-and-violence-against-women-and-children.

Rama, Ángel. *Writing across Cultures: Narrative Transculturation in Latin America*. Edited by David Frye, Duke University Press, 2012.

Ramírez-Esparza, Nairán, and James W. Pennebaker. "Do Good Stories Produce Good Health? Exploring Words, Language, and Culture". *Narrative Inquiry*, vol. 16, no. 1, 2006, pp. 211–219.

Ribeiro da Silva, Severino, and Lindomar Pena. "Collapse of the public health system and the emergence of new variants during the second wave of the COVID-19 pandemic in Brazil". *One Health*, vol. 13, 2021, pp. 1–5.

Rosenberg, Charles. "What Is an Epidemic? AIDS in Historical Perspective". *Daedalus*, vol. 118, no. 2, 1989, pp. 1–17.

Schwalb, Alvaro, et al. "COVID-19 in Latin America and the Caribbean: Two years of the pandemic". *Journal of Internal Medicine*, vol. 292, no. 3, 2022, pp. 409–427.

Shiller, Robert J. *Narrative Economics*. Princeton University Press, 2020.

Song, Zhaoli, and Alessandro Fergnani. "How Pandemic Films Help Us Understand Outbreaks: Implications for Futures and Foresight". *World Futures Review*, vol. *14*, no. 1, 2022, pp. 9–28.

Tomkins, Silvan. *Affect Imagery Consciousness: Volume 3. The Negative Affects: Anger and Fear*. Springer, 1991.

Valero, Pohl, and María Soledad Zárate. "Historias de las epidemias en América Latina. Reflexiones para pensar el presente". *Revista Ciencias de la Salud*, vol 19, 2021, pp. 1–6.

Willsher, Kim. "Albert Camus Novel the Plague Leads Surge of Pestilence Fiction". *The Guardian*, 28 March 2020, https://www.theguardian.com/books/2020/mar/28/albert-camus-novel-the-plague-la-peste-pestilence-fiction-coronavirus-lockdown.

Chapter 1

¿La Vida Volverá?

Affect in Musicians' Narrations of the Pandemic in Chile

Eunice Rojas
Furman University

Daniel Sarkela
University of Florida

Abstract

This chapter engages studies on the role of affect in social movement framing to examine the emotional mobilization strategies employed by two Chilean songs released in response to the Covid-19 crisis and its associated lockdown. While "Aburrido" (Bored/Irritated), performed by hip-hop artist Pablo Chill-E in collaboration with members from the long-standing folk supergroups Quilapayún and Inti-Illimani Histórico, reacts with irritation, frustration, and apparent resignation with a dark monochrome video, "La vida volverá" (Life will return) by the folk and Andean ensemble Illapu presents a colorful narrative of hope and optimism. Although they reflect nearly opposite emotional responses to the pandemic's disruption of both normal life and the social protests, both songs employ narratives related to the pandemic in order to promote and frame an emotional culture that fosters mobilization and bolsters the latent social movement.

Keywords: music, Chile, Covid-19, social movements, 2019 protests.

***

Introduction

When the Covid-19 pandemic began in March 2020, Chile was completing its fifth month of social upheaval over systemic inequality, government corruption, police violence, and the lingering vestiges of a dictatorship that had officially ended thirty years earlier. Chilean musicians, from street artists to international pop stars, played a prominent role in the protests, providing a soundtrack of revived songs from earlier eras and new compositions to accompany the demonstrations. Nevertheless, this musical invigoration came with a price, as the violence and instability on Chilean streets caused most concerts and gigs to be cancelled, thrusting many musicians into the same economic uncertainty already plaguing other sectors of society. Scrambling to attempt to address some of the protester's concerns, the Chilean Congress came to an agreement one month into the protests to hold a referendum to rewrite Chile's constitution. Still, neither that measure nor President Sebastián Piñera's replacement of a significant portion of his cabinet was sufficient to quell the protests that kept the centre of Santiago paralysed for several months. The pandemic and its resulting quarantine measures finally put an effective end to the effervescent massive protests, but many of the underlying social and economic issues that fuelled the upheaval were only exacerbated by the crisis brought on by the virus.

Because of the overlap between some of the issues raised by the social upheaval and those produced by the pandemic, Chilean musical responses to the health crisis are necessarily intertwined with the social movement born of the October 2019 protests. This chapter engages studies on the role of affect in social movement framing to examine the emotional mobilisation strategies employed by two Chilean songs released in response to the Covid-19 crisis and its associated lockdown. While "Aburrido",[1] performed by hip-hop artist Pablo Chill-E in collaboration with members from the long-standing folk supergroups Quilapayún and Inti-Illimani Histórico, reacts with irritation, frustration, and apparent resignation with a dark monochrome video, "La vida volverá"[2] by the folk and Andean ensemble Illapu presents a colourful narrative of hope and optimism. Although they reflect nearly opposite emotional responses to the pandemic's disruption of both normal life and the social protests, both songs employ narratives related to the pandemic in order to promote and frame an emotional culture that fosters mobilisation and bolsters the latent social movement.

Social Movement Framing and Affect

In the introduction to their *Affect Theory Reader* (2010), Melissa Gregg and Gregory Seigworth define affect as the "visceral forces beneath, alongside, or generally other than conscious knowing, vital forces that exist beyond emotion that can serve to drive us toward movement" (1). While they use the term "movement" broadly, the relevance of affect to the functioning and success of social movements is implicit within Gregg and Seigworth's explanation of the concept. More recently, sociologist Natalia Ruiz-Junco has more specifically examined the ways in which the study of emotions has been applied to the field of social movements. According to Ruiz-Junco, one of the four major emotion

---

[1] "Bored/Irritated". All translations of lyrics, song titles, and quotes in this chapter are ours.
[2] "Life will return".

concepts that has impacted contemporary social movement literature is that of emotional framing (46). Drawing on David Snow and Robert Benford's theory of social movement framing, in which movements assign meaning to certain events, figures, and conditions in ways intended to generate mobilisation, Ruiz-Junco explains that social movements employ emotion to engage in framing activities designed to resonate emotionally with the intended audience. Furthermore, in her work on mass-mediated protest music, sociologist Jeneve Brooks proposes that social movement songs employ emotional framing in order to sway public opinion and influence voting on key issues (1). Similarly, sociologist Douglas Schrock explains that "emotional mobilisation refers to processes through which feelings are suppressed, evoked, and used in multiple contexts so as to foster and/or support activism" (62). According to Schrock, the effectiveness of social movement framing largely depends on how much it resonates with potential recruits (62). Schrock therefore defines the concept of *emotional resonance* as "the link between targeted recruits' emotional lives and the emotional messages encoded in [Social Movement Organization] framing" (62).

In a special issue of *Ethnomusicology Forum* on affect and ethnomusicology, Katie Graber and Matthew Sumera reflect upon a long history of ethnomusicological literature that engages with ideas of affect, pre-dating the so-called affective turn of the mid-1990s. With regard to the concept of *resonance*, Graber and Sumera work to connect the affective use of the term with its original acoustic definition. "By returning physicality and vibration to sound and music", Graber and Sumera argue, "resonance helps return music's power and reach—not only its meaning and function in society, but also the affective intensities that support or contradict those meanings and functions" (10). In line with this idea, this chapter examines the way that the lyrics, the videos, and the music of Illapu's "La vida volverá" and Pablo Chill-E's "Aburrido" work to resonate emotionally with their intended audiences and emotively frame both the pandemic and the social protests in such a way as to keep the embers of a social movement alive even under the complicated circumstances of the Covid-19 crisis.

Illapu's "La vida volverá"

As a folk-based group influenced by the *Nueva canción chilena* (Chilean New Song Movement) and drawing on the region's Andean roots, Illapu formed in 1971 when five brothers from the Márquez family along with poet and musician, Osvaldo Torres, began performing together in Antofagasta, a port city in northern Chile's Atacama Desert. According to Andrés Márquez, one of Illapu's founding members, Salvador Allende's election in 1970 as part of the Popular Unity party and platform "brought with it a great flowering of the arts, particularly the popular arts and the work of artists who felt behind this cultural upsurge the need for art to be committed to social reality" (Márquez 8). Therefore, under President Salvador Allende's socialist government, the Chilean New Song Movement enjoyed both widespread public as well as political support, and as a result, Illapu quickly gained popularity.

After Augusto Pinochet's 1973 coup, the entire Chilean New Song Movement was thrust underground, forced into exile, or in the case of Víctor Jara, detained, tortured, and killed. The members of Illapu were initially permitted to remain in Chile and soon became part of a new musical movement dedicated to embracing and promoting local cultural values while subtly denouncing the problematic social realities of life under dictatorship (Márquez 8-9). After a brief tour in Europe in 1981, the members of Illapu were turned back by authorities upon their arrival in Chile and forced into exile. They were not permitted to return to Chile until 1988 when Pinochet allowed the return of numerous political exiles from the cultural sphere in anticipation of the October 1988 plebiscite to decide whether or not the dictatorship would continue in place. Following the group's emotional return to Chile and the subsequent return to democracy in 1990, Andrés Márquez wrote one of Illapu's most emblematic songs and one of the most poignant regarding the end of exile. According to Márquez, "Vuelvo para vivir"[3] expresses the exiles' hope of returning, reuniting with their people, and resuming their former way of life, even though for many Chileans the reality of the return did not play out quite as they had hoped (Tuñón).

While Illapu has been consistently active since its formation in 1971, despite the challenges of dictatorship, censorship and exile, its members have changed dramatically over the decades. Just two Márquez brothers from the original founding members remain, and only musical director, Roberto Márquez, has never even temporarily left the group, but the band has performed and recorded actively since its inception. In September 2020, six months into the Covid-19 crisis, Illapu released on YouTube a pandemic style music video of its members performing "Vuelvo para vivir" from their separate homes, thus equating the hope for a return to pre-pandemic existence with the hope thirty years earlier for a return to pre-dictatorship freedoms. The use of this song within the context of the Covid-19 lockdown was designed to emotionally resonate with the social protest by invoking the memory of hope for a brighter future after suffering the restrictions of dictatorship. Through its emotional resonance, the song intends to mobilise listeners to return to the protests once pandemic restrictions have abated.

On April 30, 2021, over a year into the Covid-19 pandemic, and in commemoration of the fiftieth anniversary of the group's formation, Illapu

---

[3] "I return to live".

¿La Vida Volverá?

released the song "La vida volverá" [4] simultaneously on multiple digital platforms. Like the group's famous song about return from exile thirty years earlier, by employing the future tense of the verb "volver"[5], "La vida volverá" draws on the concept of a return to an almost idyllic reality before times of trouble. The opening of the song's video alludes to the idea of an age of innocence by presenting a desk covered with watercolour paints, pastels, and markers. The scene depicts the mess created by artistic production and is composed of the bright, vibrant colours of used art implements surrounding a stack of watercolour sketches. One by one, the sketches reveal black and white moving images of Illapu's musicians playing their instruments while the music itself is represented by colourful illustrations of simplistically applied paint. The rest of the video's aesthetic continues in the same vein with monochrome video images enhanced with brightly coloured rainbows, polka dots, and wavy outlines. The effect of the video's aesthetic is to help emotionally frame the entire song with a sense of hope born of nostalgic innocence.

Using Natalia Ruiz-Junco's synthesis of social movement emotion analysis as a lens, "La vida volverá" creates a union between the emotional impacts of both the lyrical and musical content to emphasize its message and mobilize listeners to keep the movement alive. The song begins with a call and response texture to create a playful and joyous introduction with the initial call made by the bass, charango, guitar, and zampoña. In response, a quena and soprano saxophone reply with a melody in unison. After a sequence of call and responses, the ensemble comes together to play simultaneously and finish out the introduction. This opening segment is a representation of Ruiz-Junco's approach to *emotional framing*. The first group of instruments to play act as a symbol of Illapu's music in the context of social resistance and change in Chile. In the same way the instruments elicit a response from the rest of the band, the music of Illapu draws out an emotional response by framing the current Chilean political climate in an optimistic manner. Additionally, the instrumentation of the opening sequence is a representation of the different generations within the movement. The saxophone and quena playing in unison are the newest generation, and the two have several instances of prominence while the rest of the band, symbolizing the previous generation from the Chilean New Song Movement, takes a backseat.

After the melodic introduction, Verse 1 and Chorus 1 both use a chord progression that weaves between major and minor tonalities.[6] Within the realm of traditional Western musical thought, the major mode has a connotation of

---

[4] "Life will return".
[5] "Return".
[6] The full chord progression is C major, G major, A minor, E minor, F major, C major, D minor, and G major.

positive and hopeful emotion while the minor mode, in opposition, has a negative and pessimistic connotation. The progression created by the artists utilizes these associations to create a harmonic representation of the poetic voice's plea. The progression begins by establishing a major tonality for the song using C major and G major to begin the looping chords. The major tonality is then dismantled by the chords A minor and E minor, retroactively implying a minor tonality. Following this shift in mood, the F major chord then reestablishes the major tonality before returning to the tonic chord of C major, later using D minor and G major as a transition to repeat the cycle. Reflecting the lyrics' description of difficult times, this progression results in the disruption of normality through its use of an interjection of minor chords. The progression then, in a reinforcement of the song's title and the repetition of the hopeful idea of an anticipated return to laughter and people singing, returns to the original tonal area representative of joy. According to the assertions of the previously discussed social movement theorists, these connotative musical choices underpin an emotive message that pushes possible participants to mobilize in support of the cause. The listeners targeted by this song would feel motivated by their emotional response to participate in the protests according to the principles of emotional resonance.

Although the idea implicit in both the music and the lyrics of "La vida volverá" is one of optimism with regard to a return to the positive aspects of the pre-pandemic way of life, free from the shadows of quarantine and empty streets, the lyrics also offer a hopeful hint at a return to the protests of Chile's 2019 social upheaval. Some of the shadows that are expected to ultimately lift in the eventual return to normalcy are named in the opening lines of the song as "el miedo, el azote, la peste".[7] While "la peste" is a clear reference to the Covid-19 pandemic, "el azote" has a more ambiguous connotation, as it could refer to the scourge of the virus or to the beatings and other injuries protesters sustained at the hands of the police during the social unrest. These lyrics are also punctuated musically, with the A minor and E minor chords reflecting the injustices addressed before returning to the established major key. While still somewhat subtle, the song's chorus contains the clearest reference to the 2019 social upheaval by referencing the "miles buscando dignidad"[8] who are expected to return. The use of the word "dignidad" is an unmistakable allusion to Plaza Baquedano, the epicentre of Santiago's social protests that was unofficially renamed by protesters as Plaza Dignidad. In this way, the song frames the protests with the same hope and nostalgia as the desire to return to pre-

---

[7] "Fear, scourge/beating, plague".
[8] "Thousands searching for dignity".

pandemic life, which intends to serve to mobilise listeners to return to the protests once conditions allow it.

Furthermore, when the lyrics first reference the idea of the return to the search for dignity, at the very word "dignidad", the video departs for the first time from images of musicians singing and playing their instruments to an animated simplistic painting of an eye on a purple background. This eye, which appears in the video for less than two seconds—barely longer than it takes to sing the word "dignidad"—performs multiple functions. First, by briefly closing completely into a background painted with dark purple before reopening and quickly expanding until the iris occupies the entirety of the frame, the eye alludes to #Chiledespertó,[9] the common slogan and hashtag of the 2019 protests. Momentarily filling the entire screen as the eye shuts, the dark grape colour appears for the only time in the video and in contrast to the bright hues that enhance the rest of the images in the video. During the social uprising, the ubiquitous catchphrase of #Chiledespertó framed the upheaval as a popular awakening to the social inequalities caused by the implementation of a neoliberal *laissez-faire* economy under the Pinochet dictatorship, and the song's video complements this idea of awakening from a dark past to the joyfulness of a childlike painting. As the eye is closing and reopening, the song simultaneously completes its cyclical major-minor-major chord cycle, changing from E minor on "Dignidad", to F major. This creates an emotionally resonant parallel of a return, or volver, to pre-pandemic life, as well as the reinvigoration of protests in Chile. Once again, the lyrics, music, and visuals of "La vida volverá" work in tandem to create affect through emotive forces to spur listeners to mobilise in support.

Furthermore, the presence of the eye in the video alludes to the hundreds of ocular injuries experienced by protesters hit in the face with police projectiles. After the second rendition of the song's chorus, during a musical bridge, the video presents images of Gustavo Gatica, a protester who was famously blinded in both eyes in November 2019 as a result of injuries he sustained during the protests. In the video, a monochrome Gatica wearing dark glasses walks through the Plaza Dignidad, with the location evidenced only by the presence of the also monochrome Telefónica building behind him. As the scene advances, other protesters join Gatica and look toward him endearingly, and one man leans in to kiss him on the shoulder. The background throughout the Gatica scenes is painted with watercolour yellows and oranges, offering a sense of sunrise, and Gatica is filmed from below, implying an almost heavenly presence. By presenting Gatica in this way, the song emotionally frames his presence as one of joy at his return to the protests rather than sadness or anger

---

[9] #ChileAwoke.

over his injuries. The music during this section of the video returns to the idea of the saxophone and quena embodying the current *primera línea*.[10] The images of Gatica are accompanied by these two instruments playing soaring melodies while the rest of the band plays in the background. By allowing the instruments of the new generation to be in the forefront, the other band members represent the old guard passing the torch to the youth personified by Gatica. Within the wider context of the song, the joy over Gatica's return and resilience—despite his permanent disability—is presented as parallel to the anticipated joy of an end to the Covid-19 health crisis and a return to the experiences that lockdown and quarantine have prevented.

Finally, the image of the painted eye with a purple background suggests the logo of the Violeta Parra Museum, which burned three times during the social upheaval due to its location near the focal point of the protests. Parra, a singer-songwriter who was influential in the formation of the Chilean New Song Movement in the 1960s and known for her emblematic songs about social inequities in Chile, also created and exhibited tapestries both in Chile and abroad. The eye and its purple background presented in the Illapu video is reminiscent of the well-known image of an open eye in Parra's tapestries, and this is what the Museum chose to use with purple backing for its branding. The presence in the video of an eye similar to Parra's that briefly closes and then reopens is meant to resonate with listeners familiar with Parra's importance in Chile's cultural heritage. Furthermore, the closing of the eye is so brief that the focus remains on the positive connotations of its reopening rather than on its closing, implying also only a brief interruption of normal life brought on by the Covid-19 crisis. In each of its interpretations, the video's re-opening eye is intended to emotionally resonate with the protesters of the social upheaval in order to encourage them to return to the streets.

The idea of a return to childlike joy that is reflected in the bright watercolour illustrations in the video is reinforced in the lyrics of the final two verses of the song. The penultimate verse begins explicitly with the optimistic notion that hope will be reborn and then indicates that "la inocencia que fue traicionada"[11] will come again to show the way. At the same time the lyrics reference the promise of a return to the innocence of childhood that has been ripped away, the video presents images of children participating in the protests. These children carry signs containing slogans of the protest, such as "No estamos en guerra"[12], an allusion to President Piñera's statement at the start of the social upheaval that the people of Chile were at war against a powerful enemy (Andrews). The song's video therefore frames Piñera's powerful enemy as very young children armed

---

[10] "The front line [of the protests]".
[11] "The innocence that was betrayed".
[12] "We are not at war".

only with signs. Furthermore, the sign challenging Piñera's statement is itself framed with the bright colours that are characteristic of the video. At this very moment in the song, the chord progression arrives at G Major, creating tension and an expectation of change, or return, to the home chord of C Major. This functional shift is accompanied by a dynamic swelling in the band and a climbing melodic line in the vocals. All of these events apply a connotation of coming change to the image of the children, implying that they will be the agents of a great reform in the future.

At the end of the final chorus, the song isolates, highlights, and repeats the final line that promises a return of the people's voices in song. This is joined by scenes of pre-pandemic protests and imagery, including a protester marching and playing a drum with Victor Jara's face painted on the head. Jara, the most renowned singer-songwriter of the Chilean New Song Movement, was tortured and killed by the Pinochet regime in the early days of the dictatorship and has since become a symbol of a generation of protesters silenced by the regime. At the moment that Jara's image appears, the poetic voice ceases to sing while the background chorus continues to chant "volverán"[13] as the instrumental texture evolves to once again feature the quena and saxophone. The silencing of the poetic voice mirrors the tragic loss of Victor Jara, both as a musician and agent of change, and creates a musical effect that demonstrates the implied silence of the voices that will return to song. In place of Illapu's lead singer, the duo of quena and saxophone once again takes the lead aurally and demonstrates how the new generation will take up the mantle of the older one. In addition to this, the music introduces a new instrument, a deep bass drum, adding a driving rhythm to the energy of the song. This sound of the bass drum, which enters at the moment Víctor Jara's face appears in the video, affects the "other than conscious knowing" described by Seigworth and Gregg that compels the listener to become an active participant in the movement for social reform.

This outro also foreshadows the coda of the song by including an image of a protester banging on a pot, with the visual artistry accentuating the action by adding colourful lines representing spreading of the sound. At the exact moment the spoon makes contact with the pot in the video, a subtle added pang is inserted into the audio to complement the visual, blurring the line between the inserted footage of the protests and the music. Prior to this, the only images that appeared to produce audio were the clips of Illapu's members playing their instruments, making this the first time that sounds from the added imagery from the protests are heard breaking through to the song. In the final coda when the band Illapu ceases to play, this distinction between imagery and audio is destroyed as the song gives way entirely to audio and

---

[13] "They will return".

footage of the uprising, featuring the sights and sounds of protesters banging of pots and pans. This banging, known popularly as a *cacerolazo*, in reference to the *cacerola* or pot that is struck with a spoon, is a well-known characteristic of the Chilean protests. Ending on this note further emphasizes the song's overall message that the hopes for a joyful post-pandemic life run parallel to the hopes for social and political change arising from the social movement cut short by the Covid-19 crisis.

Pablo Chill-E's "Aburrido"

Positive emotions are not the only tool available to artists attempting to mobilize social change. The song "Aburrido" by Pablo Chill-E featuring the voices of Inti Illimani Histórico & Quilapayún presents an apathetic and irritated attitude toward the same events described by Illapu in "La vida volverá". Pablo Chill-E, a Chilean Latin trap artist born in 2000, recorded his first album in 2016 and included on it the self-titled track, "Pablo", in which the poetic voice describes his desire and efforts to become a drug dealer like the Colombian cartel lord, Pablo Escobar. By 2018, though, Pablo Chill-E had dedicated himself to social justice causes both as a musician and as an activist. In that year, along with Matías Toledo, he co-founded the *Coordinadora Social Shishigang*, a community solidarity organization designed to help members of Santiago's underprivileged population be of mutual service to each other. Also in 2018, Pablo Chill-E released a music video of a track with the English title "Facts", in which he samples León Gieco's famous ballad "Solo le pido a Dios"[14] in between original lyrics that denounce social inequalities in Chile and the complicity of the Piñera government in perpetuating them. In a verse calling out the proliferation of drugs in contrast with the scarcity of books in Chile's poor neighborhoods, the poetic voice sums up his personal transformation by stating: "Antes quería ser Pablo Escobar / Ahora solo quiero ser alguien major".[15]

In contrast to Pablo Chill-E's youth, the Chilean New Song groups Inti-Illimani and Quilapayún (often referred to in their shortened forms, Inti and Quila), like Illapu, date back to Chile's pre-dictatorship era. Both formed in the mid-1960s and were on tour in Europe serving as cultural ambassadors for Salvador Allende's Popular Unity government when the *coup d'état* ushered in the Pinochet dictatorship and prevented their return home. They also both suffered contentious splits after the return from exile, especially since some members of each band chose to remain in the lives they had built abroad. Ultimately, both groups had to resort to the courts to sort out their differences. While Eduardo Carrasco, one of the founding members of Quilapayún, was

---

[14] "I only ask God".
[15] "I used to want to be Pablo Escobar, but now I want to be someone better".

ultimately able to legally reserve the exclusive use of the band's original name for his ensemble, Horacio Salinas, the original musical director of Inti-Illimani, eventually found himself obligated to use the name Inti-Illimani Histórico for the band that he formed with other departed founding members of the original group. Despite these legal challenges and numerous changes in the membership of the bands, both groups have maintained an active performance schedule in the decades since their return from exile.

The generational divide and stark differences in musical genre make Pablo Chill-E and the members of Quilapayún and Inti-Illimani Histórico an unlikely pairing, but their resulting work has proven quite popular and has been able to attract listeners of a wide spectrum of ages. Eduardo Carrasco recounts that he wrote the lyrics to "Aburrido" during the Covid-19 lockdown in response to his son's challenge to him that he write a rap (Zúñiga). Eager to take up the task and do so properly, Carrasco spent time studying the form, structure, and rhyme scheme of tracks by Puerto Rican Latin trap and reggaeton megastar, Bad Bunny, before penning the original lyrics of "Aburrido". While inspired by his son's challenge and influenced by the music of Bad Bunny, Carrasco wrote the song about the feeling of boredom and irritation "porque era la situación de la pandemia, lo que estábamos todos viviendo" (Zúñiga).[16] Nevertheless, according to journalist Alexis Paiva Mack, "Aburrido", like Illapu's "La vida volverá", refers just as much to Chile's political and social realities as it does to the Covid-19 crisis.

While French film director Edouard Salier was reported to be working on an official video of the song, on November 6, 2020, Pablo Chill-E uploaded to YouTube a video of "Aburrido" complete with lyrics and set to a video backdrop of scenes from the 2019 social upheaval. This preview video, shown entirely in black and white, opens with overhead footage of one of Santiago's multitudinous marches from late 2019 and then focuses in on a protester with a sign that states, "El pueblo unido jamás será vencido". The protester is standing in Santiago's Plaza Baquedano with the Telefónica building in the background just as Gustavo Gatica appears in Illapu's "La vida volverá", and the sign references Quilapayún's internationally renowned song "El pueblo unido", which was originally written as an anthem for Salvador Allende's Popular Unity government. During the rest of the introduction to the song, the video shifts back and forth between scenes from the 2019 social upheaval, including burning barricades in the streets and throngs of protesters, and images reminiscent of the Chilean New Song Movement, such as the group Quilapayún performing on-stage with a large photograph of Víctor Jara projected behind them. Musically, "Aburrido" begins in the style of the Chilean New Song with an

---

[16] Carrasco states that he wrote the song "because it was the situation of the pandemic, what we were all living".

introduction comprised of traditional Andean instrumentation, including a quena, guitar, and cuatro among a bass and rhythm section. The march-like melody then transforms at the start of the first verse into a trap backing track that samples the quena intermittently. By beginning the song with the traditions of Chilean resistance music set to a video backdrop of the 2019 social protests, the artists harken back to the rich past before engaging with today's listeners through an urban style. This strategy both emotionally frames the protests within the political and cultural understanding of the older generation and presents the music of the past as applicable to the current social crisis. The melding of genres therefore ushers in the new age of protest music while paying homage to the past, with the persistent sampling of the introduction demonstrating solidarity between the generations and including them in today's plight. Given the emotive and affecting qualities of the song, listeners presented with these explicit and implicit connections will be motivated to engage in the political activism according to the previously mentioned social movement theories.

After the song's folk intro gives way to trap, the poetic voice's rapped lyrics hammer a repetitive message of all-encompassing boredom. With most of the lines beginning with an apostrophic "aburrido del…",[17] the poetic voice complains about the virus keeping everyone at home, Piñera's problematic leadership, drug traffickers and police, the monotony of lockdown routine, pandemic reporting, empty buses, clouds, air, and time itself. In one of several moments of self-referential irony, the poetic voice even claims to be bored of the lyrics of his own song. All the while, behind the caption of the lyrics themselves, the video displays images of throngs of people protesting in the streets of Santiago during the 2019 social upheaval. This juxtaposition of images of the uprising with lyrics regarding the Covid-19 crisis frames the protests as on hold due to the pandemic lockdown.

Later in the song, in another moment of self-referentiality, the poetic voice states that he is, "aburrido del canto del pueblo unido",[18] in an allusion to Quilapayún's famous protest song from Chilean New Song generation. In frustration, the poetic voice, through Pablo Chill-E's adolescent metal mouth, adds, "ya hubiera vencido si por mí hubiera sido".[19] Eduardo Carrasco, the original author of the lyrics, commented in an interview his intention in writing these lines: "Nos referimos a la postergación, esperamos que la alegría llegue desde el año 88" (Paiva).[20] Carrasco's reference to happiness and the year 1988

---

[17] "Bored of".
[18] The line "bored by the song of the people united" refers to Quilapayún's 1973 song "El pueblo unido" written by Sergio Ortega.
[19] "It would have already succeeded if it had been for me".
[20] "We were referring to the deferral; we have been waiting for happiness to come since [19]88".

points to the plebiscite held at that time to decide the political future of the nation. The marketing campaign for the anti-Pinochet platform promised that happiness would come with the return to democracy. Voicing a common lament during the 2019 social upheaval, Carrasco adds, "son muchos años y la cosa no llega" (Paiva).[21] Pablo Chill-E's rapped lyrics and Carrasco's commentary evidence the aggravation shared by both the older and the younger generation as communicated through the medium and messaging of music. Both the lyrics rapped by Pablo Chill-E and Carrasco's interview appear to imply that the hopeful idea of happiness to come, as embodied both in the 1988 "No" campaign and songs such as Illapu's "La vida volverá", no longer resonates with either generation. Instead of employing the emotional frame of joy and hopefulness, "Aburrido" ironically engages a frame of disenchantment to resonate with both the older and the younger demographics to mobilise them back into protest as soon as the cloud of the Covid-19 crisis lifts.

This combination of generational civil disobedience is also displayed visually during the chorus of the music video for "Aburrido". Splitting the screen into two parts, the video shows footage from a Quilapayún concert on the left side, while a slideshow of photos of young people from the 2019 protests plays on the right. Quila's concert symbolises the generation of the *Nueva canción chilena* movement, complementing the new movement's youth on the opposite side of the screen. This equivalency between the Pinochet dictatorship and the current political climate is also made on one of the protesters signs that appears in the video, which states, "No son la dictadura, pero son la mejor banda tributo".[22] By tapping into this previous generational trauma, the artists emotionally frame the current social upheaval in Chile as a continuation of the fight from decades past, and they do so with a play on words from popular music culture. Channelling this emotional power creates a springboard in the listeners' mind to strengthen the protesters' claim of injustice in modern day Chile.

Although trap music is generally not constructed with a Western tonal music theory framework in mind, the incorporation in "Aburrido" of Chilean New Song elements allows for some melodic and harmonic influence from previous generations. Within the chorus of the song, in which the poetic voice announces his intention to neither stand up nor lie down, and in no case to leave the house, the bass plays several variations of a descending pattern of the minor mode called a lament bass leading to a half cadence. This descending pattern is traditionally associated with grief and loss, while the implied harmony of the final note, the dominant chord, is representative of the

---

[21] "It has been many years, and [happiness] has not arrived".
[22] "They aren't the dictatorship, but they are the best tribute band".

strongest point of change. The use of lament bass and minor mode during the chorus, which ends with the poetic voice's lament that his pockets are empty of money, is representative of the sadness and tragedy of the poetic voice's struggles with pandemic lockdown, poverty, political and social turmoil, and boredom. By ending on the dominant note of the scale after this minor descension, Pablo Chill-E implies an impending change, subconsciously embedding the suggestion within the listener's ear through musical means.

Furthermore, during the final moments of the song, the music subverts the expectation of a finishing cadence by slowing on the greatest point of tension and having the vocalist, backing track, and instruments desynchronize and play out of time with each other. This moment of collapse is punctuated by the chorus of voices descending in a glissando, or slide, further emphasizing the deceleration. The effect of this lack of a resolving cadence represents the resignation of the poetic voice who returns to his menial life of pandemic-induced boredom previously mentioned. The musical and lyrical aloofness within "Aburrido" utilises Ruiz-Junco's theory of *emotional framing* to affect the latent beliefs of the listener. By engaging with the listeners through an emotional lens of apathy and dispassion, the artists use this song to first capture the attention of the populace in order to transform their attitude into one of engagement, mobilisation, and hope. The message of "Aburrido", despite its surface of apathy, hopes to build upon the social movement paused by the Covid-19 crisis in the future once the pandemic subsides and a semblance of normalcy returns.

Conclusion

While the artists of Illapu use harmony to create a positive emotional frame through which to view the political and social climate of Chile, Pablo Chill-E uses similar techniques to create and employ negative emotions to frame the same topic. The tragic effects of the coronavirus pandemic and the social upheaval are portrayed through the lyrics, visuals, and music of the two songs in opposite manners implying a both victorious future conclusion in the case of Illapu, and an inevitable return to the broken system in Pablo Chill-E's track. The use of inspirational and uplifting elements in "La vida volverá" creates the *emotional resonance* described by Schrock, uniting listeners' hopes for an end to the restrictions of the pandemic to the political and social aspirations for dignity and equality. Furthermore, by invoking images of childhood innocence and references to Chilean New Song artists, the song resonates with the emotions and memories of many listeners' pre-dictatorship past. By connecting the pandemic to the social upheaval through the emotional framing of hope and joy for the future, "La vida volverá" aims to foster support and inspire personal involvement in the social movement. In contrast, "Aburrido" engages with a feeling of disenchantment and frustration to paradoxically inspire both generations to continue the fight of the latent protests.

In its final verse, the poetic voice of "Aburrido" describes how the social distancing mandates have restricted his movement to wandering around his home and ordering food to be delivered online. While Seigworth and Gregg refer to affect as the vital forces that impulse individuals towards movement, the poetic voice of "Aburrido" encounters an emotional response of boredom and irritation to having his movement limited by the Covid-19 crisis. This restriction of physical movement has implicit repercussions on the broader social movement due to its hindrance on protest gatherings, and the song reminds the listener of the social protests all but silenced and squelched by the pandemic. The emotional framing of both "Aburrido" and "La vida volverá", therefore, has no immediate physical outlet with regard to social movement mobilisation but is, instead, contingent upon an eventual lifting of pandemic restrictions.

Although the massive protests of 2019 did not return after the lockdown was lifted, on October 25, 2020, Chile held a plebiscite in which its citizens overwhelmingly opted to reform the nation's constitution. Instead of the emotional mobilisation framing being channelled into greater protest participation, the resources of *estallido social* shifted to the realm of traditional politics, with many of the protests' supporters engaging with the plebiscite and the process of drafting a new constitution. The drafted constitution did not pass the ratifying vote on 4 September 2022, but the country is still undergoing a transformative shift to rewrite and restructure its most fundamental legal document. While the protests themselves have not reignited, the underlying cause supported by these two songs is still active, even as the Chilean public grapples with the potential content of a new constitution and the process for drafting it. The impact of the emotional resonance created by these songs has since shifted from the streets to the ballot box and continue to affect the population of Chile by using the transformative power of arts in protest to foster a more just and equitable society.

Bibliography

Andrews, Juan Pablo. "Presidente Piñera: 'Estamos en guerra contra un enemigo poderoso'". *La Tercera*, 20 October 2019, https://www.latercera.com/politica/noticia/presidente-pinera-estamos-guerra-enemigo-poderoso/870658/

Brooks, Jeneve. "Mass-Mediated Protest Music and Mobilization: Synthesizing the Civil Sphere's EMM-Framing Theory". *Theory in Action*, vol. 8, no. 3, 2015, pp. 1–26.

Graber, Katie J., and Matthew Sumera. "Interpretation, Resonance, Embodiment: Affect Theory and Ethnomusicology". *Ethnomusicology Forum*, vol. 29, no. 1, 2020, pp. 3–20.

Gregg, Melissa, and Gregory Seigworth, editors. *The Affect Theory Reader*. Duke University Press, 2010.

Illapu Canal Oficial. "Illapu - La vida volverá (Vídeo Oficial)". YouTube video, 10 June 2021, https://www.youtube.com/watch?v=I9rUxUQ2Lcw.

Márquez, Andrés. "When Ponchos Are Subversive". *Index on Censorship*, vol. 12, no. 1, 1983, pp. 8–10.

Pablo Chill-E. "Pablo Chill-E - Aburrido (feat. Inti Illimani Histórico & Quilapayún)". YouTube video, 6 November 2020, https://www.youtube.com/watch?v=DQlT-olEHHM.

Paiva, Alexis. "Pablo Chill-E y Quilapayún unidos por el trap: 'Es una verdadera renovación de la música popular'". *La Tercera*, 6 November 2020, https://www.latercera.com/culto/2020/11/06/pablo-chill-e-y-quilapayun-unidos-por-el-trap-es-una-verdadera-renovacion-de-la-musica-popular/

Ruiz-Junco, Natalia. "Feeling Social Movements: Theoretical Contributions to Social Movement Research on Emotions". *Sociology Compass*, vol. 7, no. 1, 2013, pp. 45–54.

Schrock, Douglas, et al. "Creating Emotional Resonance: Interpersonal Emotion Work and Motivational Framing in a Transgender Community". *Social Problems*, vol. 51, no. 1, 2004, pp. 61-81.

Snow, David E., and Robert Benford. "Ideology, Frame Resonance, and Participant Mobilisation". *From Structure to Action: Social Movement Participation Across Cultures*, edited by Bert Klandermans et al., JAI Press, 1988, pp. 197–217.

Tuñón, Carlos. "Vuelvo para vivir de Illapu: El himno post dictadura de Chile". *El Blog de Música*, 25 February 2021, https://elblogdemusica.com/2021/02/25/vuelvo-para-vivir-de-illapu-el-himno-post-dictadura-de-chile/

Zúñiga, Joaquín. "'Tenemos todo el derecho a hacer conciertos': La defensa de Inti-Illimani y Quilapayún tras más de medio siglo de vigencia musical". *The Clinic*, 17 February 2022, https://www.theclinic.cl/2022/02/17/tenemos-todo-el-derecho-a-hacer-conciertos-la-defensa-de-inti-illimani-y-quilapayun-tras-mas-de-medio-siglo-de-vigencia-musical/

Chapter 2

Putting Eggs in One Basket

Political Discourse and Action During the Covid-19 Vaccination Rollout in Chile

Kelly Bauer
George Washington University

Claudio Villalobos Dintrans
Independent Researcher

Pablo Villalobos Dintrans
Millennium Institute for Care Research

Abstract

Chile has been lauded as an international success for its efficient rollout of the Covid-19 vaccine. This chapter analyzes an original database of quotes from Chilean government officials, politicians, and medical and public health officials—using written media as source— surrounding four key events in Chile's vaccine rollout: i) securing vaccine supply, ii) government policy over eligibility and prioritization, iii) early distribution, and iv) preventative Covid-19 public health messaging in the context of high-vaccination rates. Discourse analysis of these quotes allows for assessment of variation in how different stakeholders'—government officials, politicians, public health experts, and others—understand, explain, and justify decisions regarding the vaccine and the vaccine rollout. We argue that the Piñera administration describes the vaccine rollout as technical and apolitical to advance their legitimacy and political agenda in a context of low approval ratings, ongoing protests, and upcoming elections. But despite Chile's reputation and the Piñera administration's rhetoric of technocratic governance, there is an increasingly strained relationship with medical and public health experts.

Keywords: Chile, Covid-19, vaccine, public health messaging, pandemic politics

***

Introduction

Chile has been lauded as an international success for its efficient rollout of the Covid-19 vaccine. In many ways, this is not a surprise considering Chile's pragmatic approach to securing a vaccine supply through partnerships with academic institutions and trade relationships and the rollout of the vaccination campaign by relying on existing public health capacity and prior successful campaigns (Villalobos Dintrans et al.; Aguilera et al.). However, this successful vaccination rollout came at a complicated political and public health moment in Chile. Chile saw a peak of Covid-19 cases and deaths in 2020, following a significant political uncertainty started by the October 2019 protests and the subsequent constitutional convention process (Bossert and Villalobos Dintrans; Minsal). The Piñera administration (2018-2022) had a historically low approval rating during these moments: 9% in late 2019 during protests and 12% during the Covid-19 spikes in 2020 (Cadem).

What can we learn about how public health experts and political officials communicated about the vaccine to the public? Most scholarly work on vaccine rhetoric has focused more on individual attitudes and behaviours about vaccines (and, specifically, vaccine hesitancy, anti-vaxxers' rhetoric, and pandemic nationalism) and less on how government officials, politicians, elites, and public health officials navigate, justify, debate, and communicate public health information and decision-making (Lazarus et al.; Troiano and Nardi). This focus on individuals' vaccine attitudes and behaviours overlooks the impact and role of the government's decisions and communications in shaping collective attitudes (Attwell et al.). Given its comparatively successful Covid-19 vaccine campaign and the political context at the time, Chile is a useful case to examine variations of and the significance of governmental communications regarding the Covid-19 vaccine and vaccination campaign.

Drawing on a novel database of quotes from political, medical, and public health experts in Chile, the present work describes and analyses how the vaccine rollout decision-making was publicly narrated over four stages of the vaccine campaign: securing supply, eligibility and prioritisation, early distribution, and preventing messaging. We found that the Piñera administration primarily described the vaccine rollout as technical and apolitical to advance its own legitimacy and political agenda in the context of low approval ratings, ongoing protests, and upcoming elections. But despite Chile's reputation for and rhetoric of technocratic governance, the Piñera administration's relationship with medical and public health experts was increasingly strained. The rhetoric about vaccine rollouts highlights this disconnection, with medical and public health experts increasingly expressing uncertainty and invoking collective thinking about the pandemic. In contrast with the expert's visions, officials in the Piñera administration frequently utilised positive tones, attempting to communicate certainty and trust while framing the vaccine rollout as an event of technical innovation and trade, appealing to individual responsibility to manage the complications of the evolving pandemic.

Government Communications about Vaccines: Expectations and Significance

How might we expect political officials to narrate public health information and justify vaccine decision-making to the public? The Covid-19 pandemic is a moment of political crisis, filled with threat, urgency and uncertainty complicating decision-making (Lipscy e100). The crisis layers on top of the government's pre-existing socio-political challenges and presents the paradox of limited medical knowledge about the outbreak with a dizzying spread of information. The announcement of the availability of Covid-19 vaccines changed the scenario regarding crisis management: vaccines added new alternatives to address the pandemic, opening a door for decision-makers, particularly politicians, to show leadership and success in dealing with the crisis in terms of new policies, risk communication strategies, and opportunities.

Early Covid-19 vaccination campaigns were complicated due to vaccines' high demand and limited supply, challenging governments to acquire a reliable access supply, deploy an efficient nationwide vaccination programme to ensure the fast and accurate distribution of vaccines amongst the population, and transparently communicate these decisions to the population. During these moments, how official government sources narrate public health information is incredibly significant for establishing and maintaining citizen trust (Gannon et al.), creating a collective understanding of goals for the moment (McGuire et al.), and protecting public health. Effective communication can impact individuals' vaccine attitudes and behaviours; scholars have documented that clear and efficient information can decrease vaccine hesitancy and time to vaccination. Furthermore, it has been shown that focusing on social rather than economic or altruistic benefits increases vaccination willingness (Argote et al., "Messages").

Given the significance of vaccine communications, what can we expect of how governments narrate public health information? One prominent observation is that politicians will justify decision-making by "hugging the experts". Relying on experts impacts public health outcomes; countries that rely on experts adopt containment measures quickly (Forster and Heinzel), and individuals relying on and trusting information from experts are likely to vaccinate on a quicker timeline (Argote et al., "The Shot"; Toro-Ascuy et al.) compared to when the information comes from politicians (Piazza and Schwier). However, relying on experts' knowledge potentially allows politicians to shift blame and responsibility for both implementation and outcomes. For example, Flinders warns that the presence of and/or direction of government communications strategies by public health experts in the UK is a "strategic performative act of blame-sharing and blame-displacement" that risks "senior staffs are expected to spend too much time "accounting-up" instead of focusing on "delivering-down" (11, 14).

Many politicians rhetorically rejected or challenged public health experts regarding vaccine communications. This distancing can take on many forms; one analysis concludes that Brazilian president Bolsonaro side-lined experts, Colombian president Duque leveraged, and Mexican president López Obrador limited how scientific expertise influenced decision-making (Dussauge-Laguna et al.). For example, president Bolsonaro spoke of protecting the economy while rejecting medical expertise about the pandemic, without relying on expert's claims or counter-expertise (Duarte). Scholars have analysed and demonstrated that politicians regularly prioritise ideological and political objectives, justifying through "rationalization (pseudo-science) and denunciation" (Recuero and Soares 74).

Relying on or rejecting experts and scientific expertise, however, are not necessarily dichotomous or opposite positions. Certainly, rhetorical narratives about public health information do not necessarily match decision-making, and who is presented as an expert and which knowledge and expertise do they claim is political. Scholars have long warned of the "medicalization of policy" (Degerman) and "politicization of science" (Kukkonen and Ylä-Anttila), which Bauer and Villalobos describe as the "current conceptualization of scientific and medical expertise as specialized, technical, and apolitical knowledge, perceived to be divorced from subjective or value-based decision-making, and the increased reliance on, although not necessarily a responsibility to, these forms of knowledge in politics" (67). This trend risks presenting an apolitical façade to contextual, political knowledge claims, even if coming from public health, scientific, or medical experts. Recent research provides examples of how governments relied on these expert knowledge claims during the Covid-19 pandemic. Exploring how the Chinese government relied on scientific narratives, Lemus-Delgado concludes: "This case shows that science, although generally accepted as rational knowledge based on verifiable facts and honest intellectual debate, can still be used and manipulated by governments as a tool to consolidate their hold on power and that the Chinese government is well aware of this" (12). Lasco similarly observes how the "medical populism" characterising Covid-19 responses in Brazil, the Philippines, and the United States were justified with medical knowledge claims (1417). Regardless of the validity of and responsibility for these knowledge claims, many leaders have rhetorically deployed scientific language to justify their Covid-19 decision-making.

Overall, literature on the rhetoric of Covid-19 decision-making highlights the contested, complicated nature of when, why, and how politicians rhetorically rely on scientific and public health expertise and the language through which they communicate their decision-making. Relying on scientific, public health, medical expertise and knowledge claims can reveal careful decision-making integrating content and political expertise, and/or a means of redirecting or shielding from blame and responsibility, and/or a tool to justify policy decisions to preserve or extend political power. The intentions and motivations behind these rhetorical justifications are incredibly consequential for "concealing the political decision-making behind a multi-layered bulwark of expertise, behind which accountabilities may become difficult to discern" (Degerman S66).

Research Methodology

Chile is an analytically important case to explore when, why, and how politicians narrate their Covid-19 decision-making and explore what patterns of governance are obscured during pandemic decision-making. The Covid-19 pandemic hit Chile during ongoing protests and historically low approval ratings for the Piñera administration. The Piñera administration struggled to respond to controversies over its early handling of the pandemic, with the most prominent resulting in Chile's Minister of Health Jaime Mañalich resigning in June 2020 over the definition of recovery and discrepancies in reported Covid-19 deaths ("Renuncia ministro").

Chile's vaccination campaign was incredibly successful. Within eight weeks, more than one-third of Chileans received one dose (Aguilera et al.), and, as of writing in 2023, Chile has one of the world's highest vaccination rates (about 90%). But, the "Chilean paradigm" became the "Chilean paradox" as rising vaccination rates were accompanied with rising case rates (Villalobos Dintrans et al.). Earlier than many countries, Chilean officials navigated contradictory communications strategies about the success of the vaccination campaign, responsibility for unclear and mismanaged elements of the Covid-19 pandemic (Glenn et al.), and the ongoing need for preventative measures.

To analyse justifications of decision-making in Chile, we constructed an original database of quotes from Chilean government officials, politicians, medical, and public health officials — using written media as a source. We collected more than 300 quotes from early 2020 to April 2022 newspaper articles available through Access World News Research Collection.[1] To account for potential variation in if or how different news sources quote different authorities, we also added news articles from a Google News keyword search.

---

[1] We collected quotes in articles for three keyword searches: 1: "Chile, COVID-19, Vacunas, Calendario" (72 news articles), 2: "Chile, COVID-19, Vacunas, abastecimiento" (20 news articles), 3: "Chile, COVID-19, Vacunas, priorización". For each, we limited the search to Chilean news sources, and articles published from 2020-April 2022.

Discourse analysis of these quotes allows for the assessment of variations in how different stakeholders understand, explain, and justify decisions regarding vaccination policy. This approach is relevant given the simultaneous successful vaccination rollout and concerning increases in cases; in this context of uncertainty, the public narration surrounding vaccines is a key source of information and instrument to implement public health strategies. We paid particular attention to the politicians' narratives about the vaccine rollout, drawing on Dahlstrom's definition of narrative in the context of science communication as "a particular structure that describes the cause-and-effect relationships that take place over a particular time period that impact particular characters" (13614). How do Chilean politicians justify who should take which actions and for what reasons? What role do public health and medical experts and expertise play in these justifications and narratives of vaccine decision-making? Below, we explore these questions over four key stages of Chile's initial vaccine rollout: 1) securing supply, 2) government eligibility and prioritisation policy, 3) distribution, and 4) preventative Covid-19 public health messaging in the context of high-vaccination rates.

Analysis of the stages of Chile's Covid-19 rollout

Stage 1: Securing the Supply

Chile secured vaccine access by entering negotiations and collaborations before vaccine development and authorisations were complete, which eventually secured extensive vaccine access during 2020 (Minsal). By February 2021, when Chile started its mass vaccination campaign, Chile had purchase orders for more than 35 million vaccine doses from Pfizer-BioNTech, Sinovac, AstraZeneca, Johnson & Johnson, and Covax, and was in conversations to purchase two doses of Sputnik V for the full Chilean population (Pichel). The government's success in securing the vaccine supply became the talking point of the Piñera administration, which repeatedly rhetorically narrowed the definition of successful pandemic management to its ability to secure this supply.

Two strategies secured Chile's early supply of vaccine doses: academic partnerships with laboratories, and government agreements with vaccine providers. Chile's first doses were secured as the result of academic partnerships between the Pontificia Universidad Católica (PUC) and Sinovac. In February 2020, PUC professor Alexis Kalergis contacted university officials about extending collaborative research with Chinese professors on respiratory virus vaccines. This led to PUC serving as a site for Stage 3 clinical trials, funded by four million dollars from the Chilean government and two million dollars from the Confederación de la Producción y del Comercio (CPC). In October, PUC passed the agreement to the Chilean Health Ministry to negotiate the arrival of four million doses of the vaccine by January 2021. While academic officials spoke of this collaboration as one of international collaboration and innovation, government officials highlighted the utility of this work for trade negotiations. As Rodrigo Yáñez, undersecretary in Chile's trade ministry described:

> Lo importante es que se generó un trabajo científico con la universidad desde bastante temprano con Sinovac, por lo que existía un conocimiento de la vacuna y la ciencia que tenía detrás…en paralelo, nosotros tomamos la posta de la negociación comercial, donde básicamente nos enfocamos en negociar un precio y un calendario muy ambicioso en vista de las entregas hacia el primer trimestre de 2021 (Chávez and Blanco, "Las Gestiones").[2]

This ensured Chile its first four million doses of Sinovac in January 2021, 10 million during the first three months of 2021, and 20 million doses per year for three years at a 25% discount (Piñera). Three additional laboratories carried out trials in Chile, building on the universities' expertise, public health centres, and networks of potential volunteers: Oxford-AstraZeneca and Janssen with the Universidad de Chile, and CanSino-Laval with Universidad de la Frontera (Villalobos Dintrans et al.).

Second, Chile negotiated with multiple vaccine makers, approaching, and discussing the issue as a matter of trade, technical, bureaucratic, and business tasks. Chile's strategy to diversify its negotiations and agreements, was reportedly a decision of the Ministry of Science (Luna, "La exitosa estrategia"), minimising the risk that one vaccine would not be approved or available. Government officials frequently described the strategy as "not putting all eggs in the same basket" (Piñera). Rodrigo Yáñez, the undersecretary in Chile's trade ministry, explained, "We have a huge network of international contacts…When the pandemic started, we already had many key foreign officials in our WhatsApp" (Oppenheimer). Yáñez further justified, "We considered the technical and scientific merit of each vaccine rather than political factors…" (Bartlett) and "No es conveniente que la estrategia considere más dosis de la misma plataforma, por esta razón de mitigar riesgos de apostar por una tecnología" (Gómez).[3] These agreements leveraged Chile's pre-existing trade agreements and diplomatic relationships. Discussions of vaccine supply were most commonly led by government

---

[2] "The important thing is that scientific work with the university was generated quite early with Sinovac, so there was knowledge of the vaccine and the science behind it… in parallel, we took over the commercial negotiation, where we basically focused on negotiating price and an ambitious schedule…".

[3] "The strategy of considering more doses of the same platform is not convenient, that is the reason to mitigate the risks of betting on one technology".

officials in Chile's ministries of health, science, foreign relations, and trade, revealing its approach to defining the challenge as one of innovation and trade.

This oversupply of vaccines, particularly the early access to the Sinovac vaccine, allowed Chile to weather early gaps in global vaccine supply, and the Piñera administration to redirect critiques or questions about vaccine supply to different levels of government. For example, when the EU limited vaccine exports, the Minister of Health Paris dismissed the concern explaining that, "puede generar dificultades en el arribo de vacunas de AstraZeneca, pero no esperábamos la llegada de (esas) vacunas hasta abril, así que a lo mejor de aquí a esa fecha la situación cambia. Pero con Pfizer no hay problema, y con Sinovac (fabricada en China), obviamente, tampoco" (Chávez and Herrera, "Salud Asegura")[4] As the vaccine distribution campaign developed, government communication strategies about the vaccine supply shifted in response to critiques about which vaccines were available where. For example, in April 2021 when there were reports of vaccination centres running short on supply, the head of the Departamento de Acción Sanitaria de la Seremi de la Región Metropolitana explained "definitivamente no hay un problema de stock de vacunas, sino que de logística" ("Seremi: falta de vacunas").[5] In these communication strategies, the government claimed credit for their work in securing the vaccine supply, deflecting responsibility away from the central government.

The Piñera administration's narrow definition of securing vaccine supplies as one of trade, innovation, and logistics shielded itself from responsibility to situating vaccine supplies within a broader public health strategy. The government described the first shipload of vaccines, which arrived on 24 December 2020, as a "'regalo de Navidad' para el país" (Minsal).[6] It also allowed the government to declare victory and success in accomplishing the narrow challenge of securing doses despite its less successful broader handling of the pandemic. Political analyst German Silva commented, "Se ven dos gobiernos manejando la pandemia; uno el exitoso, el que le va bien manejando la logística y distribución como si fuera una empresa… la gestión política de la pandemia donde no le ha ido nada bien" (Luna, "La exitosa estrategia").[7] Similarly, scholar Marcelo Mella observed that vaccination rollout allowed Piñera to "estrechar el resultado", but was sceptical if it was enough to "revertir el daño que en la opinión pública que

---

[4] "This may cause difficulties in the arrival of AstraZeneca vaccines, but we did not expect those vaccines to arrive until April, so perhaps between now and then the situation will change. But there is no problem with Pfizer, nor with Sinovac (made in China), obviously".
[5] "Definitely, there is not a problem of vaccine stocks, but a logistic one".
[6] "Christmas present for the country".
[7] "One can see two governments managing the pandemic; one is successful, doing well managing logistics and distribution as if it were a company… [and the other] the political management of the pandemic which has not gone well at all".

tiene el Gobierno a raíz del estallido social y la represión a las manifestaciones sociales" (Luna, "La exitosa estrategia").[8]

Stage 2: Eligibility and Prioritisation

To distribute vaccines, the Minister of Health, the Departamento de Inmunizaciones, and the National Advisory Committee on Immunisation (Comite Asesor en Vacunas e Inmunizaciones, CAVEI, an advisory committee created to provide independent, evidence-based recommendations to the Ministry of Health for immunisation programmes and policy formulation) designed a vaccination plan, drawing on the immunisation guidelines from the World Health Organisation and later revised by the Pan American Health Organization (*El programa de inmunización*). Announced by Piñera in January 2021, the plan prioritised the vaccination efforts for the higher-risk groups and "aquellas personas que desarrollan labores críticas y esenciales para el buen funcionamiento de la sociedad, el Estado, y para atender las necesidades básicas de la ciudadanía": front line health care workers, elderly citizens over 80 years old, the rest of health care workers, those working in elderly and youth government-sponsored assistance living programmes (Piñera).[9] The Minister of Health Enrique Paris justified that, based on data from similar flu vaccination campaigns, this initial phase would require approximately five million doses (Chávez, "Salud propone"). Essential personnel, citizens over the age of 65, and people with high morbidity would follow (Minsal).

Subsequent prioritisations were more controversial, with many lobbying to establish their sectors' importance in reactivating the economy. Leaders from multiple business sectors demanded to be prioritised on economic grounds. For example, the president of the Cámara Nacional de Comercio Manuel Melero commented that "nosotros hace 10 ó 15 días pedimos esto mismo al Gobierno, de que se evaluara la posibilidad de vacunar prioritariamente al comercio y el turismo. Quedaron de evaluarlo"; Ricardo Rodríguez, president of the Sindicato de Estibadores de Muellaje del Maipo framed "somos la primera línea para el abastecimiento nacional y por eso es tan relevante que nos podamos vacunar contra el coronavirus"; and president of ChilePan, Marcelo Alonso similarly justified "Creemos que los panaderos deben estar más protegidos y asegurarles una pronta inoculación" (Olivares et al.).[10]

---

[8] "Reverse the damage to public opinion that the Government has from the protests and the repression of social demonstrations… The successful process of mass vaccination…has an impact, but does not change the scorecard".
[9] "Those who carry out critical and essential tasks for the proper functioning of society, the State, and citizens' basic needs".
[10] Melero: "10 to 15 days ago, we asked the Government to evaluate the possibility of vaccinating trade and tourism as a priority. They were to evaluate". Rodríguez: "We are the first line for national supply and that is why it is so relevant that we can be vaccinated

Broad vaccination sets up the stage for a reactivation of the economy, helping workers from areas such as hotels and restaurants, some of the most impacted industries, to get back in "business".

Teachers also lobbied to be prioritised because of the high number of close contacts, and the importance of keeping the schools open to reactivate the economy. Maria Aguilar, president of Colegio de Profesores, together with Cristobal Cuadrado, of the Medical Board, argued that teachers, along with front-line health workers, should be the first to receive the vaccine, given teachers' close contact with children (Chávez, "Salud propone"). After negotiating with the Colegio de Profesores, Paris indicated teachers would indeed be included among the first to receive the vaccine in order to open schools, requiring an additional stock of 488 thousand doses (Chávez, "Salud propone").

Further political tension emerged over citizenship or residency requirements for vaccine eligibility. Government officials announced in February 2021 that they were restricting vaccine access to citizens and residents to avoid "vaccine tourism". Minister of Foreign Affairs, Andres Allamand justified "no van a tener derecho a vacunarse en Chile, los extranjeros que estén en el país con una visa de turista. Tampoco van a tener derecho a vacunarse en Chile los extranjeros que estén como turistas, pero que vengan de algún país que no se les exige visa" ("Colegio médico pide"). [11] Right-wing politicians quickly supported the announcement and mapped it onto anti-immigrant mobilisation and rhetoric by expanding from the stated goal of limiting vaccine tourism to include prohibiting irregular migrants' eligibility. For example, right wing presidential candidate José Antonio Kast, stated "Chile no es un destino turístico para vacunarse" y "quien cruza la frontera de manera ilegal, no tiene derecho a inocularse" ("Migrantes sin derecho"). [12] In contrast, leading scientific and medical experts rebuked the policy, with President of the Medical Board Izkia Siches calling to "mantener la cultura histórica de la Salud Pública Chilena brindando protección a la población migrante independientemente de su condición migratoria" (Siches).[13] Doctor Juan Carlos Said added that "pedir papeles migratorios para tratar enfermedades infecciosas o entregar vacunas, es la receta para que no logremos controlar diferentes enfermedades

---

against the coronavirus". Alonso: "We believe that bakers should be more protected and ensure prompt inoculation".

[11] "Foreigners who are in the country with a tourist visa will not have the right to be vaccinated in Chile. Nor will foreigners who are here as tourists, but came from a country from which a visa is not required".

[12] "Chile is not a tourist destination for vaccinations" and "those who cross the border illegally do not have the right to be vaccinated".

[13] "Maintain the historical culture of Chilean Public Health by providing protection to the migrant population regardless of their immigration status".

incluída #COVID19" ("'Portazo'").[14] Furthermore, multiple political figures also expressed their opposition to excluding immigrants from vaccination and hinted at the political motivations behind the policy decision; for example, current Chilean president Gabriel Boric, called for the vaccine to be "humanitaria" and for the government to "revertir esta decisión arbitraria y discriminadora" ("'Portazo'").[15] Given the strong opposition, the government quickly reversed this policy in February 2021. This policy change was communicated by several governmental authorities including Alvaro Bellolio, Director of Inmigration Service, Paula Daza, Undersecretary of Public Health, and Health Minister Paris; while announcing the change, Paris justified "Es una razón muy importante de salud pública vacunar a todos los que habitan en Chile, sean chilenos o extranjeros. Quiero aclarar las dudas y darle seguridad a la población de que los extranjeros serán vacunados cuando corresponda en el calendario" (Chávez and Cifuentes).[16] The policy change that was celebrated by the medical and scientific community.

The government also managed distribution and supply by dynamically assigning different vaccine doses to different age segments of the population. For example, when Sinovac was authorised for minors ages six and up, Chile restarted its vaccination calendar that had stopped after those all over 18 years old had been vaccinated. Previously, the Pfizer vaccine had been approved for those under 18 years old but was scarce and its distribution was logistically complicated. Showing the dynamic aspect of the vaccination schedule proposed by the CAVEI and carried out by the government, Héctor Sánchez, director of the Institute of Public Health at Andres Bello University justified:

> Si hay disponibilidad de vacunas de Pfizer para poder avanzar con las dosis de refuerzo de los menores de 55 años, y simultáneamente tenemos Sinovac para avanzar en los menores de 12 años y también para los rezagados, hay que avanzar en todos los frentes. Mientras más alto sea el porcentaje de población vacunada, más segura va a estar la gente (Chávez, "Chile Afina").[17]

---

[14] "Asking for immigration papers to treat infectious diseases or deliver vaccines is the recipe for us not controlling different diseases included #COVID19".
[15] "Humanitarian" and "reverse this arbitrary and discriminatory decision".
[16] "It is a very important for public health to vaccinate everyone who lives in Chile, Chilean or foreigner. I want to clarify doubts and assure the population that foreigners will be vaccinated when it corresponds in the calendar".
[17] "If there is availability of Pfizer vaccines to be able to advance with the booster doses for those under 55 years of age, and we simultaneously have Sinovac to advance with those under 12 years of age and also for those who are lagging behind, progress must be made on all fronts. The higher the percentage of the population vaccinated, the safer people will be".

The strategy to use of several types and providers of vaccines to quickly immunise the highest percentage of the population was also supported by medical and public health experts. This strategy exemplifies the need for rapid and efficient communication between the health experts —CAVEI in this case— and the government officials to quickly respond to the ever-changing conditions of the virus and protect the health of the population.

Stage 3: Vaccine Distribution

After acquiring sufficient vaccine stock and defining eligibility and prioritisation, the Chilean government worked to establish an efficient and reliable distribution network. Chile faced common challenges, like vaccine storage requirements, and several less common ones, including geographic logistics challenges of distributing doses across more than 6000 km and overcrowding at vaccination centres because of Chile's large supply (Minsal). However, Chile has a long successful history of vaccination programmes, including the eradication of smallpox in 1950 and poliomyelitis in 1975. As Cecilia Morales, Director of Uchile Hospital and Fonasa, highlights of how Chile drew on its healthcare network "Chile tiene un sistema de salud que está desplegado territorialmente donde se atiende el 80% de la población y que a pesar de las falencias, tiene encargada la ejecución de los programas de salud pública para el 100% de la población desde hace más de 70 años" (Luna, "2,7 Millones").[18] Current Chilean politicians recognised the contributions of past politicians and health experts in developing this vaccine infrastructure and culture. Health Minister Enrique Paris praised "los fundadores del sistema público de salud" Salvador Allende and Eduardo Cruz-Coke, demonstrating broad acceptance of the quality of Chile's vaccination culture and capacity developed over decades by political figures ranging the political spectrum (Miño).[19] This vaccination campaign network has established distribution protocols and roles for medical and administrative personnel that were quickly deployed to run 1800 vaccination sites during the Covid-19 campaign (Aguilera et al.).

Despite these advantages, politicians punted blame between levels of government for delivery delays. These delays produced crowding and long waiting lines, particularly worrisome for the elderly population during the winter. Local officials blamed national officials for not delivering doses, and national officials blamed local logistics. Tomas Vodanovic and Emilia Ríos, mayors of Maipu and Ñuñoa, complained "Le hago un llamado al ministro para que podamos organizar mejor este proceso" and "temas de descoordinación por

---

[18] "Chile has health system deployed territorially that serves 80% of the population and, despite its shortcomings, has been in charge of executing public health programmes for 100% of the population for more than 70 years".
[19] "Creators of the public Chilean system".

parte del Minsal y la oportunidad en que se ha comunicado a los municipios", respectively ("Paris se enfrenta"). [20] Meanwhile, national health authorities denied the claims of limited supply and pressured local authorities to keep vaccination centres open; Paris mentioned "No hay falta de vacunas Sinovac y menos de AstraZeneca. Es insólito que los vacunatorios cierren porque no tienen Pfizer, deberían seguir funcionando" ("Paris se enfrenta"). [21] Responding to criticisms, health officials tried to assure that waiting times would be reduced by increasing the number of vaccination centres.

In addition to punting blame between levels of government, many politicians and leaders rhetorically shifted the responsibility for managing demand and access from the government to citizens. For example, Daniela Peñaloza, mayor of Las Condes, mentioned "Las aglomeraciones se generan cuando todos llegan juntos muy temprano para asegurar dosis" (Hernández and Herrera), shifting responsibility for delays to the population rather than to organisers.[22] Public communications called on the public to follow official recommendations and the assigned vaccination schedule, frequently invoking messages of unity in the fight against Covid-19. For example, Ximena Aguilera stated "es una gran noticia. Ahora, todos a apoyar la que será la mayor campaña de vacunación de nuestra historia", while President of the Medical Board Izkia Siches reiterated calls for citizens to "colaborar para que sea un proceso ordenado y sin aglomeraciones" (Chávez and Herrera, "Vacunación masiva").[23]

Besides calling for public cooperation, official authorities presented diverse measures to avoid delays and crowding in vaccination centres, such as offering flexibility to the strict vaccination schedule presented by the government. Several of these measures also called on the public to navigate the context. For example, Paula Daza asked people to "En caso que no se encuentren en la comuna en que residen, puede acercarse al vacunatorio de donde estén" and "si por distintos motivos no pueden ir el día que le tocó según el calendario, van a poder ir después, pero les pedimos respetar el día, porque así no tenemos aglomeraciones los días siguientes" (Chávez and Herrera, "Vacunación masiva"),[24] doubling the efforts to prevent crowds and lines in vaccination

---

[20] Vodanovic: "I call on the minister so that we can better organise this process". Rios: "issues of lack of coordination on the part of the Minsal and the opportunity in which it has been communicated to the municipalities".
[21] "There is no lack of Sinovac vaccines and less of AstraZeneca. It is unusual for vaccination centres to close because they do not have Pfizer, they should continue to work".
[22] "Crowds are caused by everyone arriving together very early to secure their doses".
[23] Aguilera: "Now, everyone should support what will be the largest vaccination campaign in our history". Siches: "collaborate so that it is an orderly process and without crowds".
[24] "In case they are not in the commune in which they reside, they can go to the vaccination centre closest to wherever they are… If for different reasons they cannot go on the day that they had to go according to the calendar, they will be able to go later, but we ask them to respect the day, because that way we do not have crowds the following days".

centres. Notably, this effort was through rhetorical calls for individual responsibility. Some of this work was shifted to the staff at local health centres; for example, Edgardo Fuenzalida, the CEO of Fundación Las Rosas, one of the largest elderly-care organisations in the country, emphasised the risk of crowds in the vaccination centre for the elderly people and called on local health centres to plan and inform patients of the vaccination process (Chávez and Herrera, "Vacunación masiva").

School-aged children posed another distribution challenge. Despite the efficiency and speed of the vaccination centres, health experts also highlighted the need to include schools as vaccination hubs. There was broad support for this strategy. Francisco Moraga, former president of the Chilean Society of Pediatrics, emphasised the importance of high vaccination rates in kids to avoid case surges of the virus. Moraga, together with Humberto Soriano, advocated for vaccinating children at their schools, emphasising the risk not only for the children but to the other risk populations, such as the elderly, cancer, and transplant patients (Chávez and Gotschlich). In addition to public health benefits, this vaccination effort would facilitate parents' ability to go back to work, however, the logistics involved were complicated. For example, the Pfizer vaccine was difficult to store, thus requiring larger supplies of Sinovac and CoronaVac vaccines, easier to use and store. As Jaime Burrows, former Undersecretary of Health, declared: "es una buena estrategia ir a vacunar a los colegios para llegar a los niños que no han podido vacunarse, pero para eso hay que tener una vacuna que sea más fácil de movilizar y almacenar que la Pfizer" (Chávez and Gotschlich).[25] These strategies were promoted by government officials, who hoped to start implementation as soon as vaccines were approved.

Stage 4: Preventative Messaging

Finally, a fourth stage of Chile's vaccine rollout is the tension of high vaccination rates and high case rates, challenging officials to balance the "coexistence between the preventive message (and the need to keep basic preventive measures) with the message of victory coming from the vaccine rollout" (Villalobos Dintrans et al.). In Chile, stakeholders were either "optimistic" or "reluctant" in their communications about this tension, with most government officials communicating optimism. While the first group communicated hope in vaccines to reduce the impact of the pandemic, the second group raised concerns about this strategy, based on the effectiveness of the vaccine and/or the need to adopt a more holistic approach to address the pandemic.

---

[25] "It is a good strategy to go and vaccinate to the schools to reach children who have not been vaccinated, but for that you have to have a vaccine easier to mobilise and store than Pfizer".

Early in the vaccine rollout, politicians focused on communicating the vaccine's efficacy but were ambiguous on whether efficacy referred to cases, hospitalisations, and/or mortality. For example, in February 2021, Minister Paris commented about the positive results in other countries and the discussion on the possibility of needing several doses: "Una publicación israelita muy interesante demostró que ya con la primera dosis de Pfizer hay una protección bastante alta; entonces, ellos hicieron un grupo de estudio en el cual colocaron la segunda dosis de forma más tardía y demostraron incluso mejores resultados" (Chávez, "Consejo asesor").[26] The messaging about effectiveness was combined with the authorities' instance on vaccine safety to increase public acceptance. In April 2021, Minister Paris said: "la vacuna Sinovac es una vacuna segura y confiable. Se debe contar con total tranquilidad con esta vacuna, ha demostrado ser eficaz" (Aguirre).[27]

One of the main messages coming from the "optimistic side", in addition to vaccine effectiveness, was the need for a broad vaccination coverage to reach the so-called "herd immunity". Government health authorities set vaccine coverage as the main goal, and directly linked to the reduction or removal of stringent Covid-19 measures. For example, Minister Paris said in February 2021: "aún no lo hemos analizado bien, pero me parece que puede ser una buena idea que los municipios que tengan un alto porcentaje de inmunizados tengan mayores libertades, lo que también puede motivar a avanzar en el plan de vacunación" (Chávez, "Dieciséis comunas").[28] Similarly, Paula Daza, stated "tenemos que asegurarnos de que haya un mayor porcentaje de la población vacunada", and added that the more vaccinated people they had, the more they were able to "empezar a darles más libertades en relación al plan 'Paso a paso', principalmente a todas aquellas que tengan ambas dosis" (Chávez, "Chile es el segundo").[29] The message of the safety of the vaccines and the need to increase coverage were supported by the country's health authorities and public health experts, and repeated in discussions about vaccinating specific groups of the population, such as children and pregnant women. For example, regarding the vaccination in children, paediatrician Humberto Soriano highlighted that: "Por

---

[26] "… A very interesting Israeli publication showed that already with the first dose of Pfizer there is quite a high level of protection; so, they did a study group in which they placed the second dose later, which showed even better results".

[27] "The Sinovac vaccine is safe and reliable. You should have complete peace of mind with this vaccine, it has proven to be effective".

[28] "… It seems to me that it may be a good idea for municipalities with a high percentage of immunised persons to have greater freedoms, which may also motivate progress in the vaccination plan".

[29] "We have to make sure that there is a higher percentage of the population vaccinated" and "to start giving them more freedom in relation to the step by step plan, mainly to those with two doses".

favor, no se queden rezagados, porque no solamente están dañando a su hijo, sino que están haciendo peligrar a sus abuelos, a la persona trasplantada, a la persona con cáncer; entonces, también hay una responsabilidad muy importante por los otros" (Chávez and Gotschlich).[30] Similarly, the president of the Chilean Society of Child and Adolescent Gynecology and Obstetrics, Andrea Huneeus stated: "el Covid-19 en [mujeres embarazadas] aumenta su riesgo de enfermar y de morir (…) La vacuna se ha puesto en suficientes embarazadas que han tenido a sus hijos sin ningún problema" (Hernández).[31]

However, communications about vaccine efficacy and coverage were vague regarding how the vaccine rollout related to other preventative measures. This tension between the successes and limitations of the vaccine was clear from initial messages from Minister Paris, where he explicitly stated that preventive measures were needed, at least for a period of time, before reaching herd immunity:

> Antes del 15 de abril no vamos a notar un cambio claro (…) Hay que insistir en el lavado de manos, distanciamiento físico, uso de mascarilla, porque sabemos que no se va a acabar el virus aunque tengamos a mucha gente vacunada en marzo. Normalmente se produce el efecto rebaño cuando se vacuna al 80% de la población, con vacunas de excelente calidad como las que tenemos en Chile, y eso se va a lograr a fines de junio, por lo que no podemos bajar los brazos (Chávez and Blanco, "El 21% de la población").[32]

The quote, from February 2021, is vague regarding whether preventive measures —such as handwashing, use of facemask, and physical distancing— were needed while waiting for the coverage of the vaccine to be large enough or were even recommended after reaching 80% coverage, in June 2021. This could have influenced the declining adherence to preventive measures from 2020 to 2021 (Varas et al.).

---

[30] "Please, don't be left behind, because not only are you harming your child, but you are endangering your grandparents, the transplant recipient, the person with cancer; there is a very important responsibility for the other".

[31] "Covid-19 [in pregnant women] increases their risk of getting sick and dying (…). The vaccine has been given to enough pregnant women who have had their children without any problem".

[32] "Before April 15 we will not notice a clear change (…) We must insist on hand washing, physical distancing, wearing a mask, because we know that the virus will not end even if we have many people vaccinated in March. Normally, herd immunity effect occurs when 80% of the population is vaccinated, with excellent quality vaccines like the ones we have in Chile, and that will be achieved by the end of June, so we cannot give up".

As the rollout progressed, the transition from the Chilean paradigm (successful vaccination rollout) to the Chilean paradox (high vaccination rates and high contagion rates) raised increasing concern about the strategy of vaccines as a silver bullet. While authorities insisted on the effectiveness of the vaccines to reduce deaths and ICU utilization, messaging about the usefulness of the vaccine to prevent cases was confusing. For example, while Minister Paris insisted the vaccine would avoid health complications[33] and deaths[34], the concept of herd immunity was still used, implying that the vaccine protected against contagion.[35] This message of "hope in the vaccine" could have increased cases, as individuals' risk perceptions shifted. As public health expert Héctor Sánchez stated: "las personas, al estar vacunadas, se sienten con mayor grado de seguridad y se exponen al riesgo más allá de lo conveniente. Por lo tanto, cuando hay una circulación viral de la magnitud que estamos teniendo hoy en el país, esas personas se pueden infectar" (Chávez, "Pacientes mayores").[36]

Only at the end of May 2021 did Minister Paris explicitly established the role of vaccines and the need to complement vaccinations with other basic preventive measures, stating: "tenemos que insistir que hay que trabajar fuerte en las medidas básicas, como la mascarilla y distanciamiento físico… El virus se disemina porque la vacuna no evita el contagio, sino que las hospitalizaciones y la mortalidad" (Chávez, "Fuerte rebrote").[37] Yet, this messaging was inconsistent, with confusion still present in 2022, when Paris stated that the incentive to vaccinate was mainly "el pase de movilidad, porque para tenerlo habilitado se requiere la dosis de refuerzo, pero también hay un incentivo importante, que es evitar que la gente se enferme gravemente, que la gente muera, teniendo la posibilidad de evitarlo" (Chávez, "1.2 millones").[38]

In summary, this stage was dominated by two narratives about the vaccine: one trying to establish the vaccine as the main (and sometimes sole) strategy

---

[33] Paris argued that, at the time, more than 55% of those in intensive care units were there because they have not had their vaccines (Chávez and Neira).
[34] Paris argued that mortality in the unimmunised was more than 30% while mortality in the vaccinated dropped to 6%, what he described as a gigantic difference (Chávez, "'Diferencia gigantesca'").
[35] Paris argued that, in other countries, after increasing vaccination it was possible to see a decrease in the number of infections (Chávez, "Chile supera").
[36] "After being vaccinated, people feel more secure and expose themselves to risk beyond what is convenient. Therefore, when there is a viral circulation of the magnitude that we are having today in the country, these people can be infected".
[37] "We have to insist that we must work hard on basic measures, such as masks and physical distancing… the virus spreads because the vaccine does not prevent contagion, but hospitalisations and mortality".
[38] "The mobility pass, since the booster dose is required to enable it, but there is another important incentive, which is to prevent people from getting seriously ill, from dying, and having the possibility of avoiding it".

to emerge from the pandemic (the "optimistic" view) and one responding to this strategy (the "reluctant view"). Stakeholders in the first group, mainly government authorities, highlighted the safety and effectiveness of the vaccine which, when combined with the high vaccination coverage, would address Covid-19 in the country during 2021. On the other hand, sceptics criticised this strategy on several grounds, highlighting the nuances in the vaccine's effectiveness (cases/ hospitalisations/ mortality) and adverse effects on diminishing risk perception and the consequent increase in Covid-19 cases.

Conclusion

What can we learn from how the Piñera administration and public health experts narrated the vaccine rollout in Chile? Across the four stages of the vaccine rollout, the Piñera administration remained optimistic, defining and declaring success in securing an impressive vaccine supply and quickly rollout a vaccination campaign. However, this success was accompanied by ambiguity and deflections in other elements of the pandemic; the government punted responsibility for managing crowds and lines, on clarifying the predicted outcomes of vaccines, and on specifying the relationship between preventative public health measures and vaccination campaigns. In contrast, public health experts were more likely to caution about the limitations of seeing vaccines as a silver bullet, and to invoke a sense of unity and a collective Chile in their calls for an integrated, multifaceted approach to managing the evolving Covid-19 pandemic.

These trends highlight the communication challenges that governments face while navigating how to narrate elements of success to the public, but ongoing and shifting crises politics. As highlighted here, communication strategies reveal ambiguities in policymaking and decision-making, such as definitions of vaccine effectiveness and strategies for rolling out different vaccines to different age groups. These communication strategies also reveal clarity in decision-making priorities, such as re-establishing the economy and invoking individual responsibility.

Bibliography

Aguilera, Ximena, et al. "The Story Behind Chile's Rapid Rollout of Covid-19 Vaccination". *Travel Medicine and Infectious Disease*, vol. 42, 2021, https://doi.org/10.1016/j.tmaid.2021.102092.

Aguirre, Francisco. "Todo lo que sabemos de Coronavac, la vacuna del laboratorio Sinovac en Chile". *La Tercera*, 12 April 2021, https://www.latercera.com/que-pasa/noticia/todo-lo-que-sabemos-de-coronavac-la-vacuna-del-laboratorio-sinovac-en-chile/ZRZJ2CQQ6NFKXCDDTHFEPEY3BU/.

Argote, Pablo, et al. "Messages That Increase Covid-19 Vaccine Acceptance: Evidence from Online Experiments in Six Latin American Countries". *PloS one*, vol. 16, no. 10, 2021, https://doi.org/10.1371/journal.pone.0259059.

—. "The Shot, the Message, and the Messenger: Covid-19 Vaccine Acceptance in Latin America". *NPJ Vaccines*, vol. 6, no. 118, 2021, https://doi.org/10.1038/s41541-021-00380-x.

Attwell, Katie, et al. "Covid-19: Talk of 'Vaccine Hesitancy' lets Governments Off the Hook". *Nature*, vol. 602, no. 7898, 2022, pp 574–577.

Bartlett, John. "Chile Emerges as Global Leader in Covid Inoculations with 'Pragmatic Strategy'". *The Guardian*, 28 February 2021, https://www.theguardian.com/global-development/2021/feb/28/chile-covid-inoculations-vaccines-strategy.

Bauer, Kelly, and Claudio Villalobos. "Politics of Expertise and Blame During Covid-19 Quarantine in Chile". *Middle Atlantic Review of Latin American Studies*, vol. 4, no. 3, 2021, pp. 65–76.

Bossert, Thomas J., and Pablo Villalobos Dintrans. "Health Reform in the Midst of a Social and Political Crisis in Chile, 2019-2020". *Health Systems & Reform*, vol. 6, no. 1, 2020, https://doi.org/10.1080/23288604.2020.1789031.

Cadem. "Encuesta Plaza Pública: Especial Gobierno Presidente Piñera". *Plaza Pública CADEM*, 2022, https://cadem.cl/wp-content/uploads/2022/03/Especial-Cierre-Piñera-VF.pdf.

Chávez, Max. "1.2 millones de adultos tienen un rezago de más de 30 días en su dosis de refuerzo". *El Mercurio*, 1 March, 2022.

—. "Chile afina su estrategia de vacunación: busca reforzar con Pfizer a adultos de hasta 55 años y priorizar dosis de Sinovac en menores de 12". *El Mercurio*, 22 August 2021, https://portal.nexnews.cl/showN?valor=h3sun.

—. "Chile es el segundo país del mundo con mayor porcentaje de población completamente vacunada". *El Mercurio*, 28 April 2021, https://digital.elmercurio.com/2021/04/28/C/A53V0BUF.

—. "Chile supera récord de contagios y salud busca reimpulsar vacunación con 500 mil pacientes de 48 y 49 años la próxima semana". *El Mercurio*, 9 April 2021, https://digital.elmercurio.com/2021/04/09/C/953UMR8H#.

—. "Consejo asesor recomienda postergar por hasta 90 días aplicación de segunda dosis para ampliar cobertura". *El Mercurio*, 27 February 2021, https://digital.elmercurio.com/Ranking?date=2021/02/27&section=C&publication=mercurio&action=getRanking.

—. "Dieciséis comunas ya han vacunado a más del 25% de su población y otras 80 no superan el 10%". *El Mercurio*, 18 February 2021, https://portal.nexnews.cl/showN?valor=fn01k.

—. "'Diferencia gigantesca' de letalidad entre pacientes UCI mayores de 60 años no vacunados y aquellos inmunizados". *El Mercurio*, 28 March 2021, https://digital.elmercurio.com/2021/03/28/C/AE3UGNNC.

—. "Fuerte rebrote en RM: 86% de comunas ha aumentado infecciones en últimas dos semanas". *El Mercurio*, 29 May 2021, https://digital.elmercurio.com/2021/05/29/C/TU3VE4EM.

—. "Pacientes mayores de 60 años un UCI llegan a su nivel más alto de toda la pandemia". *El Mercurio*, 18 June 2021, https://digital.elmercurio.com/2021/06/18/C/CL3VO8EV.

—. "Salud propone sumar a 488 mil profesores a grupo prioritario de vacunación anti-Covid-19". *El Mercurio*, 24 November 2020, https://digital.elmercurio.com/2020/11/24/C/OH3SME2R.

Chávez, Max, and María José Blanco. "El 21% de la población objetivo ya fue vacunado y salud espera ver 'cambio claro' en la pandemia a mediados de abril". *El Mercurio*, 25 February 2021, https://digital.elmercurio.com/2021/02/25/C/CR3U3IAR.

—. "Las gestiones que permitieron la llegada de la vacuna del laboratorio Sinovac a Chile". *El Mercurio*, 13 February 2021, https://digital.elmercurio.com/2021/02/13/C/E93TSUKH.

Chávez, Max, and Patricia Cifuentes. "Tras críticas, gobierno retrocede y permitirá vacunar a inmigrantes en situación irregular". *El Mercurio*, 12 February 2021, https://digital.elmercurio.com/2021/02/12/C/C93TSTVN.

Chávez, Max, and Dierk Gotschlich. "Expertos llaman a vacunar en colegios para acelerar inmunización de los menores de edad". *El Mercurio*, 24 July 2021, https://digital.elmercurio.com/Ranking?date=2021/07/24&section=C&publication=mercurio&action=getRanking.

Chávez, Max, and Judith Herrera. "Salud asegura que restricciones europeas no afectarán vacunación de población de riesgo". *El Mercurio*, 30 January 2021, https://digital.elmercurio.com/2021/01/30/C/513TNA9M.

—. "Vacunación masiva parte con adultos mayores y expertos advierten riesgo de aglomeraciones". *El Mercurio*, 29 January 2021, https://portal.nexnews.cl/showN?valor=fim6q.

Chávez, Max, and Soledad Neira. "Expertos debaten sobre vacunación obligatoria para ciertos grupos y aumentar limitaciones para los rezagados del proceso". *El Mercurio*, 10 November 2021, https://digital.elmercurio.com/2021/11/10/C/2941RCIT#zoom=page-width.

"Colegio médico pide al gobierno 'formas más humanitarias' en tema de vacunas a extranjeros". *El Desconcierto*, 10 February 2021, https://www.eldesconcierto.cl/nacional/2021/02/10/colegio-medico-pide-al-gobierno-formas-mas-humanitarias-en-tema-de-vacunas-a-extranjeros.html.

Dahlstrom, Michael F. "Using Narratives and Storytelling to Communicate Science with Nonexpert Audiences". *Proceedings of the National Academy of Sciences*, vol. 111, no. 4 supplement, 2014, pp. 13614–13620.

Degerman, Dan. "The Political Is Medical Now: Covid-19, Medicalization and Political Theory". *Theory & Event*, vol. 23, no. 4 supplement, 2020, pp. S61–S75.

Duarte, Tiago Ribeiro. "Ignoring Scientific Advice During the Covid-19 Pandemic: Bolsonaro's Actions and Discourse". *Tapuya: Latin American Science, Technology and Society*, vol. 3, 2020, pp. 288–291.

Dussauge-Laguna, Mauricio, et al. "Presidential Policy Narratives and the (Mis)Use of Scientific Expertise: Covid-19 Policy Responses in Brazil, Colombia, and Mexico". *Policy Studies*, vol. 44, no. 1, 2022, pp. 1–22.

El programa de inmunización en el contexto de la pandemia de Covid-19. Organización Panamericana de la Salud, 24 April 2020, https://iris.paho.org/handle/10665.2/52055.

Flinders, Matthew. "Democracy and the Politics of Coronavirus: Trust, Blame and Understanding". *Parliamentary Affairs*, vol. 74, no. 2, 2021, pp. 483–502.

Forster, Timon, and Mirko Heinzel. "Reacting, Fast and Slow: How World Leaders Shaped Government Responses to the Covid-19 Pandemic". *Journal of European Public Policy*, vol. 28, no. 8, 2021, pp. 1299–1320.

Gannon, John, et al. "Analysing the Launch of Covid-19 Vaccine National Rollouts: Nine Case Studies". *Epidemiologia*, vol. 2, no. 4, 2021, pp. 519–539.

Glenn, Jeffrey, et al. "Public Health Leadership in the Times of Covid-19: A Comparative Case Study of Three Countries". *International Journal of Public Leadership*, vol. 17, no. 1, 2021, pp. 81–94.

Gómez, Gerardo. "El gobierno compró 36 millones de vacunas y Pfizer detalla su producto en Chile". *Pauta*, 18 December 2020, https://www.pauta.cl/actualidad/2020/12/18/chile-compra-36-millones-dosis-como-opera-vacuna-pfizer-2021.

Hernández, Manuel. "Embarazadas y vacuna por Covid-19: Se abre debate sobre ampliarla a pacientes sin factores de riesgo". *El Mercurio*, 3 May 2021, https://digital.elmercurio.com/2021/05/03/C/LU3V3RVQ.

Hernández, Manuel, and Judith Herrera. "Con más equipos y horas programadas, buscan reducir filas ante alta demanda en vacunatorios". *El Mercurio*, 15 November 2021, https://amuch.cl/prensa/el-mercurio-con-mas-equipos-y-horas-programadas-buscan-reducir-filas-ante-alta-demanda-en-vacunatorios/.

Kukkonen, Anna, and Tuomas Ylä-Anttila. "The Science–Policy Interface as a Discourse Network: Finland's Climate Change Policy 2002–2015". *Politics and Governance*, vol. 8, no.2, 2020, pp. 200–214.

Lasco, Gideon. "Medical Populism and the Covid-19 Pandemic". *Global Public Health*, vol. 15, no.10, 2020, pp. 1417–1429.

Lazarus, Jeffrey V., et al. "Revisiting Covid-19 Vaccine Hesitancy around the World Using Data from 23 Countries in 2021". *Nature Communications*, vol. 13, 2022, https://doi.org/10.1038/s41467-022-31441-x.

Lemus-Delgado, Daniel. "China and the Battle to Win the Scientific Narrative About the Origin of Covid-19". *Journal of Science Communication*, vol. 19, no. 5, 2020, pp. 1–16.

Lipscy, Phillip Y. "Covid-19 and the Politics of Crisis". *International Organization*, vol. 74, no. S1, 2020, pp. e98–e127.

Luna, Patricia. "2,7 millones de inmunizados en 15 días: las claves de Chile en su estrategia de vacunación". *France24*, 19 February 2021, https://www.france24.com/es/am%C3%A9rica-latina/20210219-chile-estrategia-vacunacion-covid19-desafios.

—. "La exitosa estrategia de vacunación chilena y el legado de Sebastián Piñera". *France24*, 11 March 2021, https://www.france24.com/es/am%C3%A9rica-latina/20210311-chile-estrategia-vacunaci%C3%B3n-legado-pi%C3%B1era-gobierno-aprobaci%C3%B3n.

McGuire, David, et al. "Beating the Virus: An Examination of the Crisis Communication Approach Taken by New Zealand Prime Minister Jacinda Ardern During the Covid-19 Pandemic". *Human Resource Development International*, vol. 23, no. 4, 2020, pp. 361–379.

"Migrantes sin derecho a vacunas: todas las críticas apuntan al canciller Allamand y la oposición lo acusa de 'empañar' el proceso de inmunización".

El Mostrador, 10 February 2021, https://www.elmostrador.cl/noticias/pais/2021/02/10/migrantes-sin-derecho-a-vacunas-todas-las-criticas-apuntan-al-canciller-allamand-y-la-oposicion-lo-acusa-de-empanar-el-proceso-de-inmunizacion/.

Miño, Rodrigo. "Ministro Paris destacó a Salvador Allende y Eduardo Cruz-Coke como 'los fundadores del sistema público de salud'". *ADN Radio*, 11 February 2021, https://www.adnradio.cl/nacional/2021/02/11/ministro-paris-destaco-a-salvador-allende-y-eduardo-cruz-coke-como-los-fundadores-del-sistema-publico-de-salud.html.

Minsal. "Covid-19 en Chile- pandemia 2020-2022". *Ministerio de Salud*, 2022, https://www.Minsal.cl/wp-content/uploads/2022/03/2022.03.03_LIBRO-COVID-19-EN-CHILE-1-1.pdf.

Olivares, R., et al. "Puertos inician vacunación y empresarios aceleran gestiones para incluir a otros sectores". *El Mercurio*, 17 February 2021, https://www.litoralpress.cl/sitio/Prensa_Cortes.cshtml?LPKey=6TMWFPY7IKPUZY45BSGGOY6KU442VEJ3IUP2TTDQV3AOCCPSHNSQ.

Oppenheimer, Andres. "Chile's Global Ties, Free-Trade Pact Help Snag Vaccines Early". *Miami Herald*, 11 February 2021, https://www.miamiherald.com/news/local/news-columns-blogs/andres-oppenheimer/article249160835.html.

"Paris se enfrenta a alcaldes por falta de vacunas Pfizer: municipios responsabilizan al Minsal y el Ministro responde que 'es insólito cerrar los vacunatorios'". *El Mostrador*, 22 July 2021, https://www.elmostrador.cl/dia/2021/07/22/paris-se-enfrenta-a-alcaldes-por-falta-de-vacunas-municipios-responsabilizan-al-Minsal-y-el-ministro-responde-que-es-insolito-cerrar-los-vacunatorios/.

Piazza, Kelly S., and Alexandria Schwier. "Ready, Set, Vaccine: The Path to Covid-19 Recovery in Latin America". *Revista Latinoamericana de Opinión Pública* vol. 10, no. 2, 2021, pp. 179–190.

Pichel, Mar. "Coronavirus en Chile: las claves que explican la exitosa campaña de vacunación contra la Covid-19 en el país sudamericano". *BBC*, 11 February 2021, https://www.bbc.com/mundo/noticias-america-latina-56026037.

Piñera, Sebastián. "Presidente Piñera presenta detalles de plan de vacunación contra Covid-19". *Prensa Presidencia*, 21 January 2021, https://prensa.presidencia.cl/comunicado.aspx?id=171125.

"'Portazo' a vacunación de grupos de extranjeros: Izkia Siches pide rectificar y excanciller cuestiona el giro 'Trumpista' del gobierno". *El Mostrador*, 10 February 2021, https://www.elmostrador.cl/noticias/multimedia/2021/02/10/portazo-a-vacunacion-de-grupos-de-extranjeros-izkia-siches-pide-rectificar-y-excanciller-cuestiona-el-giro-trumpista-del-gobierno/.

Recuero, Raquel, and Felipe Soares. "#Vachina: How Politicians Help to Spread Disinformation About Covid-19 Vaccines". *Journal of Digital Social Research*, vol. 4, no. 1, 2022, pp. 73–97.

"Renuncia ministro de salud de Chile en medio de polémica". *DW*, 13 June 2020, https://www.dw.com/es/renuncia-ministro-de-salud-de-chile-en-medio-de-pol%C3%A9mica/a-53798158.

"Seremi: falta de vacunas fue por logística y no por stock". *El Mercurio*, 27 April 2021.

Siches, Izkia [@izkia]. "Hacemos un llamado a @ministeriosalud a corregir la Resolución Exenta N136 y mantener la cultura histórica de la Salud Pública

Chilena brindando protección a la población migrante independientemente de su condición migratoria tal como lo recomienda @opsoms". *Twitter*, 10 February 2021, https://twitter.com/izkia/status/1359531706169118722

Toro-Ascuy, Daniela, et al. "Factors Influencing the Acceptance of Covid-19 Vaccines in a Country with a High Vaccination Rate". *Vaccines*, vol. 10, no. 681, 2022, https://doi.org/10.3390/vaccines10050681.

Troiano, Gianmarco, and Alessandra Nardi. "Vaccine Hesitancy in the Era of Covid-19". *Public Health*, vol. 194, 2021, pp. 245–251.

Varas, Simón, et al. "Factors Associated with Change in Adherence to Covid-19 Personal Protection Measures in the Metropolitan Region, Chile". *PloS one*, vol. 17, no. 5, 2022, https://doi.org/10.1371/journal.pone.0267413.

Villalobos Dintrans, Pablo, et al. "The Successful Covid-19 Vaccine Rollout in Chile: Factors and Challenges". *Vaccine*, vol. 9, 2021, https://doi.org/10.1016/j.jvacx.2021.100114.

Chapter 3

Covid-19, Human Rights and Denialism in Brazil

How has Former President Jair Bolsonaro Adopted a Denialist Rhetoric to Covid-19, Early Treatment and the Use of Vaccines?

Ulisses Terto Neto
Goiás State University, UEG, Brazil

Caio Augusto Guimarães de Oliveira
Federal University of Goiás, UFG, Brazil

Luciano Rodrigues Castro
Federal University of Goiás, UFG, Brazil

Ana Paula de Castro Neves
Federal University of Goiás, UFG, Brazil

Abstract

This chapter embarks on a critical-contextual discussion of key declarations made by Brazil's former President Jair Bolsonaro, from March 2020 to December 2021, on allegedly tackling the COVID-19 pandemic. Drawing on Critical Discourse Analysis the chapter presents President Jair Bolsonaro's official and non-official discourses about the Covid-19, early treatment and the use of vaccines to tackle the pandemic while comparing his statements with official documents (government reports and statistics), common populist leaders' behaviors (such as optimistic bias and complacency, ambiguity and science ignorance) and actions taken by these governments. By unveiling influences of the populist extreme right towards the fight against COVID-19, the chapter engages with the question of why President Jair Bolsonaro has presented a denialist rhetoric on COVID-19, early treatment and the use of vaccines. We present some possible answers relating to economic, political, social and legal reasons, concluding that Bolsonaro aimed to advance his anti-institutional agenda.

Keywords: Brazil, Disinformation, Populism, Bolsonarism, Critical Discourse Analysis (CDA)

***

Introduction

Brazil is a postcolonial country that has always been marked by social authoritarianism and its characteristics such as poverty, exclusion, inequality and violence (Terto Neto; Dagnino, "Culture, Citizenship, and Democracy").The (re)democratisation process that got rid of a military dictatorship (1964-1985) allowed post-1985 governments to pursue the internalisation and socialisation of international human rights laws and standards. The country was then walking the human rights walk until the 2016 parliamentary coup that removed President Dilma Rousseff and the subsequent imprisonment of – at that time former and now again – President Luiz Inácio Lula da Silva paved the way for the arrival to power of Jair Messias Bolsonaro, an extreme right-wing, sexist, homophobic, racist politician (Proner et al.; Santos and Guarnieri). This has shifted the Federal Government's (pre)disposition for implementing human rights public policies, including those directed to facing the Covid-19 pandemic.

Drawing on Critical Discourse Analysis (henceforth CDA), this chapter embarks on a critical-contextual discussion of how during his administration former President Bolsonaro adopted a denialist rhetoric in the context of dispute for hegemony over the narrative regarding tackling the Covid-19 pandemic. Within this context, the first section presents a brief description of the CDA approach and an explanation regarding the corpus utilised for the analysis in this chapter. The second section provides an analysis of President Bolsonaro's denialist[1] Covid-19 rhetoric. First, it conducts an examination of President Bolsonaro's behaviour while comparing it to those of other populist leaders. Second, it focusses on Brazilian politics, scrutinising possible internal reasons and motivations for Bolsonaro's behaviour. Then, it utilises aspects such as vocabulary, textual genre, intertextuality, and context as well as Leeuwen's techniques to interrogate President Bolsonaro's discursive representations of the Covid-19 pandemic and its social actors, early

---

[1] Particularly, with regard to the pandemic, this denialism translates into the acceptance of interventions without scientific validation, such as the dissemination and praise of a therapeutic of unproven efficacy and with extremely serious side effects such as chloroquine or the defense of an intervention strategy that contradicts the position of the World Health Organisation (WHO), called by Bolsonaro as "vertical isolation". These are in fact two solidary strategies. Because, if there is a "magic bullet" that allows a supposedly effective treatment, there would be no reason to continue maintaining the quarantine (Caponi 211). See also Löwy and Berlivet, "The Problem with Chloroquine".

treatment, and vaccines. That is, it applies the CDA methodology to the analysis. Finally, the chapter answers the question: how during his presidency has Jair Bolsonaro adopted a denialist rhetoric to Covid-19, early treatment and the use of vaccines?

Setting the Parameters of Analysis (CDA Approach)

Discourse influences all aspects of any society. As "social cognitions, socially specific ways of knowing social practices, they can be, and are, used as resources for representing social practices" (Leeuwen, *Discourse and Practice* 6). The said, silenced, manipulated, distorted, used or misused in discourses can unveil "traditions and contradictions that usually explain the set of circumstances that generate the power relations upon which societies are organized" (Terto Neto 2264–2265). This is particularly true for political discourses made in a context of dispute for the hegemony of the narrative regarding tackling the Covid-19 pandemic (Le Bart 70–71).

Discourse Analysis (hereafter DA) works according to "epistemological premises that remind the analyst that (1) researchers cannot make predictions due to the complexity and dynamism of the social world, (2) there is no neutral and unique truth in social sciences, and (3) once there are as many truths as realities, so it is not possible to reach absolute truth" (Terto Neto 2265; Nogueira 17). DA thus seeks to advance debate on discourse theory and methodology, considering language as social practice (Magalhães 2). In this sense, CDA is an approach derived from the field of DA. And what unites CDA "is neither methodology nor theoretical orthodoxy, but a common goal: the critique of the hegemonic discourses and genres that effect inequalities, injustices, and oppression in contemporary society" (Leeuwen, "Critical Discourse Analysis" 290). Being placed in the field of critical social sciences, CDA is controversial since it "involves the study of the power and the resistance, of the contestation and the fight" (Nogueira 28 qtd. in Terto Neto 2266). It thus entails that the analyst conducts critical research in the pursuit of social change (Chouliaraki and Fairclough).

By applying the CDA approach one can "comprehend the connection between the (political, economic, social, and cultural) context and the observed phenomenon (object of study)" as well as "imagine alternatives by challenging the received story, that is, it makes it possible for the analyst to construct other alternatives and implications to explain the observed phenomenon" (Terto Neto 2266). In this regard, "CDA is the appropriate framework as it does not merely explain the discourse structures but also their social and political context" (Kakisina et al. 3). This is why in the next topics we, first, explore Bolsonaro's declarations in order to verify his populist features through language, since "one way [that] researchers measure populism, and consequently determine whether a leader or party is populist, is through measuring language" (Bryant and Moffit); and, second, why we examine Brazilian politics and its context aiming to locate in time, space and circumstances Bolsonaro's speeches.

Among various available approaches to analyse former President Bolsonaro's denialist rhetoric to Covid-19, early treatment and the use of vaccines, we have chosen CDA because it entails a theoretical and methodological pluralism that allows for the results of analysis to be "compatible with several different analytical traditions, specifically bridging the positivist/post-positivist divide" (Teti 10–11 qtd. in Terto Neto 2265). In this sense, recognising the multiplicity and complexity of the authors and approaches developed under CDA's umbrella, we argue that what tie them together is the recognition of the subjectivity and reflexivity of any analytical activity as well as that research agendas should aim toward emancipatory projects as, for instance, human rights (Angermuller et al.). Hence, CDA is applied here in consonance with a human rights-based approach (Fredman).

This is to say that human rights are a major issue in this study. In the sense that, we argue, within democratic regimes a state leader must always seek the well-being of its citizens by implementing public policies that guarantee the enjoyment of their fundamental rights (Medeiros and Ramacciotti; Sunstein; Lessig and Sunstein). Irrespective of political propensities —right-wing, moderate or left-wing—, there is a contradiction when the leader's actions put in risk their constituents' lives. By making speeches advocating for ineffective medicines that form a "covid kit", not encouraging people to be vaccinated (or doing exactly the opposite, that is, telling people not to be vaccinated), and minimising some disease impacts and risks, a state leader endangers the very existence of their constituents, thus violating international human rights norms and domestic laws.[2] And the situation gets even worse when a state leader either refuses to

---

[2] At global level, the United Nations offers legal framework to understand these violations, including articles 3 and 25(1) of the Universal Declaration of Human Rights; articles 2(1) and 12(1) of the International Covenant on Economic, Social and Cultural Rights; articles 10, 11, 12 and 14 of the Convention on the Elimination of All Forms of Discrimination against Women; article 24(1) of the Convention on the Rights of the Child; article 28 of the International Convention on the Protection of the Rights of All Migrant Workers and Members of their Families, among others. At regional level, the Organization of American States provides relevant legal framework such as article XI of the American Declaration of the Rights and Duties of Man; articles 1, 4, 5, and 24 of the American Convention on Human Rights "Pact of San José, Costa Rica"; articles 10 and 11 of the Additional Protocol to the American Convention on Human Rights in the area of Economic, Social and Cultural Rights, among others. At domestic level, according to the *CPI da Pandemia* report, President Bolsonaro has committed the following crimes while (mis)handling the Covid-19 pandemic: malfeasance, quackery, epidemic resulting in death, infringement of

buy scientifically approved vaccines or tries to buy overpriced ones. In this regard, the CDA approach suits the presented research since it helps comprehend how Bolsonaro has during his time in office done such things, that is, how he has adopted a denialist rhetoric to Covid-19, early treatment and the use of vaccines, since, as explains Leeuwen, CDA is "founded on the insight that text and talk play a key role in maintaining and legitimating inequality, injustice and oppression in society" ("Critical Discourse Analysis" 290).

The CDA approach demands a *corpus* of analysis, which has been constructed having in mind the necessity to conduct a critical analysis of President Bolsonaro's talks (discourses) given in a context of political contradictions between the extreme bolsonarist right-wing conservative forces and the heterogeneous coalition of forces composed by several other groups, such as former Bolsonaro's supporters, science advocates, progressive politicians, human rights defenders and scholars. In this light, we have selected key declarations of then President Bolsonaro, from January 2020 to December 2021, regarding denialist rhetoric to Covid-19.[3] They were made during significantly challenging moments of the Covid-19 pandemic, whose mismanagement by the Federal Government brought even more political and social instability to the country, adding to a moment of collective suffering, insecurity, precariousness and grieving.

Bolsonaro's Denialist Covid-19 Rhetoric

In this section we will study speeches of then President Bolsonaro in order to characterise him as a right-wing populist leader and to connect his statements with the actions taken by other populist leaders. With the arrival of the Covid-19 pandemic, Bolsonaro worsened the level of his statements. Well-known for not being respectful on his speeches as well as attacking the press and political adversaries, the pandemic gave him a new topic to make controversial and denialist statements. For example: Bolsonaro had put distrust upon the efficacy of the vaccination, the social distancing measures, the use of masks, underestimated the coronavirus and set up science as another of his rivals. Briefly, we argue that the pandemics impacted Bolsonaro's declarations (the type of narrative we analyse throughout this chapter) by giving him new topics to attack, presenting new adversaries to him and transforming his speeches into more aggressive ones. The impacts of those more truculent speeches are seen throughout this research.

---

preventive health measures, irregular use of public funds, incitement to crime, falsification of private documents, crime of responsibility and crimes against humanity (Senado Federal).
[3] We gathered 31 key declarations during the data collection period. These have then been classified, analysed and reduced into those declarations that we examine in this study.

Bolsonaro has spread disinformation via social media to question reality (Soares et al.), especially because he has portrayed traditional media as the "enemy" (Da Silva; Recuero and Soares). Such strategy is usually employed in Western democracies by "populist leaders, as social media platforms offer affordances that are particularly important for this field, such as the possibility to influence more people" (Cesarino qtd. in Recuero and Soares 75). However, why Bolsonaro behaved like this is still unclear.

Other populist leaders around the world adopted the same position, even though they are in another ideological spectrum, as demonstrated by Bassani et al. For instance, in México, Manuel López Obrador, at the very beginning of the pandemic saw no problem in saying to his citizens to go out and hug each other (Carmo). Nicolás Maduro, President of Venezuela, posted on his Twitter account about an alleged antidote for Covid-19. A post that was after deleted by that social media. Days later Maduro seemed to have higher concerns about the virus and decreed a lockdown (Carmo). In Nicaragua, Daniel Ortega called a march named "Love in Covid-19 times" at the same moment other neighbour countries called for border restrictions (Carmo). Some other right-wing populist leaders reacted differently. Viktor Mihály Orbán, at Hungary, embraced restrictive measures from the beginning. In addition, he pushed Hungary to an emergency state allowing him to govern by decrees for two months. When the state of emergency ended, a so-called "state of danger" took place and human rights groups denounced that it would still be easy for the government to rule by decrees (Tanacs and Huet).[4]

However, Donald Trump's attitudes were quite close to those of Bolsonaro's. Trump advertised for the recommendation and liberalisation of hydroxychloroquine to fight Covid-19 (Bassani et al.), insinuated that the Chinese government might have connections with the creation of this virus and called it "kung-flu" ("President Trump Calls"), expressed scepticism about the use of masks (Victor et al.) and encouraged protests against social distancing measures (Shear and Mervosh). Actions that were also taken by then President Bolsonaro.

For Rosendo Fraga, Trump and López Obrador were concerned about their economies, even though the risks presented by the virus were more urgent (Carmo). So, López Obrador tried to align his politics with Trump's, because 85% of Mexican exports are destined to the United States of America (USA). Francisco de Santibañes remembered that those declarations have a rational aspect, aiming not to generate panic in their populations, and Guillermo Holzmann points out that this type of behaviour shows coldness by being more concerned with the economics than public health, which is a risky bet (Carmo).

---

[4] The Government of Hungary declared the state of danger on 11 March 2020.

Surely Bolsonaro shares this concern about the economic rates and, because of that, he has tried to influence his constituents to keep working and producing. Nevertheless, we argue that deeper causes relate to his attitudes. As Orbán tried and has succeeded, then President Bolsonaro attempted to become more influential in order to stay longer in power. That is, he tried to advance his extreme right-wing programme and political agenda. Even if Orbán pursued another way —combating the coronavirus— and Bolsonaro belittled the Covid-19, the goal might still be the same: to gain and concentrate power, dilute human rights and satisfy their supporters.

It is our contention that Bolsonaro has during his time in office adopted a denialist rhetoric about Covid-19, early treatment and vaccines as part of his political agenda to deconstruct democratic institutions and advance the populist extreme right programme. But before delving into this argument, we need to address some other questions that might be related with Bolsonaro's behaviour. As Leeuwen clarifies, "critical discourse analysts are seeking to explain why texts are the way they are, and why they change the way they do, and following Halliday, they look for the answers to these questions in the social, economic, and political world" ("Critical Discourse Analysis" 293). Hereupon we conduct a brief analysis thinking about the economic, political, socio-cultural and legal reasons that might help understand Bolsonaro's behaviour and speeches. And even if they do not fully explain his conduct, they nonetheless connect his declarations with the context, the facts, that is, to what was happening at those moments.

First, an economic reason cannot be left out. Bolsonaro and his government ignored several —to be exact: 101— e-mails from the pharmaceutical industry Pfizer about vaccines purchase. According to one Brazilian Senator, Randolfe Rodrigues: "The last e-mail received, on 2nd December 2020, it's a Pfizer desperate attempt asking for some information because they wanted to provide vaccines for Brazil" (Ribeiro). Senator Rodrigues was the vice-President of the Parliamentary Commission of Inquiry (PCI) created to investigate actions and omissions of the Federal Government during the Covid-19 pandemic. One of its disclosures was that the government leader at the Chamber of Deputies, Congressman Ricardo Barros, was deeply involved in schemes trying to buy overpriced vaccines. Officially, President Bolsonaro became aware of this illegal buy attempt when another Congressman, Luis Miranda, on 20th March 2021, presented him these irregularities. Bolsonaro would have said that Congressman Barros was the responsible for those actions and that he would report the situation to the Brazilian Federal Police, something Bolsonaro has never done (Senado Federal 326).

Still according to the PCI report, at the time Minister of Health —Eduardo Pazuello— and his Executive Secretary —Élcio Franco— explained that the problem in buying the Pfizer vaccine was that the pharmaceutical company did not agree to a technology transfer (Senado Federal 207). It is an odd explanation since at that time and among developing countries, Brazil was the only one against the vaccine patent breach (Senado Federal 568).[5]

That is, how could the Brazilian Government justify its refusal to buy vaccines claiming it is because the pharmaceutical industry does not agree with a technology transfer and at the same time be the one of the only developing countries against the coronavirus vaccine patent breach? What becomes clear of these disclosures is that Brazil's government had not made movements in order to buy the Pfizer vaccine but was engaged in negotiations to buy other overpriced vaccines. The government explained that the Pfizer industry would not agree with a technology transfer and would not offer guarantees relating to collateral effects. However, the whole world bought the vaccines without this agreement. A move that was after followed by Brazil, with no restrictions.

The PCI also asked what the role of the pharmaceutical industry was during the pandemic. The medicines which were part of the so-called "covid kit", advertised by President Bolsonaro, had a major increase on their sales. The company that had the biggest percentage increase regarding the ivermectin sales (1,773%), also had the biggest upsurge regarding the sales of chloroquine and hydroxychloroquine (1,458%) (Senado Federal 121-122). Other pharmaceutical companies reached a maximum increase of 24%. The biggest conclusion from that comparison is that some pharmaceutical companies made big profits selling ineffective medicine to treat the complications caused by Covid-19. These medicines are the azithromycin, ivermectin, chloroquine and hydroxychloroquine. The same drugs Bolsonaro repeatedly quoted on his statements.

Second, a political reason emerges when one considers that President Bolsonaro was notorious, before the Covid-19 pandemic, for making controversial speeches to capture the media interest. This tactic, called smokescreen, worked well during his first year of government. He tried it again during the pandemic, when he, his sons or his close Ministers were under media scrutiny about allegedly illegal acts.[6] Or when he was trying to advance his own agenda. For example, during a

---

[5] It is worthwhile to point out that Brazil has a history of production and consumption of medicines produced under the specification of the "Lei dos Genéricos" (9.787/99), which establishes that after 20 years with valid patent, the patents can be broken and generic drugs can be produced.

[6] For example, we claim that former President Bolsonaro's orientation to stop teenagers' vaccination was a smokescreen to hide the denouncements the PCI had disclosed in a dossier saying doctors connected to President Bolsonaro's "health parallel cabinet" had conducted experiments to test the "covid kit" efficacy without the patients' knowledge or consent (Moraes). President Bolsonaro also tried to create a smokescreen to hide the purchase of a six million reais mansion by his son, Senator Flávio Bolsonaro. In addition,

ministerial meeting the at the time Environment Minister Ricardo Sales, said that: "we need to make an effort while we are in this calm moment in terms of press coverage, because they are only talking about Covid-19, and push through and change all the rules and simplify norms [regarding the protection of the environment]" (Spring). But he attempted to do so behind the scenes. That is, President Bolsonaro attempted to change the media's attention and divert civil society's focus with his speeches in the hopes of achieving his own political agenda.

Third, the disinformation perpetrated by President Bolsonaro —either via smokescreens or fake news— relates to social-cultural reasons since he misguided the population. As a result, Brazilians would put aside the masks, social distancing measures and apprehensions to go out, thus continuing to consume, produce and keep the economic wheel spinning. His behaviour violated international human rights norms and domestic laws,[7] as it has influenced people to unnecessarily risk their lives, leading them to death.[8] The disinformation carried out by President Bolsonaro is not simple, nonetheless. He has been accused of commanding the "Hate Cabinet", created to spread fake news, "engage his supporters and weaken his political adversaries" (Senado Federal 667-668). Such accusations have been demonstrated by the PCI, which has also revealed that fake news "instilled distrust in part of the population, which ended up in not understanding the benefit of [social distancing] measures and, in more extreme cases, even refuting them" (Senado Federal 679). That said, it is relevant to understand that President Bolsonaro had an entire network to spread his (misguided) speeches and ideas. The pandemic denial came not only from his own words, but from several different "digital influencers" and "journalists" financed by the "Hate Cabinet".

Finally, a legal reason for President Bolsonaro's declarations: he tried to create the idea that he was not responsible for the pandemic developments, sustaining this notion after a ruling by the Brazilian Supreme Court (STF) that authorised governors and mayors to make decisions while facing Covid-19.[9] One example

---

to criticize the restrictive measures imposed to face Covid-19, President Bolsonaro said: "Stop the whining, how long are you going to cry?" (Camarotti).

[7] See footnote 2.

[8] Research comparing Brazil and other States that adopted restrictive measures and bought vaccines early point that four of each five deaths could have been avoided if the government had adopted other position. This data was presented during the PCI discussions ("Pesquisas apontam").

[9] A Fact Check conducted by the Lupa Agency demonstrated that this "information" spread by both Jair Bolsonaro and others profiles on social medias were incorrect. "The Federal Court of Justice didn't determinate that all actions were taken by governors and mayors, but that the Federal Government couldn't interfere in local actions, as lockdowns and commerce closures" (Afonso).

of then President Bolsonaro's words: "I have nothing to do with Covid-19 according to the STF. It is the governors and mayors who are up to deal with it" (Senado Federal 692). He also attempted to disassociate the economic impacts from himself by saying he was against the lockdowns. As President Bolsonaro said, on 29 April 2020: "I, since from the start, worried about lives and the employment, as the unemployment also kills. So, you have to ask the governors about this bill" ("Bolsonaro diz 'E daí?'" 00:00:40–50). Thus, if the economy went down, the one to blame would not be him, but the governors and mayors.[10] Finishing this first analysis of the reasons and the context, we follow with the examination of Bolsonaro's speeches.

Bolsonaro: A Right-Wing Populist Leader

We proceed with the analysis relating then President Bolsonaro's speeches with common behaviours adopted by populist leaders while dealing with the Covid-19 pandemic, while we also locate Bolsonaro's speeches in time, space and circumstances. To do so, we have selected key speeches made between 30 January 2020, when the World Health Organisation announced a Public Health Emergency of International Concern regarding the Covid-19 and 31 December 2021. They have been chosen because they are populist and were made in a context of disputes between the extreme Bolsonarist right-wing conservative forces and the heterogeneous coalition of forces (former Bolsonaro's supporters, science advocates, progressive politicians, human rights defenders and scholars) for hegemony over the narrative regarding facing the Covid-19 pandemics.

Lassa and Booth identified some common behaviours in how populist leaders handled Covid-19, like their optimistic bias and complacency, ambiguity and ignorance of science. The optimistic bias is related with an excessive confidence of the leaders in their abilities to handle the pandemic and with some belief that they are less susceptible to be hit by an emergency crisis. This is clearly seen in President Bolsonaro's speeches when he underestimated the coronavirus impacts, its mortality rates and by saying that the pandemic would finish soon.

On 9 March 2020, when President Bolsonaro first spoke about the coronavirus, he said: "the coronavirus, in the way I see it, its destruction power is being oversized, maybe even for economic reasons. […] Much of what's been said is fantasy, regarding the coronavirus, it's not like the media is spreading" ("Todos nós vamos morrer um dia" 00:00:07–26).

---

[10] In January 2022 Bolsonaro said the "stay at home politics" was the responsible for the rise of inflation in Brazil. Another agency check, Uol Confere, said this rise was due to the devaluation of the real and the reduction of the foreign investments, both related to the politic environment in Brazil ("Bolsonaro atribui inflação").

On 11 March 2020, he said: "what I [have] heard until now is that another type of flu killed more than this one [coronavirus]" (Coletta, "Outras gripes"). On 12 April 2020, when the Covid-19 pandemic's peak had not arrived yet, President Bolsonaro said: "it seems that the virus question is starting to go away, but the unemployment question is coming and will hit hard" ("Parece que está indo embora"). It is clear that "his move represents his resolute Covid-19 denial and indicates that the long-ailing economy is his highest priority rather than public health and safety" (Kakisina et al. 4).

On 30 October 2020 President Bolsonaro said again that the pandemic was almost over. He did so because the first vaccines were being negotiated and he wanted to minimise both the efforts of São Paulo's Governor —João Dória— to buy them and the vaccines' possible positive results: "The pandemic is finishing. I think he [João Dória] wants to force people to be vaccinated because the pandemic is going away and then he would say: 'it's over because of my vaccine'. Ok? What is finishing is his government, I'm sure" (Gullino). To specifically discredit João Dória, President Bolsonaro displayed the "Us/Them polarization, vilifying the other, using the communicative acts, and attacking the other's characteristics" (Kakisina et al. 4).

The second common behaviour found is the leadership ambiguity. The PCI report contains a quote by Andrew Roberts connected with this type of behaviour: "there is a tendency to think of leadership as something inherently good, but this is something actually morally neutral, i.e., you can lead people into the abyss or the mountains" (Senado Federal 132). For Lassa and Booth populist leaders utilise fake news and misinformation campaigns, since they are not able to adopt evidence-based deliberation as a strategy, which creates a space where we cannot see clear boundaries between truth and lies. Not listening to experts, utilising symbols and blind faith to calm people, diminishing the virus consequences, attacking the press and putting him/herself as an establishment target are good patterns. The authors present President Bolsonaro as an example: "Bolsonaro labelled the Covid-19 pandemic a 'little flu', a 'media trick' and an 'absurd' campaign intended to force him out of power" (Lassa and Booth).

On 5 June 2020, the Brazilian Government changed the schedule to publicise the daily death toll by Covid-19. When asked about it, President Bolsonaro said: "It's over, the *Jornal Nacional* reportage" (Fonseca). *Jornal Nacional* is the broadcast journal with the most audience in Brazil and belongs to a big Brazilian media corporation —Rede Globo— which has constantly received hostilities made by Bolsonaro. This change led the Brazilian media to create a consortium for gathering data about deaths and cases relating to Covid-19 in Brazil. Some days later, on 11 June 2020, President Bolsonaro mislead the population by asking his supporters to film hospitals to check if hospital beds were really occupied (Prazeres). This happened the same day Brazil became the second country with most deaths by Covid-19 and a few days after some Congressmen connected with President Bolsonaro had already invaded a field hospital (Trindade).

President Bolsonaro has also misled his constituents regarding vaccines. On 16 December 2020, he said: "Some stupid people are saying that I'm giving a bad example [for saying he will not be vaccinated], I already had the virus, I already have the antibodies, so why would I take it again?" (Marcello). Before that, he created some controversies about the development and purchase of vaccines. First, he said he would not buy the CoronaVac because the vaccine should first be scientifically proven ("Bolsonaro diz que governo"). Later, he declared that even if the CoronaVac were approved by the ANVISA (Brazilian Health Regulatory Agency) he would not buy it ("Bolsonaro diz que governo não comprará"). His, at the time, Minister of Health —Eduardo Pazuello— said: "one commands and the other obeys", trying to justify why he blindly obeyed President Bolsonaro's order to cancel the purchase of 46 million doses of CoronaVac.

President Bolsonaro even celebrated when the CoronaVac tests were paused in Brazil because some adverse incident: "Death, disability, anomaly. This is the vaccine that Dória wanted to force all Paulistanos to take. The president said the vaccine could never be mandatory. One more that Jair Bolsonaro wins" (Mazui). Afterwards it was proven that the incident had no connections with the quality of the vaccine.

In addition, President Bolsonaro had portrayed himself as a target. His declaration happened a day before Brazil had registered, for the first time, four thousand deaths daily, the chief of the Federal Police had been replaced and the STF had established a deadline for the Minister of Justice explain why he authorised the use of the National Security Law against President Bolsonaro's criticisers. On 7 April 2021, while speaking during a nomination event, Bolsonaro said: "Let's not cry over spilled milk. We are still going through a pandemic that, in part, is used politically. Not to defeat the virus, but to try to bring down the President. We are all responsible for what happens in Brazil" (Soares).

Moreover, neither faith nor religion was a major issue in Bolsonaro's speeches vis-à-vis Covid-19. Still, Bolsonaro acted to keep the support of what Souza and Chéquer call conservative Christians, whom Bolsonaro has tried to please since his baptism in 2016, while he was seeking the Presidential role (Souza and Chéquer 127). For instance, he acted to calm his conservative Christian supporters down when he issued the Decree 10.292, on 25 March 2020, recognising that religious activities are essential and thus they should proceed during the Covid-19 pandemic (Diário Oficial da União). This attempt to calm them down may have had more than just religious motivations. It was instrumental since, as argued by Macedo (qtd. in Gracino Junior et al. 557), the reason of the concern of many church pastors apropos the closure of temples during the Covid-19 pandemic was the reduction in tithes and offerings during the religious services.

The last common behaviour is the science denial. In fact, "research suggests populist governments' tendency to deny scientific knowledge around complex issues, such as health and the environment, for economic and political gain is deeply entrenched" (Lassa and Booth). This is clearly seen in the previous President Bolsonaro's declarations about the vaccines. His refusal to work together with science to fight Covid-19 was also highlighted by the Human Rights Watch's World Report 2022: "President Bolsonaro continued to flout scientific recommendations to prevent the spread of the Covid-19 virus" (109). On vaccines, President Bolsonaro even said: "In the Pfizer contract, it is very clear that they [Pfizer] are not responsible for any side effects. If you turn into an alligator, that's your problem. If you become Superman, if some woman grows a beard or some man's voice gets feminine, they [Pfizer] have nothing to do with it" ("Bolsonaro: Se tomar vacina" 00:00:34–01:00).

But there are even graver speeches when we analyse President Bolsonaro advocating for some medicines that are not effective to combat Covid-19, like those present in the "covid kit". Bryant and Moffitt point that populist leaders often promote "a sense of crisis (whether true or not), and present themselves as having the solution to the crisis". Even though this crisis were not created by President Bolsonaro, the defence of these medicines can be seen as his solution for the problem. An easy and rapid solution for a complex issue. On 7 July 2020, at a press conference after revealing that he had Covid-19, Bolsonaro asked the journalists to move away, took of his mask and said he was fine. After, he said that he had taken the "covid kit" by doctor's prescription. Bolsonaro also said that many people are dying at their homes, because they are afraid of going to the hospitals due to the coronavirus. Thereby, the number of deaths were rising up, but caused for other reasons, since the panic also kills. About the hydroxychloroquine, he also declared: "I endorse what doctors are saying all around Brazil —I'm not a doctor, I'm an Army's Captain— when the hydroxychloroquine is used at the first moments, the success' rates are near of 100%" ("Entrevista com o presidente Jair Bolsonaro" 00:15:08–23:55).

On 5 May 2021, after two of his former Ministers of Health testified at the PCI, President Bolsonaro declared: "a scoundrel is someone who is against the early treatment [the one made with the "covid kit"] and does not present alternatives, he is a scoundrel. What I took everyone knows. I dare to say that millions of people have had this treatment" ("#AoVivo: Abertura" 00:46:55–47:13). At the same day, former Minister of Health Nelson Teich declared he left the government because he disagreed with President Bolsonaro about the chloroquine use.

At the previous day, former Minister of Health Luiz Henrique Mandetta said the government refused to make an official campaign to combat the Covid-19 virus and that the Presidency had sent a draft proposing ANVISA to make chloroquine recommended for treating Covid-19. Even in his speech at the United Nations, President Bolsonaro advocated for chloroquine and early treatment:

> Since the pandemic's beginning, we supported the doctor's autonomy in its search for the early treatment following our Federal Medicine Council. Myself was one of those who took this treatment. […] We can't understand why many countries and major part of the media put themselves against the early treatment. The History and the science will know how to charge each one ("Confira discurso de Bolsonaro" 00:11:05–49).

President Bolsonaro also tried to misdirect the population when he quoted data without references and mentioned unreliable research. When asked about the death toll in Brazil, on 20 April 2020, he said: "I'm not a gravedigger". Earlier that day, he declared: "About 70% of the population will be infected. There's no way out. It's a fact. Are you afraid of the facts?" ("Bolsonaro sobre número de mortos" 00:00:09–01:40). On 7 January 2021, he said: "Do you know how many Brazilians are going to get vaccinated? As far as I know, less than half is going to" (Fagundes). According to information provided by the Ministry of Health: "Brazil closes 2021 with more than 90% of the Campaign's target audience, of 177 million Brazilians, vaccinated with the first dose and 80% with the complete vaccination schedule" ("Retrospectiva 2021"). It follows that by "disseminating incorrect statements, President Bolsonaro has attempted to influence the public opinion and assure the recipients to firmly believe that the media has manipulated them" (Kakisina et al. 5).

Every Thursday on YouTube President Bolsonaro made live speeches. On one occasion he talked about some research made in a German University about the use of masks. According to him "the collateral effects of the masks were appearing": "A German university says they are harmful to children. It considers several items: irritability, headaches, difficulty to concentrate, decreased perception of happiness, refusal to go to school or day care, discouragement, impaired learning ability, vertigo and fatigue" ("Bolsonaro usa enquete alemã"). In fact, what President Bolsonaro had quoted were the results of an online survey, not of scientific research.

Finally, we cannot forget that populist leaders try to present themselves as outsiders, being against the usual politics and the establishment. They also seek to put themselves near the common people, being their speakers, their representative and knowing what they desire. As Lassa and Booth summarise: "populism can be understood as an ideology organized around two core beliefs: 1. anti-establishment society is divided into two opposing groups: 'the people' (pure) and 'the elite' (corrupt); 2. politics should express the 'general will' of 'the people'".

This happened when President Bolsonaro had portrayed himself as a target; when he was against the Brazilian Supreme Court, governors and mayors; when he ignored the science and resorted to common believes and wrong data; when he was sexist and disrespectful in his speeches; and when he presented the solution for the crisis but some tried to boycott his proposals. The fact is that President Bolsonaro's declarations are often connected with more than one aspect and even with the possibilities we presented in the previous topic (economic, social, etc.). Even though they are a science ignorance example, they can also be a smokescreen for another situation. Or even a President Bolsonaro's demonstration of his real agenda. We follow the analysis utilising the aspects and techniques developed by Leeuwen, such as vocabulary, textual genre, intertextuality and context.

Representing Characters

We have already pointed out some thoughts connected with the answer to our question of "how has former President Jair Bolsonaro adopted a denialist rhetoric to Covid-19, early treatment and the use of vaccines?" by demonstrating that economic, social and legal aspects may have influenced him, and also that his behaviour is deeply linked to populist actions.

Now we advance the analysis further, utilising the aspects and techniques developed by Leeuwen, such as vocabulary, textual genre, intertextuality, and context. Then, departing from some of Leewen's tools for CDA's practice, we shall interpret some aspects of President Bolsonaro's discursive management of the Covid-19 pandemic, specifically exploring the representation of social characters as well as social actions. This is done in the pursuit of a better understanding of how President Bolsonaro deployed specific discursive formations to further his own agenda. To conduct these examinations, we will explore —in this section— the representation of characters in Bolsonaro's speeches. In the next section we look over to how Bolsonaro represented the social distancing and the vaccines using the "activation" concept. And before the conclusion we look at the Bolsonaro's discourses in order to think about his reasons/motives through the lens of the "legitimation" concept.

The first point to which we must draw attention is the personalisation of President Bolsonaro's speeches. In technical terms, this is represented by the immense incidence of the deictic "I" as a structuring axis of the actions and social actors represented discursively. Between the (at least theoretically) impersonal stance of a Head of State and the affirmation of his positions as a private choice that should, moreover, also be available to Brazilian citizens,

President Bolsonaro opts for the latter. When representing the social actions of social isolation and vaccination, his speech is structured around his figure. Around it, two poles would gravitate: a pole signalled as an enemy, marked by abjection and obstruction; another flagged as productive, needing defence.

The personalisation is present in basically every sentence previously analysed. Some occurrences are very explicit, as for what he said on 9 March 2020: "the coronavirus, in the way *I* see it, its destruction power is being oversized (…)" ("Todos nós vamos morrer um dia" 00:00:07–26). In others, the personalisation is even clearer, as for what he said on 20 March 2020: "After the stabbing, a flu is not going to take *me* down" (Mazieiro). Here, the allusion to the attempt of murder suffered during his presidential campaign (largely capitalised for the construction of his mythic image) is evoked.

Important discursive conclusions arise. The first is that while constantly pointing to his opinions and putting himself on the centre of the stage, President Bolsonaro makes clear the alliance between his authoritarian way of managing institutions and the neoliberal rationality. Authors such as Brown, and Dardot and Laval have stressed that neoliberalism is much more than a simple economic mode of production, that is, it involves a rationality, a new way of self-governing. The viability of neoliberalism rests upon the production of subjects and subjectivities shaped in the market's image. In this sense, individuals are like companies and must govern themselves through the rules of free markets.

As Brown notes, this logic has been associated with the conservatism from the very beginning. Since Hayek's formulations, she points, moralism has been central to the functioning of neoliberal markets. There is no surprise that individualism plays a central rule there (59–61).

President Bolsonaro affirms his personal visions while in opposition to some actors. His conservative version of authoritarian individualism includes the affirmation of hegemonic masculinities (Connel). On 10 November 2020 he clearly stated: "We cannot escape reality, we have to stop being a country of sissies" ("#AoVivo: Lançamento" 01:05:23–30). The statement, in itself, is a clear demonstration of how authoritarianism in Brazil is not simply an institutional phenomenon but includes social and cultural determinations (Dagnino, "Os movimentos sociais"; Schwarcz), such as homophobia. This becomes clearer in other of President Bolsonaro's formulations, as for what he said on 26 March 2020: "(…) Brazilians should be studied. They don't contract anything [diseases]. You see someone jumping in a sewage. He goes out, dive and nothing happens to him" ("Brasileiro mergulha no esgoto").

Through homophobic statements and a depreciative depiction of the underprivileged,[11] President Bolsonaro depicts what he sees are the flawed aspects of the country. Those are not the only "enemies" he elects in his way of representing things, especially in politics. Among the institutional actors, the media (mainly Rede Globo), the STF (one of the crucial institutions that has acted to curtail his authoritarian outbursts) and some governors who took actions to promote social distancing and import vaccines are the most prominent.

This dispute between President Bolsonaro and the mayors and governors has already been demonstrated. Regarding the contest with the STF, some aspects have also been shown, but we will examine other situations in order to demonstrate how Bolsonaro challenged this institution which may be related with his authoritarian features.

The main official tension with the STF occurred when President Bolsonaro declared he had no intention of imposing sanctions on the population in regard to the vaccines. After that, the STF ruled that vaccination was mandatory. On another occasion, on 19 April 2020, President Bolsonaro strained even more when, in front of a manifestation demanding a military "intervention" and the STF's closure, he said that people could count on him "to do whatever it takes to keep our democracy and guarantee what is most sacred among us, which is our freedom" ("Bolsonaro discursa em Brasília"). It was a clear message upholding the STF as an enemy of the people and freedom, and highlighting to his supporters he was willing to undermine formal democratic institutions, if necessary.

On 7 September 2021, Brazil's Independency Day, President Bolsonaro and his supporters organised large rallies to demonstrate support to the Federal Government (Peixoto; Ferraz et al.). In one of those manifestations, he said: "Any decision by Mr. Alexandre de Moraes [STF Justice], this President will no longer obey. The patience of our people has run out. He still has time to ask his resignation and mind his own business" (Peixoto). President Bolsonaro also declared: "To those who want to make me ineligible in Brasilia: only God can get me out of there. I will leave only arrested, dead or with victory" (Peixoto). It is relevant to mention that Justice Moraes is the rapporteur in several cases in which President Bolsonaro and his family are under investigation. These speeches made clear President Bolsonaro's authoritarian bias and his quarrels with the STF.

---

[11] Important to remark, in accordance with Leeuwen (*Discourse and Practice*), that those actors are represented through processes of generalization – they are not nominated, but loosely affirmed as "sissies" or "Brazilians".

Representing Social Distancing and Vaccines

Following the analysis with Theo van Leeuwen's tools and thoughts, social distancing and vaccination are strongly represented through the process he describes as activation. According to him "actions and reactions can be activated, represented dynamically, or deactivated, represented statically, as though they were entities or qualities rather than dynamic processes" (Leeuwen, Discourse and Practice 63). It should be borne in mind, however, that while processes of activation are usually related to representations that validate some social actions, it is not the case in our analysis.

Former President Bolsonaro's enunciations characterise social distancing and vaccination as excessive and overestimated social processes being forced against a majority violated in their freedom of choice. See, for instance, his statement on 20 April 2020: "There has been a potentiation of the virus consequences"; he also said: "they [the media] brought fright to the public, hysteria" (Gomes). On 31 August 2020 he declared: "to impose obligations is definitely not in the plans" (SecomVc). The image of vaccination as an illegitimate imposition calls for clarifications: what is imagined as target and how does President Bolsonaro function in this dissent?

The imagined target, as President Bolsonaro repeatedly stated, was the "economy". Portrayed as passive and endangered, the defence of jobs and salaries was a strong part of his denialist rhetoric. He advocated against the lockdowns and the social distancing measures because he was trying to keep the economics still running. He was aiming to reach good economic rates in order to say he did a good work and protected the jobs, families and salaries in Brazil. Even though, he was putting them in risk by influencing the citizens to go out and continue to assemble during the Covid-19 pandemic.

Former President Bolsonaro also presents himself as a protector for his supporters against institutions such as the STF and the media. His discourse frames his actions as defences of freedom against the arbitrariness of the Courts (mainly STF) and mass hysteria promoted through news and information. The constant attacks on media are illustrated by the way he characterised Rede Globo, on 5 June 2020: "Funeral TV". He also changed the way information regarding the number of deaths were made public, in a clear attempt to hit Rede Globo and its most watched broadcasted journal: "It's over, the *Jornal Nacional* reportage" (Fonseca).

From the beginning former President Bolsonaro had demonstrated some sympathy for a quick and easy resolution for the pandemic. Even when some medicines were still being tested to know if they could fight the Covid-19, Bolsonaro expressed hope that they could work. But this hope was materialised in discourses asking people to not isolate themselves, that the pandemic would finish soon and that the vaccines were not necessary. So, he defended the "early treatment" at the expense of vaccination. Focusing mainly on Chloroquine, his discourse started to oppose vaccination (and its alleged side effects) to Chloroquine (which after was scientifically discredited as a possible treatment for Covid-19).

It is important to say that President Bolsonaro's characterisation of vaccination as a risk involved a particularly homophobic discourse, characteristic of his authoritarian style: "If you turn into an alligator, that's your problem. If you become Superman, if some woman grows a beard or some man's voice gets feminine" ("Bolsonaro: Se tomar vacina" 00:00:34–01:00). And as we have demonstrated before, Bolsonaro said that Brazil needs to stop being a country of "sissies" and face the pandemic. Until now, we have seen how Bolsonaro portrayed the characters and how he characterised the social distancing and the vaccines in his speeches. In the next section we explore the last one of Leeuwen's tool, the legitimation, in order to understand how Bolsonaro tried to justify what he was saying.

Legitimation

To justify his opinions, then President Bolsonaro was constantly invoking economic issues, as it was one of his imagined targets, perhaps the principal.[12] While doing so, he was constantly pointing towards the legitimate characters that should be protected —they are, almost invariably, portrayed as economic actors. For example, while commenting the measures taken by some governors, he stated, on 17 March 2020: "So, this hysteria leads to a shock in the economy. Some merchants end up having problems" ("Bolsonaro volta"). On another occasion, on 29 April 2020, he stated: "I deeply regret the deaths. I knew they would happen. I, since from the start, worried about lives and the employment, as the unemployment also kills" ("Bolsonaro diz 'E daí?'" 00:00:40–50). He constantly portrays the protection of jobs and of "honest workers" as the justification of his actions. That is, he tried to demonstrate that the protection of the economy was also the protection of the workers' lives.

Regarding his choices towards vaccination, he constantly presents it as a matter of private choice, something outside the purview of presidential duties. When asked what he planned on doing to stop the deaths, on 28 April 2020, he

---

[12] Justification involves the elements that Theo van Leeuwen describes as motives and legitimation. According to the author: "Apart from the "what for", the purpose, recontextualizations may also add the "why" to their representations of social practices, that is, they may add legitimations, reasons that either the whole of a social practice or some part of it must take place, or must take place in the way that it does. Texts not only represent social practices, they also explain and legitimate (or delegitimate, critique) them" (Leeuwen, *Discourse and Practice* 20).

answered: "I'm Messias, but I do not perform miracles" ("Sou Messias").[13] On another occasion, on 7 January 2021, he stated: "Do you know how many Brazilians are going to get vaccinated? As far as I know, less than half is going to (…) But, for those who wish to, they [the vaccines] are going to arrive in January" (Fagundes).

He went to extremes to justify freedom of choice at the expense of public health and bad institutional coordination to manage the pandemics. When governors and mayors took actions to contain the spread of the disease, he threatened to use the Armed Forces to guarantee the freedom of movement, on 23 April 2020, by saying:

> People talk about Article 142 of the Constitution, which ensures law and order. We should not intervene. What am I prepared for? I'm not going into details, a chaos in Brazil. What I have said: this politics, lockdown, quarantine, stay at home, curfew, this is absurd (…) I'm the chief of the Armed Forces. Our military, our Armed Forces, if necessary, we are going to the streets not to keep the people inside their houses, but to re-establish the Article 5 of the Constitution. (…) Our Armed Forces can go to the streets one day (…) to ensure Article 5. The right to freedom of movement, end this cowardice of curfew (…). An excessive power that unfortunately the Supreme Court has delegated (Coletta, "Bolsonaro afirma que Exército").[14]

This declaration let no doubts about former President Bolsonaro's intentions. He tried to push his authoritarian agenda further, willing to discover how extreme far he could go. With his speeches he could not only feel the ground to know what he may do, but also please his supporters.

Though President Bolsonaro may have never tried to govern by decrees as Orbán or agitate his supporters to invade governmental buildings —however he did so with hospitals, as we already explained— something similar to the Capitol attack happened in Brazil on 8 January 2023. Bolsonaro's supporters broke into the Brazilian Congress, the Brazilian Supreme Court and the Brazilian Presidential Palace. Although Donald Trump evidently encouraged his supporters to attack the Capitol, until now there is no sufficient evidence that Bolsonaro did the same with his followers. Nevertheless, Bolsonaro had

---

[13] Bolsonaro performed a wordplay with his middle name: Messias (in English: Messiah).
[14] "Article 142. The Armed Forces, comprised of the Navy, the Army and the Air Force, are permanent and regular national institutions, organized on the basis of hierarchy and discipline, under the supreme authority of the president of the Republic, and are intended for the defense of the Country, for the guarantee of the constitutional powers, and, on the initiative of any of these, of law and order" (Federal Supreme Court).

presented ambiguous behaviour since he lost the 2022 Brazilian elections for President Luiz Inácio Lula da Silva, which might have given hope to or misled the people who did not accept the election results. Beyond that, Bolsonaro made several declarations putting in doubt the electoral process in Brazil and the electronic voting machines' reliability. That happened even in the elections which Bolsonaro won.[15] This might have created a perception on his supporters that if someday Bolsonaro was not elected, it was because the process was somehow corrupted.

During his presidency, Bolsonaro faced problems, such as pressure from Congressmen, parliamentary investigations (as the PCI), corruption accusations targeting him and his family, but he had continued politically strong. As the Covid-19 pandemics waled to an end —like his government which finished at the end of 2022— we could see how much stronger or weaker he got during the pandemics and what his last moves were. For instance, Bolsonaro used the government machine aiming to favour himself in order to compete with Lula during the presidential elections.

In fact, Bolsonaro expanded social benefits in the last months of 2022, even though he did not allocate enough budget to keep the same amount for expenditures related to social benefits in 2023.[16] He also contended with state governors at reducing the states' tax revenues in order to lower the oil prices and sustain the inflation rates in 2022. Further, near the election day, Bolsonaro pressured Petrobras to artificially hold the oil prices.[17] In addition, the Federal Highway Police (FHP) conducted several approaches and blockages in some highways in the elections day, creating obstacles for people to vote in Northeast, a region of the country where Lula had the great majority of supporters.[18] And we

---

[15] Aos fatos, an investigative journalist platform, identified 84 Bolsonaro's allegations of fraud regarding the electronic voting machines and allegedly fragility in the voting process in Brazil (Ribeiro and Menezes). Folha de São Paulo, a traditional Brazilian newspaper, made an article presenting 25 times that Bolsonaro attacked the Brazilian electoral system without proofs ("Relembre alguns ataques"). CNN Brazil remembered five of Bolsonaro's speeches questioning the Brazilian elections ("Relembre vezes em que").

[16] Bolsonaro's government granted a rise to some social benefits amidst the elections period. Also, that rise was not a secured right for the Brazilian population. In the 2023 budget, there was not any money allocated to keeping paying the difference. That is, the rise would last until the end of 2022. In that way, this rise was seen like a movement to increase Bolsonaro's approval ratings during the election period (Pinzer).

[17] Petrobras is a Brazilian company accountable to produce and distribute oil. Its prices policy was, at that time, bounded with the oil international prices. That is, if the international oil prices rise, internally it would happen the same. However, due to Bolsonaro's pressure, the company froze intern prices, even though there was an international increase ("Petrobras segura reajuste").

[18] These actions from the Federal Highway Police raised concerns for some reasons. First, because the highest number of blocks was performed in a region where Lula is historically strong. Second, in the day before the elections, Justice Alexandre de Moraes

cannot let aside the so-called "orçamento secreto (secret budget)" —called secret since there is no requirement to explain and detail to where some public money was allocated— which contributed to the high re-election percentage of Congresspersons, who gave support to Bolsonaro in their respective election zones (Carrança). Even with those illegal or unethical moves, Bolsonaro was not able to secure his re-election. He could neither face-up to the Brazilian memory about the former Lula's governments nor erase his behaviour as a state leader during the facing of the Covid-19 pandemic.

Conclusion

The CDA approach has been undertaken to critically analyse elected key declarations of former President Jair Bolsonaro from January 2020 to December 2021. This has made possible the contextualisation of his denialist rhetoric to Covid-19, early treatment and the use of vaccines.

Returning to our initial question, "how has former President Jair Bolsonaro adopted a denialist rhetoric to Covid-19, early treatment and the use of vaccines?", it is our contention that Bolsonaro has adopted a denialist rhetoric about Covid-19, early treatment and vaccines as part of his political agenda to deconstruct democratic institutions and advance his populist extreme right programme.

As the analysed data shows, Bolsonaro's discourses had the purpose of further advancing his anti-institutional agenda. The Brazilian political scientist Leonardo Avritzer stated that anti-politics has been one of the most important traits of President Bolsonaro's political behaviour (*Política e Antipolítica: A crise*). Hence, acting from within the democratic institutions, Bolsonaro has tried to corrupt and weaken them. This has been shown throughout this paper, especially when we demonstrate how Bolsonaro behaved during the election period. Furthermore, his discursive representation of the pandemics, social distancing and vaccination reveals strong links to his intentions to delegitimise democracy itself. He gave signals of his support to a so-called military "intervention" and deliberately obstructed the flow of information to halt the work of liberal press, which —as we have demonstrated— Bolsonaro has considered to be his enemy.

More important to note is the way he has chosen to do so. Advancing a discourse based on personalism, free market and absolute individual freedom, he undermined the necessity of collective participation and deliberation. This agenda was furthered to the extreme. President Bolsonaro's discourse

---

prohibited any operation related to public transport during the elections. Third, the at the time General Director of the FHP —Silvinei Marques— declared support to Bolsonaro. Also, an official document produced by him convoked officers to the duty and created ambiguous explanations about what should be stopped and what should proceed (Schreiber; "Policiais dizem que ofício de diretor").

portrayed the Covid-19 pandemic and collective health as something outside his presidential duties and advanced representations that framed vaccination, social distancing, and early treatment as private choices. He was also involved with corruption accusations, the defence of ineffective medicines and an initial denial to buy vaccines.

Now, if we think about whether President Bolsonaro has meant what he has said, there is no conclusive answer. If he only used polemic statements to distract the public from issues such as criminal investigations against him, his sons and allies, to keep the economic wheel spinning, to induce the purchase of some medicines or if he really believed in what he had said, we are not able to give a definitive answer. Probably many of these questions and possible answers are mixed together. But the fact remains: many of his outrageous statements coincide with criminal investigations and scandals; and that his misguided behaviour and opinions have been constant during the period analysed.

It is also not possible —at least not within the purview of this research— to say that he was furthering an economy-based agenda exclusively with electoral purposes. Nonetheless, it can be argued that President Bolsonaro advanced the economic discourse aimed at impoverished workers at the expense of hundreds of thousands of lives and to his own advantage. As Avritzer argues, his management of the Covid-19 pandemic and the insistence on an anti-institutional solution were responsible for a significant decline of his approval rates ("Política e antipolítica").

The question of the approval ratings cannot be underestimated. President Bolsonaro faced a huge reduction in his approval ratings, voting intentions and government evaluation since the pandemic started. One of the reasons he may have worsened the level of his statements, attacked science and the press could be to please his supporters, as their loyalty remained high during the same period. Therefore, he relied on them.

During the elections Bolsonaro kept his level of discourse, intercalating with some minor moments of soft declarations and calm reactions, especially during the broadcasted debates. That seemed to be enough to reward his supporters and secure Bolsonaro even more votes in 2022 (58,206,354) than when he was elected in 2018 (57,797,847). However, this voting rate —the second biggest in the history— was not enough to defeat Lula, who got 60,345,999 votes, the biggest voting rate in Brazilian history.

In a clear demonstration that speeches and narratives can build worlds, shape contexts and influence people's everyday lives, we can realise that with his declarations Bolsonaro managed to raise more votes for himself. He was also able to postpone the purchase of vaccines and stimulate social gatherings, which led to the deaths of thousands of people. He contributed to the devaluation of science as well as to the source of disaffections between people who were once cherished to each other, like members of the same family. He surely built a negative image of some Brazilian Institutions. And, in short, he created a context in which Covid-19 was not tackled as it should have been, leading to unnecessary deaths, redundant public spending and an atmosphere of conflict in Brazil.

In this way, Bolsonaro strategy may have worked as a double-edged sword. On one side, Bolsonaro and the right-wing remained strong and loyal. On the other side, his poor behaviour and aggressive speeches during the pandemic helped gather together different groups, giving Lula a large support base and his meaningful vote numbers. The Brazilian right-wing (and even the extreme-right and the Bolsonarism) cannot be belittled at this point, nonetheless. Even being defeated at the elections, their number got bigger. However, Bolsonaro seems to have been losing strength.

After losing the elections, Bolsonaro took a long time to recognise Lula's victory. Also, a big part of his supporters felt betrayed by him (since he did not thank them for their assistance). In addition, he went to the United States of America, where he stayed 89 days: taking part in right-wing conferences, giving interviews and facing accusations regarding the time when he was President (ranging from the incorporation of some Presidential gifts to his private collection to disinformation). Those accusations might have contributed to the deterioration of Bolsonaro's image, since he started avoiding the media and the public scrutiny. This, also, can be a strategy to stay off the radar and preserve his public perception.

Only in the next electoral period will we see how much stronger Bolsonaro remains when he capitalises again on his image and supporters. Likewise, only the future will let us know Bolsonaro's intentions: a state leader who really believed in what he had said or a state leader who is capable of saying anything to change the focus on his mistakes and possible crimes in order to perpetuate his rule.

Bibliography

Afonso, Natháli. "É falso que STF afastou Bolsonaro do controle de ações estratégicas contra pandemia de Covid-19". *Lupa*, 1 July 2020, https://lupa.uol.com.br/jornalismo/2020/07/01/verificamos-stf-bolsonaro-covid/.

Angermuller, Johannes, et al. "Introduction". *The Discourse Studies Reader: Main Currents in Theory and Analysis*, edited by Johannes Angermuller, et al., John Benjamin Publishing Company, 2014, pp. 1–15.

"#AoVivo: Abertura oficial da Semana das Comunicações". *YouTube*, uploaded by CanalGov, 5 May 2021, https://www.youtube.com/watch?v=Qlz0UuP AVjc&ab_channel=CanalGov.

"#AoVivo: Lançamento da Retomada do Turismo". *YouTube*, uploaded by CanalGov, 10 November 2020, https://www.youtube.com/watch?v=LtKUvVE6QcI.

Avritzer, Leonardo. *Política e Antipolítica: A crise do governo Bolsonaro*. Todavia, 2020.

—. "Política e antipolítica nos dois anos de governo Bolsonaro". *Governo Bolsonaro: Retrocesso democrático e degradação política*, edited by Leonardo Avritzer, et al. Autêntica, 2021, pp. 13–20.

Bassani, Ana Taís, et al. "SARS-COV-2: Pandemia, negacionismo científico populista de extrema direita e a utilização off label de medicamentos". *Revista de Políticas Públicas*, vol. 25, no. 1, 2021, pp. 228–244.

"Bolsonaro atribui inflação a medidas de isolamento; economistas discordam". *UOL*, 12 January 2022, https://economia.uol.com.br/noticias/redacao/2022/01/12/bolsonaro-inflacao-medidas-covid-19.html.

"Bolsonaro volta a chamar medidas contra coronavírus de histeria". *CNN Brasil*, 17 March 2020, https://www.cnnbrasil.com.br/politica/bolsonaro-volta-a-falar-em-histeria-e-diz-que-medidas-contra-coronavirus-afetam/.

"Bolsonaro discursa em Brasília para manifestantes que pediam intervenção militar". *g1*, 19 April 2020, https://g1.globo.com/politica/noticia/2020/04/19/bolsonaro-discursa-em-manifestacao-em-brasilia-que-defendeu-intervencao-militar.ghtml.

"Bolsonaro diz 'E daí?' e depois troca acusações com Doria sobre Covid-19". *YouTube*, uploaded by Jornal O Globo, 29 April 2020, https://www.youtube.com/watch?v=4HFbUzzpUoE&ab_channel=JornalOGlobo.

"Bolsonaro diz que governo federal não comprará vacina CoronaVac". *agênciaBrasil*, 21 October 2020, https://agenciabrasil.ebc.com.br/politica/noticia/2020-10/bolsonaro-diz-que-governo-federal-nao-comprara-vacina-coronavac.

"Bolsonaro diz que governo não comprará Coronavac mesmo se vacina for aprovada pela Anvisa". *O Globo*, 22 October 2020, https://oglobo.globo.com/saude/coronavirus/bolsonaro-diz-que-governo-nao-comprara-coronavac-mesmo-se-vacina-for-aprovada-pela-anvisa-1-24705798.

"Bolsonaro: 'Se tomar vacina e virar jacaré não tenho nada a ver com isso'". *YouTube*, uploaded by UOL, 18 December 2020, https://www.youtube.com/watch?v=lBCXkVOEH-8&ab_channel=UOL.

"Bolsonaro sobre número de mortos por Covid-19: 'Não sou coveiro'". *YouTube*, uploaded by UOL, 21 April 2020, https://www.youtube.com/watch?v=aIpUbYjjdn0&ab_channel=UOL.

"Bolsonaro usa enquete alemã distorcida para criticar uso de máscaras". *g1*, 26 February 2021, https://g1.globo.com/bemestar/coronavirus/noticia/2021/02/26/bolsonaro-usa-enquete-alema-distorcida-para-criticar-uso-de-mascaras.ghtml.

"Brasileiro mergulha no esgoto e não acontece nada, diz Bolsonaro". *A Gazeta*, 26 March 2020, https://www.agazeta.com.br/brasil/brasileiro-mergulha-no-esgoto-e-nao-acontece-nada-diz-bolsonaro-0320.

Brown, Wendy. *In the Ruins of Neoliberalism: The Rise of Antidemocratic Politics in the West*. Columbia University Press, 2019.

Bryant, Octavia and Benjamin Moffit. "What Actually Is Populism? And Why Does It Have a Bad Reputation?". *The Conversation*, 5 February 2019, https://theconversation.com/what-actually-is-populism-and-why-does-it-have-a-bad-reputation-109874.

Camarotti, Gerson. "Bolsonaro tenta dividir sociedade e criar cortina de fumaça para mansão do filho, avaliam aliados". *g1*, 5 March 2021, https://g1.globo.com/politica/blog/gerson-camarotti/post/2021/03/05/ao-falar-de-mimimi-bolsonaro-tem-metodo-dividir-a-sociedade-com-intencao-eleitoral-e-criar-cortina-de-fumaca-para-mansao-do-filho.ghtml.

Caponi, Sandra. "Covid-19 no Brasil: Entre o negacionismo e a razão neoliberal". *Estudos Avançados*, vol. 34, no. 99, 2020, pp. 209–224.

Carmo, Marcia. "Coronavírus: Por que Bolsonaro e líderes de esquerda na América Latina adotam postura parecida". *BBC News Brasil*, 20 March 2020, https://www.bbc.com/portuguese/internacional-52042531.

Carrança, Thais. "Bolsonaro derrotado: 10 armas usadas sem sucesso na tentativa de reeleição". *BBC News Brasil*. 30 October 2022, https://www.bbc.com/portuguese/brasil-63419897.

Cesarino, Letícia. "How Social Media Affords Populist Politics: Remarks on Liminality Based on the Brazilian Case". *Trabalhos Em Linguística Aplicada*, vol. 59, no. 1, 2020, pp. 404–427.

Chouliaraki, Lilie, and Norman Fairclough. *Discourse in Late Modernity: Rethinking Critical Discourse Analysis*. Edinburgh University Press, 1999.

Coletta, Ricardo Della. "Bolsonaro afirma que Exército pode ir para a rua acabar com 'covardia de toque de recolher'". *Folha de S. Paulo*, 23 April 2021, https://www1.folha.uol.com.br/poder/2021/04/bolsonaro-afirma-que-exercito-pode-ir-para-a-rua-acabar-com-covardia-de-toque-de-recolher.shtml.

—. "Outras gripes mataram mais do que coronavírus, diz Bolsonaro". *Folha de S.Paulo*, 11 March 2020, https://www1.folha.uol.com.br/equilibrioesaude/2020/03/outras-gripes-mataram-mais-do-que-coronavirus-diz-bolsonaro.shtml.

"Confira discurso de Bolsonaro na Assembleia-Geral da ONU". *YouTube*, uploaded by BBC News Brasil, 21 September 2021, https://www.youtube.com/watch?v=EmiKQDVtDds&ab_channel=BBCNewsBrasil.

Connel, Raewyn W. *Masculinities*. University of California Press, 2005.

Da Silva, Yago. *Bolsonaro and Social Media: A Critical Discourse Analysis of the Brazilian President's Populist Communication on Twitter*. 2020. Uppsala Universitet, Master Thesis, https://uu.diva-portal.org/smash/get/diva2:1448385/FULLTEXT01.pdf.

Dagnino, Evelina. "Culture, Citizenship, and Democracy: Changing Discourses and Practices of the Latin American Left". *Cultures of Politics/Politics of Cultures Re-Visioning Latin American Social Movements*, edited by Sonia E. Alvarez, Evelina Dagnino and Arturo Escobar, Westview Press, 1998.

—. "Os movimentos sociais e a construção da democracia no Brasil: Tendências recentes". *Journal of Iberian and Latin American Studies*, vol. 7, no. 1, 2001, pp. 75–104.

Dardot, Pierre and Christian Laval. *The New Way of the World: Neoliberal Society*. Verso Books, 2014.

De Moraes, Marcelo. "Orientação para suspender vacinação é mais uma cortina de fumaça; leia análise". *Estadão*, 16 September 2021, https://www.estadao.com.br/saude/orientacao-para-suspender-vacinacao-e-mais-uma-cortina-de-fumaca-leia-analise/.

Diário Oficial da União. *Decreto Nº 10.292*, 25 March 2020, https://www2.camara.leg.br/legin/fed/decret/2020/decreto-10292-25-marco-2020-789872-publicacaooriginal-160178-pe.html.

"Entrevista com o presidente Jair Bolsonaro". *YouTube*, uploaded by CanalGov, 7 July 2020, https://www.youtube.com/watch?v=Q_q0DTmOpfw&t=1366s&ab_channel=CanalGov.

Fagundes, Murilo. "'Pelo que sei, menos da metade da população vai tomar vacina', diz Bolsonaro". *Poder 360*, 7 January 2021, https://www.poder360.com.br/governo/pelo-que-sei-menos-da-metade-da-populacao-vai-tomar-vacina-diz-bolsonaro/.

Federal Supreme Court. *Constitution of the Federative Republic of Brazil*, 5 October 1988, https://www.stf.jus.br/arquivo/cms/legislacaoConstituicao/anexo/brazil_federal_constitution.pdf.

Ferraz, Adriana, et al. "'Ou ele (Moraes) se enquadra ou pede para sair', ameaça Bolsonaro em discurso golpista". *Estadão*, 7 September 2021, https://www.estadao.com.br/politica/quero-dizer-aos-canalhas-que-eu-nunca-serei-preso-diz-bolsonaro-em-novo-discurso-golpista/.

Fonseca, Pedro. "'Acabou matéria do Jornal Nacional', diz Bolsonaro sobre atraso em divulgação de casos de Covid-19". *UOL*, 5 June 2020, https://economia.uol.com.br/noticias/reuters/2020/06/05/acabou-materia-do-jornal-nacional-diz-bolsonaro-sobre-atraso-em-divulgacao-de-casos-de-covid-19.htm.

Fredman, Sandra. "A Human Rights Approach: The Right to Education in the Time of Covid-19". *Child Development*, vol. 92, no. 5, 2021, pp. e900–e903.

Gracino Junior, Paulo, et al. "'Os humilhados serão exaltados': Ressentimento e adesão evangélica ao Bolsonarismo". *Cadernos Metrópole*, vol. 23, no. 51, 2021, pp. 547–579.

Gomes, Pedro Henrique. "'Não sou coveiro, tá?', diz Bolsonaro ao responder sobre mortos por coronavírus". *g1*, 20 April 2020, https://g1.globo.com/politica/noticia/2020/04/20/nao-sou-coveiro-ta-diz-bolsonaro-ao-responder-sobre-mortos-por-coronavirus.ghtml.

Gullino, Daniel. "Bolsonaro diz que pandemia 'está acabando' e ironiza pressa de Doria para comprar vacina". *O Globo*, 30 October 2020, https://oglobo.globo.com/brasil/bolsonaro-diz-que-pandemia-esta-acabando-ironiza-pressa-de-doria-para-comprar-vacina-1-24721013.

Kakisina, Peggy A., et al. "Discursive Strategies of Manipulation in COVID-19 Political Discourse: The Case of Donald Trump and Jair Bolsonaro". *SAGE Open*, vol. 12, no. 1, 2022, pp. 1–9.

Lassa, Jonatan A., and Miranda Booth. "Are Populist Leaders a Liability during Covid-19?". *The Conversation*, 8 April 2020, https://theconversation.com/are-populist-leaders-a-liability-during-covid-19-135431.

Le Bart, Christian. *Le discours politique*. Presses Universitaires de France, 1998.

Leeuwen, Theo van. "Critical Discourse Analysis". *Encyclopedia of Language & Linguistics*, edited by Keith Brown, Elsevier, 2006, pp. 290–294.
—. *Discourse and Practice: New Tools for Critical Discourse Analysis*. Oxford University Press, 2007.
Lessig, Lawrence, and Cass R. Sunstein. "The President and the Administration". *Columbia Law Review*, vol. 94, no. 1, 1994, pp. 1–123.
Löwy, Ilana, and Luc Berlivet. "The Problem with Chloroquine. Epistemologists, Methodologists, and the (Mis)Uses of Medical History". *História, Ciências, Saúde – Manguinhos*, 6 May 2020, https://www.revistahcsm.coc.fiocruz.br/english/the-problem-with-chloroquine-epistemologists-methodologists-and-the-misuses-of-medical-history/
Magalhães, Izabel. "Introdução: A analise de discurso critica". *D.E.L.T.A.*, vol. 21, Especial, 2005, pp. 1–9.
Mazieiro, Guilherme. "Depois da facada, não vai ser gripezinha que vai me derrubar, diz Bolsonaro". *UOL*, 20 March 2020, https://noticias.uol.com.br/politica/ultimas-noticias/2020/03/20/depois-da-facada-nao-vai-ser-gripezinha-que-vai-me-derrubar-diz-bolsonaro.html.
Mazui, Guilherme. "'Mais uma que Jair Bolsonaro ganha', diz presidente sobre suspensão de testes da CoronaVac". *g1*, 10 November 2020, https://g1.globo.com/politica/noticia/2020/11/10/mais-uma-que-jair-bolsonaro-ganha-diz-o-presidente-ao-comentar-suspensao-de-testes-da-vacina-coronavac.ghtml.
Marcello, Maria Carolina. "Bolsonaro diz que ninguém pode obrigar vacinação e chama de imbecil quem o considera mau exemplo". *Reuters*, 18 December 2020, https://www.reuters.com/article/instant-article/idLTAKBN28R3A2/.
Medeiros, Marcelo, and Bárbara L. Ramacciotti. "O estado de bem estar social e seus reflexos na estruturação da organização política administrativa brasileira". *Revista de Estudios Interdisciplinares*, vol. 3, no. 4, 2021, pp. 89–112.
Nogueira, Conceição. "A análise do discurso". *Métodos e técnicas de avaliação: Novos contributos para a prática e investigação*, edited by L Almeida and E Fernandes, Centro de Estudos Educação e Psicologia, 2001, pp. 15–47.
Organization of American States. American Declaration of the Rights and Duties of Man. April 1948. *Organization of American States*, www.oas.org/en/iachr/mandate/Basics/declaration.asp.
—. American Convention on Human Rights "Pact of San José, Costa Rica". November 1969. *Organization of American States*, www.oas.org/dil/treaties_B-32_American_Convention_on_Human_Rights.htm.
—. Additional Protocol to the American Convention on Human Rights in the area of Economic, Social and Cultural Rights. 17 November 1988. *Organization of American States*, www.oas.org/juridico/english/treaties/a-52.html.
"'Parece que está indo embora', diz Bolsonaro sobre vírus em live com religiosos". *O Tempo*, 13 April 2020, https://www.otempo.com.br/politica/parece-que-esta-indo-embora-diz-bolsonaro-sobre-virus-em-live-com-religiosos-1.2323878.
Peixoto, Guilherme. "Ataques ao STF e promessa de desobedecer Moraes: o 7/9 de Bolsonaro". *Estado de Minas*, 7 September 2021, https://www.em.com.br/

app/noticia/politica/2021/09/07/interna_politica,1303432/ataques-ao-stf-e-promessa-de-desobedecer-moraes-o-7-9-de-bolsonaro.shtml.

"Pesquisas apontam que 400 mil mortes poderiam ser evitadas; governistas questionam". *Senado Notícias*, 24 June 2021, https://www12.senado.leg.br/noticias/materias/2021/06/24/pesquisas-apontam-que-400-mil-mortes-poderiam-ser-evitadas-governistas-questionam.

"Petrobras segura reajuste nos preços dos combustíveis antes do 2° turno". *Exame*, 26 October 2022, https://exame.com/economia/petrobras-segura-reajuste-nos-preco-dos-combustiveis-antes-do-2-turno/.

Pinzer, Pedro. "Orçamento de 2023 prevê Auxílio Brasil de R$ 405, mas equipe econômica promete negociar manutenção dos R$ 600". *Rádio Senado*, 31 August 2022, https://www12.senado.leg.br/radio/1/noticia/2022/08/31/orcamento-de-2023-preve-auxilio-brasil-de-r-405-mas-equipe-economica-promete-negociar-manutencao-dos-r-600.

"Policiais dizem que ofício de diretor da PRF deu 'carta branca' a operações". *BBC News Brasil*, 30 October 2022, https://www.bbc.com/portuguese/brasil-63450698.

Prazeres, Leandro. "Bolsonaro pede a apoiadores que entrem em hospitais para filmar leitos". *O Globo*, 11 June 2020, https://oglobo.globo.com/saude/coronavirus/bolsonaro-pede-apoiadores-que-entrem-em-hospitais-para-filmar-leitos-24475348.

"President Trump Calls Coronavirus 'Kung Flu'". *BBC News*, 24 June 2020, https://www.bbc.com/news/av/world-us-canada-53173436.

Proner, Carol, et al. *A resistência ao golpe de 2016*. Projeto Editorial Praxis, 2016.

Recuero, Raquel, and Felipe Soares. "#Vachina: How Politicians Help to Spread Disinformation about Covid-19 Vaccines". *Journal of Digital Social Research*, vol. 4, no. 1, 2022, pp. 73-97.

"Retrospectiva 2021: as milhões de vacinas Covid-19 que trouxeram esperança para o Brasil". *Ministério da Saúde*, 30 December 2021, https://www.gov.br/saude/pt-br/assuntos/noticias/2021/dezembro/retrospectiva-2021-as-milhoes-de-vacinas-covid-19-que-trouxeram-esperanca-para-o-brasil.

"Relembre alguns ataques de Bolsonaro oa sistema eleitoral sem apresentar provas". *Folha de S. Paulo*, 8 January 2021, https://www1.folha.uol.com.br/poder/2021/01/veja-o-que-bolsonaro-ja-disse-sobre-urnas-eletronicas-e-fraude-em-eleicao-sem-apresentar-provas.shtml?utm_source=twitter&utm_medium=social&utm_campaign=twfolha.

"Relembre vezes em que Jair Bolsonaro questionou o sistema eleitoral". *CNN Brasil*, 26 April 2023, https://www.cnnbrasil.com.br/politica/relembre-vezes-em-que-jair-bolsonaro-questionou-o-sistema-eleitoral/.

Ribeiro, Amanda and Luiz Fernando Menezes. "Como a desinformação sobre urnas abasteceu a artilharia de Bolsonaro contra o sistema eleitoral". *Aos Fatos*, 6 June 2022, https://www.aosfatos.org/noticias/desinformacao-urnas-abasteceu-artilharia-bolsonaro-contra-sistema-eleitoral/.

Ribeiro, Bruno. "Ao todo, 53 e-mails da Pfizer ao governo Bolsonaro ficaram sem resposta, diz Randolfe". *Estadão*, 4 June 2021, https://politica.estadao.com.br/noticias/geral,ao-todo-53-e-mails-da-pfizer-ao-governo-ficaram-sem-resposta-diz-randolfe,70003737162.

Santos, Fabiano, and Fernando Guarnieri. "From Protest to Parliamentary Coup: An Overview of Brazil's Recent History". *Journal of Latin American Cultural Studies*, vol. 25, no. 4, 2016, pp. 485–494.

Schreiber, Mariana. "O que se sabe sobre ações da PRF que contrariaram proibição do TSE?". *BBC News Brasil*, 30 October 2022, https://www.bbc.com/portuguese/brasil-63451402.

Schwarcz, Lília. *Sobre o autoritarismo brasileiro*. Companhia das Letras, 2018.

SecomVc [@secomvc]. "O Governo do Brasil investiu bilhões de reais para salvar vidas e preservar empregos. Estabeleceu parceria e investirá na produção de vacina. Recursos para estados e municípios, saúde, economia, TUDO será feito, mas impor obrigações definitivamente não está nos planos". *Twitter*, 1 September 2020, https://twitter.com/secomvc/status/1300838424526626820.

Senado Federal do Brazil, Comissão Parlamentar de Inquérito da Pandemia. *CPI da Pandemia. Relatório Final*. 26 October 2021, https://legis.senado.leg.br/comissoes/mnas?codcol=2441&tp=4#:~:text=26/10/2021-,Relat%C3%B3rio%20Final%20apresentado%20pelo%20Relator,-Relat%C3%B3rio%20final%20apreciado.

Shear, Michael D. and Sarah Mervosh. "Trump Fans Protest Against Governors Who Have Imposed Virus Restrictions". *The New York Times*, 17 April 2020, https://www.nytimes.com/2020/04/17/us/politics/trump-coronavirus-govenors.html.

Soares, Felipe B., et al. "Research note: Bolsonaro's firehose: How Covid-19 disinformation on WhatsApp was used to fight a government political crisis in Brazil". *Harvard Kennedy School Misinformation Review*, 29 January 2021, https://doi.org/10.37016/mr-2020-54.

Soares, Ingrid. "Bolsonaro sobre aumento de mortes: 'Não vamos chorar o leite derramado'". *Correio Braziliense*, 7 April 2021, https://www.correiobraziliense.com.br/politica/2021/04/4916781-bolsonaro-sobre-aumento-de-mortes-nao-vamos-chorar-o-leite-derramado.html.

"'Sou Messias, mas não faço milagre', diz Bolsonaro sobre mortes por coronavírus". *CNN Brasil*, 28 April 2020, https://www.cnnbrasil.com.br/politica/e-a-vida-diz-bolsonaro-sobre-mortes-por-coronavirus/.

Souza, Catiane and Priscila Chéquer. "Fundamentalismo religioso e político na pandemia: 'É isso mesmo', 'e daí?'". *Caderno Teológico*, vol. 5, no. 2, 2020, pp. 123–37.

Spring, Jake. "Brazil Minister Calls for Environmental Deregulation While Public Distracted by Covid". *Reuters*, 22 May 2020, https://www.reuters.com/article/us-brazil-politics-environment-idUSKBN22Y30Y.

Sunstein, Cass R. "Well-Being and the State". *Harvard Law Review*, vol. 107, no. 6, 1994, pp. 1303–1327.

Tanacs, Gabor, and Natalie Huet. "Hungary Ends Emergency Powers, But New Law Opens Up Potential to Re-Apply Them". *Euronews*, 16 June 2020, https://www.euronews.com/2020/06/16/hungary-debates-end-to-emergency-powers-but-new-law-opens-up-potential-to-re-apply-them.

Terto Neto, Ulisses. "Making the Human Rights Talk Matter: Are the Brazilian State's Practices Really Following Its Rhetoric Towards the Protection of

Human Rights Defenders in the Country?". *Revista Quaestio Iuris*, vol. 9, no. 4, 2016, pp. 2263–2311.

Teti, Andrea. "Democracy Without Social Justice: Marginalization of Social and Economic Rights in EU Democracy Assistance Policy after the Arab Uprisings". *Middle East Critique*, vol. 24, no. 1, 2015, pp. 9–25.

"'Todos nós vamos morrer um dia': veja falas de bolsonaro sobre o coronavírus". *YouTube*, uploaded by UOL, 2 May 2020, https://www.youtube.com/watch?v=oegOQ_IakoU&ab_channel=UOL.

Trindade, Luciano. "Deputados invadem hospital de campanha do Anhembi e causam tumulto". *UOL*, 4 June 2020, https://www1.folha.uol.com.br/cotidiano/2020/06/deputados-invadem-hospital-de-campanha-do-anhembi-e-causam-tumulto.shtml.

United Nations, General Assembly. Universal Declaration of Human Rights. Resolution 217 A, 10 December 1948. *United Nations*, www.un.org/en/universal-declaration-human-rights/.

—. International Covenant on Economic, Social and Cultural Rights. Resolution 2200 A, 16 December 1966. *United Nations*, www.ohchr.org/en/instruments-mechanisms/instruments/international-covenant-economic-social-and-cultural-rights.

—. Convention on the Elimination of All Forms of Discrimination against Women. 18 December 1979. *United Nations*, www.un.org/womenwatch/daw/cedaw/text/econvention.htm.

—. Convention on the Rights of the Child. Resolution 44/2, 20 November 1989. *United Nations*, www.ohchr.org/en/instruments-mechanisms/instruments/convention-rights-child.

—. International Convention on the Protection of the Rights of All Migrant Workers and Members of Their Families. Resolution 45/158, 18 December 1990. *United Nations*, www.ohchr.org/en/instruments-mechanisms/instruments/international-convention-protection-rights-all-migrant-workers.

Victor, Daniel, et al. "In His Own Words, Trump on the Coronavirus and Masks". *The New York Times*, 2 October 2020, https://www.nytimes.com/2020/10/02/us/politics/donald-trump-masks.html.

World Report 2022: Events of 2021. Humans Right Watch, 2022, https://www.hrw.org/sites/default/files/media_2022/01/World%20Report%202022%20web%20pdf_0.pdf.

Chapter 4

"Monstruos" and "Mujeres Callejeras"
Covid-19, Gender-based Violence and Discourses of Blame in Peru

Saskia Zielińska
King's College London

Abstract

Despite growing public and state recognition that sexual and gender-based violence (GBV) is a serious problem in Peru, discourses of blame continue to portray women and girls as responsible for the violence they experience. Looking at four different cases studies, this chapter will examine several individualising discourses of blame with regards to GBV before and during the COVID-19 pandemic in Peru, including how the state contributes towards these narratives. Firstly, it will examine how, depending on their social location, some women are portrayed as 'undeserving' victims of violence. On the other hand, it will examine how in the cases where blame is attributed to the perpetrators for the violence they have committed these perpetrators are dehumanised as 'monsters' and are perceived of as anomalies. In all these cases, the chapter examines how such discourses obscure the structural causes of GBV and therefore contribute to its perpetuation.

Keywords: Gender-based violence, sexual violence, feminicide, discourses of blame, Peru

* * *

Introduction

Peru consistently reports high levels of sexual violence and gender-based violence (GBV), yet discourses of blame continue to portray women and girls as responsible for the violence they experience.[1] For instance, in the days before the pandemic, Peruvian news Channel AV Noticias portrayed the young

---

[1] This chapter focuses on cisgender women and girls, but it should be noted that in Peru, as elsewhere, the trans community suffers from particular vulnerability to GBV (see notes 8 and 12).

Venezuelan murder victim, Jocelyn Daniela Vázquez Hernández, as a "chica mala"[2] who "enjoyed parties". At the same time, Peruvian feminists confronted blame culture, performing "Un violador en tu camino"[3] during the final pre-pandemic 8-M[4], denouncing state complicity and deeply rooted patriarchal inequalities. The quarantine shed light on the nature of GBV in Peru as it became clear through increased calls to domestic violence hotlines during the sanitary emergency (Agüero et al. 3) that the perpetrators of GBV were largely within women and girls' own homes. Nevertheless, diverse discourses of blame persisted and were subtly modified to fit with the particular circumstances of lockdown. When in the early months of the pandemic, the Peruvian newspaper La República reported that 557 women had disappeared since the quarantine began, public response varied. Whilst some expressed outrage, others blamed the women. What were they doing outside of their house during the quarantine? Had they provoked the violence by being "mujeres callejeras"?[5] On the other hand, in the case of child-rapists, such as the "Monstruo de Chontalí",[6] a man who was arrested for sexually abusing and attempting to burn alive his 13-year-old daughter, blame was directed at the perpetrator. Yet, the perpetrator was conceptualised in the public imagination as non-human and thus an isolated anomaly, unrelated to the continuum of structural, gendered violence in society. In both cases, blame is individualised and attention is turned away from the gendered inequalities that make such violence possible in the first place.

This chapter will examine the multiple narratives of blame with regards to GBV during the Covid-19 pandemic in Peru, including how the state contributes towards these narratives. Whilst discourses of blame certainly existed before the pandemic, the moment of pandemic itself presents an interesting opportunity with which to study these discourses. Firstly, as aforementioned, the pandemic represents a high point of sexual and GBV given that women and girls were largely quarantined with their aggressors. Secondly, whilst the nature of lockdown challenged the erroneous bases of many of the pre-existing discourses of blame, (such as dressing "provocatively") as will be demonstrated, it did not eradicate them, demonstrating the staying power and malleability of such narratives. It will also examine how such discourses obscure the structural causes of GBV and contribute to its normalisation and hence reproduction.

The chapter principally focuses on discourses emanating from the mass media, given that mass media are amongst the principle sources of contemporary

---

[2] "Bad girl".
[3] "A rapist in your path".
[4] 8 March, International Women's Day.
[5] "Women of the street".
[6] "Monster of Chontalí".

"ideological, moral, and cultural norms" (Ogden 78). As Ogden argues, mass media, more so than the state, has become an important source of promoting individualised "reproductive responsibility" and constructing "neoliberal selfhood" (77–78). The impact of such constructions is that blame for sexual transgression may be individualised, given that the neoliberal subject assumes responsibility for their action. In the cases that will be discussed below, blame for sexual violence is always individualised, but depending on the circumstances, may be attributed to the victim or the perpetrator. These narratives of blame are important for the lived experience of women and girls for several reasons. Firstly, they may further traumatise those who have already experienced sexual or GBV. Secondly, the misdirection of blame towards victims rather than perpetrators contributes to the normalisation and hence reproduction of GBV. Given that many of the discourses that will be discussed below are also sexualised insults in themselves, they also represent part of a continuum of violence.

Rather than attempt to provide a large-scale media analysis of discourses of blame which is out of the scope of this study, this chapter will reflect on four specific case studies, three of which pertain to different instances of sexual and GBV, one before and two during the pandemic. Through these three case studies both the representation of GBV and its victims in the media will be examined. The three case studies from the media were chosen for analysis given that they each received widespread media coverage in Peru over several weeks, and as such received high levels of engagement in social media. The particular cases were chosen for this chapter as they demonstrate both the variety of different co-existing blame narratives abounding in the public discourse, albeit connected by a common "individualising" logic. As well as examining how the cases themselves were constructed in the media, public Facebook comments[7] on the cases were also analysed to see how different narratives of blame purveyed through public discourse. Facebook was chosen over other social media sites as it is the most widely used social media platform in Peru. Of 28.1 million social media users in the country in January 2022, Facebook adverts reached a maximum of 24.8 million (*Digital 2022: Peru*).

The chapter will later examine campaign materials from the state's own public information campaign to combat GBV during the pandemic, and consider how state discourse similarly promotes an individualised approach to GBV, that further supports the individualisation of blame. It will conclude that although

---

[7] No direct quotes from Facebook comments are given in this chapter. This is due to the fact that although comments are made in a public forum and are therefore publicly visible and available, it is not implied that such comments were made with the express consent of being directly quoted in research or otherwise. As a result, I will only be using short, generalised, and aggregate comments from Facebook users, rather than specific quotes from individual Facebook users, to protect individual identities of Facebook users.

the events of the pandemic did much to shine a light on the widespread nature of GBV in Peru (as in the rest of the world), such events did not lead to a radical reconceptualization of GBV in the public discourse; on the contrary, the adaptability and prevalence of discourses of blame surrounding GBV continued to obscure the structural causes of the phenomena, namely intersecting inequalities including those based on gender, and thus help to normalise, invisibilise and reproduce sexual and GBV.

Sexual and Gender-based Violence in Peru and Beyond

Reflecting on the nature of GBV, Heise explained in her seminal work that "[t]he setting may change as well as the abuse, but all forms of gender violence share a common theme: they are violent acts that are socially tolerated in part because the victims are female" (223).[8] It is for this reason that domestic and inter-personal violence between men and women is conceptualised as *gender-based violence* rather than *violence against women*. Whilst the latter term conceptualises of a phenomenon where women are the victims, the former understands that women are victims *because* they are women, namely that the violence is gendered, and hence this violence actively contributes to the continuation of female subordination in the gendered hierarchy.

In Peru, as in many places in Latin America and the world, the bodies of women, adolescent girls, and female children, have long been sites of patriarchal violence and control. Indeed, there is a recent history of mass sexual and reproductive rights abuses in Peru, the legacy of which can be felt to this day. For instance, during the internal conflict between the guerrilla organisation Sendero Luminoso[9] and state forces in 1980s, thousands of women, mainly poor and indigenous, were subjected to widespread sexual abuse at the hands of both state and guerrilla forces (Boesten, "Wartime Rape" 87). Moreover, during the regime of President Alberto Fujimori in the 1990s, between 200,000 and 300,000 women and a small proportion of men, once again principally poor and indigenous, were forcibly or coercively sterilised (Boesten, "Free Choice" 13), one of the worst mass violations of the reproductive rights of women in Peruvian history. In the years following the internal conflict, high instances of GBV persist in peacetime Peru. The last full ENDES[10] survey conducted before the pandemic in 2019 (published in 2020), noted how in the 12 months prior to

---

[8] Whilst Heise's work focuses on women and girls, it should be noted that the transgender community is particularly vulnerable to GBV and faces a higher lifetime prevalence of IPV (Peitzmeier et al. e1).

[9] Shining Path.

[10] *Encuesta Demográfica y de Salud Familiar* (Demographic and Family Health Survey), conducted yearly by INEI (*Instituto Nacional de Estadística e Informática* – National Institute of Statistics and Informatics).

the study 35-50.8% of all women had experienced "family violence" on behalf of a spouse or partner (*Encuesta demográfica*); however it is interesting that ENDES chose to conceptualise of this as "family" rather than GBV, a conceptual choice that, as will be discussed below, negates the underpinning gendered power inequalities that contribute to the violence. Indeed, as Hunnicut notes, conceptualising such violence as "family violence" highlights perpetrators as "sick individuals" rather than highlighting the "sick social arrangements" that facilitate and normalise sexual violence (556).

Sexual and Gender-based Violence in Peru During the Pandemic

As in many parts of the world, the pandemic and subsequent lockdown measures acted as aggravating factors to already normalised and routinised levels of GBV in Peru. Instances of physical intimate partner violence rose by around 56% from 2019 to April/May 2020, and calls to the Linea 100 emergency call line almost doubled from March 2020 until 2021, clearly demonstrating the impact of the pandemic on GBV (Agüero et al. 1,3). Feminist organisations in Latin America began to talk of "la otra pandemia"[11] of GBV, as women and girls[12] were largely confined with their aggressors (Medina Lopez and Rivas); nevertheless, the Peruvian government promoted a discourse of "home" as a "safe place" during the sanitary emergency. Furthermore, from the beginning of the quarantine on 16 March 2020 to the end of August 2020, 49 feminicides were registered to the Ministerio de la Mujer y Poblaciones Vulnerables (MIMP).[13] The numbers are likely to be much higher given that levels of sensitisation to issues surrounding GBV amongst the Peruvian judiciary and police are low (Medina Lopez and Rivas), and indeed many policemen have themselves been perpetrators of GBV violence. Of the 49 officially documented feminicides, two-thirds of the perpetrators were the partners of the victim.

Nevertheless, despite the evident intensification of GBV, women' and girls' recourse to help and support was severely curtailed, by government policy and inaction on the part of state institutions. Due to lockdown regulations from the beginning of the quarantine in March 2020 until June 2020, the government closed Centros de Emergencia Mujer[14] (CEMs) for women experiencing acute cases of domestic and sexual abuse (*Violencia de Género en Pandemia* 4), as well as other in-person services for domestic violence (Agüero et al. 2). In police stations across Peru, staff refused to receive complaints of domestic violence or

---

[11] "The other pandemic".
[12] Again, the trans community also faced specific vulnerabilities and a disproportionate burden of GBV during the pandemic, especially during the implementation of gendered lockdown policies in April 2020 (Perez-Brumer and Silva-Santisteban).
[13] Ministry of Women and Vulnerable Populations.
[14] Emergency Centres for Women.

to detain aggressors, because of the sanitary emergency (*Violencia de Género en Pandemia* 3). Despite the State of Emergency being declared in mid-March, it took more than six weeks before a protocol was established by the Peruvian executive to tackle GBV in the context of the pandemic. On 27 April 2020, the Executive approved Legislative Decree no. 1470 that established measures to guarantee attention and protection from violence for women and dependents during the sanitary emergency, to clarify the specific responsibilities on the part of the judiciary, family court and national police, and also define mechanisms to prevent violence against children and to attend to child victims of violence during the pandemic (*Violencia de Género en Pandemia* 7). A further Health Decree, no. 094-MINSA/2020/DGIESP, guaranteed the rights of women and girls to access family planning, obstetric care, and specialist attention following sexual violence. However, it did *not* guarantee women and girls the right to effectively access contraception, the Kit de Emergencia[15] or therapeutic abortion during the pandemic and the subsequent collapse of the healthcare system (*Violencia de Género en Pandemia* 8). As a result, women and girls who were exposed to sexual abuse and rape were also potentially exposed to STIs, as well as unwanted pregnancy, thus reviolating their sexual and reproductive rights.

"*Los trapos sucios se lavan en casa*": Gender-based Violence and Discourses of Blame

Narratives of rape and violence are important to the lived experience of violence; as Alcoff notes, how we experience sexual violence is "discursively and historically constituted" (56). Whilst not the root cause of GBV, dominant narratives surrounding GBV certainly contribute to its naturalisation and endurance. According to Berns, political discourse and narratives surrounding GBV in the media – in her study, US men's magazines – downplay the role of male violence by "degendering" the problem of GBV, removing from view the gendered power imbalances that contribute to the violence (262). Nevertheless, Berns found that at the same time, the media employed a second tactic of "gendering the blame" by placing responsibility for sexual and domestic abuse onto the female victims; this occurred by overtly gendering the victim and blaming them for violence, portraying victims as overstepping socially permitted behaviours for women (262).

Despite rising public recognition of GBV in Peru, and campaigns on behalf of the state and feminist organisations, several discourses prevail that place the blame for GBV onto the victims themselves. A 2019 survey of public opinion

---

[15] The Emergency Kit is an emergency healthcare package legally mandated to be available to victims of rape and sexual assault and designed to protect them from STIs and unwanted pregnancy. The kit normally contains medicines and injections to protect against diphtheria and tetanus, STI tests, the morning after pill and pregnancy tests.

conducted in three departments —Lima, rural and urban Ayacucho, and rural and urban Ucayali—, shed light on some of the prevailing attitudes regarding blame and GBV in Peru. In urban Ayacucho and Ucayali, over a third —34% and 36% of respondents respectively— agreed with the statement that women who go out alone at night were culpable in the case that they were raped (*Percepción de la violencia* 12). In rural Ayacucho, this increased to almost half of those surveyed (47%). The survey also shows that well over half of respondents in urban and rural Ayacucho (55% and 57%) and urban and rural Ucayali (60% and 52%) agreed with the statement "women who dress provocatively invite disrespect". In both cases, blame is apportioned to the victim, and women's behaviour is portrayed as either "inviting" or "provoking" sexual violence. Furthermore, whilst public opinion is changing, it remains the case that almost one in five respondents from rural Ayacucho and rural Ucayali (17% and 22% respectively) agreed with the statement "there are occasions in which women deserve to be hit" (*Percepción de la violencia* 10). Such figures demonstrate that in such cases GBV is not only normalised, but seen as a productive way to discipline women and to consolidate patriarchal power.

Discourses of blame, however, are not only directed at the women themselves, as some element of the blame —depending on the particular nature of the violence, as will be discussed below— is directed at the perpetrator. The manner in which such perpetrators are often described as "deranged" or "mentally unwell", as will be demonstrated in the second case study below, serves to create a distracting narrative that obscures the structural causes of GBV and the continuum of violence. Indeed, in the 2019 survey, around two thirds of respondents from Lima, and urban and rural Ucayali (72%, 76% and 70% respectively) agreed with the statement that "only a mentally ill man is capable of beating his wife" (*Percepción de la violencia* 10). As Jimena Sánchez writes, this characterisation of aggressors as "mentally unwell" works to "exculpar a los maltratadores y de ocultar la manera en que las construcciones sociales de relaciones de poder entre hombres y mujeres han posibilitado que la violencia sea aprendida y normalizada en nuestra sociedad" (*Percepción de la violencia* 13).[16]

Finally, the survey also noted how in Ucayali and Ayacucho between 71-83% of respondents agreed with the statement that "problems of violence between a partner are issues that only they should resolve between themselves" (*Percepción de la violencia* 10). This demonstrates how a significant majority of the population in these departments still see GBV as a *private* rather than a public matter. As Sanchez notes, this discourse is reflected in the popular Peruvian

---

[16] "Exculpate perpetrators and to hide the way in which social constructions of the relations of power between men and women have facilitated the normalisation of violence in our society".

adage that "los trapitos sucios se lavan en casa"[17] meaning that one's "dirty laundry" (in this case GBV) should not be aired in public (*Percepción de la violencia* 13). Indeed, in my own research on teenage pregnancy in Huaraz and in Ayacucho itself, practitioners frequently commented that both teenage pregnancy and GBV are often conceptualised as being an isolated problem of "*that* particular family" rather than a problem in society as a whole. Such discourses are damaging for two principle reasons. Firstly, making violence a "private" matter negates the structural, societal factors that contribute to such violence in the first place, placing the blame within a single family unit, hence exonerating wider society (including the state). Secondly, by characterising the violence as "family" violence, it similarly negates the gendered power dynamics that underpins GBV. As a consequence, such discourses may be purposefully deployed by reactionary, anti-feminist movements. In July 2022 in Peru, MIMP rejected the Proyecto de Ley[18] 1229/2021-CR that proposed changing its name to from Ministry of Women and Vulnerable Populations to "Ministry of the *Family* and vulnerable populations", a change that, according to MIMP the change would not only "invisibilise women (...) pretending to relegate them to the space of the family, reproducing a traditional conception of their roles" but would also negate the "structural discrimination" based in gender that contributes to issues such as GBV ("¿Por qué se quiere cambiar el nombre...?").

This chapter will now present three different case-studies of GBV in Peru; firstly, the murder of young Venezuelan migrant, Joselyn Daniela Vasquez Hernandez, in pre-pandemic 2020, secondly the case of the "Monster" of Chontalí who attempted the rape and murder of his young daughter at the beginning of lockdown, and finally the disappearances of over 500 women in the quarantine by June 2020. The chapter will examine the different manifestations of discourses of blame used in the media and in the public reaction to these stories, demonstrating how these subtly different discourses each contribute in their own way to the obfuscation of the wider structural inequalities behind GBV in Peru. It will also look at an example of campaign materials produced by the Peruvian government designed at tackling GBV during the pandemic, and how these campaigns themselves propagate discourses surrounding how GBV should be tackled and even contribute towards these discourses of blame.

¡La buena vida de la chica mala! The Murder of Joselyn Daniela Vásquez Hernández

In the twilight days before the pandemic in February 2020, Peruvian news was ablaze with headlines over the murder of 22-year-old Venezuelan migrant

---

[17] "Dirty clothes are washed at home".
[18] Law Project.

Joselyn Daniela Vasquez Hernandez. Her body had been found hours after she and a friend had left a club in Chorrillos, with a bullet wound in the head and lesions on other parts of her body; Jocelyn left behind a daughter of five years ("Esto fue lo que hizo la Venezolana asesinada"). The press thought nothing of sharing images of Jocelyn's murdered body. On 27 February, Peruvian News Channel, AV News featured a segment on Joselyn, with the headline "¡La buena vida de la chica mala!"[19] showing pictures of Jocelyn partying on a boat, with the tagline "Bella venezolana asesinada disfrutaba de lujos".[20] As a result, the public response to Jocelyn's murder was less than empathetic. Reactions to the story on Facebook page of Peruvian newspaper Perú 21 concentrated on her status as an illegal Venezuelan migrant, with public indignation hinging more on the fact that she had managed to return illegally to Peru after being deported rather than on the fact that a young woman had been murdered.

There are several layers to the character assassination that Jocelyn faced in the press treatment of Jocelyn and the public response was predicated on multiple layers of Jocelyn's identity; her gender, and principally her migrant status, especially as a Venezuelan. Jocelyn, in the eyes of the Peruvian media and many members of the public, was undeserving of public empathy; discourses of blame surrounding her death pointed towards Jocelyn herself for being a "chica mala". The way in which Jocelyn was framed aligns with Bern's idea of "gendering the blame" as Jocelyn was openly criticised as a "femme fatale" figure, beautiful but bad, who should have been at home rather than enjoying luxuries and parties. Indeed, El Nacional's article entitled "Esto fue lo que hizo la Venezolana asesinada en Perú en su último noche de vida"[21] invited the general public to pass judgement on Jocelyn's final night as she attended a disco with her friend. However, as aforementioned, Jocelyn's gender was only one of different intersecting factors that contributed to the lack of public empathy. Her Venezuelan nationality and her illegal migrant status played into the discourses of blame. The El Nacional headline feeds into this discourse by emphasising that she was a Venezuelan in Peru. Hence, discourses of blame are not universal, but also depend on the social location of the victims and aggressors, and incorporate stereotypes and prejudices based on intersecting identities, including class, race, ethnicity and gender.

El Monstruo de Chontalí: José Felizardo Zoriano Arias

In the early days of the pandemic, another story of sexual and GBV, and incest hit the headlines, of a father, Jose Felizardo Zoriano Arias, against his own 13-year-old daughter, that became known in the press as the case of "El Monstruo

---

[19] "The good life of the bad girl".
[20] "Beautiful, assassinated Venezuelan used to enjoy luxuries".
[21] "This is what the assassinated Venezuelan girl (in Peru) did on her last night of life".

de Chontalí". In April 2020, Zoriano Arias was apprehended by force in Cajamarca after torturing and attempting to rape his daughter. In May, he was freed and returned to the house to threaten the family, who were subsequently granted protective measures. Nevertheless, on 16 June, Zoriano Arias was liberated once more, and subsequently returned to the house to find his daughter. Entering the house through the roof when her mother was out, Zoriano Arias beat his daughter with a stick and attempted to burn her alive. According to the young girl, her father wanted to kill her: "mis brazos, mis dedos, se han quemado. Mis pelitos se han quemado. Se han quemado mis cositas, mis tareas, todo se ha quemado. Me golpeó mi cabeza y me tiró alcohol. Ya yo no quiero estar acá, tengo miedo ("Sujeto que abusó sexualmente de su hija").[22]

The girl gave her statement at the local police station in Chontalí, but the police were largely indifferent, even though several police officers were witness to the fire. Zoriano Arias had eight previous complaints of sexual violence against him before the attack on his daughter; nevertheless, the local judiciary in Jaen declared the sentence of nine months of preventative prison against Zoriano Arias "unfounded", leaving him free to return to the home and attempt to burn her alive. The case thus exposed the structural failures within the Peruvian police and justice systems, as both institutions ignored or underplayed the danger that Zoriano Arias posed ("Sujeto que abusó sexualmente de su hija").

Contrary to the public reception of Jocelyn's murder, the public response to the Zoriano Arias case was one of outrage. In reaction to La República news articles on Facebook on 23 June 2020, members of the public largely called for the death penalty for Zoriano Arias. In the public discourse, Felizardo was described as an "animal", "monstruo" and a "degenerado".[23] He soon became known in the press and in the public eye as the Monster of Chontalí. Given the severity of the crimes and the attempted crimes that Zoriano Arias committed against his daughter, it is not difficult to understand the public outrage. Nevertheless, conceptualising such men as "monsters" is problematic on several levels.

Zoriano Arias' case was emblematic in the sense that during the pandemic, women and girls were most likely to be quarantined with their aggressors. However, by identifying certain perpetrators as "monsters", dehumanising discourse paints certain aggressors as "anomalies". Whilst the violence perpetrated by Zoriano Arias against his daughter (and in the eight other charges of sexual violence) was perhaps amongst the most shocking cases of sexual and GBV perpetrated in the public eye, it is also part of a continuum of violence that escalates from more seemingly innocuous, albeit far more omnipresent forms

---

[22] "Wanted to kill me. My arms, my fingers, they were burnt. My hair was burnt. He burnt all my things, my homework, everything was burnt. He hit me over my head, and he threw alcohol over me. I don't want to be here anymore, I'm scared".
[23] "Animal", "monster", "degenerate".

of sexual and GBV (Kelly 74,137). As abovementioned, Berns noticed that "degendering" GBV obscures the structural inequalities that contribute to GBV in the first place (262). However, in this instance, the public discourse goes a step further by *dehumanising* the perpetrator; not only is the violence "degendered" but also is now seen as "exceptional" and an "anomaly" meaning that its place in the continuum of GBV is obfuscated; this makes it harder to understand how seemingly "lesser" acts of violence may escalate to the very serious acts of violence committed and attempted by Zoriano Arias against his daughter.

Secondly, by fixing blame in the "monstrous" individual, it locates the cause of such violence in the psychological field and negates the structural causes of GBV. If such crimes are the result of "deranged" individuals, then deep-rooted structural inequalities may be ignored and exculpated; this alleviates, to some extent, the state from the responsibility of tackling GBV as a *structural* and societal problem. Indeed, we are again reminded of the high percentage of respondents (70-76% of residents in Lima and Ucayali) who agreed with the statement that "only a mentally ill man is capable of beating his wife" (*Percepción de la violencia* 10), demonstrating again the prevalence of such attitudes. Finally, this discourse is also one side of a coin of a discourse that allows some women and girls to be "deserving" victims, powerless at the hands of deranged individuals, whilst excusing the murders of others, such as Jocelyn, who "should have known better" than to get involved with a "bad" crowd. While public outrage in the case of the "Monstruo de Chontalí" allowed his daughter to be a "deserving" victim, Jocelyn's status as an illegal Venezuelan migrant excluded her from public empathy, denied her victimhood, and subsequently held her responsible for her own murder.

Where Are they? Explaining Disappearing Women During the Pandemic

As the pandemic continued to unfold, Peruvian media reported on the increasing number of women who had disappeared, despite the quarantine and despite the strict curfew. On 7 June 2020, two and a half months into the pandemic, La República published a news piece online concerning the 557 that had disappeared (so far) during the quarantine, and asking where they were. The article lamented how the women "podrían ser las hijas, madres o hermanas de cualquiera de nosotros" and how "las familias de estas mujeres deben enfrentar una ardua búsqueda diaria" ("¿Dónde están ellas?").[24] However, such framing negates the fact that the aggressor may have originated from within the family.

The following day on 8 June 2020, La República shared the story on its Facebook page, prompting significant public engagement. Whilst some members of the

---

[24] "They could be the daughters, mothers, or sisters, of any one of us"; "the families of these women have to face an arduous daily search".

public recognised that perpetrators were most likely to originate from within the home, others were dumbfounded; just what had happened to these women and girls if everyone was supposed to be at home? However, the connection between the violence and the confinement with one's family was not obvious. Many comments suggesting that families should better protect their daughters from aggressors that lurked in the streets – theories of paedophile rings and kidnappers also emerged – demonstrated the lack of awareness of the issue. Of those who did recognise that perpetrators often originated from within the family, some demonstrated the opinion that such problems should be resolved *within* the family, reminding us of how "los trapos sucios se lavan en casa". Other Facebook users commented that these women "should have been at home before the curfew" or that they were "mujeres callejeras" who should have known better than to be wondering the streets in a quarantine; such comments further fed into discourses of blame that women were responsible for their own disappearances. A final subset of commentary denied the credibility of the story, calling the article "fake news", part of a feminist conspiracy to "invent violence".

The many different approaches to explain away the gendered nature of the disappearances demonstrates how there is a repertoire of discourses that obscure the true nature of GBV. It should be noted that amongst the discourses were those who recognised that such a level of disappearances amounted to a societal problem, with its roots in gender-based inequalities and most likely perpetuated by the victims' own partners and families. Nevertheless, we also see many different discourses that negate such factors. Firstly, we see evidence of gendering the blame in the accusations that the victims were "mujeres callejeras", a gendered and sexualised insult to rebuke women (without proof) for venturing out of the home. In these cases, the Covid-19 pandemic, the quarantine and the curfew are used as a reason to blame the women. However, the specific insult of "mujeres callejeras" uncovers the misogyny behind the comments, with connotations of sexual "transgression". Secondly, in this case, amongst the multiple voices we see conceptualisations of GBV as both a public and a private issue. For those who expressed the view that such issues should be dealt with within the family the disappearances remain a *private* issue. However, in commentary that theorises about paedophile rings or trafficking groups, there is some appreciation of the disappearances as a *public* issue, yet the aggressors are sensationalised and imagined; they may well be similar "monstruos" in the public eye such as Zoriano Arias, but they are divorced from the reality that most aggressors are individuals known to the victims.

"Stress management": "Individualisation" and State Discourses Surrounding Gender-based Violence

From the beginning of the lockdown, the Peruvian state did attempt to instigate measures to protect the rights of women, girls (and also transgender individuals) during the pandemic, especially in the case of GBV. For example, in response to "la otra pandemia" of domestic violence, a widespread initiative was made to increase awareness of the Línea 100 emergency phone line, where victims of domestic violence could seek help and support. However, as evidenced above by the failure to protect women and girls' sexual and reproductive rights throughout the pandemic, the state response was inadequate. Part of state failure to fully implement effective responses to GBV lay in the discourses used in campaigns produced during the pandemic. Medina Lopez and Rivas noted that the predominant focus of Peruvian state campaigns on the issue centred on "stress management". As they elaborate:

> This approach portrays feminicide and GBV as a result of personal interactions and relations. The 'individualisation' of these acts (Segato, 2016) and the focus on the emotional responses of men to the lockdown and the emergency measures as the main triggers of violence against women work to ignore the structural and historical circumstances which create the facilitating conditions for gendered forms of violence to take place (Medina Lopez and Rivas).

Such individualising discourses may be found in public-facing materials produced by MIMP during the pandemic. In April 2020, MIMP released campaign materials entitled "Manejo de conflictos y orientación de emociones".[25] In one campaign image, a cartoon woman is pictured alone and in distress during the confinement; in the same artwork, a cartoon MIMP representative advises that "la ansiedad y el estrés son emociones normales en un contexto de aislamiento y distanciamiento social. Esto puede incrementar los conflictos en los hogares y pone en mayor riesgo a las mujeres. No permitamos que esto se convierta en violencia" (*Manejo de conflictos 1*).[26] As noted above by Medina Lopez and Rivas, this campaign located GBV in the individual sphere, by suggesting that it can be avoided simply by the management of personal feelings. Moreover, it is surprising to note how in a campaign that is supposedly targeted at eradicating GBV is almost entirely gender-blind. Whilst the victim in the image is clearly female and the campaign notes the increased dangers to women due to the

---

[25] "Conflict management and emotional orientation".
[26] "Anxiety and stress are normal emotions in a context of social distancing and isolation. This can increase conflicts in the home and put women at greater risk. Let's not permit that his turns into violence".

quarantine, the (male) perpetrator of GBV is inexplicably absent from the campaign; once again, even in a campaign designed to prevent *gender-based violence*, we can see traces of both elements of "degendering the problem" and "gendering the blame". In the absence of the presence of the male perpetrator, violence has been "degendered" and as such all the gendered power inequalities that contribute to GBV are invisibilised. Furthermore, in the deafening absence of a male perpetrator, the suggestion that "let's not permit that this turns into violence" implicitly suggests that the "us" is women, once again putting responsibility (and hence the blame) for preventing GBV on women and the victims themselves.

In a second campaign image, a cartoon representative of MIMP is shown giving six tips on how to address and prevent violent situations. The tips include "reflexiona cómo te hace sentir esa situación" and "realiza actividades que contribuyen a estados de relajación como el deporte, la meditación, algún hobby, entre otras" (*Manejo de conflictos 2*).[27] Again, there is an absence of the acknowledgement of any form of structural cause of GBV and the gendered dynamics of victims and perpetrators is absent. Indeed, the insinuation that "playing sports" or "practicing meditation" can protect victims of GBV from their aggressors is reflective of a "stress management" approach to GBV (Medina Lopez and Rivas). This once again places the responsibility of eradicating GBV on the individual, be that the female victim, the male perpetrator, or the individual family unit as a whole. Furthermore, advice such as "listening attentively to others" and "remembering that we don't always agree on everything" to avoid violence feeds into narratives that women "provoke" domestic abuse, by insinuating that doing the reverse, namely not listening or refusing to compromise, are behavioural factors that cause GBV.

Conclusion

From the early stages of the pandemic, feminist activists and scholars within and outside of Peru argued that for many women and girls, aggressors came largely from *within* the home itself (Boesten, "Rethinking Home"). The pandemic did much to showcase this through the sheer number of calls to domestic violence hotlines, and daily reports of growing feminicides both within and outside of Peru. Women could no longer be accused of "seeking" trouble by "dressing provocatively" or "partying" given the lockdown restrictions of the pandemic. Indeed, the quarantine measures of the pandemic shed light on what feminist scholars and activists had long known; that home is not necessarily a safe place. Cases such as that of the "Monstruo de Chontalí" are

---

[27] "Reflect on how the situation makes you feel" and "do activities that contribute to relaxing states such as sport, meditation, or some hobby, amongst other things".

prime examples of this. However, the increased reports of disappeared women, and of increases in calls to domestic abuse hotlines during lockdown did *not* drastically change public discourse surrounding sexual and GBV in Peru.

Through looking at four brief case studies, several different manifestations of blame can be found in the media, the public and even in the state discourse surrounding GBV. Firstly, as in the case of Jocelyn in the pre-pandemic days, and of the disappeared women during the lockdown, certain discourses of blame simply paint victims of violence as "chicas malas" or "mujeres callejeras" directly placing the blame on these women and girls themselves. This discourse falls into Berns' category of "gendering the blame" as such women are censured for breaking social norms of expected behaviour. The responses to the three instances of violence against women and girls above thus ask us to consider, who "deserves" victimhood in the public discourse? In the case of the "Monstruo de Chontalí" Zoriano Arias' daughter was accepted as a victim; however, Jocelyn was seen as undeserving in the public eye, a manifestation of her multiple intersectional identities as a young, Venezuelan illegal migrant and teenage mother. The nameless cohort of the 557 disappeared women were also blamed *en masse* for their disappearances by some commentators, perhaps a reflection of much more deeply misogynistic attitudes towards women, that it must have been their supposed transgressive behaviour that led to their disappearances rather than the fault of the perpetrators.

A second discourse, somewhat related to Bern's "degendering" the perpetrator, is a discourse that rather *dehumanises* and thus *exceptionalises* the perpetrator, as can be seen within the case of the "Monstruo de Chontalí". In such discourses, because the aggressor is seen as "deranged" or in some way "not human", the structural reasons behind GBV are obscured, and the conceptualisation of GBV as a *social* problem is negated. A third, related and cross-cutting discourse is that of individualisation, of placing the blame for GBV or responsibility to avoid it within the sphere of the individual, whether that be the perpetrator or the individual family unit. This can be seen across all four case studies; in Jocelyn's case, the blame was directed at her as an individual, for not acting as a woman should, and for being an illegal migrant. In the case of the "Monstruo de Chontalí", blame was focused on Zoriano Arias, but his actions were seen as those of a "monster". In the case of the 557 disappeared women, some characterised them as "mujeres callejeras" themselves responsible for their disappearances, or part of violent families who should sort their problems amongst themselves. In the Peruvian state campaign, GBV was tackled on the individual level, but suggesting that people avoid conflict by doing stress-relieving activities, without mentioning the inequalities that underpin GBV. Finally, accompanying the discourses of blame and individualising narratives are also voices that simply deny GBV, either as a concept by re-categorising the phenomena as "family violence", thus negating the gendered power imbalances, or by simply rejecting media reports.

Whilst the three cases of GBV (Jocelyn's murder, the Zoriano Arias' abuse of his daughter, and the hundreds of disappeared women) are less frequent manifestations of GBV (compared, for example to more everyday sexual harassment or physical abuse in the home), they must be recognised as part of a continuum of violence. Although these manifestations of GBV are comparatively infrequent (and hence more sensationalised in the media), their root causes lie in the same patriarchal inequalities that make more normalised and routinised everyday instances of GBV possible. Indeed, the fact that over 550 women were reported as disappeared within the first two and a half months of the pandemic (and many more perhaps were not officially reported) demonstrates that these are not isolated occurrences, but represent a social issue. It is true that some left-leaning news organisations, such as the investigative journalism corporation Wayka tried to highlight the more structural nature of GBV, both during the pandemic and beyond. Nevertheless, the overall tendency of the mainstream media to sensationalise GBV, rather than uncovering the systematic levels of GBV experienced by many Peruvians, contributes to perpetuation of a narrative that sees GBV as isolated instances, perpetrated by disturbed individuals and experienced by undeserving women.

The pandemic and the moment of quarantine may itself be seen as both exception and unexceptional in relation to GBV. The exceptional nature of quarantine, the restrictions placed on daily lives, the subsequent economic crises all acted as aggravating factors for GBV. However, it was also unexceptional in sense that the pandemic only aggravated *existing* structural factors that contributed to GBV in the first place, in Peru and beyond. The pandemic may have been an opportunity to shed light on the structural causes of GBV and a re-evaluation of "home" as a safe place, highlighting the fact that the vast majority of perpetrators of GBV are partners, or family members of the victims themselves. The focus on a few, sensational cases in the mainstream media, without making reference to the wider context of GBV in Peru, did much to obscure the escalation of other more routinized and widespread forms of GBV during the pandemic. The contribution of the media and the state to these narratives of blame only adds to the further normalisation of GBV in Peru.

Bibliography

Agüero, Jorge, et al. "COVID-19, Job Loss and Intimate Partner Violence in Peru". *SSRN*, 2021, pp. 1–35, http://dx.doi.org/10.2139/ssrn.3998964.

Alcoff, Linda Martín. *Rape and Resistance*. Polity Press, 2018.

Berns, Nancy "Degendering the Problem and Gendering the Blame: Political Discourse on Women and Violence". *Gender & Society*, vol. 15, no. 2, 2001, pp. 262–281.

Boesten, Jelke. "Free Choice or Poverty Alleviation? Population Politics in Peru under Albert Fujimori". *European Review of Latin American and Caribbean Studies*, no. 82, 2007, pp. 3–20.

—. "Rethinking Home". *Feminist Perspectives*, 11 June 2021, https://www.kcl.ac.uk/rethinking-home.

—. "Wartime Rape and Peacetime Inequalities in Peru". *Feminism and the Body*, edited by Catherine Kevin, Cambridge Scholars Publishing, 2009, pp. 84–98.

Digital 2022: Peru. DataReportal, 16 February 2022, https://datareportal.com/reports/digital-2022-peru.

"¿Dónde están ellas? Ya son 557 mujeres desaparecidas en plena cuarentena". *El Nacional*, 7 June 2020, https://larepublica.pe/sociedad/2020/06/07/mujeres-desaparecidas-en-cuarentena-donde-estan-las-personas-que-desaparecieron-durante-estado-de-emergencia-en-peru-defensoria-del-pueblo.

Encuesta Demográfica y de Salud Familiar 2019. Instituto Nacional de Estadística e Informática, Estado Peruano, 2020, https://www.inei.gob.pe/media/MenuRecursivo/publicaciones_digitales/Est/Endes2019/.

"Esto fue lo que hizo la venezolana asesinada en Perú en su última noche de vida". *El Nacional*, 27 February 2020, https://www.elnacional.com/mundo/esto-fue-lo-que-hizo-la-venezolana-asesinada-en-peru-en-su-ultima-noche-de-vida/.

Heise, Lori. "Gender-based violence and women's reproductive health". *International Journal of Gynaecology and Obstetrics*, vol. 46, no. 2, 1994, pp. 221–229.

Hunnicutt, Gwen. "Varieties of Patriarchy and Violence Against Women: Resurrecting 'Patriarchy' as a Theoretical Tool". *Violence Against Women*, vol. 15, no. 5, 2009, pp. 553–573.

Kelly, Liz. *Surviving Sexual Violence.* Polity Press, 1988.

Manejo de conflictos 1. Ministerio de la Mujer y Poblaciones Vulnerables, Estado Peruano, 1 April 2020, https://cdn.www.gob.pe/uploads/document/file/662880/Manejo-de-conflictos-1.png.

Manejo de conflictos 2. Ministerio de la Mujer y Poblaciones Vulnerables, Estado Peruano, 1 April 2020, https://cdn.www.gob.pe/uploads/document/file/662881/Manejo-de-conflictos-2.png.

Medina Lopez, Claudia, and Althea-Maria Rivas. "No Lockdown on Violence Against Women and Girls during COVID-19: A View from Peru". *Feminist Review Journal Blog*, 7 August 2020, https://femrev.wordpress.com/2020/08/07/no-lockdown-on-violence-against-women-and-girls-during-covid-19-a-view-from-peru/.

Ogden, Rebecca. "Teenage Pregnancy and Neoliberal Subjectivity in Mexican Television Series *La Rosa de Guadalupe*". *Bulletin of Latin American Research*, vol. 42, no. 1, 2022, pp. 67–80.

Peitzmeier, Sarah M., et al. "Intimate Parnter Violence in the Transgender Populations: Systematic Review and Meta-analysis of Prevalence and Correlates". *American Journal of Public Health*, vol. 110, no. 9, 2020, pp. e1–e14.

Percepción de la violencia de género en Lima, Ayacucho, y Ucayali. Instituto de Opinión Pública de la Pontificia Universidad Católica del Perú, 21 November 2019, https://repositorio.pucp.edu.pe/index/handle/123456789/168793.

Perez-Brumer, Amaya and Alfonso Silva-Santisteban. "COVID-19 Policies can Perpetuate Violence Against Transgender Communities: Insights from Perú". *AIDS and Behaviour*, vol. 24, no. 9, 2020, pp. 2477–2479.

"¿Por qué se quiere cambiar el nombre del Ministerio de la Mujer? Conoce cómo podría afectar al MIMP". *La República*, 7 July 2022, https://larepublica.pe/sociedad/2022/07/06/ministerio-de-la-mujer-por-que-se-le-quiere-cambiar-el-nombre-por-ministerio-de-la-familia-y-como-afectaria-mimp-congreso/.

"Sujeto que abusó sexualmente de su hija de 13 años intentó quemarla tras su liberación en Cajamarca". *La República*, 17 June 2020, https://larepublica.pe/sociedad/2020/06/17/chontali-sujeto-que-abuso-sexualmente-de-su-hija-de-13-anos-intento-quemarla-tras-su-liberacion-en-cajamarca/.

Violencia de Género en Pandemia: Reporte y análisis de la Red Interdistrital de Mujeres de Lima Metropolitana Contra la Violencia de Genero. Demus Estudio, 2020, http://www.demus.org.pe/wp-content/uploads/2021/06/Violencia-de-g%C3%A9nero-en-pandemia-Reporte-y-an%C3%A1lisis-de-la-Red-Interdistrital-Diciembre-2020-comprimido.pdf.

Chapter 5

Aborting in Isolation

Testimonial Narratives, Affect and Feminist Political Identities in Covid-19 Argentina

Lea Happ
King's College London

Abstract

How has Covid-19 shaped the experience of abortion as a personal and political act in Argentina? I ask this question before the backdrop of Argentina's legalisation of abortion in December 2020. Prior to the legalisation, abortion was illegal in almost all cases. In response to this, a wide network of feminist activists formed, dedicated to providing medical abortions outside the healthcare system as safely as possible. Whilst the legalisation of abortion has been celebrated as a landmark shift towards reproductive justice, issues about de facto access are predicted to persist. Socorristas en Red, the most prominent network offering abortion support, have stated that of over 9,900 people seeking their support in 2021, only 2,377 opted for an abortion within the healthcare system, while 7,523 chose to have a self-managed abortion at home.

In this chapter, I analyse the narratives around abortion and Covid-19 presented in a collection of 52 testimonies published by Socorristas en Red. These testimonies by people who aborted during lockdown, prior to legalisation, with the Socorristas' support are centred around the ambiguous emotions invoked by the experience of aborting in isolation — from fear, sadness and loneliness to hope, community and empowerment. Focusing primarily on the affective work invoking those feelings in testimonial narration does, I provide an account of how Covid-19 has shaped the experience of abortion as a personal and political act for both abortion seekers and activists. To this end, I consider the following key questions: how do affects circulate among this group? How do they shape understandings of individual and collective political identity among those involved? And how does this in turn determine how abortion is experienced in the extraordinary circumstances created by the confluence of Covid-19, the legalisation of abortion and ever-adapting feminist activism?

Keywords: abortion, accompaniment, Argentina, affect, feminism

***

Introduction

The current moment is an extraordinary time for investigating the experience of abortion in Argentina. On the one hand, the Covid-19 pandemic has created new challenges and exacerbated existing inequalities in relation to abortion. On the other hand, the legalisation of the voluntary interruption of pregnancy ("interrupción voluntaria del embarazo", henceforth IVE) in December 2020 is radically changing the context in which people experience abortions. This chapter traces the experience of people who had abortions with the support of feminist activists during the first months of the pandemic through the analysis of testimonial narratives. Reading narrative depictions of abortion by those who experienced abortions during the pandemic allows us to trace how feminist identities are constructed through practices of narrating and sharing testimonies.

Formed in 2012, Socorristas en Red (henceforth SenRed) is a nationwide network of feminist collectives that accompany abortions in Argentina. Since the mid-2010s, it has been the most prominent organisation of its kind (Burton, "Prácticas feministas"; McReynolds-Pérez, "No doctors required"). In 2021, the first year after the legalisation of abortion, SenRed accompanied 9,900 people, of whom 2,377 decided to obtain an abortion in the healthcare system, while 7,523 people preferred a self-managed abortion with activist accompaniment (SenRed, "A un año [...], tenemos motivos"). These statistics are indicative of the persistent need for feminist abortion accompaniment and illustrate the continuities between activism before and after the legalisation of IVE. Prior to the legalisation of IVE, the legal interruption of pregnancy ("interrupción legal del embarazo", henceforth ILE) permitted abortions in the case of rape or a risk to the life or health of the pregnant person. This regulation continues to be in effect for abortions after the 14th week of pregnancy. Beside accompanying self-managed abortions, activist groups like SenRed have also supported abortion seekers in procuring an abortion on the basis of one of these indications. The holistic interpretation of health as encompassing physical, mental, and social health opened up avenues for activists to facilitate access to abortions within the healthcare system by framing unwanted pregnancy as detrimental to the pregnant person's mental and social health (*Protocolo*). The increasing importance of this aspect of their activism even prior to the introduction of IVE is reflected in the fact that, in 2020, SenRed already accompanied 6,430 out of 15,297 people in the healthcare system, a steep increase from the previous year (SenRed, "Sistematización 2020"; "10 datos de acompañamientos"). Thus, informing about and enabling access to ILE within the healthcare system already constituted an important part of feminist activist abortion accompaniment prior to the Covid-19 pandemic. Due to these pre-existing links to institutional actors, activists were able to shift their work to primarily accompanying abortions within the healthcare system during the pandemic.

It is crucial to acknowledge that after the legalisation, people continue to face barriers to accessing an IVE within the healthcare system for many reasons, including, but not limited to, lack of information, as well as various forms of obstetric violence (SenRed, "A un año [...] Falta de información"; "A un año [...] Información falsa"; "A un año [...] Prácticas crueles"). This illustrates that rather than a matter of legalisation, abortion access is a holistic issue requiring sustained activist mobilisation. Many barriers people faced prior to the pandemic have intensified due to Covid-19 and associated policies of isolation, for instance financial precarity, lack of access to information, and vulnerability to domestic and intimate partner violence. This has reduced people's access to community, as well as sources of information, often leaving them in positions where their main social contacts are family members or partners who may not know about or approve of their abortion. Therefore, analysing abortion with feminist activist accompaniment in the early days of the pandemic may provide insight into the social, economic, and cultural barriers to accessing abortion that are likely to persist until long after the introduction of IVE. Activist practices in response to this provide important pointers to how feminist identity may be reconceptualised in response to the rapidly changing current circumstances. Narratives are a key constituent of this response and the identities constructed through it.

Drawing on an analysis of a collection of 52 testimonies published by SenRed in summer 2020, this chapter investigates how Covid-19 has shaped the experience of abortion and how narratives about pandemic abortion experiences have in turn shaped the construction of feminist political identities. Throughout these narratives, written by people who had abortions with the group's support, emotions play a key role in describing abortion seekers' experiences. Drawing on affect theorists like Sara Ahmed, Clare Hemmings, Cecilia Macón, Mariela Solana and Nayla Luz Vacarezza, I investigate these emotions as vehicles for constructing individual and collective political identities. Focusing on the affective work done by invoking feelings in abortion narratives, my reading of the testimonies considers how affects circulate among those involved in feminist-accompanied abortion; and what constructions of individual and collective political identity this enables. In addressing these questions, I hope to offer a perspective on the importance of narrative practices for feminist identities in relation to abortion support in the current context of recently legalised abortion and increasingly normalised pandemic, as well as add to a rapidly growing body of literature on abortion during Covid-19.

This chapter is divided into three sections. First, I provide a brief contextualisation of narratives of feminist-accompanied abortion during the

Covid-19 pandemic. Subsequently, I trace some of the key affects expressed in the narratives and how they circulate among the various actors involved in feminist abortion accompaniment. Lastly, I discuss how the circulation of these affects makes possible the deliberate as well as accidental construction of individual and collective political identities, pertaining to abortion seekers and activists alike.

Contextualising narratives of abortion

In January 2021, Argentina underwent a seismic shift: with law 27.610 coming into effect, voluntary abortion up until the 14th week of pregnancy, free of charge and within the public healthcare system became a legal entitlement (Honorable Congreso). This achievement was underpinned by years of mobilisation from feminist activists, most prominently those under the umbrella of the National Campaign for Legal, Safe and Free Abortion, launched in 2003 (Sutton and Borland). The legalisation has been celebrated as a landmark victory, not only in Argentina, but all over Latin America and the world. A 2021 report by Mariana Romero and colleagues, part of Proyecto Mirar, which monitors the process of implementation of and compliance with law 27.610, provides a first comprehensive overview of abortion access in Argentina one year after the legalisation. In the first semester of 2021, 25,894 people accessed an abortion through public health services (Romero et al. 20). While emphasising that, at this point, findings about the implementation can only be preliminary, the report identifies unequal access among provinces, as well as insufficient access to information as some of the persisting challenges. It frames the implementation of the law as continuing a previously existing trend towards safer abortion, among others due to the availability of misoprostol —an abortifacient pharmaceutical— and the increasing willingness of healthcare services to provide abortion in accordance with the previous legislation. Further, the report also situates the implementation in the context of the Covid-19 pandemic, which restricted the access to healthcare services, increased geographical barriers to access, and complicated accompaniment due to social distancing. These continuities between abortion access before and after the legalisation, as well as during the initial phase of the pandemic and now, resonate with activist strategies employed to support abortion seekers, as well as the kinds of identities constructed in response to the current situation.

Pioneered by Brazilian feminists in the 1980s and made possible by the growing availability of misoprostol from the early 1990s onwards (De Zordo; McReynolds-Pérez, *Misoprostol for the masses*), a growing number of feminist activists have not only campaigned for legal abortion, but also facilitated access to safe, medical abortion within and without the healthcare system. Early versions of such support services distributed information on "do-it-yourself" medical abortions via hotlines, the first of its kind being organised by Lesbianas y Feministas por la Descriminalización del Aborto (Drovetta; Fernández Romero). From the mid-2010s, Socorristas en Red network emerged as the most prominent network of abortion companions in Argentina (Burton, "Prácticas feministas"). As Socorrista and feminist scholar Ruth Zurbriggen and colleagues lay out, the network has acquired the medical and activist skills to provide supportive, women-centred accompaniment outside the formal healthcare system. While most Socorristas do not have formal medical training, they "undergo extensive training in feminist principles and medical guidelines to be able to provide high-quality information and support" (Zurbriggen et al. 109). This is accomplished through studying relevant materials, as well as shadowing and being supported by other Socorristas. Socorristas also receive training by other regional and international organisations, as well as medical professionals to ensure they are able to identify when medical care is needed (Zurbriggen et al. 109). Through the acquisition of this otherwise gate-kept knowledge, activists are able to perform an "act of providing this feminist model of care" (Zurbriggen et al. 113). This practice constitutes a strategy by which feminist activists may "subvert dominant medical and political discourses that depoliticise issues of reproductive rights" (McReynolds-Pérez, "No doctors required" 371). According to Zurbriggen and colleagues, the Socorrista network subscribes to three key feminist principles. These include the commitment to "compassionate abortion accompaniment care in spaces where women will not be judged or mistreated" (Zurbriggen et al. 109). Further, activists commit to collaborating with medical professionals to "generate empathetic bonds with women who have abortions and to reinstate abortion treatment in health establishments in an antidiscriminatory manner". Lastly, they "[s]upport and advocate for the accessibility of legally sanctioned abortions". These principles are reflected in the practices narrated in abortion seekers' testimonies and underpin a persistent commitment to conceptualising their activism as a practical, as well as epistemic intervention. This is reflected by a high number of activist-scholars involved in feminist abortion accompaniment, as recently reviewed by Julia Burton ("Los estudios").

Prior to the Covid-19 pandemic, abortion seekers would initially reach out to the network via a telephone hotline (Zurbriggen et al.). During this initial contact, Socorristas would seek to calm abortion-seekers anxieties, provide reassurance, and affirm their decision. The next step would involve an in-person group meeting during which abortion-seekers get a chance to discuss their feelings around abortion and receive extensive informational material. Besides providing information, these meetings' aim is to highlight abortion as a collective experience, as well as something that may happen to anyone. During the abortion itself, telephone support is provided by a Socorrista. After the abortion, abortion-seekers are encouraged to have a routine check-up carried out by a medical professional. A significant aspect of this feminist project, which underpins and simultaneously transcends abortion as a healthcare provision, was activists' ability to gather in person, both with each other and abortion seekers (SenRed, "Capítulo 1"). Confronted with the restrictions on gatherings imposed as a result of the pandemic, "new tactics"[1] for shifting abortion seekers' perspective on abortion as a normal, collective, and safe experience had to be devised.

First and foremost, this meant shifting their support and accompaniment to entirely virtual. Activist-accompanied abortion can be conceptualised as the centre of a web of affective ties that create a loose community of activists, health practitioners, abortion seekers, families, and friends. During the Covid-19 pandemic, communication via phone calls, texts and WhatsApp messages has emerged as a key vehicle for maintaining these ties across the barriers imposed by the virus and subsequent policies of isolation. Key sites of affective circulation are interactions with SenRed, healthcare professionals, friends and other people they connect with while pursuing access to an abortion, as well as the testimonies that form the object of this analysis themselves. Since affects are the key for "understanding the transformation, as well as the conservation of the dominant orders of gender and sexuality" (Solana and Vacarezza 2), these circulations are crucial for destabilising persisting hegemonic narratives around gender norms and abortion. They make possible the reimagining of political identity outside and beyond those narratives. The following sections provide insight into the specific affects mobilised among narrators, activists and others, as well as the constructions of both individual and collective political identities made possible through them.

Affective Circulation and the Experience of Abortion During Covid-19

Storytelling is an important way through which affective and embodied knowledge production about the experience of abortion, feminist activist abortion support, and individual and collective identity may be communicated. Elizabeth Borland identifies storytelling as an important form of feminist activist identity formation and a "fruitful way to consider how [people] define their activism" (502). Narratives can furthermore be understood as attempts to "vindicate [feminists'] power of collective fabulation and [...] the invention of a logic that defies what is considered 'political' rationality" (Gago 50). As such, testimonies about experiences that are seldom present within structures of power are an important form of producing feminist knowledge. Argentine scholars like Verónica Gago and Solana and Vacarezza have emphasised the

---

[1] This and all following direct quotations from Spanish language primary and secondary sources were translated by myself.

importance of collective, feminist storytelling in "dismantling, critiquing, and tearing apart the origins that consecrate our secondary place" (Gago 50). The collective element of narrative storytelling becomes particularly important when established ways of collectively engaging in political life are challenged by the isolation and atomisation imposed by Covid-19-caused confinement. The testimonial narratives of abortion during the Covid-19 pandemic ought to be interpreted as participating in and contributing to this process of dismantling when other ways of doing so became impossible.

Narrators who shared their story with Socorristas en Red frequently relate their experience of abortion in four key moments, each associated with specific affective regimes: finding out about an unwanted pregnancy, their initial contact with the activists, the abortion itself, and the post-abortion moment. Many of the feelings the narrators describe are in tension with each other: grief, defeat, fury, pain, hope and pride. Though often contradictory, positive as well as negative emotions function as vehicles for resistance that have the potential to provide an "opening of other futures" (Solana and Vacarezza 10). Their mobilisation within the feminist movement has demonstrated "the contagious power of a renovated affective-political repertoire" (10). This is evident in the various and often conflicting emotions narrators recount in relation to their experience of abortion during the Covid-19 pandemic. Indeed, it is through these complexities and contradictions that a political identity that posits abortion seekers as agentic beings with complex inner lives and reasonings — in contrast to hegemonic constructions of pregnant people as passive and infantilised— emerges.

Upon finding out they are pregnant, most narrators report feelings of distress. These range from anxiety to anguish to outright fear. One narrator describes her initial response as passing through "many doubts, many questions, much anxiety", while another recounts "[wanting] to die because I didn't want what was in my body, I didn't feel it was mine, I cried every night, I didn't sleep" (SenRed, "Capítulo 1"). The implied disconnect between one's bodily and mental state is a recurrent theme throughout the narratives, and the realignment of the two through the termination of pregnancy is a key way in which people conceptualise their abortion journey. Many narrators also speak of finding out about their pregnancy as a moment of shock in which life grinds to a hold, with a feeling of having their normal course of life suspended and threatened. What constitutes "normal life" varies among narrators, with many of them mentioning their education, family and already existing children, as well as travel plans. All of these are perceived as threatened by the unwanted pregnancy, which would fundamentally and permanently alter one's life, body, and —in many cases— sense of self.

This explains many abortion seekers' intuitive certainty that they would obtain an abortion. Some narrators mentioned their current economic position being "very precarious" or circumstances such as living with their family and not having "a place for having a baby" as reasons (SenRed, "Capítulo 1"). Meanwhile, others simply speak about an intuitive knowledge and feeling that they did not want to carry this pregnancy to term, as in the case of a narrator who states "I know myself. I am sure. I feel it in every part of my being. It's not my moment. I don't want it like this" (SenRed, "Capítulo 4"). Even those who feel reservations about having an abortion recount how, despite their doubts, after some consideration they arrived at the certainty that an abortion was the correct way forward. This causes a sense of urgency reflected in many of the narratives. For instance, one narrator recounts her persistence in contacting SenRed by describing her urge to "know if misoprostol is available" in the current situation (SenRed, "Capítulo 5"). Feelings of certainty are juxtaposed by many narrators' living situation during the Covid-19 pandemic, which frequently involves obstacles to accessing abortion, due to confinement in usually heteronormative family units, causing a lack of support, increased difficulty to do things alone, and less access to feminist circles. This induces high levels of uncertainty, interlinked with a feeling of loneliness also intensified through the Covid-19 pandemic. Some abortion seekers speak of the support they received from the people in their immediate environment, such as one woman who emphasises that she was "very accompanied by her family and her boyfriend" (SenRed, "Capítulo 3"). It is noteworthy that the people who become significantly involved in narrators' experience of abortion are almost exclusively women. This is the case whether it applies to "the women in my family who surrounded me were there [for me], unconditionally" or to the friends who "joined in accompanying this decision from afar" (SenRed, "Capítulo 2"). While some recount feeling supported by the people they live with, the vast majority of narrators recount how they had to hide their plan to obtain an abortion from them, be it parents or partners. For instance, one woman states that a key memory of her abortion is "leaving the house quietly so the family doesn't find out", while another deliberately had her abortion at night "so that [her] family wouldn't find out" (SenRed, "Capítulo 4"). In a situation in which it was close to impossible to connect with people outside of one's own home —usually meaning one's nuclear family— unnoticed, this left people seeking to obtain an abortion feeling isolated and clueless who to turn to.

The Covid-19 pandemic is furthermore likely to have exacerbated feelings of shame and stigma. Abortion seekers recall both internalised stigma and concern about stigmatisation anticipated from other people around them. One narrator recalls her reluctance in contacting the activists again after a previous abortion because she felt "full of shame for being insensible" (SenRed, "Capítulo 4"). During confinement, worry about being stigmatised for seeking an abortion is exacerbated by being confined to living in close proximity of people abortion seekers feared stigmatisation from, and them being the only in-person contacts. This stigmatisation through people in the narrators' immediate and wider community majorly contributed to feelings of loneliness and isolation, sentiments that were already present due to social distancing and orders to stay at home. This has not only had the effect that abortion-seekers were not able to meet up with people or visit services that might support them in their decision to have an abortion in the same way as prior to the pandemic, but also that many people's only in-person contact was to people who they knew to be strongly opposed to abortion. This creates an additional layer of clandestinity, in which abortion must be kept secret from people in one's immediate environment in a situation in which there is little to no excuse to leave this environment. Narrators also report feelings of guilt for not having taken better care with contraception and feeling a moral obligation to carry the pregnancy to term. This was the case even for narrators who are in favour of abortion, such as one woman who explains that "despite [her] personal ideologies, [she] often felt guilty [and] selfish" but also emphasises that she "knew very well that it was not [her], but society that puts that chip in you so that you feel guilty about the decision you are making" (SenRed, "Capítulo 2"). In the context of increased isolation and atomisation, feminist activists' dedicated effort to build networks and create collectivity became all the more urgent.

Upon getting in contact with Socorristas en Red, most narrators describe the above outlined feelings of distress being abruptly alleviated, due to gaining the "security and tranquility" that they would be accompanied during the whole process (SenRed, "Capítulo 2"). Crucially, the information they receive from them is new to most abortion seekers, despite the public attention abortion has received in recent years due to feminist mobilisation and public debate. Many are unaware of the services already available to abortion seekers prior to the legalisation, such as the 0800 sexual health line, a government operated hotline that provides information about ILE. It is important not to presume widespread awareness of current abortion legislation solely due to it having been prominent in public debate. The main channels through which abortion seekers learn about Socorristas en Red is through friends or via the internet, with fewer people already being vaguely or fully aware of their work from their involvement with feminist spaces, such as marches or activist groups. Upon initial consultation, narrators describe how the Socorristas share knowledge, give abortion seekers space for asking questions and expressing their worries, and providing lay expertise. Julia McReynolds-Pérez, in her analysis of the activism of Lesbianas y Feministas por la Descriminalización del Aborto, finds that "[m]isoprostol activists used expertise about pharmaceutical abortion, along with peer education, to position themselves as lay experts on safe abortion in a context of illegality" ("No Doctors Required" 371). There are two immediate affective consequences of this initial knowledge-sharing. On the one hand, it communicates a sense of care to abortion seekers, centring them as the protagonist of this moment of their lives. This challenges medical authorities and stands in contrast to heteropatriarchal narratives of pregnancy, in which the foetus is centred as protagonist (Petchesky; Sutton and Vacarezza; Lewis). This became at once more challenging and more urgent during the pandemic, as abortion-seekers were in closer contact with medical authorities reinforcing such normative narratives of pregnancy. The Socorristas' engagement with pregnant people in a way that respects them as autonomous directors of their own lives gives rise to a sense of safety, protection, and freedom. This became particularly urgent during Covid-19, which destabilised people's sense of autonomy and certainty in general, but especially in the context of experiences at the margins of legality and social acceptability, like abortion. Thus, their activism directly contradicts previously experienced feelings of fear and uncertainty.

On the other hand, narrators describe that this knowledge exchange prompts in them a sense of tranquillity, as exemplified by one narrator stating that being in contact with SenRed "gave [her] a lot of security and tranquillity [because she knew] that this was going to end and everything would return to 'normal'" (SenRed, "Capítulo 4"). The clarity conveyed through this knowledge transfer provides a sense of resolution to the situation of chaos caused by unwanted pregnancy that was previously perceived as threatening to overturn the narrators' lives. In that sense, knowledge transfer is a key vehicle for enabling routes to re-establishing one's prior sense of self. The knowing that there is a resolution to their situation causes a shift that is both affective and embodied. This is reflected by feelings of relief being "as much physical as emotional" (SenRed, "Capítulo 2"). Socorristas en Red's presence, despite not being *there* physically is described by one narrator as "fundamental for alleviating in some way the physical and psychological sufferings" caused by the process (SenRed, "Capítulo 4"). Relief is by many described as manifesting physically and intuitively, as in the case of a woman who after finding out about the activists, felt like "[her] soul returned into [her] body [and she] could breathe again" (SenRed, "Capítulo 5"). The embodied and interpersonal nature of this sense of relief highlights the importance of proximity in SenRed's work and draws attention to that which is communicated nonverbally, through presence and emotions. Recreating virtually the sense of proximity usually brought about by physical presence has been a primary challenge for activists during the Covid-19 pandemic, illustrated by the title of the testimony collections: *Estamos cerca*—we are near. The focus on presence and proximity highlights the centrality of opening up different ways of feeling and knowing about one's body and self within their work, drawing attention to their epistemic interventions being as crucial as their practical ones.

The experience of the abortion itself is retold by most narrators as a moment of intense stress and pain (SenRed, "Capítulo 1"; "Capítulo 2"). Pain is a key affect for feminist politics and the associated vulnerability can constitute an important "point of departure for powerful forms of political resistance" (Solana and Vacarezza 7). Many narrators express that they find it important to communicate the pain they experienced, for instance by stating "it was very painful, I won't deny it" (SenRed, "Capítulo 1"). A major motivation in describing their pain is to inform others who may have abortions in the future what to expect, but giving testimony of the endured pain also seems to be an important aspect of describing this part of the abortion experience. Importantly, pain described both by those who had abortions within and without the healthcare system. Pain, alongside more positive emotions people describe in relation to the support they experience and the relief they feel about being able to abort safely, constitutes an equally important vehicle for shaping individual and collective political identity in relation to abortion. While more celebratory abortion discourses highlighting "women's autonomy and ability to make their own reproductive decisions" (McReynolds-Pérez, *Misoprostol for the masses* 157) are important for reversing repressive narratives that function through the attribution of fear and shame, reclaiming the pain that is involved in the experience is also important. In doing so, a more complete picture of abortion as a multifaceted, complex, and ultimately normal experience emerges. It also allows people who pass through the experience to emerge as capable of holding these complexities.

After the abortion, or in some cases after having received a post-abortion check-up, narrators recount experiencing a moment of catharsis. Many of the narrators describe feelings of relief, happiness, joy, luck, and contentment. These feelings of joy are often expressed as calm emotions, connected to contentment and peacefulness, rather than more energetic forms of happiness. Another sentiment shared among many of the narrators is a sense of reaffirmed purpose upon resuming their "normal life" after the abortion. As one narrator tells, the activists gave her the "tranquillity of being able to decide over [her] body, [...] and to be able to continue to be here, standing, alive for [her] other two children and to go ahead with what [she wants]" (SenRed, "Capítulo 1"). This is communicated through feelings of strength, autonomy, and certainty in ones' beliefs and choices and embodied through "feeling" oneself again, as in the case of one woman who recounts "I felt my body returning to normality" (SenRed, "Capítulo 1"). This is attributed to having overcome severe obstacles and taken significant risks in order to pursue this purpose. Further, various narrators describe the experience of abortion as having had a politicising effect on them. This may be expressed in the form of demonstrating support for the campaign for legal abortion or feminism, reproductive justice, and bodily autonomy more generally. One narrator closes her testimony with the statement

"We will continue to fight so that there will be not one less and that it will be law" (SenRed, "Capítulo 4"), referencing to the feminist slogans "Ni Una Menos" and "Que Sea Ley".

Abortion, Affect and Political Identity

The emotions narrated in relation to abortion during the Covid-19 pandemic shed light on abortion-seekers' perception and construction of political identity, particularly after the abortion, as well as activists' political identity during this particular time. While only few of them explicitly discuss how they thought about themselves as political agents prior to the experience, many imply their feelings about their political identity have changed or intensified as a consequence of the abortion. One narrator explains that while she was not in favour of abortion previously, "now that it happened to [her], [she understands] what women are fighting for" (SenRed, "Capítulo 1"). This illustrates the politicising impact the experience of feminist-accompanied abortion has on many people. In publishing this volume of narratives around this experience, SenRed mobilises this impact for constructing their own collective feminist identity during a time of fragmentation and individualisation due to the imposition of Covid-19-related confinement.

Knowledge production has long been conceptualised by feminist scholars as an important ground of contestation over authorities of meaning making. Verónica Gago particularly draws on Carole Pateman's criticism of social contract theory being underpinned by the sexual contract that renders women "natural, pre-political, and generally muted" (50). It is on this basis that "the male body is revealed as a rational and abstract body with the capacity to create order and discourse" (51). Thus, the figure of the individual emerges as explicitly different from female and feminised bodies. Solana and Vacarezza further draw on Pateman to criticise the exclusionary and gendered nature of "the constitutive binary pairings of the philosophical tradition —mind/body, passion/reason, public/private, culture/nature" (2). In this context, femininity becomes associated with "the body, the passions, the private sphere and the natural" (Solana and Vacarezza 2). Therefore, feminist projects are also by necessity always projects of producing knowledge that contests the gendered nature of political identity. Affects play a crucial role in producing such alternative knowledge about subversive political identities. For this reason, it is important to understand personal emotions as intimately connected to the maintenance and challenging of structures of power (Solana and Vacarezza). Feminists have long mobilised a broad affective repertoire for political resistance and social transformation. Having historically been attributed to and used to "justify the oppression of racialised, colonised and sexually dissident groups" (Ahmed 2), emotionality has been emphasised by feminist thinkers as constituent of all gendered identities. Emphasising the self as constructed through the emotions that circulate between subjects also highlights the body as a crucial site of feminist productions of knowledge about oneself, one's experiences and one's community (Ahmed).

In the context of abortion, many narrators describe their emotional response to the whole experience as articulated through their body. Some describe early pregnancy symptoms as are commonly known, such as nausea and painful breasts, while others refer to a gut feeling that they would obtain an abortion. Various narrators describe the link between their body and mind, for instance by recounting that "my head and my body were afraid" or that after the abortion, their "heart and [...] body" are recovering (SenRed, "Capítulo 1"). One narrator states that "[her] womb, [her] whole Body understood that [this was] not part of [her] plan" and her decision therefore being unequivocal (SenRed, "Capítulo 2"). In locating these feelings in the body, narrators situate their knowing that abortion is the right thing to do not only in their rational contemplation as privileged by hegemonic knowledge production, but also conceptualise it as emotional and embodied. Ahmed highlights that only philosophical approaches which do not assume that the body can be transcended may account adequately for the "contingency, locatedness [and] worldliness of being" (41). In line with that, the testimonies reflect a political identity that is contingent, located, and grounded in abortion seekers' lived experience of the real world. Relationality is key to Ahmed's conceptualisation of embodiment, emotions and the self, expressed through the notion of inter-embodiment, the "understanding of embodiment as lived experience which moves beyond the privatised realm of 'my body'" (47). Similarly, feminists have long insisted on the "centrality of the body in the reproduction and transformation of culture" (Jaggar and Bordo 4). Thus, the nexus of body and emotions emerges as crucial for intellectual insight, particularly about the formation of individual and collective identities. Highlighting the embodied nature of such intellectual insight becomes all the more urgent in relation to the Covid-19 pandemic, which in many ways removed inter-embodiment from daily experience.

For many, the experience of abortion is an instance that shifts their perception of themselves as individuals and in relation to others. This is owed to gaining both first-hand and structural insight into the experience of abortion, as well as the barriers imposed by social, medical and political institutions. In various narrators' cases, their own abortion is the first time they encounter activists who openly discuss abortion and offer a perspective on the topic that diverges from hegemonic perceptions of gender and sexuality. Not despite, but rather because of the extensively acknowledged pain, fear and sadness, they describe the experience as ultimately vindicating and transformative, affirming ones bodily and political autonomy. One woman summarises her experience as "simply magical, painful, transformative and wise" (SenRed, "Capítulo 2"). Community is central to many narrators' experience. This is expressed in emphases on how important it was not to be alone, feelings of sisterhood and friendship, but also by stating their intention as wanting to let others know that it will be alright. As such, perceptions of individual identity in the context of abortion are inextricably intertwined with a feeling of embeddedness in a wider community. This community is not so much consolidated by a shared identity but rather a commitment to a shared feminist project, thus putting into action what Clare Hemmings refers to as "affective solidarity", the potency of which is encapsulated by Cecilia Macón's notion of "affective agency". Through their presence via digital communication, activists are able to establish themselves as non-judgmental listeners, who are simply "there" throughout the process, thus prompting a rethinking of notions of proximity and support. However, it is important to point to the limitations of virtual forms of proximity and care during the Covid-19 pandemic, as is demonstrated by several women who opted for breaking quarantine rules and undertaking their abortion in the physical proximity of a friend or Socorrista.

Various narrators describe feelings of love for oneself and others, prompted by the support they received from Socorristas en Red, which is perceived as generous and altrusitic. This love for others does not only extend to people who offer support in the situation of abortion, but also to others who have experienced abortion in similar circumstances or will do so in the future. Narrators describe that it is from these sentiments that a sense of community emerges, often expressed through notions of sisterhood, friendship and comradery. Furthermore, many people who had abortions with the support of Socorristas en Red during the Covid-19 pandemic emerge from the experience with an increased awareness of the need for feminist mobilising and a sense of connectedness to a wider, loosely defined feminist community. From abortion-seekers' narratives, three dimensions of the Socorristas' role emerge: they are "psychologist, medic, and friend" all at once (SenRed, "Capítulo 4"). Having previously explored how emotions shape knowledge production, here we see the reverse is true, too. The command of knowledge about abortion invokes particular ways of feeling about others within this community, thus shaping its relational collective identity. This, too, describes a distinct political identity that is attributed to both individual Socorristas, but also describes their community as a wider entity. This three-fold characterisation adequately encompasses three key facets of their work and political identity. The "psychologist" encompasses their ability to respond to abortion-seekers fears and anxieties, providing a space in which they can safely ask questions, express worries, and find answers to them. The second facet of their identity, the "medic" speaks to the crucial importance of lay expertise and the challenge to medic's exclusive authority over knowledge in relation to abortion. These two identity facets are backed up by the professionalism most narrators mention, expressed through discretion, clarity, efficiency and responsibility. Lastly, for many abortion-seekers, the Socorristas are also a friend. Various narrators describe the activists they were in touch with as immediately likeable and uncomplicated to have informal conversations with. It was frequently mentioned that their dedication and commitment to their work immediately communicated a sense of trust and intimacy, leading to various narrators saying that communicating with the Socorristas throughout their abortion experience often felt like a virtual hug. One narrator relates that her abortion led her to discover "rebellious and courageous people, like the women […] who help other women to have an abortion, with the love of a sister who only embraces and listens" (SenRed, "Capítulo 4"). This reflects the political identity SenRed seek to construct for themselves, in their day-to-day-interactions with abortion seekers, as well as in cultural and informative productions like this collection of testimonies.

I hope to have shown how the affects circulating among abortion seekers and feminist activists and shared via testimonial narratives enable the construction of a highly politicised identity that stands in sharp contrast to heteronormative understandings of political identity as atomistic, rational, and abstract, which were reinforced through the Covid-19 pandemic. Instead, it centres embodied, collective, and emotional experience as the source for constructing dissident identities, emerging out of the experience of abortion.

Conclusion

The pandemic altered social life beyond what would have been imaginable in 2019. The experience of abortion has been subject to changes to a particular extent, not only due to Covid-19 but also because of the introduction of IVE in early 2021. While some barriers have been removed in this time and others have newly occurred, yet others have emerged as persistent issues throughout these changes. To tackle these persisting challenges, a vigilant feminist movement willing and able to disrupt restrictive narratives about abortion and people who have them is necessary. The work of Socorristas en Red, particularly in response to the Covid-19 pandemic, exemplifies this kind of activism, enacted through activist practices of feminist (health) care. Analysing narratives of abortion experiences with them illustrate that feminist politics of knowledge production and sharing, as well as affective circulations, are crucial for this.

The pandemic has posed a significant challenge to the models of care feminist activist abortion accompaniment relies upon. SenRed is dedicated not only to the provision of an essential healthcare service, but rather to holistic intervention into societal and political perceptions of abortion and people who have them, as is evident from their aim to repostulate abortion as normal, collective, and safe (Zurbriggen et al.). In line with theorisations of knowledge production as affective and embodied, being physically present enables possibilities of experiencing abortion as supportive, caring, affirmative. This in turn shapes how people who have had an abortion feel about their own identity in relation to the experience, as well as their position within wider social and political hierarchies. The onset of the Covid-19 pandemic required an urgent reconfiguration of the tools of their feminist model of care. In practice, this has meant moving interactions between activists and abortion seekers online, which is in some ways more distant than in-person interaction, but has also given their abortion support a new level of immediacy due to their (virtual) presence at every step along the way. In requiring the urgent rethinking of proximity, care, and accompaniment, the pandemic has brought to the fore the substantive ways in which feminist abortion accompaniment challenges heteropatriarchal conceptions of identity ascribed to pregnant people and enables instead the construction of feminist identities. The activist practices used for subverting dominant, depoliticising discourses around abortion in medicine, politics, and society function as much as a practical intervention as an epistemic one.

Narrative storytelling in the form of testimonies about the experience of abortion produces knowledge about pregnant people's political identity and location that is absent from structures of power. In narrating their experience of feminist accompanied abortion, the people who shared their stories with SenRed contest narratives of abortion that presuppose the experience as always a tragic and traumatic last resort. This assumption reproduces heteronormative notions of motherhood as universally desired, tapping into narratives that equate womanhood and motherhood and ultimately render pregnant people's position as apolitical, passive, and, as Verónica Gago points out, secondary. Narratives of the feminist care women experienced in the context of their abortion give rise to the construction of a feminist political identity that contradicts this. The link between knowledge and emotions is crucial for enabling these kinds of constructions. As discussed in this chapter, the relationship between the two goes both ways: activists' mastering of lay expertise about safe, pharmaceutical abortion and their sharing of this knowledge with abortion seekers makes it possible for abortion seekers to move from feelings that range from distress to outright panic about being pregnant to feelings of tranquillity, relief, and joy. At the same time, the feelings experienced in relation to abortion generate, often embodied and affective, forms of knowledge. From this reciprocal interaction between knowledge and emotions, a distinctly feminist political identity emerges. The range of often conflicting feelings that emerge in the interactions between activists and abortion seekers —ranging from fear, pain, and uncertainty to affirmation, care, and happiness. In a context in which the association of abortion with negative emotions and suffering is employed to render pregnant people as passive and apolitical, these emotions take on a subversive function. Aligning with Solana's and Vacarezza's notion of "other futures" opened up by the complex feelings associated with abortion, they make possible a different way of constructing one's own political identity that accounts for and does justice to the humanity of people who have abortions. Ultimately, feminist activist accompanied abortion gives rise to a vocal and vigilant identity that understands abortion access as being determined by and standing for a more comprehensive issue about the political identity of people who may become pregnant. A feminist movement that subscribes to these characteristics is crucial for monitoring the lasting implementation of the entitlement to IVE. Only in contesting and transgressing the repressive heteronormative definitions of political identity that govern abortion access today, the substantive implementation of the right to legal, safe and free abortion can be ensured.

Bibliography

Ahmed, Sara. Strange Encounters: Embodied Others in Post-Coloniality. Routledge, 2000.

Borland, Elizabeth. "Storytelling, Identity, and Strategy: Perceiving Shifting Obstacles in the Fight for Abortion Rights in Argentina". Sociological Perspectives, vol. 57, no. 4, 2014, pp. 488–505.

Burton, Julia. "Prácticas feministas en torno al derecho al aborto en Argentina: aproximaciones a las acciones colectivas de Socorristas en Red". Punto Género, no. 7, 2017, pp. 91–111.

—. "Los estudios sobre aborto en Argentina. Un estado de la cuestión". Cadernos PAGU, no. 63, 2021, pp. 1–22.

De Zordo, Silvia. "The Biomedicalisation of Illegal Abortion: The Double Life of Misoprostol in Brazil". História, Ciências, Saúde-Manguinhos, vol. 23, no. 1, 2016, pp. 19–36.

Drovetta, Raquel Irene. "Safe Abortion Information Hotlines: An Effective Strategy for Increasing Women's Access to Safe Abortions in Latin America". Reproductive Health Matters, vol. 23, no. 45, 2015, pp. 47–57.

Fernández Romero, Francisco. "'We Can Conceive Another History': Trans Activism Around Abortion Rights in Argentina". International Journal of Transgender Health, vol. 22, no. 1-2, 2020, pp. 126–140.

Gago, Verónica. Feminist International: How to Change Everything. Verso Books, 2020.

Hemmings, Clare. "Affective Solidarity: Feminist Reflexivity and Political Transformation". Feminist Theory, vol. 13, no. 2, 2012, pp. 147–61.

Honorable Congreso de la Nación Argentina. Acceso a la interrupción voluntaria del embarazo, 15 January 2021, https://www.argentina.gob.ar/normativa/nacional/ley-27610-346231/texto.

Jaggar, Alison M., and Susan Bordo. Gender/body/knowledge: Feminist Reconstructions of Being and Knowing. Rutgers University Press, 1989.

Lewis, Sophie. Full Surrogacy Now: Feminism Against Family. Verso Books, 2021.

Macón, Cecilia. Desafiar el sentir. Feminismos, historia y rebelión. Omnívora, 2022.

McReynolds-Pérez, Julia Ana. Misoprostol for the masses: the activist-led proliferation of pharmaceutical abortion in Argentina. 2014. University of Wisconsin-Madison, PhD dissertation.

—. "No Doctors Required: Lay Activist Expertise and Pharmaceutical Abortion in Argentina". Signs: Journal of Women in Culture and Society, vol. 42, no. 2, 2017, pp. 349– 375.

Pateman, Carole. The Sexual Contract. Polity Press, 1988.

Petchesky, Rosalind Pollack. "Fetal Images: The Power of Visual Culture in the Politics of Reproduction". Feminist Studies, vol. 13, no. Summer 87, 1987, pp. 263–92.

Protocolo para la atención integral de las personas con derecho a la interrupción legal del embarazo: Actualización 2019. Ministerio de Salud y Desarollo Social, 2019.

Romero, Mariana, et al. Proyecto mirar: a un año de la ley de aborto en Argentina. Proyecto Mirar, 2021, https://proyectomirar.org.ar/reporte/PROYECTO_MIRAR_reporte_aniversario_ley_VF.pdf.

Solana, Mariela, and Nayla Luz Vacarezza. "Sentimientos feministas". Estudos feministas, vol. 28, no. 2, 2020, pp. 1–15.

SenRed. "Capítulo 1. Miedos y tristezas". Estamos Cerca, 2020, https://socorristasenred.org/wp-content/uploads/2020/08/Miedos-y-tristezas_c.pdf.

—. "Capítulo 2. Esperanza". Estamos Cerca, 2020, https://socorristasenred.org/wp-content/uploads/2020/08/Esperanza.pdf.

—. "Capítulo 3. Acompañarnos, acuerparnos". Estamos Cerca, 2020, https://socorristasenred.org/wp-content/uploads/2020/08/Acompanarnos-acuerparnos.pdf.

—. "Capítulo 4. Abortar en cuarentena". Estamos Cerca, 2020, https://socorristasenred.org/wp-content/uploads/2020/08/Abortar-en-cuarentena.pdf.

—. "Capítulo 5. Apoderadxs: que sea ley". Estamos Cerca, 2020, https://socorristasenred.org/wp-content/uploads/2020/09/Apoderadxs-que-sea-ley.pdf.

—. "Sistematización 2020". Socorristas en Red, 2021, https://socorristasenred.org/download/sistematizacion-2020/.

—. "10 datos de acompañamientos a abortar (2020)". Socorristas en Red, 2021, https://socorristasenred.org/10-datos-de-acompanamientos-a-abortar-2020/.

—. [@socenredarg]. "A un año de la ley de aborto en Argentina, tenemos motivos para seguir luchando por abortos cuidados. Entre el 20 de enero y el 30 de octubre de 2021 acompañamos a 9.900 personas en sus abortos. >> 2.377 decidieron que las acompañemos en la solicitud en el sistema de salud. >> 7.523 decidieron que las acompañemos en la autogestión de un aborto. . . . .#IVE". Instagram, 29 December 2021, https://www.instagram.com/p/CYElzk1rfmS/.

—. "A un año de la ley de aborto en Argentina, tenemos motivos para seguir luchando por abortos cuidados. >> Falta de información sobre el acceso al aborto: No hay campañas masivas de difusión del derecho a abortar.

Tampoco los espacios de salud cuentan con información accesible, sencilla y comprensible, en distintas lenguas y soportes para facilitar la solicitud y concreción del aborto". Instagram, 1 January 2022, https://www.instagram.com/p/CYMVqqvLWni/.

—. "A un año de la ley de aborto en Argentina, tenemos motivos para seguir luchando por abortos cuidados. >> Información falsa por parte de profesionales de la salud para desalentar la decisión de abortar. Joven de 17 años de una localidad de Chaco, solicita una Interrupción Legal del Embarazo, durante la atención profesionales de la salud ofrecieron que diera en adopción, argumentaron sobre los riesgos de un aborto en segundo trimestre de gestación. No le informaron los riesgos de la continuidad del embarazo y dieron parte a sus familiares sobre la solicitud del aborto. La desalentaron y obligaron a maternar". Instagram, 4 January 2022, https://www.instagram.com/p/CYUTsVbrpks/.

—. "A un año de la ley de aborto en Argentina, tenemos motivos para seguir luchando por abortos cuidados. >> Prácticas crueles especialmente en abortos en segundo trimestre de gestación. 'Me ponían 3 pastillas en la vagina y 1 por boca, cada 5 ó 6 horas. Entré a las 9 de la mañana y expulsé a las 6 de la mañana del día siguiente. Les supliqué que hagan algo por mis dolores. Me pusieron calmantes por el suero a las 3 de la mañana'. (Karina, 19 años, Misiones)". Instagram, 12 January 2022, https://www.instagram.com/p/CYpRwuTDLrz/.

Sutton, Barbara, and Elizabeth Borland. "Queering Abortion Rights: Notes from Argentina". Culture, Health & Sexuality, vol. 20, no. 12, 2018, pp. 1378–93.

Sutton, Barbara, and Nayla Luz Vacarezza. "Abortion Rights in Images: Visual Interventions by Activist Organizations in Argentina". *Signs: Journal of Women in Culture and Society*, vol. 45, no. 3, 2020, pp. 731–757.

Zurbriggen, Ruth, et al. "Accompaniment of Second-Trimester Abortions: The Model of the Feminist Socorrista Network of Argentina". Contraception (Stoneham), vol. 97, no. 2, 2018, pp. 108–115.

Chapter 6

When Community Utopias Neutralise Biomedical Morals

The Poetry of Covid-19 in Peru and Chile

Daniel A. Romero Suárez

Pontificia Universidad Católica del Perú

Abstract

This article proposes that the poetry of Covid-19 written in Peru and Chile shows that the pandemic has been a communal experience of illness interwoven with social advocacy movements. On the one hand, massive protests in countries such as Chile, Colombia, and Peru indicate that people were willing to put their health at risk during a pandemic to demand better political and economic conditions. On the other hand, governments and conservative sectors have applied models of "sanitary citizenship" (Briggs and Martini-Briggs 2003) to delegitimize protests and condemn political dissent. In this context, poetry constitutes an emerging corpus that materializes what Rebecca Solnit (2009) refers to as the utopian hope that arises from disasters. Specifically, the poetic reformulations of biomedical concepts of health and disease suggest utopian ways of living focused on community and social justice.

Keywords: Poetry, Sanitary Citizenship, Disasters, Covid-19, Utopia

***

Poetry cannot help cure a pandemic, but if poetry did not exist, everything would be over.

Raúl Zurita.

Would it be an exaggeration to say that if we all read poetry, we might not have been harmed by Covid-19? Not at all.

Elena Poniatowska.

Introduction

Literature is an archive of narratives and metaphors that record human life during epidemiological crises. In fact, the literary tradition of Greco-Latin roots begins with an epidemic scene: the god Apollo sends a plague to the crowded Greek troops in *The Iliad*. After the famous calling to the Muses, the narrator relates the origin of the dispute between Achilles and Agamemnon:

> What god drove them to fight with such a fury?
> Apollo the son of Zeus and Leto. Incensed at the king
> he swept a fatal plague through the army—men were dying
> and all because Agamemnon spurned Apollo's priest (Homer 9–12).

Agamemnon's offense is twofold because, while refusing to act according to Chryses' requests, he also uses words to offend him. The priest's response is to raise a prayer to his protector, who initiates the outbreak. Much of the first book is epidemic dialogues: the characters discuss the causes, consequences, and solutions to the plague, all expressed in dactylic hexameters. The danger does not fade away until Chryses, in a sacred lyrical language —a ritual prayer— pleads to Apollo for him to stop.

Is poetry as vital to human life during a pandemic as Raúl Zurita and Elena Poniatowska suggest? In the realm of pandemic language, poetry is essential. It is clear that poetry cannot reduce the viral load in infected lungs or stop the mutations of SARS-CoV-2 proteins. However, two crucial pandemic disciplines —science communication and public health— are, to a large degree, language. The pandemic involved the emergence, intersection, and contestation of explanatory narratives. Given the lack of familiar precedents, on more than one occasion such narratives resorted to literary figures to explain health protocols and concepts. In this context, poetry is a valuable archive of collective memory that stores metaphorical uses that thread personal experiences with global narratives. The study of the imagery that emerged in March 2020 offers insights into the victories and failures of pandemic health policies.

Covid-19 poetry in Peru and Chile produces narratives about communities with a history of economic and health precariousness. Giving importance to collective ways of being is a way of challenging the fragmenting impulse of hegemonic biomedicine. When contagion intersects with racist or aporophobic imaginaries, the biological event is transformed into a social and moral failure that pushes the infected people aside. In contrast, poetry depicts collective identities that neutralise the exclusionary discourses that permeate biomedicine and, instead, establishes a community founded on the inequality that existed before the arrival of the coronavirus and, ultimately, envisions a utopian hope in the midst of disaster.

The reformulation of the concept of sanitary citizenship (Briggs and Martini-Briggs 10) is vital in the poetry of Covid-19. The concept refers to the set of rules that people must comply with in order to be considered healthy and, therefore, fully citizens. In poetry, as well as in other pandemic narratives, a common step is to formulate a critique of neoliberal healthcare. However, Latin American poems also depict poetic subjects that seek to be part of communities stigmatised and excluded by hegemonic health discourses. By doing so, poetic utopias prioritise solidarity over being considered healthy.

Metaphorical Virology, Protests, and Rituals of Disinfection

The semantic field of virology was notoriously fertile during the pandemic. Very quickly, authors used terms such as infection, mutation, and virus to make visible other social crises that had gone largely unnoticed. For example, due to their global nature and transmission, poverty and gender-based violence became events with epidemiological reminiscences. Using terms associated with Covid-19 in other areas is a starting point for reformulating concepts of health and disease. In the wake of the massive state and private efforts to halt the spread of infections, the neglect of other urgent problems generated indignation. For vulnerable communities, the pandemic meant worsening previously existing precarious conditions; in other words, it was more of the same. The threat of the new virus paled when inserted into the daily routine of death and neglect that characterised the lives of large portions of the Latin American population.

Yonofui ["It was not me"] is an Argentine political and social organisation that offers one of the most relevant discourses for understanding viral metaphorical potential. In the manifesto "We are a plague", socioeconomic precariousness is represented as a biopolitical mechanism that keeps at bay unwanted communities that are seen as viral agents:

> Somos el tipo de personas que no entran en el plan de emergencia. Cuerpos extraños. El descarte de una sociedad que nos trata en cualquier circunstancia como ciudadanxs de segunda. Para ellxs, nosotrxs somos el virus. Lo sabemos. Nos hacemos cargo. Mutamos, sobrevivimos y por eso, no hay anticuerpo que nos detenga. Estamos inmunizadxs a cualquier mierda, porque hemos pasado la mayor parte de nuestras vidas expuestas a la pobreza, al hambre, al consumo, a la vida en la calle, a la cárcel, a los síntomas y a las secuelas del capitalismo; sobre su efecto en nuestras vidas podemos escribir largo y tendido. Por eso no hay cuarentena ni obediencia que nos aseguren una vida visible bajo los parámetros de una sociedad de la que pareciéramos no ser parte (Yonofui).

[We are the kind of people who do not fit into the emergency response plan. Strange bodies. The discarded of a society that treats us in all circumstances as second-class citizens. For them, we are the virus. We know it. We take responsibility for it. We mutate and survive; therefore, no antibody can stop us. We are immune to any shit because we have spent most of our lives exposed to poverty, hunger, consumption, street life, prison, and the symptoms and after-effects of capitalism; we can write long and deep about its impact on our lives. That is why no quarantine or obedience can assure us a livable life under the parameters of a society of which we seem not to be a part].

The medicalisation of poverty and otherness is a long-standing practice. Susan Sontag has shown that disease was already associated with poverty and exoticism, turning poor places into primitive and infectious sites in nineteenth-century texts (139). The metaphorical novelty of the manifesto is that the author —a we-voice— is affirmatively accepting some viral characteristics.

A virus is a set of nucleic acids (DNA or RNA) stored inside a protein coat that has developed extraordinary survival capabilities. The term "survive" establishes a fundamental characteristic: viruses cannot reproduce by themselves (they need to infect a cellular host) and, therefore, are not considered living beings. Yonofui speaks from the point of view of an "us", defined as a set of "strange bodies" that are belittled and excluded as if they were a virus. However, far from rejecting the association, the text accepts it and claims that it has been able to stay alive thanks to that virus. Vulnerable communities have not been annihilated because they have been able to adapt —like viruses— to harsh conditions, including capitalism. Thus, public health mandates feel alien to them since quarantines aim to ensure the continuity of a livelihood they do not feel part of. By identifying with a virus, Yonofui confronts the hegemonic discourse and common sense that assures that it is better to stay away from infectious agents.

The protests that occurred during the pandemic also contested traditional ideas of health. To understand this reformulation, we must first consider one of the ways in which neoliberalism has constructed a picture of the healthy based on state regulations that hide, within medical terminology, civil and moral guidelines. Charles Briggs and Clara Mantini-Briggs coined the concept of sanitary citizenship to explain the process by which modern states classify their inhabitants through biomedical codes:

> Sanitary citizenship is one of the key mechanisms for deciding who is accorded substantive access to the civil and social rights of citizenship. Public health officials, physicians, politicians, and the press depict some

individuals and communities as possessing modern medical understandings of the body, health, and illness, practicing hygiene, and depending on doctors and nurses when they are sick. These people become sanitary citizens. People who are judged to be incapable of adopting this modern medical relationship to the body, hygiene, illness, and healing—or who refuse to do so—become unsanitary subjects (10).

Given that the criteria to be granted sanitary citizenship have been established by the elite able to meet them —thanks to their privileged access to knowledge, money, and medical technologies— our ideas of what healthy is has functioned as an exclusion mechanism hidden under medical concepts.

In the interconnected world of the late twentieth century, the precepts of health and disease were strongly influenced by international institutions. Consequently, health guidelines have overlooked particular traditions and needs. In addition to economic gaps and the lack of solid public health programs, many Latin American communities maintain the stigmatised category of unhealthy subjects.

The pandemic protests in Chile (2020-2021), Peru (2020), and Colombia (2021) were events in which people set aside hierarchies established by sanitary citizenship to prioritise social justice.[1] Although the demonstrations had different origins, in all three cases, we notice that citizens were willing to take to the streets to protest, even if it meant risking their health. By mid-2020, there was already evidence to claim that protests were not superspreader events, thanks to epidemiological studies of mass demonstrations led by the Black Lives Matter movement in the USA (Neyman and Dalsey 3). However, some factors definitely increased the risk of suffering severe symptomatology: shouting, lack of physical distance between demonstrators, misuse of masks, physical trauma, and inflammation of the respiratory system caused by tear gas. That is, catching a deadly disease such as Covid-19 (or at least weakening the organism) in the midst of a pandemic in countries with precarious healthcare systems was a risk taken by thousands of people in Latin America.

The three scenarios generated debates about the legitimacy of mass demonstrations during a pandemic. The opposing views were mainly articulated

---

[1] In Chile, the pandemic demonstrations were the continuation of the *estallido social* ("social outburst") of October 2019, which, at the time of writing this paper, led Chile to the rejection of a second draft for a new constitution in December 2023. In Peru, the people took to the streets in November 2020 to oppose the illegitimate president Manuel Merino, who resigned five days after assuming office thanks to a coup. Finally, Colombian citizens protested against the neoliberal reforms carried out by President Iván Duque. In all three cases, international human rights organizations reported violence by police officers who arrested, injured, and killed numerous demonstrators.

by conservative sectors that sought to minimise the importance of social demands. In their arguments, the minimal risk of contagion was sufficient to qualify the protests as illegitimate since they violated the code of sanitary citizenship. From this perspective, it was not justifiable for a community to protest because all citizens should put social activism on hold to collaborate with a greater good: the reduction of positive cases of Covid-19.

When states impose strict ideals of sanitary citizenship, they perpetuate the long history in which medical institutions have been used to justify social coercion. In contrast, pandemic protests are a practice that reduces the importance of hegemonic health values. Now, sanitary citizenship is less relevant because people recognise that the concept is part of the system they are protesting. Moreover, if obtaining that citizenship requires access to high-quality services to check our wellbeing, it is important to note that many people who took to the streets had never had such an opportunity. With or without demonstrations, therefore, the precariousness of public health systems had already turned a large part of Latin American communities into unsanitary subjects.

Valeria Román Marroquín published a text in April 2020 that examines the limitations of sanitary citizenship. The poem "limpieza" takes as its starting point the duties of disinfection to explore its connection to labour and social hierarchies:

> la limpieza es el principio,
> lo que sigue no tiene límite.
>
> 5 litros mezcla agua-clorox,
> tecnología cabeza de familia
>
> amable para con la estructura
> y la estética de su empleador
>
> esto es, manos de amas de casa
> fabricadas en cadena. muchacha
>
> provinciana. chica minúscula que hace
> la limpieza del hogar. sus pisos y sus
>
> habitantes. 5 litros mezcla agua-clorox
> organiza los días, equilibra la sanidad
>
> de los ciudadanos, desinfecta al colectivo (Román 107).

> [cleaning is the beginning,
> there is no limit to what follows.

5 liter water-clorox mixture,
head-of-household technology

gentle to the structure
and aesthetics of their employer

that is, the hands of housemaids
manufactured in a production line. rural

girl. minuscule girl who
cleans the home, its floors, and its

inhabitants. 5 liter water-bleach mixture
organises the days, balances the sanitation

of the citizens, disinfects the collective]

The disinfection of surfaces was fundamental in the first months of the pandemic, especially when the debate around the airborne nature of SARS-CoV-2 transmission had not yet concluded. In the text, the poetic voice weaves a testimonial narrative with the power relations constructed around domestic cleaning jobs. Social stratification is highlighted when the disinfecting agent is, on the one side, gentle with the employers' aesthetics, but, on the other, the cleaners' hands are distanced from beauty, for they are inert pieces manufactured in a chain.

Dehumanisation is also seen in the fetishization of the workers' bodies: only their hands are worthy of mention as they achieve the employers' goals. In the poem, the figure of the "muchacha provinciana" [rural girl] is a racial and infantilising stereotype used by Lima's wealthy classes for female domestic workers. In conformity with the concept of sanitary citizenship, hygiene goes beyond the purely epidemiological sphere and becomes the central axis of life: it organises the days and balances our wellbeing. In this way, the poem depicts a ritual of cleanliness that surpasses the individual character of the one who performs it and disinfects a collective.

Román's poem traces a history of exploitation through the image of disinfection. The culture of cleanliness is inescapable even for the poetic voice, as revealed in the use of the first-person perspective. A shadow of pessimism covers the text because no change is in sight:

la limpieza es el principio, y la limpieza es

la fuerza que impone el orden, gobernaje
de los sujetos. la limpieza es forjador para

mis cadenas. 5 litros mezcla agua-clorox
hubiesen sido en su momento 5 litros

mezcla vinagre-agua oxigenada, algo
ha cambiado. ¿algo ha cambiado?

a diferencia de quienes han ido antes
en la secuencia temporal de la categoría

que me reconfigura, poseo propiedad.
para mí: 5 litros mezcla agua-clorox,

un balde y una escobilla y una habitación
propia donde contabilizo la marca del

producto desinfectante... (Román 107–8)

[cleanliness is the principle, and cleaning is

the force that imposes order, governing
of the subjects. cleanliness is the forger of

my chains. 5 liters of water-clorox mixture
would have been at the time 5 liters of

vinegar-hydrogen-peroxide mixture, something
has changed. has anything changed?

unlike those who have gone before
in the temporal sequence of the category

that reconfigures me, I own property.
for me: 5 liters of water-bleach mixture,

a bucket and a brush and a room of my own
where I record the brand name of the

disinfectant product]

Cleanliness is a control mechanism—the imperative of disinfection chains the subjects. The restraint goes beyond Covid-19 protocols, as the poem highlights that the yoke previously existed. First, the text reminds us that domestic workers have always been exposed to chemically unstable mixtures, such as vinegar and hydrogen peroxide. The sanitising method can be effective but harmful for those who perform the role of cleaners. Second, while cleaning products may change, the subordination is permanent. The rhetorical question "Has anything changed?" suggests disbelief that some economic improvement has resulted in substantial variation. Now, the poetic subject owns a bucket, brush, and room. However, the possessions bring the speaker back to a condition of submission to cleaning. The room, far from suggesting privacy or autonomy, shows confinement and the omnipresent need for disinfection.

The obsession with hygiene takes place in a repetitive and decadent world. Furthermore, the monotony of cleaning paves the way for the normalisation of exploitation, which the poetic voice expresses with a new image of restraint:

> ... tallo cerámico,
> porcelanato. tallo para mí con belleza y
>
> felicidad. tallo con felicidad en el fin de los
> tiempos. un movimiento único oscilando,
>
> arriba abajo, arriba abajo, arriba abajo. toda
> mi labor, arriba abajo. ¿algo ha cambiado?
>
> sustancialmente, de los desinfectantes
> y su composición, ¿algo ha cambiado?
>
> sustancialmente, de las usuarias y su
> composición, ¿algo ha cambiado? no
>
> tengo respuesta: tengo 5 litros agua-clorox,
> un balde y un limpiavidrios multiusos de alto
>
> brillo *streak-free!* en vidrios, espejos, acero
> inoxidable, pantallas. décadas domésticas,
>
> tengo horas teórico-prácticas en el cautiverio.
> tengo un único y extenso ventanal: observo
>
> el movimiento arriba abajo del mundo moderno
> y sus iguales. observo la tranquilidad de su
>
> encierro y decadencia... (Román 108–9)

> [... I carve ceramic,
> porcelain tiles. I carve for myself with beauty and
>
> happiness. I carve with happiness at the end
> of time. a single oscillating movement.
>
> up down, up down, up down, up down. All
> my labor, up down. has anything changed?
>
> substantially, about disinfectants
> and their composition. has anything changed?

substantially, about the users and their
composition, has anything changed? no

I have an answer: I have 5 liters of water-clorox,
a bucket and a multi-purpose glass cleaner of

high gloss streak-free! on glass, mirrors, stainless
steel, screens. domestic decades,

I have theory and practice hours in captivity.
I have a single large window: I observe

the up-and-down movement of the modern world.
and its equals. i observe the tranquility of their

confinement and decadence]

The ambiguity of the Spanish term *tallo* allows for a double interpretation. On the one hand, if we consider the *tallo* as a part of a plant [stem], we discover that the only natural element is made of ceramic. Even if it is vicarious in nature, the poetic voice can recognise and admire it. This interpretation offers an optimistic perspective since the "chains" have not been able to strip the subject of its ability to be moved by nature. Beauty neutralises labour alienation, at least for a few moments; an intimate connection is established with the porcelain representation of the plant kingdom. On the other hand, the Spanish verb *tallar* [carving] suggests that it is impossible to escape from work. Beauty is possible in ceramics, but only if the subject keeps labouring with a "single oscillating movement". In this pessimistic view, the manual labour of carving becomes a minor consolation in the context of exploitation.

The poetic voice questions whether domestic labour has changed, and the answer is no. The ritual of cleaning that goes from top to bottom reflects the monotony of the modern world. But it also portrays the confinement that existed before the pandemic. In that direction, the decadence mentioned in the poem pinpoints that the subject has not been able to free herself from the labour confinement and disinfecting tasks.

Hygiene anxiety results in dehumanisation. The cleaner becomes an entity that correctly fulfils a single function:

... ¿algo ha cambiado?
la limpieza es el principio. del principio yo

soy su dispositivo: una autómata disciplinada,
contentada y contenida en su labor. enterada

del progreso, nueva fórmula clorox potenciador
del remojo paños húmedos lyssol [sic] mata el 99%

de virus y bacterias, publicidad bien ejecutada.
bien ejecutada mi función y bien ejecutado el

conocimiento de mis límites: un gran ventanal,
una habitación propia, dos manos y un balde.

lo que sigue no tiene límite (Román 109–10).

[. . . has anything changed?
cleanliness is the principle. I am a device

of the principle: a disciplined automaton,
content and restrained in her work. aware

of progress, new formula clorox booster
of soaking wet wipes lyssol [sic] kills 99%

of viruses and bacteria, well-executed advertising.
well executed my function and well executed the

understanding of my limits: a large window,
a room of my own, two hands, and a bucket.

what follows has no limit]

Meticulous compliance with the imperative of cleanliness turns the subject into a disciplined automaton. Repetition is not always identical. Progress involves perfecting sanitation with new methods or products, like Lysol disinfectant wipes. However, the poetic subject cannot escape from the automatization that leads to domestication, which makes one conform to the established limits. Even if there is a world outside, the maid's room and the cleaning equipment must suffice.

The poem destabilises the biomedical concept of sanitary citizenship because it evidences its connection with discrimination. The anxiety of disinfection, first exclusive to employers, has now been internalised by female workers. In the former, hygiene signifies modernity and commitment to the common good. In the latter, cleaning is a heavy workload. Domestic workers are the ones who enable employers to comply with the hygiene requirements of sanitary citizenship, but the cleaners do not gain access to that status. Even the privacy of the room functions to continue the preparation of cleaning tasks. The confinement perpetuates the exploitation of young female labourers with indigenous roots, and the poetic voice decides to join that community when using the plural "we". Therefore, the text shows that sanitary citizenship can be set aside in favour of solidarity with exploited communities.

Hope in Disaster

The pandemic was a twofold community event. First, the public health crisis established epidemiological equality. In May 2020, Paula Canelo explained the unexpected and unwanted bonds created between people:

> [La pandemia] nos devolvió una cierta sensación de igualdad, de pertenencia a una misma comunidad. Alteradas las rutinas cotidianas y las certidumbres, el "enemigo invisible" nos igualó. Hoy nos percibimos todos igualmente vulnerables ante su amenaza, todos igualmente inseguros, todos igualmente temerosos (18–19).

> [The pandemic gave us back a certain sense of equality, of belonging to the same community. By altering our routines and certainties, the "invisible enemy" put us on an equal footing. Today we all perceive ourselves as equally vulnerable to its threat, all equally insecure, all equally fearful]

In addition, equality was visible in the undermining of the belief that a subject is sufficient unto itself: "El Covid-19, su invisibilidad devastadora, puso en cuarentena la autoconfianza del individuo liberal en su capacidad de salvarse a sí mismo sin ayuda del Estado, de lo público y de lo común" (Forster 57) [Covid-19's devastating invisibility quarantined the liberal individual's self-confidence in his ability to save himself without help from the state, the public, and the commons]. As an effect of mandatory quarantines, all people had to rely on the other members of society, whether neighbours, relatives, or state officials. The problem was communal. Even if monetary abundance and political power allowed some people to bypass restrictions, life on the planet became more interconnected than before, not only because of local actions but also because of dependence on scientific information and vaccine development.

However, epidemiological equality cannot really exist since each new infection occurs in a specific socioeconomic context. Judith Butler noted that "social and economic inequality will make sure that the virus discriminates. The virus alone does not discriminate, but we humans surely do, formed and animated as we are by the interlocking powers of nationalism, racism, xenophobia, and capitalism" ("Capitalism"). Thus, the prejudices and privileges that shape our lives determined the political action and imagery of the pandemic. The continuation of these exclusionary narratives must be neutralised in the future, as they could become the starting point for public health reform. According to Rita Segato, communities that are already being discriminated against will carry the blame for the severity of the pandemic:

> El furor y odio hacia toda y cualquier persona asociada a la plaga cunde entre sectores reaccionarios de la sociedad, que pretenderán, a futuro, imponer ese orden social frente a lo que puedan definir como "amenaza pública": enfermos, migrantes, no-blancos, delincuentes, inmorales, etc. (Segato 82).
>
> [The rage and hatred directed towards any person associated with the plague spread among reactionary sectors of society, which will seek, in the future, to impose this social order against what they can define as a "public threat": sick people, migrants, non-whites, criminals, immoral people, etc.]

Segato outlines how epidemiological fear is expressed through political, racial, and moral exclusions. Here, sanitary citizenship determines what is considered a "public threat" in times of "plague", but the criteria used are far from exclusively medical.

Second, the pandemic is an event that makes visible and empowers community relations through an optimistic view of the future. Utopian hope announces a radically different social order, even in the devastation generated by the pandemic. Moving away from a tradition of utopian thinking that imagines a better future through abstract ideals or elite-generated knowledge, Judith Butler and Rebecca Solnit find the seeds of change in communal solidarity.

Butler explains two types of hope during a public health crisis. The first reflects a common acceptance of the term. In hopelessness, subjects look for solace to cling to (Butler, "The World" 00:27-1:00). The second hope that emerges in pandemic times is the confidence that movements seeking social transformation will be able to accomplish what they envision (1:00-1:53). When asked if she has hope for future social change, Butler responds "I am encouraged by the radical democratic ideals embodied in social movements" ("Interview" 6).

Solnit has examined in depth the possibility of building utopias in the midst of disasters. In April 2020, the author underlined the opportunity that arises in times of crisis: "At moments of immense change, we see with new clarity the systems—political, economic, social, ecological—in which we are immersed as they change around us. We see what's strong, what's weak, what's corrupt, what matters and what doesn't" ("The impossible"). As a first step for change, social groups must have a turning point that allows them to evaluate their current life. The emergency then leads to experiencing an alternative future in the community:

I have often thought that the wave of privatisation that has characterised our neoliberal age began with the privatisation of the human heart, the withdrawal from a sense of a shared fate and social bonds. It is to be hoped that this shared experience of catastrophe [the pandemic] will reverse the process (Solnit, "The impossible").

Solnit yearns for "a new awareness of how each of us belongs to the whole and depends on it" to demonstrate that radical and sudden changes are possible. In other words, the collective solidarity and love shown in the pandemic by many people should be the starting point for imagining more inclusive futures.

Solnit's approach to the pandemic is grounded in previous research on utopian communities that emerge in disasters. In *A Paradise Built in Hell* (2009), Solnit posits that natural disasters are events in which collective ways of living —or desires to achieve these new ways of living— are empowered and become central to survival. These communal experiences originate a liminal frame in which the anxieties of the past and the future temporarily disappear, as people's minds are focused on the day-to-day (Solnit, *A Paradise* 166–7). It is in this new temporality that the opportunity to formulate utopias arises. Disaster allows us to envision new ways of living in the world. However, the definitive goal is to recognise that those new desires and possibilities can materialise in ordinary times (307).

The utopia of a pandemic community incorporates biomedical language to neutralise the moral acceptance of concepts such as sanitary citizenship and transform them into a vocabulary of solidarity. María Galindo envisions a future in which societies abandon individualism and eating is celebrated as a communal act: "¿Qué pasa si pasamos del abastecimiento individual a la olla común contagiosa y festiva como tantas veces lo hemos hecho?" (126) [What if we move from individual food provision to the contagious and festive communal pot as we have done so many times before?]. This utopia is defiant, for it uses the adjective "contagious" positively in March 2020, when the pandemic was saturating health systems worldwide.

The desire to participate in a community described with such a terrifying adjective is understandable when we consider that their lives have never been immune to disease outbreaks nor food insecurity. The physical distancing advised by institutions was an inaccessible luxury to people who depended on community life outside their private homes. Galindo builds a utopia rooted in the networks that allow the existence of communal pots that save thousands of people from the daily disaster of poverty and malnutrition.

Utopia does not dismiss the threat generated by Covid-19. When contagion and death are imminent, one can choose either submission or love. Galindo advocates for the latter: "Que la muerte no nos pesque acurrucadas de miedo obedeciendo órdenes idiotas, que nos pesque besándonos, que nos pesque haciendo el amor y no la guerra. Que nos pesque cantando y abrazándonos, porque el contagio es inminente" (127) [May death does not catch us crouching in fear obeying idiotic orders; may it catch us kissing and making love, and not war. May death catch us singing and holding each other because the contagion is imminent]. In the disaster of Covid-19 infections and a government that gives idiotic orders, eroticism and community solidarity provide a glimpse of a radically different way of living. Thus, the poem conceives a metaphorical reality that excludes the common understanding of the pandemic as war.

Chile experienced a unique pandemic. Not long before the quarantines, the country had plunged into a massive revolutionary process. The curfews established by the government were, in fact, mandatory physical distancing restrictions. In the southern nation, two meanings of "disaster" coexisted: social and epidemiological. Solnit explains that a revolution is reminiscent of disaster because social disorder provides a glimpse of new possible orders for the world:

> If a revolution is a disaster—which many who oppose them would heartily endorse—it is so because a disaster is also a utopia of sorts; the two phenomena share aspects of solidarity, uncertainty, possibility, and the upending of the ordinary systems governing things—the rupture of the rules and the opening of many doors (*A Paradise* 160).

The social outburst that shook Chile in October 2019 was a time of utopias. During daily protests in the streets, collectivities emerged capable of imagining a new Chile that would take shape in a constituent assembly.

Kakín Buchui Plaza published the poem "Somos" in April 2021. The search for collective identity amid a social revolution and pandemic begins by acknowledging the lineage of violence in history by stating that Chileans are children of merciless spectacles (Buchui 371). In the final stanzas, identity is constructed through biopolitical language:

No somos bestias antropomorfas
De trompas selladas.
Por muy carnívora que sea la planta
> Debe pasar hambre
> Cuando toman las moscas
> La mierda para organizarse.
Somos, seremos
Y venceremos.
Somos las hogueraspara quemar las impurezas
> Del sistema políticobacterial (Buchui 372).

[We are not anthropomorphised beasts
With gagged trunks.
As carnivorous as the plant may be

    It must starve
    When the flies take to
    The shit to organise.

We are, we will be
And we will win.
We are the bonfires
to burn the impurities

    Of the political-bacterial system]

The plural poetic voice refuses to be considered a beast, but assumes without resistance the identity of a plague. The "we" is identified with flies capable of neutralizing a carnivorous plant. Paradoxically, the poetic subject is also purifying fire. The image of disinfection confronts the current institutions that must be incinerated since they are a source of political-bacterial transmissions. The organisation of the flies and the collective disinfection, therefore, are the two mechanisms that will lead to the announced victory.

In "Asepsia", a text by Gonzalo Robles published in April 2021, the criticism of state neglect is translated into verses that refer to Chilean social and pandemic outbreaks. The poem begins with a description of the privileges of the Minister of Health:

La pulcritud de los muros
de la residencia del ministro
no desentona con su delantal médico.
Las alacenas rebosantes de alientos
hasta el aire que respira es limpio (Robles 254).

[The neatness of the walls
of the Minister's residence
matches his medical apron.
The cupboards overflowing with food
even the air he breathes is clean]

The distance between the state official and the rest of the population is such that one can even breathe clean air in his residence. As suggested in the first verse, the walls and the clothing are immaculate. In contrast, life outside the upper-class neighbourhood is associated with hunger, dirt, and overcrowding:

> Ministro, en los conventillos que usted no ve
> chilenos sufren por el hambre
> huelen a orines y las zonas pudendas
> duelen por el hacinamiento (Robles 255).

> [Minister, in the tenements that you do not see
> Chileans suffer from hunger
> they smell of urine, and their pudendal zones
> hurt from overcrowding]

This stanza is a poetic statement that would work perfectly to describe the Chilean social fabric in both October 2019 and March 2020. The fragment includes scatological images that reinforce the representation of filth but also suggest that in the poor tenements there is a lack of bodily control, which is a failure in the expectations of sanitary citizenship.

The figure of blindness is not fortuitous. In a previous stanza, the Minister was described as someone who causes ocular damage and myopia, which prevents people from seeing beyond their noses (Robles 254). The social revolt of October has, as one of its tragic legacies, more than 400 victims of ocular trauma, produced mainly through weapons fired by police forces. The magnitude of state violence was such that the press already described the police tactics as a public health emergency in November 2019. Various media presented excessive eye injuries as an "epidemic". In this context, Robles' poem suggests that the inability to see inequality is the "origin of the eye damage" that has affected the Chilean population.

The last two stanzas encapsulate the hybrid disaster that Chile experienced in recent years:

> Los ojos de esos que no conoce
> tropiezan con las mismas caras
> día a día hasta la psicosis
> el Covid-19 debilita sus pulmones
> la peste abraza sólo a los márgenes.

> No se trata de alienígenas
> ni de chavistas venezolanos
> los que remecieron conciencias en octubre
> son aromas pestilentes, emergen
> ante su descaro de reconocerlos
> cuando la carne ha sido infectada
> y no se le arruga la piel
> en vociferar al país el sincericidio (Robles 255).

[The eyes of those you do not know
stumble over the same faces
day by day until psychosis
Covid-19 weakens their lungs
the plague clings only to the margins.

It is not about aliens
nor Venezuelan Chavistas
those who shook consciences in October
are pestilent aromas, they emanate
when you refuse to recognise them
when the flesh has been infected
and its skin does not wrinkle
when vociferating the brutal honesty to the country]

The communities on the margins live a daily life that leads to psychosis. The mortality generated by Covid-19 corroborates the continuity of their precarious life: its most severe effects occur in marginal areas. The disconnect between the government and the citizens is such that the poem recalls Chilean First Lady Cecilia Morel who claimed that the October protests resembled an alien invasion. The hyperbole works to dramatically contrast a Minister breathing clean air and a population emanating pestilence. The cleanliness at the poem's beginning collides violently with the infected flesh at the end.

The utopian spirit of the poem pales in the face of the depiction of the suffering and indifference of the state official. However, the poem's end announces a community whose skin does not wrinkle as it speaks out with radical sincerity. It is then that the text offers a new representation of the world. Now, the sick and overcrowded bodies are capable of shaking consciences.

Gabriela Contreras constructs a different kind of pandemic utopia, centred on tenderness and eroticism. The poetic voice of "La enfermedad es una sola", published in late 2020, reworks epidemiological language to speak of gender inequality in Latin America:

Las que portamos el virus de la pobreza
y nuestros olores nos delatan
sabemos de encierros y cuarentenas
mucho antes de esta estética apocalipsis
antes que llegaran
las ficciones televisadas
nuestras vecinas mueren
sus hijos las odian

la enfermedad es una sola
está erguida en los barrios del hambre (Contreras 158).

[We, who carry the virus of poverty,
to whom our smells give us away
we know about confinement and quarantine
long before this aesthetic apocalypse
before the arrival
of televised fictions
our neighbors die
their children hate them
the disease is only one
it is standing in the neighbourhoods of hunger]

A pandemic is a familiar event because vulnerable communities previously knew about narratives of confinement and quarantine: there was already an endemic of poverty and hunger. In the poem, death and hatred fragment society, and, later on, the poetic voice enunciates a pessimistic statement: there is no improvement possible, even less compassion (Contreras 158).

In this context, utopian language does not aspire to eliminate any reference to poverty or sick bodies. On the contrary, the poetic subject conceives a utopian hope through a narrative that builds on frustration and precariousness to celebrate future solidarity and eroticism.

somos expertas
tenemos otras estrategias
para nunca soltarnos la mano
infectadas de rabia (Contreras 159)

[we are experts
we have other strategies
to never let go of our hands
infected with rabies]

Rage, understood as resentment towards those responsible for inequality, was one of the motivations for the demonstrations in Chile. In the poem, anger is a desirable infection that spreads a communal worldview rooted in previous social solidarity.

Towards the end, the poem calls for a utopia in favor of pleasure that disregards the threat of infections. In a context that announces the possibility of dying tomorrow, the poetic voice puts eroticism above prophylactic practices:

si mañana seremos ruinas
si me estoy acabando por latir
quiero deshacerme en tus piernas
vaciar mi aliento en tu pubis
así, cuando nos encuentren
prendan fuego de una vez (Contreras 159).

[if tomorrow we will be ruins
if I am running out of heartbeats
I want to melt in your legs
pour my breath on your pubis
so that when they find us
they set fire already]

The last two lines show that the desire to be in a community is above the imperatives of cleanliness proposed by sanitary citizenship. Erotic love is celebrated even if it means becoming the target of epidemiological-moral disinfection campaigns. Again, as in Galindo's text, fear of future infection does not justify the abandonment of social ties. On the contrary, the pandemic crisis allows us to rework an intimate poetics of solidarity.

The Latin American Poetry of Covid-19

Jesús Sepúlveda synthesises the opportunity of building a utopian hope in the midst of the pandemic disaster and the pursuit of greater social justice. In the poem "Es un río que ha perdido su luz", the first pandemic year is a time that enables a perfect vision of the world (Sepúlveda 15). This privileged perception offered by 2020 is the glimpse of a new world that Solnit described as possible in times of disaster. The poetic voice represents, in addition to the pandemic, the police brutality in the U.S. and Chile that spread like a viral infection.

The poem contains the germ of utopia in the following lines: "insurrección, pandemia, incendio / Trinidad que antecede la nueva dimensión" (Sepúlveda 18) [insurrection, pandemic, fire / Trinity that precedes the new dimension]. The three elements of the trinity are ambiguous: they generate death and destruction. However, a crisis is when we imagine new possibilities as "reality collapses" and "the wronged rise" (Sepúlveda 18). Similarly, the river that had lost its current now recovers its strength and kisses the light (19). The end of the poem makes us relive police brutality in the U.S., but it also lets us see a glance of new possibilities:

No puedo respirar
no puedo
puedo
res
pi
rar (Sepúlveda 19).

[I cannot breathe
I cannot
I can
brea
the]

The poem elaborates on multiple images related to asphyxia and anxiety. But, now, even in a versification that resembles the spasms of coughing, it is possible to breathe again.

The corpus of Covid-19 poetry is still under construction. However, the texts published offer three conclusions. First, the poetry questions and neutralises hegemonic narratives of biomedical concepts such as sanitary citizenship. Poetic subjects know that sanitary citizenship is a difficult requirement to fulfil in Latin America. Therefore, this concept loses value among precarious communities. Moreover, being part of stigmatised communities may be metaphorically desirable because they live in solidarity away from biomedical demands.

Second, utopian hope in times of crisis responds to a social logic opposed to neoliberal individualism. While capitalism focuses on the idea of scarcity to establish imperatives of production and competition, other forms of socioeconomic organisation establish their basis on the principles of generosity (Solnit, *A Paradise* 89). The possibility of imagining a positive future in the pandemic can be read, as Judith Butler proposes, as confidence that the work of social justice movements is achieving victories that will soon spread. This proposal offers a valuable hypothesis for the study of Covid-19 poetry in the Latin American region because it allows us to insert the poetic texts into the broader context of the work of grassroots organizations to promote social justice.

Finally, we must consider that poetry would have circulated faster than other arts during the pandemic, since its material conditions allow it to do so. Requiring no more resources than a notebook or a word processor, the pandemic generated an explosion of anthologies and virtual poetry recitals that quickly began to process global infections metaphorically. Thus, poetry is a crucial archive for understanding, amid the rush and incomprehension of what it meant to live in a pandemic, the anxieties and imaginaries that spread through Latin America.

Bibliography

Briggs, Charles L., and Clara Martini-Briggs. *Stories in the Time of Cholera. Racial Profiling During a Medical Nightmare*. University of California Press, 2003.

Buchui Plaza, Kakín. "Somos". *Una invitación. Un poema. Memoria poética de la pandemia y el estallido social*, edited by Carolina Pezoa and Dante Cajales. Rumbos Editores, 2021, pp. 371–372.

Butler, Judith. "Capitalism Has its Limits". *Verso Books: Blog*, 30 March 2020, https://www.versobooks.com/blogs/4603-capitalism-has-its-limits.

—. "Interview with Judith Butler, Philosopher and Activist". *Peace in Progress*, no. 39, 2021, pp. 2–6.

—. "The World After Coronavirus: The Future of Hope". *Youtube*, uploaded by BU Pardee Center, 24 July 2020, https://youtu.be/6K-rYp4mqsw.

Canelo, Paula. "Igualdad, solidaridad y nueva estatalidad. El futuro después de la pandemia". *El futuro después del COVID-19*. Jefatura de Gabinete de Ministros, 2020, pp. 17–25.

Contreras, Gabriela. "La enfermedad es una sola". *Encerrar y vigilar. Escrituras bajo amenaza*, edited by Alberto Moreno y Ibarra Samuel. Marcianos Editores, 2020, pp. 157–159.

Forster, Ricardo. "Más allá del neoliberalismo. El Estado social el día después". *El futuro después del COVID-19*. Jefatura de Gabinete de Ministros, 2020, pp. 56–63.

Galindo, María. "Desobediencia, por tu culpa voy a sobrevivir". *La sopa de Wuhan. Pensamiento contemporáneo en tiempos de pandemia*, edited by Pablo Amadeo. Aspo, 2020, pp. 119–127.

Homer. *The Illiad*. Trans. Robert Fagles. Penguin Books, 1991.

Neyman, Gregory, and William Dalsey. "Black Lives Matter protests and COVID-19 Cases. Relationship in Two Databases". *Journal of Public Health*, vol. 43, no. 2, 2021, pp. 1–3.

Poniatowska, Elena. "Mi tema no soy yo". Interview. *The San Diego Union-Tribune*, 28 November 2021, https://www.sandiegouniontribune.com/en-espanol/espectaculos/gente/articulo/2021-11-28/elena-poniatowska-mi-tema-no-soy-yo.

Robles, Gonzalo. "Asepsia". *Una invitación. Un poema. Memoria poética de la pandemia y el estallido social*, edited by Carolina Pezoa and Dante Cajales. Rumbos Editores, 2021, pp. 254–255.

Román, Valeria. "limpieza". *Durará este encierro. Escritoras peruanas en cuarentena*, edited by Anahí Barrionuevo, Ana María Vidal and Victoria Guerrero. Cocodrilo ediciones, 2021, pp. 107–111.

Segato, Rita. "Coronavirus: Todos somos mortales. Del significante vacío a la naturaleza abierta de la historia". *El futuro después del COVID-19*. Jefatura de Gabinete de Ministros, 2020, pp. 76–88.

Sepúlveda, Jesús. *Pax Americana*. El Sur es América, 2023.

Solnit, Rebecca. *A Paradise Built in Hell. The Extraordinary Communities That Arise in Disaster*. Viking, 2009.

—. "The Impossible Has Already Happened. What Coronavirus Can Teach Us About Hope". *The Guardian,* 7 April 2020. https://www.theguardian.com/world/2020/apr/07/what-coronavirus-can-teach-us-about-hope-rebecca-solnit.

Sontag, Susan. *Illness as Metaphor & AIDS and Its Metaphors.* Picador, 1989.

Yonofui. "Somos plaga". *(E)laboraciones sociales en tiempos de pandemia. Biopolítica,* edited by Andrea Torrano. Universidad Nacional de Córdoba, 12 April 2020, https://elaboraciones.sociales.unc.edu.ar/somos-plaga-colectivo-yonofui/.

Zurita, Raúl. "Discurso Raúl Zurita". *Premio Reina Sofía de Poesía Iberoamericana,* 31 November 2020, Universidad de Salamanca, https://saladeprensa.usal.es/filessp/Discurso_Ra__l_Zurita.pdf.

Chapter 7

Pasajeras

A Lockdown Anthology as Female Solidarity Across Borders

Katie Brown

University of Exeter

Abstract

Pasajeras: Antología del cautiverio (2020) brings together poems, essays, diary entries, reflections and images created during lockdown by 60 Venezuelan women living across the world. The book was made available for free online and complemented by regular interviews with the contributors shared on Facebook, further growing the sense of community. Building on studies of the political and social power of anthologies, this chapter explores the significance of various aspects of *Pasajeras*: creating an all-female anthology with space for older women in a male-dominated and youth-oriented literary culture; countering the isolation not just of the lockdown, but of Venezuela's ongoing social and economic crisis; and crossing borders between the book and the digital. The analysis will explore the creation and publication process as well as the content of the book, with a focus on what is shared between the 60 contributions.

Keywords: anthologies, women's writing, life writing, Venezuela, digital communities

* * *

Introduction

The spread of Covid-19 across the globe in 2020 and the subsequent lockdowns imposed sparked a trend in anthologies of women's writing documenting the extraordinary circumstances and women's experience thereof. Examples include *Diarios de encierro* [Confinement Diaries], three volumes of accounts from Spanish-speaking women; *Stories from the Inside: Ascolta Women Write COVID-19 Tales 2020*, from an Italian-Australian community; *Keep Walking: Real Covid-19 Lockdown Stories from the Women I Know*, and *Pasajeras*, the subject of this chapter, which unites texts by 60 Venezuelan women within the country and the diaspora. As the editors of these volumes outline in their introductions and blurbs, reading and writing collaboratively provided much needed community in a time of enforced isolation. In this way, narratives do not only offer a reflection of these women's experience of the pandemic; they also shaped *how* they experienced this period. In addition, the all-female nature of these collections responded to distinctly gendered experiences of the pandemic. Lauren McKeon, author of *Women of the Pandemic: Stories from the Frontlines of COVID-19*, starts her blurb with the claim, "The story of the pandemic is the story of women". In public, women were at the forefront of vaccine development and key workers in healthcare, service and education; in the domestic sphere, they assumed the bulk of extra caring responsibilities and experienced an "acumulación de microtraumas" (Tello de la Torre and Vargas Villamiza 390).[1] In her reflection on women's writing in the pandemic, Biviana Unger Parra reminds readers that many women do not enjoy the material conditions that would allow them to write, highlighting that, "la pandemia puso sobre la mesa una situación incómoda a la que no todas habíamos puesto suficiente atención: el cuidado y el trabajo no remunerado sigue siendo una responsabilidad mayoritariamente femenina" (11).[2]

Building on critical studies of anthologies, this chapter explores the significance of various aspects of *Pasajeras* as a case study of an anthology of women's writing in the pandemic. I will discuss the creation and publication process as well as the content of the book, with a focus on what is shared between the 60 contributions. *Pasajeras* is a rich and varied document, presenting more themes than can be covered in one chapter. I will therefore limit the focus firstly to what this all-female anthology tells us about women's creative processes at the outbreak of the pandemic, the wellbeing benefits of reading and writing, and the challenges the pandemic posed for writing, especially for women. Enforced domesticity is a recurring theme in many of the pieces in *Pasajeras*, so I will consider how this relates to the authors' ability to write. As many of the authors were in their sixties or older, I will discuss the intersections of gender and age here. Secondly, I will consider the Venezuelan specificities of the text, particularly how the effects of the pandemic are portrayed as only worsening an already volatile political, social and economic situation. While it is mainly writers still resident in Venezuela who discuss this context, some of the texts also present lockdown as a further isolation for those who have experienced migration or exile as part of the now nearly eight-million strong Venezuelan diaspora. Finally, I will consider *Pasajeras* as a "digital window", presenting both the digital —and completely free— publication of the anthology and its afterlife on websites and social media as a concerted effort to build community against these multiple forms of isolation.

---

[1] "Accumulation of microtraumas".
[2] "The pandemic brought to the table an uncomfortable situation to which not all of us had paid enough attention: care and unpaid work continues to be a mostly female responsibility".

Jeffrey Di Leo highlights that editing an anthology is "grounded in commitments" and "always already implicated in various political and cultural agendas" (2). Lesbia Quintero, who proposed and co-edited *Pasajeras*, is grounded in commitment to Venezuela and to celebrating women's voices. She is the managing editor of Lector Cómplice, a Caracas-based publishing house dedicated to publishing and promoting Venezuelan literature. After publishing *Pasajeras*, she has gone on to lead the project *Hacedoras*, bringing together contributions from 1,000 Venezuelan female creatives, the first volume of which was published in October 2021. This work encapsulates Biviana Ungar Parra's notion of "sisterhood" within women's writing: "La sororidad se presenta como una práctica política, como un quehacer ético que quiere desmontar los hábitos patriarcales que han determinado las relaciones humanas" (14-15).[3] In a male-dominated literary culture, not only sharing and promoting women's voices, but also making clear the barriers that women face to creativity, is a radical act. PEN and UNESCO are currently carrying out research into gender disparities in publishing in Latin America. Though they have not yet reported on Venezuela, they have found that, in the five countries studied to date, around three men are published for every woman (*Women Seizing the Word*). They note, however, that during the Covid-19 pandemic, the use of digital platforms and self-publishing or independent publishing played an important role in recalibrating cultural activities and increasing women's participation in the literary field. Discussing *Pasajeras* on the podcast *Blanco y en botella*, Quintero explained that she wanted the anthology to showcase Venezuelan women's experiences of the pandemic as women are more used to being enclosed than men, and more so in Venezuela during its current crisis ("Episodio: Pasajeras").

The end credits page of *Pasajeras* states that the anthology "se realizó en medio del desconcierto y el miedo de una cuarentena inédita" (Quintero and Bonnet 270).[4] The project began when, at the start of the Covid-19 lockdown in Venezuela, Quintero reflected on "aislamientos literariamente fecundos" (Quintero 7), that is, how previous periods of isolation had been highly productive for writers such as Marcel Proust. She noted, however, that this productivity usually was made possible by unrecognised female labour. Consequently, she became curious as to how other creative women were coping with the pandemic and whether they were still able to write. This curiosity became the seed of the anthology, as well as an excuse to maintain or

---

[3] "Sorority is presented as a political practice, as an ethical task that wants to dismantle the patriarchal habits which have determined human relationships".
[4] "[the anthology] was put together in the midst of the confusion and fear of an unprecedented quarantine".

ignite contact with a creative community of women to counter the isolation of the lockdown. Quintero explains in the introduction to the anthology:

> Esta indagación entre el cautiverio y los procesos de la creación artística, poética, literaria es una forma de convocar lo ausente, la libertad de andar por cualquier calle, hoy desierta y marcada por la muerte que acecha. Es puente y vaso comunicante, manos que destejen distancias para propiciar la cercanía mediante voces y miradas (9).[5]

Editing this collection, then, shaped how Quintero experienced the pandemic, as it provided an antidote to social isolation. Quintero co-edited *Pasajeras* with her frequent collaborator Graciela Bonnet, also working closely with poets Edda Armas and Belkys Arredondo Olivo on the selection of authors. Armas describes the pain of missing hearing other voices during lockdown, recounting that Quintero would counteract this by calling authors to check on the progress of their texts ("Episodio: Pasajeras"). She asserts, however, that this was not about creative control, as writers were given total freedom to submit whatever they wanted. Quintero was interested in what people were feeling and how that conditioned their writing. The project allowed Quintero and her collaborators to reconceive the pandemic and lockdown as a topic for their writing, providing an outlet through which to process the experience as they lived through it.

Rather than sending out an open call, the group invited around 100 women who already had a trajectory of published texts to send in a submission, as they believed these women's texts would need little editing and the anthology could be published quickly. Quintero affirms that "en Venezuela, sobra talento" ("Episodio: Pasajeras"),[6] so they were confident in the quality of texts they would receive. Sixty women responded to the call with texts (others were either committed to other projects already or did not feel capable of writing in the context). The anthology brings together writers of all ages, inside and outside the country, with a notable presence of women in their sixties and seventies. This is significant not only because it counters perceived ageism in publishing, but especially because older people were more "vulnerable to a range of negative health and social outcomes" during Covid-19 (Brooke and Jackson 2044). Brooke and Jackson consider both the "openly ageist discourse" (2044), which emerged from the fact that the risk of mortality increased with age and contributed to feelings of worthlessness among older people, and the effects of

---

[5] "Delving into the [effects of] captivity and the processes of artistic, poetic, and literary creation is a way of summoning the absent, the freedom to walk down any street, today deserted and marked by lurking death. It is a bridge and a communicating vessel, hands that unravel distances to promote closeness through voices and gazes".
[6] "In Venezuela, there is a surplus of talent"

social isolation, such as increased risk of anxiety, depression or even mortality. To counter these effects, they recommended the creation of social networks and creative activities, both of which the *Pasajeras* project provided. We could also speculate that the preponderance of older contributors is a reflection of different experiences of the pandemic. While these women were more likely to have been isolated during the lockdown, women with younger families may have had fewer opportunities to write, as discussed below.

Pasajeras takes its title from Julio Cortázar's 1973 novel, *Libro de Manuel*, which features the phrase "pasajeros de la ausencia".[7] The full phrase —changed to the feminine *pasajeras*— was the working title shared with authors in the call for submissions, evolving over the process to simply *Pasajeras*, taking on a dual meaning as a collective noun for travelling women and adjective for temporary or fleeting. *Pasajeras* was written, edited and published all within the three months of March to May 2020. Almost all of its texts were previously unpublished, which Quintero calls generous, beautiful and important ("Episodio: Pasajeras"). The result is a multi-genre anthology, bringing together poems, prose, diary extracts, letters, and even a collection of Facebook posts. It is divided into two sections, "Visiones" (poetry) and "Narrativas" (everything else). In her study of multi-genre anthologies by communities of women, Cynthia G. Franklin argues that "their crossing of generic boundaries enabled the unfixing of other boundaries as well" (5). In the case of *Pasajeras*, we could think about the boundaries between those in Venezuela and those in the diaspora, and between those affected by Covid-19 in different ways. Franklin adds, "The anthologies' format opens up the definition of what constitutes publishable material as it narrows the gap between public and private, between professional and non-professional writing, and between oral and written expression" (13). The inclusion of diary entries, letters, Facebook posts and scattered thoughts allows for an intimate portrait of life during the pandemic, encourages women to write when they may not have the time or state of mind to craft full texts, and challenges readers' understanding of what is considered literature.

Although a multiplicity of genres and styles is valued as a symbol of an inclusive community, Anne Ferry warns that readers may be put off by the "discontinuousness produced by [an anthology's] many, varied, short entries" (4). It was therefore important for the text to have a unified style, symbolising togetherness in isolation. This was aided by the book's design, featuring watercolour feathers —"plumas viajeras"— by Belkys Arredondo. The 60 pieces also share a depth of feeling, whatever their genre. Arinda Engelke describes the texts as "Melancólica a veces, encendida otras. Repletas de experiencias, de nostalgias, de profundos sentimientos de amor, dolor, miedo, incertidumbre,

---

[7] "Passengers of absence"

tristeza".[8] Each text offers an honest and intimate portrait of life under lockdown. Beyond the separation between poetry and prose, there is no obvious order to the texts: they are not arranged alphabetically by authors or title, nor separated by the age or location of the author. Sharing the pages of the anthology lends the texts new meaning, or "gives a different direction to the experience of reading a [text]" (Ferry 2). Recurring aspects of the texts take on increasing significance with each reappearance, including: images of clouds and trees; paying attention to nature; time not passing; not knowing what day it is; being used to isolation but this being different; lockdown worsening the already difficult situation in Venezuela; and experiencing or fearing a loss of identity.

Women Writing and Reading in the Pandemic

Publicising *Pasajeras*, Graciela Bonnet wrote "convocamos a muchas escritoras venezolanas con la idea de contarnos qué estábamos haciendo, sintiendo y pensando durante esta cuarentena".[9] This use of the first person plural and feminine agreements recurs throughout the anthology. For example, Ana Teresa Torres asserts, "Quiero decir que en este abril de 2020 mirar el futuro exige mucha imaginación, pero si somos escritoras estamos obligadas a tenerla" (92),[10] and Dinapiera di Donato recounts, "Me anima una invitación, como si hubiera un *nosotras*, todavía" (51).[11] This suggests that the contributors are talking, first and foremost, to each other, reinforcing a community of Venezuelan women writers, though a wider readership is of course very welcome. The present tense and use of gerunds again emphasizes that the process of writing was an integral part of how these authors positioned themselves and responded to the pandemic.

Diverse attitudes towards and experiences of writing and reading are represented in the anthology. Firstly, we can see writing as a refuge, or an act of defiance. Ana Teresa Torres refers to the lockdown as "una orden de detención", but affirms that "la orden no incluye detener la creación, no impide seguir pensando y escribiendo" (93).[12] Her text reads like a call to arms (a call to pens) to her fellow writers, urging them to keep writing. Ana María Velázquez, meanwhile, sees writing as coming from an inner strength that cannot be beaten by the pandemic, asserting, "Se refina la expresión creativa, se hace más pura. La creatividad ahora es esencia, desprendida de todo lo que la contaminaba. Nace

---

[8] "Sometimes melancholic, sometimes heated. Full of experiences, nostalgia, deep feelings of love, pain, fear, uncertainty, sadness"
[9] "We brought together many Venezuelan [female] writers with the idea of telling each other what we were doing, feeling and thinking during this quarantine".
[10] "I want to say that in this April 2020, looking into the future requires a lot of imagination, but if we are writers we are obliged to have that".
[11] "An invitation encourages me, as if there were an *us* still".
[12] "A detention order", "the order does not include stopping creation, it does not prevent us from continuing to think and write".

de nuestras fuentes secretas" (63).[13] In her poem "Ábaco negro" (83–89) — written as one or two lines every few days and littered with quotes and references— Jacqueline Goldberg writes:

> Llevo contabilidades de cautiverio.
> Días. Domingos. Almuerzos. Libros.
> Muertos no puedo. No puedo.
> [...] Soy libros.
> Los que he comprado, leído, editado, escrito.
> Los que vendrán (86–87).[14]

Goldberg is one of only two writers in the anthology to use the term "cautiverio", despite it being in the subtitle of the collection. Her captivity is not just being contained in the home, but being subjected to the constant news of Covid-19's effects and the fear and sorrow it causes. Both reading and writing become an escape from this captivity for her.

This refuge in reading is shared by Lena Yau, Mariela Cordero, Geraudí González Olivares and Graciela Yáñez Vicentini, among others. Yau writes, "Me aislé dentro del aislamiento, esculpí un silencio lleno de estímulos, me cerré al intercambio social para poder dialogar con gente que amo en los libros que escriben" (59).[15] In this way, narratives become a way to counter the social isolation of lockdown, to be with people in spirit if not in person. This affective relationship with reading is present in Cordero's desire to "volver a saborear las letras que me expulsan a una morada caliente e inequívoca" (68)[16] and in González Olivares and Yáñez Vicentini's identification with the authors and books they are reading—Eugenio Montejo, Samanta Schweblin and Carlos Fuentes for the former (172–177), *Diary of a Body* by French author Daniel Pennac for the latter (157–162). Yáñez Vicentini confesses that she is struggling to concentrate in general but is reading obsessively, like she did when she was young. She recognises herself in Pennac's story of loss focused on bodies, which gives her a way to process her own feelings of loss —including the loss of contact with friends— during the lockdown.

For others, writing proves important for their psychological wellbeing, in the face of a loss of identity. In "Cuarentena entre ficciones" (26–27), Gladys Ramos

---

[13] "Creative expression is refined, made purer. Creativity is now essence, detached from everything that contaminated it. It is born from our secret sources".
[14] "Black Abacus": "I keep captivity accounts / Days. Sundays. Lunches. Books. / Not the dead. I can't / [...] I am books / Those that I have bought, read, edited, written / Those that will come".
[15] "I isolated myself within isolation, I sculpted a silence full of stimuli, I closed myself off from social exchange to be able to dialogue with people I love in the books they write".
[16] "To savour again the words that push me to a warm and unmistakable home".

writes a description of herself in relation to the pandemic, repeating "soy yo" as if committing it to paper makes her identity more stable. She calls herself:

> La misma que se niega a actuar
> como protagonista y víctima
> de este teatro oscuro en el que
> deambulamos cabizbajos (27).[17]

The same urge to be active, to use writing as a weapon against the pandemic, is present in Belkys Arredondo Olivo's poem "Salambó" with the line "Cuenta algo diferente y te salvarás" (17).[18] Like many of the authors in the collection, Sonia Chocrón struggles to write during the lockdown, but when she does, it feels like a victory: "Los días buenos logro completar una idea. O un verso. Un fragmento de algo. Y entonces siento que lo venzo, al pavor" (55).[19] While so much is out of control during the pandemic, writing allows these women to feel some agency.

Nonetheless, the pandemic presents many obstacles to creativity. For Blanca Elena Pantin, the monotony of lockdown is stifling: "Apenas breves anotaciones, puedo. Una sucesión de imágenes traduce los días que se pasan la posta uno tras otro sin solución de continuidad" (64).[20] In "La atrofia del músculo" by Inés González, it is the writing muscle that has atrophied from lack of use. The pandemic has given her time to write but, as such, has proven to her that she has lost the habit of writing out of fear, fear of what her stories and characters might turn into, and fear that her writing will not find a place for itself. The "free time" that comes from forced lockdown also cannot be used for creativity when one is preoccupied with worries about not being able to do paid work and running out of money, as Dulce María Ramos recounts in "Solitude" (155–156). In this very frank text she states, "Debo confesar que el pánico, el insomnio y la depresión me alejan de la escritura. [...] De ahí que no existan momentos ideales para la escritura y tampoco la utopía del cuarto propio" (156).[21]

Unsurprisingly, Virginia Woolf's "room of one's own" looms large in this collection. Aglaia Berlutti (106–116), notably, describes in detail her first encounter with Woolf aged 11, how this fuelled her writing, and how she asked

---

[17] "Quarantine among fictions", "I am me", "The same person who refuses to act / as protagonist and victim / of this dark theatre in which / we wander with our heads down".
[18] "Tell a different story and you'll save yourself".
[19] "On good days, I manage to complete an idea. Or a verse. A fragment of something. And then I feel that I overcome the dread".
[20] "All I can manage is brief notes. A succession of images translates the days that pass the post one after another without any continuity".
[21] "I must confess that panic, insomnia and depression keep me from writing. [...] Hence, there is no such thing as ideal moments for writing, nor the utopia of a room of one's own".

her bemused parents for her own room for writing (separate from her bedroom) —eventually being gifted a desk of her own. Berlutti is one of several authors in the anthology who reflect on having chosen isolation throughout their lives to focus on their writing, but who now suffer from Covid-19 having taken away this choice, making isolation compulsory.

Throughout the anthology, we see a re-evaluation of the domestic space. Architect Cathy Smith highlights that in the pandemic "the binaries that once distinguished domestic, public and commercial spaces and their attendant subjectivities have been rendered obsolete" (166). When all aspects of life are removed to the domestic sphere, having "a room of one's own" becomes difficult, if not impossible, if one has caring responsibilities. In "En pausa", Silda Cordoliani describes in detail how the pandemic makes writing more difficult for women.

> Muy al contrario de lo que se supone, quizás el tiempo para la creación escasee en estos días, principalmente para las mujeres. Ella tiene familia y personas queridas fuera de las fronteras de su casa, gente por quien se preocupa de manera especial en semejantes circunstancias [...] De seguro es ella quien cuida de que en la casa se cumplan todos los complicados protocolos de higiene recomendados, esos que fácilmente pueden duplicar las tareas domésticas. [...] Ella recurre constantemente a su creatividad, sí, pero solo para hacer menos tedioso y difícil el encierro de los seres que la rodean (99).[22]

Cordoliani makes visible the labour that can go unnoticed within the domestic sphere, challenging the common refrain that lockdown was an opportunity for creative productivity.

Reflecting on the confinement to the domestic space during the pandemic, Cathy Smith notes:

> In cultural and architectural discourses, interior spaces and particularly domestic interiors are often negatively associated with enclosure, containment, and the oppression of women more generally. At the same time, interior spaces may also be sites of resistance and positive

---

[22] "On pause", "Quite contrary to what one might think, the time for creation is scarce these days, especially for women. She has family and loved ones outside the borders of her home, people for whom she cares in a particular way in such circumstances [...] Surely it is she who makes sure that all the complicated recommended hygiene protocols are followed in the house, which can easily double the housework. [...] She constantly resorts to her creativity, yes, but only to make the confinement of the beings that surround her less tedious and difficult".

identification for women and families if they can be made and occupied in ways that challenge the 'normative structurations of space' (171).

Both sides are present in *Pasajeras*. In her "Arrebato" (35)[23], Liliana Fasciani imagines the violent destruction of everything in the house and the surrounding area, before floating on a cloud and shouting at God. She is embarrassed by her desired outburst, as women are conditioned to accept confinement to the domestic and to not cause a scene. By contrast, in "La casa: lugar de la escritura" (81), which is illustrated with a photo of a living room with a hammock and traditional artefacts on wall, Marisol Marrero demonstrates positive identification with the domestic space. Using terms which symbolise care and comfort, she states, "En este confinamiento al que hemos estado sometidas la casa se ha convertido en nido, caparazón, refugio, madre, lugar de sueños, recuerdos y evocaciones" (81).[24] Taking root in the house and its memories provide inspiration for her writing.

As encapsulated in "Dos casas" by Olivia Villoria Quijada (31–34), many women are caught between the inspiration and the obligations of the home:

> Una casa luminosa habita en mí.
> Es la casa alucinante de la poesía,
> la casa inspiradora de la fecundidad.
> [...]
> Mientras, mi alma femenina
> no se cansa de pronunciar el verbo cuidar.
> Yo me cuido. Yo te cuido.
> Cuídate tú. Cuida de mí (33–34).[25]

The Pandemic in Venezuela

As well as the isolation, fear, difficulty concentrating and weight of domestic and caring responsibilities that will be recognisable to readers across the world, *Pasajeras* reveals the distinct experience of the pandemic in Venezuela. A recurring theme in the collection is that the pandemic did not present a sudden

---

[23] "Outburst".
[24] "The house: a place of writing", "In this confinement to which we have been subjected, the house has become a nest, a shell, a refuge, a mother, a place of dreams, memories and evocations".
[25] "Two houses", "A bright house dwells within me. / It is the hallucinating house of poetry, / the inspiring house of fertility. / Meanwhile, my female soul / never tires of saying the verb care. / I take care of myself. I take care of you. / Take care yourself. Take care of me"

Pasajeras 145

change, rather a worsening of an already difficult situation. Aglaia Berlutti, for example, claims:

> Por veinte años, […] pasamos a ser una población traumatizada y pesimista que siempre espera lo peor. De modo que la gran crisis mundial, es otra de las tantas. Una de las tantas formas que toma el caos en nuestras vidas (110–111).[26]

In March 2020, President Nicolás Maduro was entering his eighth year in office, despite the leader of the National Assembly, Juan Guaidó, declaring himself interim president and being recognised by almost 60 countries over a year earlier. Hyperinflation was rife, though easing somewhat having hit 500,000% in 2019 and over 900,000% in 2018 (according to the IMF; the figures put out by the National Assembly were even higher). Food, medicine, and even oil — Venezuela's national resource— were scarce. All of this is present in María Luisa Lázzaro's "Desterrada cuerpo" (124–126), an account of scarcity, fear, mistrust and isolation, where "la miseria humana se puede estudiar psicológicamente mientras se esperan tres o cuatro días para surtir el vehículo" (125).[27] The emotive lexical field of Cinzia Procopio's "Resistenica en días eternos" (128–133) —"resignación", "obligariedad", "oscuridad", "ansiedad", "fragilidad"— stems as much from the Venezuelan crisis as the pandemic.[28] In Carmen Rosa Orozco's surreal story "Cautiverio", Covid-19 is one of many causes of death:

> En un país donde la cuarentena es la extensión de la muerte y el hambre, y las arenas más livianas invaden las casas de fantasmas ya idos; me miro al espejo como quien busca una sombra y le pregunto a ese espejo que me mira: —¿Estoy viva o estoy muerta? (75).[29]

Orozco's story powerfully evokes the loss of identity and sense of reality that results from living in prolonged crisis. Other texts highlight the separation from the rest of the world in terms of how Covid-19 is experienced. Krina Ber, for example, writes:

---

[26] "Over twenty years, […] we have become a traumatized and pessimistic population that always expects the worst. In this way, the great global crisis is another of many. One of the many forms that chaos takes in our lives".
[27] "Uprooted body", "Human misery can be studied psychologically while waiting three or four days to fuel your car".
[28] "Resistance in eternal days", "resignation", "compulsion", "darkness", "anxiety", "fragility"
[29] "In a country where quarantine is the extension of death and hunger, and the lightest sands invade the homes of ghosts who have already gone; I look in the mirror like someone looking for a shadow and I ask the reflection who looks at me: - Am I alive or am I dead?"

> Tengo la sensación de que las ciudades del mundo libre se han estrellado desde la altura de unos diez o quince pisos sobre el duro pavimento de la cuarentena, pero aquí, en Caracas, el impacto no se ha sentido tanto porque estamos acostumbrados a vivir en caída (187).[30]

Similarly, Silda Cordoliani notes the privilege of those who have only discovered privation through the pandemic:

> Son muchos los que consideran una gran revelación de esta pandemia, o al menos un gran aprendizaje, el haber descubierto que se puede vivir con menos. Eso me hace sonreír. Sin duda es gente que jamás ha vivido una guerra o ha sido víctima de un cataclismo natural. Sin duda no son venezolanos (100).[31]

The prevalence of older contributors is significant here again, as this demographic has been one of the worst affected by the crisis in Venezuela, as has been widely reported (see Taladrid, for example). The informal dollarization of the country has made pensions and savings in bolivares worth even less, and many pensioners are now facing malnutrition. They are also increasingly likely to experience isolation, as younger generations leave the country in search of work abroad.

The conditions in Venezuela have sparked a mass exodus, particularly since 2017. Venezuela's migrant population is now one of the biggest in the world, approaching eight million people, over one fifth of the population, having left the country. Migration presents a different form of isolation, as migrants often leave family, friends and support networks behind. In her submission, Erika Reginato, for example, suggests the isolation of the pandemic is not new for migrants, who "se acostumbran al silencio" (79).[32] The combination of pandemic and socio-economic crisis in Venezuela still reaches those who have left loved ones in the country. In her frank and moving text "Dos cuarentenas", Gisela Kozak Rovero describes her mother's passing during —though not because of— the pandemic in Venezuela while Kozak was living in Mexico. Her text presents the breakdown of public services in Venezuela, only worsened by Covid-19, and the struggles to help her mother access healthcare from abroad: "Con una

---

[30] "I have the feeling that the cities of the free world have crashed from the height of about ten or fifteen storeys onto the hard pavement of the quarantine, but here, in Caracas, the impact has not been felt as much because we are used to living in freefall"
[31] "There are many who consider it a great revelation of this pandemic, or at least a great lesson, to have discovered that you can live with less. That makes me smile. Without a doubt, they are people who have never lived through a war or been the victim of a natural disaster. They are certainly not Venezuelans".
[32] "get used to silence".

mezcla de ira y tristeza constaté, una vez más, el envilecimiento de la existencia en mi país, la impotencia apenas enfrentable con dólares y privilegios" (169).[33] Kozak's text is a scathing attack on the 'Bolivarian Revolution', in which, she affirms, "se ha producido un aislamiento vivamente buscado con fines de control".[34] Kozak refuses victimisation, instead reaffirming the importance of mutual support, stating, "en esto momento aislarse [...] no significa quebrar los lazos sino hacerlos más fuerte".[35] She embraces the different possibilities for connection offered by digital platforms, including a WhatsApp group set up to mourn her mother.

Virtual Windows

Throughout *Pasajeras*, windows are celebrated as an escape from isolation within the home. Many of the texts are accompanied by photographs looking through windows, often at trees. In her contribution, Ana Teresa Torres states "las que escribimos venimos de esa herencia, de las que miran por la ventana" (92),[36] and gives examples of books by women involving looking out of the window. Moreover, Inés Muñoz Aguirre's text is an ode to windows:

> En este confinamiento cada ventana es un tesoro, es el regalo de la luz, del aire, del paisaje por el que no transitas. De la luna colgada en una esquina del cielo o el sol brillante que lo vence todo. La ventana es el hilo de mi conexión con el universo (143).[37]

The windows that Muñoz Aguirre celebrates are not just physical, but also virtual windows, the access to world news and to communities afforded by the internet. Reflecting on online book launches and reading groups during the pandemic, Biviana Unger Parra claims, "Habíamos conquistado un nuevo espacio, una habitación propia llena de ventanas virtuales" (14).[38]

---

[33] "With a mixture of anger and sadness, I confirmed, once again, the debasement of existence in my country, the impotence that can just about be faced with dollars and privileges".
[34] "an isolation has been produced which [the government] eagerly sought for the purpose of control".
[35] "At this moment, isolating [...] does not mean breaking ties, but rather making them stronger".
[36] "Those of us who write come from that heritage, from those who look through the window".
[37] "In this confinement each window is a treasure, it is the gift of light, of air, of the landscape through which you do not travel. From the moon hanging in a corner of the sky or the bright sun that conquers everything. The window is the thread of my connection with the universe".
[38] "We had conquered a new space, a room of own room, full of virtual windows".

The anthology itself is a digital window, giving a view into the intimacy of these 60 women. In a Facebook post advertising the anthology, Quintero describes the texts as "Ventanales líricos, narrativos y visuales" (Editorial Lector Cómplice, "Pasajeras es un aleph"), [39] echoing Paul Auster's claim that an anthology is "a threshold opening on to a new space" (Di Leo 2). Auster's comment refutes the common conception of an anthology as the creation of a cannon, viewing an anthology instead as an invitation to readers to get to know writing from a certain context with the understanding that there is always more to explore. *Pasajeras* does not claim to be a cannon or definitive selection of Venezuelan women writers. Rather, it offers a glimpse into 60 lived experiences of the pandemic and the diverse writing styles of a range of women. For readers, this offers the potential discovery of writers who may enter their "personal cannon", as reader Humberto Fermín Bueno noted in his letter to Quintero, shared on the Lector cómplice website (Editorial Lector Cómplice, "Correo para pasajeras"), as well as a sense of shared intimacy with already familiar writers. Fermín Bueno enthuses that "Un libro gratuito con lo mejor de la narrativa y la poesía venezolana es un milagro, sobre todo para los lectores que aún vivimos en un rincón olvidado del país donde estamos ayunos de novedades".[40] In Venezuela, print publishing is monopolised by the state, which runs three publishing houses, a national printing press and a distribution network, all subsidised by oil income (Brown). Printing and distributing books outside the state system can be difficult and costly, and many independent bookshops have closed down in the last decade. For the editors, then, it was of the utmost importance that the book be published digitally, in a free and easily available format. Graciela Bonnet outlines in her blog post about *Pasajeras*:

> La idea me pareció estupenda, pero sobre todo el hecho de que fuera virtual y de libre acceso a todo el mundo. Es decir, todo el que tenga una conexión a Internet y lea en español puede acceder a su lectura. El libro no tiene costo alguno y se puso especial énfasis en que no hubiera ninguna dificultad para descargarlo y leerlo. [...] Cuanto más se haga, mejor será para todos y más lo agradeceremos.[41]

---

[39] "Lyrical, narrative and visual windows".
[40] "A free book with the best of Venezuelan narrative and poetry is a miracle, especially for readers who still live in a forgotten corner of the country where we are starved of new works".
[41] "I thought the idea was great, but above all the fact that it was virtual and freely accessible to everyone. That is, everyone who has an Internet connection and reads in Spanish can read it. The book is free of charge and special emphasis was placed on making it easy to download and read. [...] The more that is done, the better it will be for everyone and the more we will appreciate it".

This insistence on reaching readers, wherever they may be, reinforces the idea that the aim of the book was to build a community of writers and readers, countering the isolation of both the pandemic and Venezuela's crisis. To aid this aim further, the credits page notes that all of the contents of the anthology can be reproduced in other media, as long as credit is given to the author and the anthology. Consequently, extracts appeared in publications including *El Universal, Letralia, Revista Muu,* and *Comunicación continua,* as well as on contributors' personal websites.

Moreover, following the publication of the anthology, Quintero regularly posted to Facebook interviews with the contributors about their experience of participating in the anthology and their creative processes during Covid, tagging all of the contributors and other interested readers (including me). This was a concerted effort to build community beyond the pages of the anthology, encouraging contributors and readers to follow each other and keep each other company during the pandemic. Many contributors have noted just how valuable this community building was for them. For example, Yurimia Boscán posted the following comment on the "Correo para pasajeras" post:

> Lo más hermoso de ser una pasajera en este libro ha sido la grata e inmensa compañía de quienes han escrito en sus páginas o sobre ellas... la travesía por ese mar de palabras ha diluido un tantico los sinsabores de este tiempo donde las respuestas y las preguntas son olas que revientan en nuestras orillas.[42]

On the "Blanco y en botella" podcast, Edda Armas described getting to know other authors through the project and feeling "en presencia de algo vivo",[43] while Belkys Arredondo affirmed that "Me sentí unidos desde algún punto con todos los escritores que en cuarenta movimos nuestros lapices", adding, "Una forma de salvarnos es crear" ("Episodio: Pasajeras").[44] It is therefore clear that writing as part of this collaborative project shaped these women's experience and perceptions of the pandemic.

---

[42] "The most beautiful thing about being a passenger in this book has been the pleasant and immense company of those who have written in or about its pages... the journey through that sea of words has somewhat diluted the troubles of this time where the answers and questions are waves that break on our shores...".
[43] "In the presence of a living thing".
[44] "I felt united from some point with all the writers who moved their pencils during the quarantine", "One way to save ourselves is to create".

Conclusion

While anthologies can be seen as exclusionary and cannon-forming, multi-genre anthologies such as those written by groups of women during the Covid-19 lockdowns can be valuable "places to find or create homes or communities" (Franklin 9). *Pasajeras* creates a community of Venezuelan women united by their vocation for writing —complicated during the pandemic by fear, money worries, caring commitments, and isolation, yet presented by many as an integral part of their identities and vital for their mental wellbeing. These women share with other women around the world many of their reactions to Covid-19, yet are unique in how the experience of political, social and economic crisis and mass migration in Venezuela colours their experience of the pandemic and lockdown. Community building was at the heart of the project, from its conception to its afterlife online, particularly in the insistence on free and wide online distribution of the text. For readers outside of this community (not women and/or not Venezuelan), the anthology still invites us to feel close to these 60 authors through the intimate, frank and sometimes very moving texts they share, as an antidote to isolation.

Bibliography

Arredondo Olivo, Belkys. "Nadie quiere a los heridos". *Pasajeras: Antología del cautiverio*, edited by Lesbia Quintero and Graciela Bonnet, Lector Cómplice, 2020, pp. 17–18.

Ber, Krina. "Mis posts en Facebook, marzo y abril 2020". *Antología del cautiverio*, edited by Lesbia Quintero and Graciela Bonnet, Lector Cómplice, 2020, pp. 185–189.

Berlutti, Aglaia. "Un castillo de la memoria en medio del silencio". *Pasajeras: Antología del cautiverio*, edited by Lesbia Quintero and Graciela Bonnet, Lector Cómplice, 2020, pp. 106–117.

Bonnet, Graciela. "Pasajeras, una antología desde el cautiverio: Un libro para descargar libremente". *Grupo Li Po*, 12 June 2020, http://grupolipo.blogspot.com/2020/06/pasajeras-una-antologia-desde-el.html?m=1.

Brooke, Joanne, and Deborah Jackson. "Older people and COVID-19: Isolation, risk and ageism". *Journal of Clinical Nursing*, vol. 29, 2022, pp. 2044–204

Brown, Katie. "'There Can Be No Revolution without Culture': Reading and Writing in the Bolivarian Revolution". *Bulletin of Latin American Research*, vol. 38, no. 4, 2019, pp. 438–452.

Callipari, Fortunata, et al., editors. *Stories from the Inside: Ascolta Women Write COVID-19 Tales 2020*. Ascolta Women, 2021.

Chocrón, Sonia. "Intermezzo". *Pasajeras: Antología del cautiverio*, edited by Lesbia Quintero and Graciela Bonnet, Lector Cómplice, 2020, pp. 53–55.

Cordero, Mariela. "Días extraños". *Pasajeras: Antología del cautiverio*, edited by Lesbia Quintero and Graciela Bonnet, Lector Cómplice, 2020, pp. 67–68.

Cordoliani, Silda. "En pausa". *Pasajeras: Antología del cautiverio*, edited by Lesbia Quintero and Graciela Bonnet, Lector Cómplice, 2020, pp. 98–101.

D'Ambrosia, Linda. "Pasajeras". *El Universal*, 8 June 2020, https://www.eluniversal.com/el-universal/72449/pasajeras.

Di Donato, Dinapiera. "Espero que te encuentres bien". *Pasajeras: Antología del cautiverio*, edited by Lesbia Quintero and Graciela Bonnet, Lector Cómplice, 2020, pp. 49–53.

Di Leo, Jeffrey R. *On Anthologies: Politics and Pedagogy*. University of Nebraska Press, 2004.

Editorial Lector Cómplice. "Pasajeras es un aleph hecho por 60 miradas femeninas…" *Facebook*, 2 June 2020, https://www.facebook.com/452553068429714/posts/pfbid02LfMhy969hhx1SEwymbFkRxGsVpYCesx9BzDXweQ2DNHyiKUzZRrHKz2xYDjuQUB8l/?app=fbl

—. "Correo para pasajeras". 26 June 2020, http://lectorcomplice.blogspot.com/2020/06/correo-para-pasajeras.html?m=1

Engelke, Arinda. "'Pasajeras': Antología del cuativero". *Comunicación Continua*, 8 June 2020, https://comunicacioncontinua.com/pasajeras-antologia-del-cautiverio/.

"Episodio: Pasajeras". *Blanco y en botella, porque la vida es la leche*, hosted by Silmar Jimenez, podcast ed., *PL Radio*, 21 June 2020, https://www.ivoox.com/en/podcast-porque-vida-es-leche-pasajeras-audios-mp3_rf_52266330_amp_1.html.

Fasciani, Liliana. "Arrebato". *Pasajeras: Antología del cautiverio*, edited by Lesbia Quintero and Graciela Bonnet, Lector Cómplice, 2020, pp. 34–35.

Ferry, Anne. *Tradition and the Individual Poem: An Inquiry into Anthologies*. Stanford University Press, 2001.

Franklin, Cynthia G. *Writing Women's Communities: The Politics and Poetics of Contemporary Multi-Genre Anthologies*. The University of Wisconsin Press, 1997.

González Olivares, Geraudí. "Pasajera y ausente en tiempos de pandemia". *Pasajeras: Antología del cautiverio*, edited by Lesbia Quintero and Graciela Bonnet, Lector Cómplice, 2020, pp. 171–177.

González, Inés. "La atrofia del músculo". *Pasajeras: Antología del cautiverio*, edited by Lesbia Quintero and Graciela Bonnet, Lector Cómplice, 2020, pp. 177–178.

Goldberg, Jacqueline. "Ábaco negro". *Pasajeras: Antología del cautiverio*, edited by Lesbia Quintero and Graciela Bonnet, Lector Cómplice, 2020, pp. 83–90.

Hernández, Marina, and Carla Santángelo. *Diarios de encierro*. Indigo Editoras, 2020.

Kozak Rovero, Gisela. "Dos cuarentenas". *Pasajeras: Antología del cautiverio*, edited by Lesbia Quintero and Graciela Bonnet, Lector Cómplice, 2020, pp. 168–171.

Lázzaro, María Luisa. "Desterrada cuerpo". *Pasajeras: Antología del cautiverio*, edited by Lesbia Quintero and Graciela Bonnet, Lector Cómplice, 2020, pp. 123–126.

Letralia. "La antología Pasajeras reúne a 60 autoras en torno al tema de la cuarentena". 2 June 2020, https://letralia.com/noticias/2020/06/02/pasajeras-antologia-del-cautiverio/.

Liverpool, Judith, et al. *Keep Walking: Real Covid 19 Lockdown Stories from the Women I Know*. Lulu.com, 2022.

Marrero, Marisol. "La casa: lugar de la escritura". *Pasajeras: Antología del cautiverio*, edited by Lesbia Quintero and Graciela Bonnet, Lector Cómplice, 2020, pp. 80–83.

McKeon, Lauren. *Women of the Pandemic: Stories from the Frontlines of COVID-19*. McClelland and Stewart, 2021.

Muñoz Aguirre, Inés. "Diario de a bordo". *Pasajeras: Antología del cautiverio*, edited by Lesbia Quintero and Graciela Bonnet, Lector Cómplice, 2020, pp. 140–149.

Orozco, Carmen Rosa. "Cautiverio". *Pasajeras: Antología del cautiverio*, edited by Lesbia Quintero and Graciela Bonnet, Lector Cómplice, 2020, pp. 74–77.

Pantin, Blanca Elena. "Días de pandemia, el aire apenas". *Pasajeras: Antología del cautiverio*, edited by Lesbia Quintero and Graciela Bonnet, Lector Cómplice, 2020, pp.63-65.

PEN International. *Women Seizing the Word*. 2023, https://www.pen-international.org/research/women-seizing-the-word.

Procopio, Cinzia. "Resistencia en días eternos". *Pasajeras: Antología del cautiverio*, edited by Lesbia Quintero and Graciela Bonnet, Lector Cómplice, 2020, pp. 127–133.

Quintero, Lesbia, and Graciela Bonnet, editors. *Pasajeras: Antología del cautiverio*. Lector Cómplice, 2020.

Quintero, Lesbia. "Punto de partida". *Pasajeras: Antología del cautiverio*, edited by Lesbia Quintero and Graciela Bonnet, Lector Cómplice, 2020, pp. 6–9.

Quijada, Olivia Villoria. "Dos casas". *Pasajeras: Antología del cautiverio*, edited by Lesbia Quintero and Graciela Bonnet, Lector Cómplice, 2020, pp. 30-34.

Ramos, Dulce María. "Solitude". *Pasajeras: Antología del cautiverio*, edited by Lesbia Quintero and Graciela Bonnet, Lector Cómplice, 2020, pp. 154–156.

Ramos, Gladys. "Cuarentena entre ficciones". *Pasajeras: Antología del cautiverio*, edited by Lesbia Quintero and Graciela Bonnet, Lector Cómplice, 2020, pp. 26–28.

Reginato, Erika. "Hay que renacer del silencio". *Pasajeras: Antología del cautiverio*, edited by Lesbia Quintero and Graciela Bonnet, Lector Cómplice, 2020, pp. 77–79.

Revista Muu. "Pasajeras. Antología de cautiverio". 14 April 2021, https://revistamuu.com/2021/04/14/pasajeras-antologia-del-cautiverio/

Smith, Cathy. "A Screen of One's Own: The Domestic Caregiver as Researcher During Covid-19, and Beyond". *Australian Feminist Studies*, vol. 36, no. 108, 2021, pp. 165–179.

Taladrid, Stephania. "Aging and Abandoned in Venezuela's Failing State". *The New Yorker*, 12 April 2022, https://www.newyorker.com/culture/photo-booth/aging-and-abandoned-in-venezuelas-failing-state.

Tello de la Torre, Claudia, and Óscar Hernán Vargas Villamizar. "Género y trabajo en tiempos del Covid-19: una mirada desde la interseccionalidad". *Revista Venezolana de Gerencia*, vol. 25, no. 90, 2020, pp. 398–393.

Torres, Ana Teresa. "A través de la ventana". *Pasajeras: Antología del cautiverio*, edited by Lesbia Quintero and Graciela Bonnet, Lector Cómplice, 2020, pp. 91–93.

Unger Parra, Biviana. "Lecturas y escrituras feministas: Alianzas y sororidad en tiempos de Covid". *AnDanzas: Revista de teleología feminista*, vol. 1, no. 1, 2021, pp. 9–16.

Velázquez, Ana María. "El rezo de las salamandras". *Pasajeras: Antología del cautiverio*, edited by Lesbia Quintero and Graciela Bonnet, Lector Cómplice, 2020, pp. 61–63.

Woolf, Virginia. *A Room of One's Own*. Penguin Classics, 1st ed., 2002.

Yáñez Vicentini, Graciela. "Diario de un confinamiento". *Pasajeras: Antología del cautiverio*, edited by Lesbia Quintero and Graciela Bonnet, Lector Cómplice, 2020, pp. 156–162.

Yau, Lena. "Agua que vas". *Pasajeras: Antología del cautiverio*, edited by Lesbia Quintero and Graciela Bonnet, Lector Cómplice, 2020, pp. 55–61.

Chapter 8

Nothing is Normal, Everything is Normal

Disruption and Continuity in Guayaquil's Pandemic Experience

Andrea Espinoza Carvajal

University of Exeter

Luis Medina Cordova

University of Birmingham

Abstract

This chapter offers a critical reflection on the meanings of the "new normal" in Ecuador. Our analysis focuses on the first months of 2020 as they transpired in Guayaquil, the Andean country's economic capital. The experience of Guayaquil offers a compelling opportunity to address some of the issues raised by the discourses of normality in a time of crisis. We explore how the pandemic caused an unprecedented disruption in the imaginary configurations of everyday life in Ecuador while, at the same time, it facilitated the continuity of patterns of gender-based violence normalised in Ecuadorian society. In this light, we argue that the pandemic shaped a context where what was "new" and what was "normal" coexisted and clashed simultaneously to articulate a paradoxical order that was disruptive and continuous at once.

Keywords: Ecuador, Covid-19, gender, narration

* * *

Introduction

Ecuador announced its first case of Covid-19 on 29 February 2020 and its first fatality barely two weeks later ("Ministra de Salud confirma"). By the end of March 2020, 70% of the 2302 confirmed cases were identified in the Guayas province, whose capital and most populated area is Guayaquil, a port city with 2.7 million inhabitants that soon became the epicentre of the pandemic in the Andean country (COE, "Informe de situación" 7). The high number of confirmed cases, which nearly tripled by mid-April, resulted in a notorious increase in excess mortality in the province. Local media reported that, under normal circumstances, Guayas averages 2000 deaths per month, but it documented

6703 deaths in the first half of April alone ("En los primeros 15 días"). The unprecedented demand quickly surpassed the capacity of Guayaquil's health and mortuary services, and the city became an early sign of the havoc the pandemic would cause in Latin America.

In March and April 2020, photos and videos of cardboard coffins and corpses abandoned on the streets and sidewalks of Guayaquil became a common sight that circulated globally via social media. International news outlets reported the story with the connotations of an extraordinary occurrence unseen elsewhere. The BBC referred to a "coronavirus nightmare" in the city, while The Guardian compared the "virus-ravaged" area with a warzone where "there were dead in the streets, dead in homes, there were dead outside the hospitals" (Collyns). A year later, The New Yorker summarised the events by noting that "the whole city had become a cemetery, a spectacle for all the world to see" (Alarcón).

The necro-spectacle of Guayaquil in the early months of the pandemic made headlines suggesting significant disruptions of everyday life in the city. Yet for as much disruption, Guayaquil also experienced the continuation of types of violence common long before Covid-19. During the pandemic, quality healthcare proved to be inaccessible for large segments of the population. At the same time, the measures to curb the spread of the virus exposed victims of gender-based violence to mandatory confinement with their aggressors. The conditions created by the pandemic were new, but the violence it enabled to continue was not. In this light, what was "new" and what was "normal" coexisted and clashed to articulate a paradoxical order that was disruptive and continuous at once: the so-called "new normal", a term that became familiar not only in Ecuador but across the world.

This chapter interrogates the meanings, disconnections and overlaps between discourses of normal and new normal in Ecuador. By focusing on the case of Guayaquil, we discuss how the Covid-19 crisis caused an unprecedented disruption in the imaginary configurations of everyday life in Ecuador while, at the same time, it facilitated the continuity of patterns of structural and gender-based violence normalised in Ecuadorian society. Our purpose is to examine and contrast official and non-official narratives during the pandemic to argue that, while the Ecuadorian government insisted on the need for the population to adapt to the so-called new normal living conditions, alternative discourses reminded us of pre-existent structural vulnerabilities in Guayaquil that made violence anything but new.

Our analysis juxtaposes an example of literary production that questions normality during the health emergency, the poem "¿Es normal?"[1] by the visual artist Diana Gardeneira (Guayaquil 1981), with statements issued by the

---

[1] "Is it normal?". All translations of quotes in this chapter are ours.

Ecuadorian government regarding the new normal. As diverse as they are, we read these sources as texts that offer different perspectives on the narration of the pandemic in Guayaquil during the first months of 2020. By focusing on forms of violence disruptive and continuous at once, our reading highlights the ambiguities raised by the new normal in Ecuador while providing an alternative insight into the narration of the Covid-19 outbreak in Ecuador. We propose to reflect on the crisis not as statistical representations —something the Ecuadorian government pursued by repeatedly announcing the daily number of cases, hospitalisations and deaths— but, above all, as lived experience.

This chapter first overviews the ways in which the Ecuadorian government referred to the new normal at the onset of the outbreak. We outline how the official narrative delimited the new normal as explicitly related to the measures introduced to stop the spread of the virus. The following subheading examines Gardeneira's poem to problematise the official discourse on the new normal. We look at how "¿Es normal?" allows us to question the pandemic's impact on the understanding of normality beyond the changes precipitated by the procedures to reduce the virus transmission. Lastly, we conclude that the contrasting narratives analysed here signal that the pandemic exceeded a threshold of normalised violence in Ecuador to become deserving of a new designation.

The New Normal, Officially

The global spread of Covid-19 brought change into far more than healthcare. Social, cultural, economic and educational practices were also forced to adapt to self-isolation, social distancing, face covering and similar measures introduced worldwide since the World Health Organisation declared the outbreak a public health emergency of international concern in January 2020 and a pandemic barely two months after. Narratives about the new normal quickly emerged to describe how different facets of life were to be organised during —and likely after— the time of SARS-CoV-2. The rhetoric about settling into life in the new normal became commonplace in media outlets, politicians, scientific publications, NGOs and policy reports, among others. Reading, hearing and talking about the new normal ways of working, communicating, meeting friends and family, teaching and learning became pervasively normal.

Following the devastating first wave of the pandemic and early lockdowns, Ecuador announced its entry into the new normal on 4 May 2020. The government aimed to reactivate economic life, transitioning from isolation to self-distancing while acknowledging that daily life would be different from pre-pandemic times ("Gobierno anuncia"). The Comité de Operaciones de Emergencia Nacional[2], the governmental institution coordinating the country's responses to

---

[2] National Emergency Operations Committee.

Covid-19, referred to transitioning into the new normal as a process in which people became aware and accepted that regular activities needed to be different to those they knew (COE, "Distanciamiento" 4). Their definition alluded to integrating and coming to terms with behaviours that, in the first months of 2020, were new to most people in the country. Not only using face coverings regularly, limiting human contact and maintaining distance from others, but also navigating a colour-coded Ecuador divided into green, yellow and red areas depending on the risk of contagion present in each.

The new normal conditions in Ecuador seem to entail a change of social paradigms that all people had to acknowledge. The virus had made life different, and everybody was to understand it and behave accordingly. Nevertheless, the official narrative limited the differences to specific behaviours people had to follow. In a press briefing where she explained what the new normal meant, María Paula Romo, a senior minister in the Ecuadorian government, argued that the most significant changes to most Ecuadorians' daily life were using face coverings and keeping a minimum distance of 1.5 meters from each other on the streets, in the workplace and stores (Cañizares). Compliance with these measures in Guayaquil was monitored by municipal authorities, who often stopped people in public places to demand the use of face coverings and shut down businesses for failing to ensure customers complied with social distancing rules ("Ante irrespeto"). In this sense, the new normal was explained —and enforced— as directly connected to personal actions and responsibilities in the collective effort to stop the virus from spreading.

The government's definition of the new normal, however, fell short of explaining the full extent of what it entailed. Noting that there was more to the new normal than social distancing and face coverings, Francisco Hidalgo argues that, in the name of responding to the crisis, the Ecuadorian government pursued neoliberal economic and political measures they had not been able to implement in the past, including the expansion of labour flexibility, the dismissal of employees from both public and private companies and the downsizing of the state through privatisation (147). Moreover, limiting the new normal to sanitary measures also ignores the contradictions the term raises. For example, the argument that with the economic unevenness of global capitalism alongside racism, nationalism and the climate crisis already provoking thousands of deaths every year, the world order before Covid-19 was already lethal and, thus, far from anything we could consider "normal" (Gabriel). In this light, as the Ecuadorian government insisted on the need for the population to accept and adapt to the new normal living conditions, alternative sources emerged to question what was normal and what was new in the pandemic context.

Disruption and Continuity

Diana Gardeneira's poem "¿Es normal?" exposes the ambivalence surrounding the new normal discourses in Ecuador. The text —a free verse composition conveying rich visual imagery of how the daily routines of Guayaquil juxtaposed with the unprecedented scenarios created by the spread of the virus— appeared in the 2020 dossier *Ciudad y Pandemia*[3] published by the University of the Arts of Guayaquil, which gathered a selection of essays, first-person accounts, illustrations and photos by local creators giving testimony to the strong response of the city's cultural production to the pandemic. By intertwining references to everyday life in Guayaquil with the extraordinary circumstances the city's inhabitants experienced during the pandemic, Gardeneira blurs the line between the normal and the new. In doing so, her work counters the official narrative to reveal the new normal as far more than self-distancing and face coverings —"¿Es normal?" therefore lays bare the new normal as a regime of disruption and continuity.

The text starts with references to sadness, fear and uncertainty: "Es normal sentirme triste / Es normal sentir miedo / Es normal la incertidumbre"[4] (Gardeneira 107). The strategy remains the same throughout; each line is a statement about the ordinary experience of people living in Guayaquil during the time of Covid-19, particularly in those initial months when the city made international headlines due to the severity of the outbreak. While the first lines of "¿Es normal?" evoke sentiments globally familiar when the pandemic started, as the text goes on, it begins to explore how the virus altered the relationship between Guayaquil and its inhabitants by unsettling the understanding of what was possible and feasible in its living, that is, by unsettling the city's regime of subjectivity. Achille Mbembe and Janet Roitman refer to regimes of subjectivity as shared ensembles of imaginary configurations of everyday life:

> Imaginaries which have a material basis; and, systems of intelligibility to which people refer in order to construct a more or less clear idea of the causes of phenomena and their effects, to determine the domain of what is possible and feasible, as well as the logics of efficacious action. More generally, a regime of subjectivity is an ensemble of ways of living, representing and experiencing contemporaneousness while, at the same time, inscribing this experience in the mentality, understanding and language of a historical time (324).

---

[3] City and Pandemic.
[4] "It's normal to feel sad / It's normal to feel uncertainty".

In March and April 2020, Guayaquil transformed into something unrecognisable to its inhabitants, a city where previously unthinkable actions became a material reality (Medina Cordova 109). The failures of the health network are quick to surface in the poem: "Es normal tener que ingeniármelas para enterrar a mis familiares"[5] (Gardeneira 110) hints at the struggles people in Guayaquil had to face to bury their deceased family members when morgues were full and unable to take in more bodies. Gardeneira continues to discuss this issue by adding: "Es normal que los muertos aparezcan en las calles"[6] (111); and "es normal que sientas ganas de llorar cuando ves muertos en una banca en la vereda. Con un parasol. Con un letrero que diga 'lo intentamos todo, pero nunca nos ayudaron'" (113).[7] The text portrays Guayaquil as a chaotic city in the early days of the pandemic, with death palpable on the streets for everyone to see.

Finding bodies on curbs and benches on Guayaquil's streets was, of course, uncommon before the arrival of the virus. Yet by combining references to normality with the disruptions Covid-19 caused in the city's everyday life, the text lays bare the extent of a crisis which, building on Mbembe and Roitman, produced a lack of coincidence between the practice of life and the corpus of significations or meanings available to explain and interpret what was happening (324). That is to say, Guayaquil's inhabitants were referring to pre-pandemic frameworks to understand their city during the first lethal wave of the pandemic; they assumed that funerary practices were to be the same but soon discovered that the health emergency had radically disrupted them. In this sense, the crisis was not only being unable to bury the dead, but also inhabiting a city that had become unknown and unpredictable.

The rupture in the regime of subjectivity extended to the official narrative about the crisis of Guayaquil. While the city's inhabitants struggled to find beds in local hospitals, witnessing family and friends die in their homes and fighting to give them a proper burial, the Ecuadorian president at the time, Lenin Moreno, was twitting about what seemed like an alternative reality. His Twitter account became a communication outlet providing regular updates about the government's actions to mitigate the impact of the health emergency. On 31 March, Moreno twitted he was committed to guaranteeing the population's tranquillity, and his office was taking care of the healthcare workers fighting against the spread of the virus and of those who deserve "un adiós digno"[8] (Moreno). However, Guayaquil's casualties of the virus in March and April 2020 were far from accessing the so-called dignified farewell that the government

---

[5] "It's normal to have to find ways to bury my relatives".
[6] "It's normal for the dead to appear in the streets".
[7] "It's normal to feel like crying when you see dead people on a bench on the sidewalk, with a parasol and a sign that reads 'we tried everything, but they never helped us'".
[8] "A dignified farewell".

was referring to. Not only were some people forced to abandon the bodies of dead relatives on the streets, but there were also reports of bodies being misplaced in the morgues that, even years later, remained unreturned to their families (Ponce); or of people showing up at their own wakes, where their families were mistakenly bereaving the ashes they had been told belonged to their supposedly deceased relatives (Léon Cabrera). To a large extent, the pandemic precipitated the city's inhabitants into unimaginable situations facing experiences that had little correspondence to what was officially alleged.

"¿Es normal?" highlights the mismatch between official discourse and life experience in this context. The poem bluntly says that how "normal" it is "que haya funcionarios de morgues hospitalarias que cobraban hasta $400 por entregar cuerpos a familiares"[9], "que se pierdan los cuerpos de personas fallecidas en los hospitales públicos"[10] and "que las morgues estén saturadas"[11] (Gardeneira 114). In doing so, Gardeneira's work counters Lenin Moreno's discourse and, once again, sheds light on the extent of the disruption provoked by the coronavirus outbreak, which broke expectations in the city's social order and exposed authorities' claims as fiction. We are not by any means saying that in normal circumstances Guayaquil's population is trustful of what governmental officials promise, but that the health emergency created special circumstances where the incompatibility of the political discourse and the practice of everyday life was too evident to go unnoticed and too palpable to ignore. In this sense, both as a geographical space and as a cultural entity, the city became somewhat unrecognisable to those living in it.

Yet, for as much disruption engendered by Covid-19, Gardeneira's work also brings to light the continuity of structural violence, which was normal to the city long before the virus, during the crisis. In this context, structural violence refers to "the avoidable limitations that society places on groups of people that constrain them from meeting their basic needs and achieving the quality of life that would otherwise be possible" (Lee 123). While it could be seen as a misnomer for inequality and injustice, the concept of structural violence aims to unveil the power that overarching political, economic, religious, cultural or legal structures exercise over vulnerable individuals (Lee 123). One example offered by Johan Galtung in 1969 remains illustrative: if a person died from tuberculosis in the eighteenth century, it would be hard to conceive of this as violence since it might have been unavoidable, but if that person died from it today, despite all the medical resources in the world, then we can discuss it as a form of violence (168). It becomes violence because access to healthcare is possible but structural problems in the state (such as lack of funding for

---

[9] "Hospital morgue officials charging up to $400 for returning bodies to their families".
[10] "The loss of the bodies of deceased persons in public hospitals".
[11] "That morgues are overcrowded".

medicine) and society (such as isolation and discrimination of vulnerable populations) restrict it.

"¿Es normal?" explores structural violence through images of Guayaquil in the Covid-19 emergency that resonate with pre-pandemic Guayaquil, reminding readers that the catastrophic scenarios of Covid-19 crisis were already familiar to populations unable to afford private healthcare. "Es normal que te enfermes y vayas al hospital y te digan que te regreses a tu casa porque no hay camas libres"[12] (111), for example, brings up a common issue during the initial stages of the pandemic. But however severe it was then, struggling to get hospital beds and medicines was not new to vulnerable groups. In 2005, for instance, Guayaquil's hospitals did not have enough beds to treat all patients needing hospitalisation during an outbreak of dengue fever, a recurrent public health issue in the city ("Sin camas"). In this sense, Gardeneira's poem speaks of the Covid-19 pandemic as a crisis that raises the question of whether it could be normal to be sick —be that of dengue or Covid-19— and not having a space in the healthcare system to receive treatment. In Guayaquil, the answer before and during the pandemic could be the same: "es normal".

The interplay of disruption and continuity keeps featuring in the poem's contrasting portrayal of Guayaquil as a city silenced by the virus on the streets on the one hand, and where violence loudly continues behind closed doors on the other. Garderneira lays out the strangeness of Guayaquil in the time of Covid-19 by bringing to focus how uncommon it is to experience "la soledad de la ciudad inhabitada"[13] (108). As Ecuador's principal port and a city historically associated with commercial activity, Guayaquil is rarely empty. Retail and wholesale trade make up important sectors of the urban economy, and particularly in the city centre, street vending is prime among informal commercial activities (Villacres and Geenen 5). However, the mandatory lockdowns radically changed Guayaquil's urban landscape, which, despite continuous gentrification efforts of municipal authorities, has historically featured people buying and selling on the streets. In this sense, when Gardeneira suggests how normal it is "que no haya embotellamientos"[14] (109), her poem is not only referring to deserted avenues usually full of road traffic during working hours. It also signifies an alien and alienating experience in a city unaccustomed to staying still.

In contrast to the disruption of Guayaquil's outdoors, "¿Es normal?" highlights that the pandemic enabled gender-based violence to continue indoors with normality. Gardeneira remarks how normal it is "que haya 5200 denuncias de

---

[12] "It's normal to get sick and go to a hospital where they tell you to go home because there are no available beds".
[13] "The loneliness of an uninhabited city".
[14] "That there are no traffic jams".

violencia intrafamiliar contra las mujeres, durante el primer mes de cuarentena"[15] (112). The large number of reports was hardly new to pandemic times in a country where, according to national statistics, 20 out of every 100 women have experienced some type of violence in the family environment, and 43 out of 100 women have experienced some type of violence from an intimate partner (INEC). These numbers have been consistent for the last ten years, yet during the pandemic authorities were unprepared to understand the impact of lockdown and isolation in a society with high levels of intrafamily violence (Espinoza Carvajal). In this sense, Gardeneira's work presents violence against women as a significant but unattended problem before and during the pandemic, noting that "es normal que, a 2 meses de cuarentena, haya habido 12 femicidios"[16] (117).

Violence against women might have looked particularly extraordinary during the pandemic but global statistics tell a different story. At least one in three women in the world has suffered physical or sexual violence at some point in her life, mainly from a partner, prompting organisations like the United Nations to call violence against women a pandemic that causes more deaths than tuberculosis, malaria and all types of cancer combined (René and CINU México). While violence against women was already established as a worldwide problem, the Covid-19 pandemic gave it more visibility (*The Shadow Pandemic*). The UN popularised the title of "shadow pandemic", reinforcing the idea that gender-based violence is invisible and private, and it framed its discussion in the Covid-19 timeline, presenting it to some extent as another by-product of the health crisis rather than a worsening issue rooted in already existing gender inequalities and discriminations. By reminding readers that violence against women was "normal" at its core, not just in Ecuador but also globally, Gardeneira's work presents a critical view of continuity and unveils the negligence embedded in thinking about gender-based violence as a new or extraordinary phenomenon.

"¿Es normal?" outlines how women in Guayaquil faced Covid-19 in a health context that was already prone to be violent with them. Obstetric violence, for example, emerges when Gardeneira notes that "es normal que te dé preeclampsia y estés en coma por violencia obstétrica"[17] (111). Obstetric violence is defined in Ecuador as any action or omission that limits the right of pregnant or non-pregnant women to receive gynaecological-obstetric health services, and national statistics suggest that 48 out of every 100 women have experienced it at least once throughout their lives (INEC). Furthermore, the poem offers a

---

[15] "Having 5200 reports of intrafamily violence against women during the first month of the quarantine".
[16] "It's normal that, after 2 months of quarantine, there have been 12 femicides".
[17] "It's normal to get preeclampsia and fall in a coma due to obstetric violence".

poignant verse about the restriction of women's body autonomy by limiting access to sexual and reproductive health: "Es normal *tener* que estar embarazada"[18] (115, my emphasis), which not only refers to the lack of access to contraceptives or reproductive health services during the pandemic (*Informe de resultados*) but also to limitations on women aiming to decide over their bodies. Gardeneira's use of the verb *tener* [to have] is not a coincidence. Choosing pregnancy and motherhood is central to ongoing Latin American feminist campaigns for decriminalising abortion, the recognition of women's autonomy and the experience of their full citizenship across a region where abortion is entirely or highly restricted by law in most countries.

Gardeneira's poem does not present novel scenarios by mentioning obstetric violence or alluding to women's struggle for bodily autonomy. Instead, it refers to figures suggesting normalised abuse in Ecuadorian society on the one hand, and builds on long-standing local, national and transnational demands of feminist groups on the other. That is, the poem signals that the violence and the demands for change might have worsened and become more necessary respectively during the health emergency, but they were there before it arrived. Therefore, "¿Es normal?" lays bare how pre-pandemic experiences and real-time pandemic experiences resonate in women's lives, portraying a different yet continuous story of pain, discrimination and inequality where "es normal estar furiosa"[19] (110) and "es normal estar herida"[20] (112).

Our analysis in this section highlights the ways in which "¿Es normal?" foregrounds how disruption and continuity coincided in Guayaquil's pandemic experience. Through references to structural and gender-based violence, the poem tells readers that the Covid-19 crisis unravelled in historically constituted, structurally conditioned sites of inequality, domination and powerlessness (Kabel and Phillipson 8). However, at the same time, it enables them to see how the pandemic unsettled Guayaquil's regime of subjectivity and transformed it into an unrecognisable city for its inhabitants. In this light, Gardeneira's work shows the continuity of violence coexisting with the disruptiveness of the pandemic in Guayaquil, thereby articulating a regime where the normal and the new not only clash and bleed into each other but also inform and reinforce one another. The new normal is revealed as never entirely new or normal; instead, it is a term serving to accommodate a different type of everyday life horror in normalised patterns of violence.

---

[18] "It's normal *to have* to be pregnant".
[19] "It's normal to be angry".
[20] "It's normal to be hurt".

Conclusion

Whereas the narrative of the Ecuadorian government presented the new normal as sanitary measures to cut the transmission chain of the virus, Gardeneira's poetry conveys an alternative picture in which the violence underlying life in Guayaquil before and during the outbreak structures normality, new and old. In doing so, the poem not only allows readers to see and make sense of a catastrophic reality that, while novel and extraordinary in many ways, is also commonplace in many others. It raises questions about the level that violence needs to reach to be considered disruptive. That is, in the discourse of the Ecuadorian government considered here, the pandemic and the need to counter it prompted the call for adapting to a new normal; structural and gender-based violence take part of a common normality that does not deserve special treatment. The new normal, as Gardeneira's work suggests, proposes that the exceptional circumstances brought about by the Covid-19 outbreak demand people to adapt to more of the same painful inequality they experience on a daily basis, which will remain after the virus is contained.

Reflecting on the Ecuadorian government's narrative on the new normal alongside Gardeneira's work at a time when the World Health Organisation has stopped considering Covid-19 a global health emergency enables us to see that life in Ecuador has resettled to the known patterns that intensified but never went away during the disruption caused by the pandemic. Three years after the first reported case of Covid-19 in Ecuador, there may be no more improvised coffins in the streets of Guayaquil or the unnerving silence of a quarantined city, but the precarity, the anger, and the disappointment are still there. The social distancing and the face masks are a memory; the violence, however, endures: vulnerable populations still struggle to access quality healthcare, women continue to experience abuse. The new normal has returned to the same old normal, revealing —as "¿Es normal?" proposes— that they were not so different from the beginning. Furthermore, that the narratives about the new normal need to be critically examined as they not only tell us about the pandemic, but help us to understand how they contributed to shaping the experience of living and surviving it in Latin America.

Bibliography

Alarcón, Daniel. "A Pandemic Tragedy in Guayaquil". *The New Yorker*, 7 March 2022, https://www.newyorker.com/magazine/2022/03/14/a-pandemic-tragedy-in-guayaquil.

"Ante irrespeto al distanciamiento social en sector de la Bahía de Guayaquil, Cabildo intensifica controles". *El Universo*, 21 May 2020, https://www.eluniverso.com/guayaquil/2020/05/21/nota/7847649/ante-irrespeto-distanciamiento-social-sector-bahia-guayaquil/.

Cañizares, Ana María. "Ecuador iniciará fase de distanciamiento físico de forma paulatina el 4 de mayo". *CNN Español*, 24 April 2020, https://cnnespanol.cnn.com/2020/04/24/ecuador-iniciara-fase-de-distanciamiento-fisico-de-forma-paulatina-el-4-de-mayo/.

COE. "Distanciamiento, el camino hacia la nueva normalidad". *Comité de Operaciones de Emergencia Nacional*, 2020.

—. "Informe de situación COVID-19 Ecuador No. 024". *Comité de Operaciones de Emergencia Nacional*, 2020.

Collyns, Dan. "'Like the horror of war': mayor of virus-ravaged Ecuador city calls for drastic response". *The Guardian*, 22 April 2020 https://www.theguardian.com/world/2020/apr/22/ecuador-guayaquil-mayor-.

"En los primeros 15 días del mes de abril, Guayas contabiliza 6703 fallecidos". *El Universo*, 16 April 2020, https://www.eluniverso.com/guayaquil/2020/04/16/nota/7815114/que-va-mes-abril-guayas-contabiliza-6703-fallecidos/.

Espinoza Carvajal, Andrea. "COVID-19 and the Limitations of Official Responses to Gender-Based Violence in Latin America: Evidence from Ecuador". *Bulletin of Latin American Research*, vol. 39, no. S1, 2020, pp. 7–11.

Gabriel, Markus. "El orden mundial previo al virus era letal". *El País*, 7 March 2020, https://elpais.com/cultura/2020/03/21/babelia/1584809233_534841.html.

Galtung, Johan. "Violence, Peace, and Peace Research". *Journal of Peace Research*, vol. 6, no. 3, 1969, pp. 167–191.

Gardeneira, Diana. "¿Es normal?". *Ciudad y pandemia: Escrituras de la catástrofe*, edited by Andrea Alejandro, Universidad de las Artes, 2020, pp. 107–121.

"Gobierno anuncia 'nueva normalidad' en Ecuador desde el 4 de mayo del 2020; ¿finaliza la cuarentena por el Covid-19?". *El Comercio*, 24 April 2020, https://www.elcomercio.com/actualidad/politica/ecuador-normalidad-distanciamiento-social-coronavirus.html.

Hidalgo, Francisco. "In the Face of the Pandemic: The Potential of Rurality and Peasant Agriculture". *Alternautas*, vol, 8, no. 1, 2021, pp. 146–157.

INEC. "Encuesta Nacional sobre Relaciones Familiares y Violencia de Género contra las Mujeres". *Instituto Nacional de Estadísticas y Censos*, 2019.

Informe de resultados del monitoreo del estado de los servicios de salud sexual y salud reproductiva durante la emergencia sanitaria por COVID-19 en Ecuador. Surkuna, January 2021.

Kabel, Ahmed, and Robert Phillipson. "Structural violence and hope in catastrophic times: from Camus' The Plague to Covid-19". *Race & Class*, vol. 62, no. 4, 2021, pp. 3–18.

Lee, Bandy. *Violence: An Interdisciplinary Approach to Causes, Consequences, and Cures*. John Wiley & Sons, 2019.

Moreno, Lenin [@Lenin]. "Otra intensa jornada de trabajo Guayaquil. Nuestro compromiso con la población es no escatimar esfuerzos para garantizar su tranquilidad. ¡Nos ocupamos de quienes día a día salen al campo de batalla a enfrentar al #Covid19, y también de quienes merecen un adiós digno!". *Twitter*, 31 March 2022, https://twitter.com/Lenin/status/1244818638202458113.

Léon Cabrera, José María. "'Los que no aparecen': la búsqueda de los cuerpos extraviados en Ecuador durante la pandemia". *El País*, 7 December 2021, https://elpais.com/internacional/2021-12-07/los-que-no-aparecen-la-busqueda-de-los-cuerpos-extraviados-en-ecuador-durante-la-pandemia.html.

Mbembe, Achille, and Janet Roitman. "Figures of the Subject in Times of Crisis". *Public Culture*, vol. 7, no. 2, 1995, pp. 323–352.

Medina Cordova, Luis. "Narrating a Global Crisis from Guayaquil in Real Time: Early Literary Responses to the COVID-19 Outbreak in Latin America". *Bulletin of Latin American Research*, vol. 39, no. S1, 2020, pp. 108–111.

"Ministra de Salud confirma muerte de paciente por COVID-19". *Ministerio de Salud Pública*, 13 March 2020, https://www.salud.gob.ec/ministra-de-salud-confirma-muerte-de-paciente-por-covid-19/.

Ponce, Isabela. "La gente que reclama sus muertos". *GK*, 5 December 2021, https://gk.city/2020/04/03/cadaveres-guayaquil-coronavirus/.

René, Pierre-Marc, and CINU México. "La violencia de género es una pandemia mundial". *Naciones Unidas*, 25 November 2016, https://news.un.org/es/audio/2016/11/1418021.

"Sin camas para casos de dengue". *El Universo*, 30 April 2005, https://www.eluniverso.com/2005/04/30/0001/12/51F481AD6161436089DC951100C11495.html?amp.

The Shadow Pandemic: Violence against women and Girls and COVID-19. UN Women, April 2020, https://www.unwomen.org/sites/default/files/Headquarters/Attachments/Sections/Library/Publications/2020/Issue-brief-COVID-19-and-ending-violence-against-women-and-girls-Infographic-en.pdf.

Villacres, Lisette, and Sara Geenen. "Framing street vending in Guayaquil – Ecuador". *IOB Discussion Papers*, no. 02, 2020, pp. 5–28.

Chapter 9

The End of The World

Decoding the Ideological Framework of Latin American Pandemic Narrative Today[*]

Barbara Ann French

Germanna Community College

Abstract

As the widespread effects of the Covid-19 pandemic were growing, society sought understanding and meaning. The study of Latin-American pandemic narrative provides valuable insights into the societal and ideological constructs that have governed not only its rhetoric but also the public's interpretation of this historical catastrophe. Modern pandemic narrative alludes in many ways to the religious paradigms that were established under colonial rule. Unable to free themselves from these imposed ideals, many communities have continued to propagate these teachings, generating a vast and complex series of narratives that enter dialogue with early epidemiological prose. This chapter examines the ideological frameworks relevant for decoding Latin-American pandemic narratives. It discusses the way in which ideological frameworks forged during the Vice Royal period not only remain relevant for Latin-American citizens today, but how they have served to shape the lens through which the current pandemic is perceived and understood by many.

Keywords: pandemic, narrative, colonial, ideology, Latin America

***

Introduction

Contemporary narrative forms, combined with vastly growing digital platforms have allowed pandemic narrative in both Latin America and around the world to be experienced in ways in which not many people would have imagined even a short time ago. From social media platforms to tweets and online news forums, pandemic survivors have created and integrated a series of *locus*

---

[*] This research was funded as part of a grant provided by the Mellon/ACLS Community College Faculty Fellowship.

communis or commonplaces, used to discuss and formulate meaning surrounding the world's current pandemic. While it is easy to think that prose narrative production during this time was shaped by the pandemic and the topics it brought to light, it is important to highlight that the accessibility and instantaneous nature of the internet, amongst other social forums, have also allowed narrative to influence the way in which the Covid-19 pandemic was perceived during diverse moments of its development. The study of narrative text produced in Latin America sheds understanding on societal and communal reactions, contention strategies, as well as explains broad spectrum beliefs surrounding the illness and seeks to comprehend the diverse interpretations that were associated with the outbreak crisis. In its broadest sense, we can understand pandemic narrative as the stories or expressed reasons that have been set forth by individuals or governments to explain or otherwise give meaning to the pandemic. This definition expands on the concept of narrative set forth by Robert Shiller. In his study, Shiller explores the economic implications of a diverse range of narratives and defines narrative "to mean a simple story or easily expressed explanation of events that many people want to bring up in conversation or on news or social media, because it can be used to stimulate the concerns or emotions of others, and/or it appears to advance self-interest" (4). These texts, as they circulate on public forum and from receptor to receptor, serve to compile a collective societal image of the pandemic, its policies for containment, as well shape the way communities perceive individuals who have fallen ill, their lifestyle choices, and overall shape the way that societies respond to the messages being set forth by official governing channels. This constant exchange between narrative content and the construct of human experience during the pandemic is an essential key to understanding how far reaching the power and influence of narrative prose can be regarding communal action.

While epidemiological narrative has been present since medieval times, and before, the continual evolution and rupture with tradition present in both the narrative forms and in the symbolic figures used to create literary constructs on the topic, have changed significantly over time. The examination of a range of narrative texts produced during the Covid-19 pandemic better equips us to comprehend the way in which today's epidemiological narratives have been influenced not only by traditional factors, but also how popular culture (including outbreak literature), and film affected the public's perception of the current situation and the way different communities have chosen to live out these circumstances as a result of narrative influence. The type of texts that were analysed for this study include news narratives, informative narratives produced by organizations such as UNICEF and governmental organizations, and other miscellaneous prose writings produced in Latin America during the Covid-19 pandemic.

Cultural framework plays a decisive role in the way in which the pandemic has been perceived and ideologically interpreted by a diverse range of nations and their people. Each epidemic takes on meaning and interferes in the lives of citizens in different ways, changing profound and intimate aspects of daily life, such as coexistence, ways of interacting and the beliefs of survivors. José Luis Beltrán Moya explains that:

> Cualquier enfermedad, cualquier epidemia sólo adquiere sentido e importancia dentro de un contexto humano por las formas en que se infiltra en la vida de sus gentes, por las reacciones que provoca y por el modo en que da expresión a los valores culturales y políticos de una época determinada, que trata de enfrentarse colectivamente a aquélla. La propia etimología de la palabra griega *epidemos* (sobre el pueblo) lo confirma (12).[1]

Thus, to comprehend the phenomena more wholly, it is necessary to use historical contextualization as a fundamental tool for its interpretation.

This study seeks to highlight the influence of historical prose in the constitution of pandemic narrative and considers colonial era writers as a source of ideological frameworks that shaped the way the current outbreak has been portrayed and understood across Latin America by mainstream channels, as well as individual perceptions shared on public forums. To reach this end, my chapter highlights the influence of narrative historical interpretations of various outbreaks produced between the sixteenth and eighteenth centuries in diverse moments of Latin American history and narrative writings produced during the Covid-19 pandemic. The corpus studied for this analysis focuses primarily on text that originated in New Spain, although the ideologies reflected can also be observed in other territories as a means of political justification, for example the use of *translatio imperii* to justify conquest rule, and the religious perspectives the narratives contain are common within the Catholic church of the time. As a result of the analysis, I identified two main ideologies that laid the foundations for the symbolic and narratological representation of modern epidemics: divine destruction and the punishment for deadly sins. The historical and bibliographical texts used to conduct this study have not been uniformly studied and present valuable insights into the social and ideological constructs surrounding epidemiological narrative. Ranging from testimonies, historical chronical, iconographical religious representations, to

---

[1] "Any disease, any epidemic, only acquires meaning and importance within a human context by the ways in which it infiltrates the lives of its people, by the reactions it provokes, and by the way in which it gives expression to the cultural and political values within a determined epoch". Translations from Spanish are by this chapter's author throughout.

other miscellaneous works, these narratives all serve to help generate a collective image of the way in which colonial paradigms regarding the projection of epidemics in societal narrative were and continue to be echoed in current pandemic narrative throughout different parts of Latin America.

Publilius Syrus, a classical Latin writer, once wrote that death is the great equalizer of all, however, a review of colonial era works shows that the most vulnerable populations experienced the epidemics in a very different way than those belonging to social classes that had access to more resources and possessed understanding of what was happening. This position holds true today in many countries, where the stigmatization of the unvaccinated or those who fell ill with Covid-19 runs perhaps more rampant than the illness itself. The propagation of social stigmas relating to the virus led to the publication of flyers and other documents to be released in 2020 as a conjoined effort by countries such as Colombia, Uruguay and organizations such as UNICEF, the United Nations and the Red Cross in order to educate communities and social groups on the way in which social stigma not only harms those who are ill, but also describes how it can thwart efforts to contain the virus. This happens by inadvertently encouraging those who have the virus to hide it to avoid social isolation (*La estigmatización social* 1). Perhaps one of the most interesting examples for texts put forth to explicitly help shape Covid-19 narrative and the framework for the representation of individuals suffering from the virus is that of the *La estigmatización social asociada a la Covid-19: Guía para prevenir y abordar la estigmatización social.*[2] This document was published by UNICEF in Uruguay and disseminated in various regions in Latin America and is listed as a conjoined effort publication of UNICEF, the Red Cross and the World Health Organisation. This document proved of particular interest as it focuses on the impact narrative stories had on society and communal interactions during the heath crisis.

In the aforementioned document, journalists are encouraged to adapt their narrative strategies to avoid stigmatization by doing the following: speak openly about the spread of the virus, but do not associate it to a specific population or ethnic group/subgroup or population; avoid language with negative connotations such as suspicious cases, or suspects who may have the virus; choose words like people who contract the virus not spread or transmit (*La estigmatización social* 3). In short, the document at hand seeks to modify the lexical field surrounding pandemic narrative to avoid the creation of social stigmatization and the propagation of ideological frameworks that are damaging to people, contention strategies and communities that have been affected by the illness.

---

[2] The title of the publication translates to "Social Stigmatization Related to Covid-19: Guide for Preventing and Addressing Social Stigmatization".

In the section of the document dedicated to actionable ideas on how to discuss the current pandemic, the authors set forth concrete suggestions on how to shape the narratives surrounding the outbreaks in different communities. Amongst those strategies are the engagement of religious figures to promote reflection on the support of those affected by the illness, assuring that different groups are equally represented in reports, avoiding placing emphasis on blame or the identification of sources of communal outbreak (*La estigmatización social* 4–5). The authors go on to state that media sources should communicate or share compassionate narratives and stories that humanize the experiences and struggles of individuals or groups affected by the novel coronavirus (*La estigmatización social* 5). The inclusion of this directive regarding what types of narratives to publish bears witness to the power and influence these texts have and continue to possess regarding the ways in which the pandemic was and continues to be experienced by Latin American communities and others around the world.

The study of early narratives aides in better understanding the origin of some of these ideals being combatted and how modern rhetoric has manipulated them to fit into current situations in various places, often serving to generate fear amongst those who find relevancy in its message, making necessary the publication of guides and other efforts to change the way in which pandemic narrative was being framed. In many instances, outbreak fiction, movies, and other pop culture elements have reinforced these ideals that further project, albeit inadvertently, cultural paradigms formed under Spanish rule. In many cases, early narratives have the sick appear in the texts as condemned figures, punished for their sins, amongst other images of negative relation. These differences reflect not only the inequality that existed in terms of castes at the time, but also reveal the way authorities, writers of the time and, above all, the religious community formed the ideologies and discourse that circulated regarding the outbreaks and projected negative imagery relating to those who contracted diseases, thus creating social stigmas surrounding outbreak patients. This imagery aided in the consolidation of an ideological framework that served as a fundamental concept for the broad social construction of different epidemics in the territory. These narratives serve as distant echoes of the lives lost, the attempts to understand what was happening, and above all the search to make sense of those tragedies. Although epidemiological narrative did not originate in New Spain, its cultivation has been seen in various literary genres throughout its history.

Understanding the ideologies that constitute the framework for the understanding and meaning of the epidemics allows us to illuminate the social beliefs that surrounded these events, especially in terms of the causes and implications of the epidemics at various times in New Spain's history and the way in which society saw those who fell ill. Also, understanding the different narrative works that talk about these important moments, allows us to better understand how the outbreaks were incorporated into daily life, history, and the collective image of destiny for New Spain itself.

The ideology that epidemics come from God and are a part of divine providence can be observed in the early narratives as a means of demonstrating the favouritism shown to the Spanish forces. However, this initial conception of disease had repercussions that lasted for many centuries regarding the ideological framework of epidemics in the territory, some of which are still valid in the narrative of the Covid-19 pandemic. Approaching this literature implies immersing ourselves not only into its words but also in the ideologies and worldviews that make it up. The epidemiological texts that are discussed herein give us a luxurious window to understanding more fully the ideological frameworks that prevailed at that time and that serve as key elements for understanding references and common spaces used in pandemic narrative today. These narratological projections of the epidemics became part of an imperial discourse that served to justify the Spanish intervention in the colony and finally the Conquest itself.

Epidemiological narratives, from very early times, framed the waves of pestilence within a sacred discourse, interpreted through the powerful lens of the Old Testament. Such a decision set in motion a series of symbolic relationships that would not only come to have implications in the narrative throughout the viceregal period but also in today's pandemic discourse, positioning patients as sinners, punished individuals, agents of blame, etc. Despite evidence of conscience efforts to distance the pandemic from these interpretations, they continue to appear on popular platforms and even in news related media.

Although Catholicism provided authors with a powerful weapon to interpret the events, it was the vision of the writers, who promoted an image and meaning for the outbreaks, and directed their narrative towards a vision of the sick as condemned figures. History is interpreted through the eyes of the historian who records it. The narrative works they create reflect not only the facts regarding events that occurred but have cultural baggage and an ideology interwoven in the plot that allows the writer to order, interpret, and give meaning to a later audience. This allows the historian to explain, using their own personal lens, why an event occurred. Historical narrative is no exception because it is part of the same tradition and creative process. For its creation, the author seeks to use prose narrative structures to unite chronological events in a way that, according to his own worldview, explains what occurred. Thus, it is extremely important to recognize that these works, products of a process of narrative re-elaboration, reflect ideological frameworks that circulated at the time. When passing from the tangible historical fact to the narrated story, these writings underwent an interpretive process, which allowed the historian/writer to highlight the meaning, the implicit teaching in the story, and reflect their own ideals or cultural paradigms in the produced text.

Hayden White specifically points out this relationship when he declares that narrative is an essential part of historical discourse, because it requires a narrator to tell it and it is he who interprets, orders, and relays it to an audience. White explains:

> Cuando se trata de proporcionar una narrativa de acontecimientos reales, hemos de suponer que existe un sujeto que proporcione el impulso necesario para registrar sus actividades [...] Si toda narración dota a los acontecimientos, reales o imaginarios de una significación que no poseen como mera secuencia, parece posible llegar a la conclusión de que toda narrativa histórica tiene como finalidad latente o manifiesta el deseo de moralizar sobre los acontecimientos que trata. (24).[3]

Colonial authors, most of whom were religious, sought to insert New Spain into universal history, often merging events with scenes of great importance, such as episodes from the Bible. These ideological frameworks became so intertwined with breakout theory, religious beliefs, and cultural paradigms that many of them still carry relevance today.

Divine Destruction: The Rise of Apocalyptical Interpretations and Pandemic Narrative

Around the globe, insinuations that Covid-19's intercontinental spread was a sign that the end of the world was near, circulated from early on in news articles, social media, in religious spaces, and more. From references to the zombie apocalypse, to biblical prophecy, writers on a myriad of platforms took to describing the novel experience of widespread illness, isolation, and public shutdowns. These references and assimilations were not limited to social media and other popular platforms, but rather slowly made their way into mainstream media, being included in newspapers, and even reflected in discourse shared by government endorsed officials. On 3 July 2020, *El sol de México* released an article titled "Coronavirus: ¿El fin del mundo está cerca?", where it discussed various elements and theories that have contributed to the spread of the novel Coronavirus as a sign related to the Apocalypse. A quick

---

[3] "When it comes to providing a narrative of real events, we have to assume that there is a subject that provides the necessary impulse to record their activities (...) If all narration endows events, real or imaginary, with a significance that they do not possess as a mere sequence, it seems possible to reach the conclusion that all historical narrative has as its latent or manifest purpose the desire to moralize about the events it deals with".

glance at the article's abstract shows a powerful link between apocalyptic discourse and the narrative validated by Mexican President López Obrador: "El pastor evangélico más cercano a AMLO piensa que el anticristo está cerca y los testigos de Jehová creen que las profecías se están cumpliendo" (Hernández).[4] The author, Saul Hernández, goes on to sight the following:

> La pandemia de Covid-19 ha puesto a más de uno a pensar que quizá el fin del mundo está cerca. Internet se llena de teorías de la conspiración, #Apocalipsis es tendencia en redes y en YouTube abundan los videos que explican cómo la Biblia, Nostradamus, Los Simpson y hasta un niño indio astrólogo predijeron la enfermedad que azota al mundo.[5]

The article goes on to reveal how accompanying calamities have served to reinforce the apocalyptic interpretation of recent events. Many of these ideals, particularly those originating from Latin America, not only share deep ties to the Catholic and overall Christian faith, but also to the rich tradition and cultivation of epidemiological literature that has circulated in their communities for centuries. In an article published in Argentina, Santiago Roggerone shares a similar sentiment with regards to the correlations made between the Pandemic and the Apocalypse. In his work, Roggerone explains that in part, this vision is related to the propagation of the idea that Covid-19 had forever changed the way the world would operate, and profoundly impacted sectors of society thought to be invulnerable (38). The assimilation of these two ideals led many to the conclusion that the pandemic was the end of the world as we knew it, marking a before and after in how people were able to carry out their day to day lives.

Epidemiological narrative produced in Latin America during the Covid-19 pandemic looks to familiar cultural paradigms and religious context to explain many of the happenings during the height of the global crisis. Although the writing of epidemiological themes did not originate among the Americas, its production in New Spain sheds light on its evolution as it relates to the adaptations and appropriations of the genre in this new context. For example, in New Spain, not only the narration of local historical components is observed, but also the use of symbolic associations that are new and charged with meaning for the Novohispanic communities can be found and are used consistently by

---

[4] "The evangelical pastor closest to AMLO thinks that the antichrist is near, and Jehovah's Witnesses believe that the prophecies are being fulfilled".

[5] "The Covid-19 pandemic has made more than one think that perhaps the end of the world is near. The Internet is full of conspiracy theories, #Apocalypse is a trend in social networks and videos abound on YouTube that explain how the Bible, Nostradamus, The Simpsons and even an Indian astrologer child predicted the disease that is plaguing the world".

authors to generate a unified vision and discourse surrounding the outbreaks. These are reflected as cultural references in distinct narratives relating to the current pandemic and are also present in other cultural spaces such as film, break out literature, religious genres, etc. As a literary topic, apocalyptic narrative can be observed in a wide range of prose throughout Latin America. Outside of fictional narrative, it continues to be disseminated as a means of warning and comprehension of world events. Geneviève Fabry observes that:

> Un breve repaso por una serie de publicaciones recientes procedentes de campos tan disímiles como la historia, la filosofía y la ecología da cuenta de la presencia de múltiples avatares del mito apocalíptico y de sus ambigüedades en los discursos sociales y culturales actuales (2).[6]

This recent study queries diverse approaches to the comprehension of apocalyptic narrative in Hispano-American literature, focusing predominately on those works produced in the twentieth century. It examines the external factors, including historical and philosophical sources that may have influenced literary themes in that epoch.

The ideological framework of epidemics as a force of divine destruction, found primarily in viceregal works produced during sixteenth and seventeenth century texts and deeply related to the narratives of the Conquest, was born from an assimilation of the historical facts with the biblical description of the destruction of Egypt and Jerusalem. Some authors, particularly those associated with Conquest's religious narrative, such as Miguel Sánchez, went further to associate the events surrounding it, including outbreaks of various illness with the apocalyptic battle foretold in *Revelations*. It is evident when examining some early works, that there was an intentional conformation through narrative prose of sacred discourse regarding the Conquest, the fall of the Mexica Empire, and finally the death of those who were infected with the diseases that the Spaniards brought to these lands. In this context, the authors framed different episodes of illnesses in service not only as a tool of God to defeat the Mexica empire, but also to consolidate the power of the Spanish Crown, who tried to liberate the indigenous people from the power of the Satan.

As has been commented, within the sacred chronicles that recount the history of the fall of Tenochtitlan, numerous parallels are observed that link its history with two biblical accounts of destruction: that of Jerusalem and of Egypt. By inserting the history of New Spain within this context, the authors generated a discourse focused on divine providence and victory that justified

---

[6] "A brief review of a series of recent publications from fields as dissimilar as history, philosophy, and ecology reveals the presence of multiple incarnations of the apocalyptic myth and its ambiguities in current social and cultural discourses".

the role the conquerors and the Spanish crown played in the conquest of the territory. This apology for the Conquest generated certain symbolic and theological relationships in the early narrative works that would last for several centuries. As a central element, many of the authors saw the importance of highlighting the omens that Moctezuma had seen before the Conquest. The omens were interpreted both as evidence that the hand of God was already present and controlling the history of the indigenous people and that omens announced their destiny. In current pandemic narrative, numerous authors have sought this strategy as a means of retrospectively demonstrating the path of historical events. This can be observed in a 2022 publication by Pablo Batalla Cueto, a Spanish historian, whose study focuses on the relation between Aztec omens and extreme phenomena observed in today's world that has provoked climatic charge or other extreme life altering events. In his recent publication Batalla Cueto highlights this specific relation between the interpretation of pre-Columbian omens, the catholic lens through which they were later understood and the signs that pointed to pandemic. He states that there is:

> Un mensaje de Dios en, por ejemplo, la ola de calor que sacudió la costa occidental de Canadá el año pasado, provocando la muerte, cocidos literalmente en sus conchas, de miles de mejillones en los pedreros del área de Vancouver, cuya putrefacción llenó durante días el aire de un olor pestilente; algo que los aztecas sí habrían interpretado como advertencia divina. Tampoco lo vemos en los cielos anaranjados, diabólicos, de una tormenta de polvo sahariano en lugares a los que nunca había llegado el polvo sahariano. Ni en las inundaciones monstruosas que devastaron Alemania en 2021 (Batalla Cueto).[7]

In large part, the use of omens in current pandemic narrative has served two ends: to show how current events relate to apocalyptic predictions and to give meaning or purpose to global disaster.

The Florentine Codex as well as Book III of Mendieta's work speak of several signs that were seen in Tenochtitlan before its destruction; among them is the comet that several authors deciphered as a sign of its destruction. Similar descriptions appear in Toribio de Benavente, better known as Motolinía, who narrates:

---

[7] The text by Batalla Cueto can be interpreted as stating that there was a message from God in, for example, the heat wave that swept the western coast of Canada last year, causing thousands of mussels to die, literally cooked in their shells, in the Vancouver-area quarries, whose putrefaction filled for days the air of a pestilential odor; something that the Aztecs would have interpreted as a divine warning. Batalla Cueto also makes reference to the orange, "devilish skies" of a Saharan dust storm in places where Saharan dust has never reached, and the "monstrous floods" that devastated Germany in 2021.

La espiriençia nos enseña y la Escritura Sagrada lo aprueua que quando alguna gran tribulación a de venir, o Dios quiere demostrar alguna cosa notable, primero muestra Dios algunas señales en el cielo o en la tierra, demostratiuas de la tribulación venidera [...]. Y daquí es que comúndmente, antes de las mortandades y pestilençias suelen aparesçer cometas, e antes de las grandes hambres anteçeden terremotos o tempestades, e antes de las destruyçiones de los rreynos y prouinçias, aparesçen terribles visiones. Y ansí leemos que en tiempo de Antiocho, antes de la destruyción de Jerusalém y del templo, por espaçio de quarenta días fueron vistos por el ayre cauallos que discurrían y gentes armadas con lanças, y rreales y esquadrones de gentes, e otras muchas cossas, como en el dicho capítulo paresçe [...]. Bien ansi aconteçió que antes de la destruyción de México de la conquista desta Nueua España antes que los cristianos entrasen en esta tierra fueron vistas en el ayre gentes que parescían pelear vnas con otras y desta señal, nunca vista en esta tierra los indios quedaron muy marauillados (*Memoriales* 311).[8]

As described by Motolinía, the fall of the Mexica empire was inscribed within the biblical context of the Old Testament through a series of very specific associations.

The meticulous description of the omens and their meanings provide an important context for their interpretation in the history of New Spain. In this case, Motolinía begins by explaining how these omens originate within sacred tradition and the meaning that they received in the past. His text serves to assert to the reading public that the meaning of these signs was verified both within History itself and Holy Scripture and gives an example of one of the most significant cases such as the destruction of Jerusalem. He ends his description with the narration of the signs seen in Tenochtitlan before the arrival of the Spaniards and explicitly exposes the relationship with this tradition of omens as coming from the Old Testament. It is of particular interest that the writer not only associates the comet as a sign of destruction, but also defines it as a

---

[8] "Experience and the Holy Scriptures demonstrate that when there is a great tribulation coming or God wants to show something noteworthy, first he shows signs in the sky or on the land, demonstrating that the tribulation is coming (...) commonly, before the fatalities and pestilences, comets tend to appear, and great periods of hunger are preceded by earthquakes or storms, and before the destruction of kingdoms and providences, terrible visions appear. And so we read that in the time of Antiochus, before the destruction of Jerusalem and its temple, for 40 days were seen in the air running horses and armed men with spears and squadrons of people and many other things, as they are told appear in that chapter (...) That is how it was before the destruction of Mexico from the Conquest of New Spain before the Christians entered the land. They were seen as people who appeared to be fighting others in the air, and this sign, as it had never been seen in the land by the natives before, left many amazed".

warning of the pestilences that would come later. This is an element that served to link the events of the Conquest with the epidemics that would break out among the indigenous population later and frame them in a single divine plan, to thus initiate the decline and finally the fall of the Mexica civilization. This relationship reveals, albeit in a veiled way, the guilt of the Mexica empire because the reason for God's wrath in this biblical episode lies in its idolatry.

It is evident that the representation of epidemics as a divine punishment had already been consolidated in the narratives of the sixteenth century, although within this same discourse, differences can be found between the visions presented by each author in their respective work. By focusing on different writings by Motolinía, it is possible to understand the way in which his discourse developed in greater detail these ideas and the link that they share with contemporary and later works. It is interesting that the author does not develop a single symbolic line, because, in the same way that he relates the story of the Conquest with the destruction of Jerusalem, he also fuses it with the biblical episode of the destruction of Egypt. This duality of biblical images is perhaps due to the content of each episode; for example, the destruction of Jerusalem is used to highlight the loss of life due to battle and the taking of the city, while the destruction of Egypt is used to indicate the plagues that led to its end.

It should be noted that the fusion of the history of the Conquest with the destruction of Jerusalem was not exclusively developed by Motolinía, as it appears in various texts of the time. One of the most notable examples can be found in the chronicle by Gonzalo Fernández de Oviedo y Valdés, who takes up this biblical image also to symbolically illustrate the violent nature of the Conquest. The chronicler builds important parallels between the city of Tenochtitlan and the destruction of Jerusalem, thanks to the level of death and destruction caused by battles between the two groups. Either by following a similar logic or because this biblical image had already been assimilated into the narrative tradition of the time, another great chronicler, Bernal Díaz del Castillo, evokes the same biblical image when he writes:

> Yo he leído la destrucción de Jerusalén; mas si fue más mortandad que ésta, no lo sé cierto, porque faltaron en esta ciudad tantas gentes, guerreros que de todas las provincias y pueblos sujetos a México que allí se habían acogido, todos los más murieron que, como ya he dicho, así el suelo y laguna y barbacoas todo estaba lleno de cuerpos muertos y hedía tanto que no había hombre que lo pudiese sufrir (175).[9]

---

[9] "I have read the destruction of Jerusalem; but if it was more mortality than this, I do not know for sure, because so many people were missing in this city, warriors that from all the provinces and towns subject to Mexico who had taken refuge there, all of them died

It is worth dwelling briefly on his words as they highlight essential ideas and cultural knowledge for understanding the consolidation process of this ideological framework. Despite the apparent simplicity of the quote, the author's reference to a literary work that circulated during the period escaped critical study for many years, because it was believed that it referred to the subject and not a literary work. However, thanks to the study of Oviedo's work by recent scholars and other sources of the period, it is known that the author refers rather to a book of wide circulation in the period.[10] For many years, literary criticism was not able to identify it as a book, perhaps thanks to the few copies that have reached our hands. Its inclusion in Bernal's chronicle reveals not only the relevance of this biblical episode but also sheds some light on the literary works of the time that influenced the consolidation of this ideology.

For a modern audience, it was not easy to capture the book cited by the chronicler as a literary reference, a fact that is verified when reviewing *Los libros del conquistador*, whose list does not include it. Upon further examination of what Bernal Díaz del Castillo writes about the graphic scene of the taking of Tenochtitlan, one realises that his words take us back to the text of *La destrucción de Jerusalem*. By evoking it in his account of the destruction and the degree of violence that Tenochtitlan suffered, the destruction of the Holy City is merged with the historical account of the fall of the Mexica city. In this way, they are fused in the collective memory of the period and become one of the central components in the ideology regarding the historiography of the Conquest.

The second biblical reference used by various authors in relation to the epidemics in New Spain, insert us into another history of destruction: that of Egypt, land of idol worshipers, and oppressors of the children of Israel. In this story, we find two fundamental parallels to unravel the interpretations of these historical events. The first relates to the idea of the oppression of those chosen by God. The second refers us to the belief that plagues, or epidemics are part of a divine judgment and punishment for the idolatries of the people. By relating New Spain's history to this context, it reveals an important belief: The oppression suffered by the indigenous people while they were under the control of the devil was not their fault, but rather the result of an act of subjugation. It can be seen in the literature produced around the cult of Our Lady of Guadalupe during the time that the belief prevailed that a trick of the devil founded the Mexica Empire and therefore, the Conquest and everything

---

that, as I have already said, like this the ground and lagoon and barbecues everything was full of dead bodies and it stank so much that there was no man who could suffer it".

[10] Enrique Flores, in his article "La destrucción de Jerusalén: fantasma, violencia y conquista en un libro de cordel del siglo XVI", talks about the nature of this little-known book.

suffered during it was against the monarchy, and not on the people themselves. Ultimately, the belief served to free them from Satan's control and to bring the light of Catholicism. Just as the plagues were unleashed on Egypt because of the pharaoh's denial, the indigenous populations of New Spain suffered as part of the divine plan to free them from the evil that ruled them. In this way, the work of the Conquest and the punishment of the plagues was inscribed within an ideology of liberation and at the same time, condemnation. Marian narrative largely defends the concept of New Spain's destiny as the place chosen by God for the foundation of a new Jerusalem, a sacred city. This vision is consolidated with the appearance of the Virgin of Guadalupe, a central figure in the development of the Creole identity discourse and whose discourse culminates with the narration of the birth of the Creole church after the apocalyptic battle. As for its origin story, perhaps one of the best-known versions is that of Miguel Sánchez, who narrates:

> La idolatría en la gentilidad de México, tubo su principio de siete naciones, que sacó el Demonio de ciertas partes retiradas, y lexos, que oy llaman Nuevo México, y vinieron a poblar diversos sitios de toda estar comarcha, el último fue aqueste de México, cuyas señas fueron las aguas (…) Con el tiempo se apoderó el rey de los mexicanos, sujetando y avasallando a si todos los otros reyes, fundando en Mexico imperial monarchia de siete coronas (10).[11]

The wise words of the Creole writer show us two fundamental ideas that circulated at the time regarding the foundation of the indigenous territory. First, its foundation was in times of their gentility, that is, before the word of God had even reached them. Second, idolatry was something imposed by the king, who gradually took over the different groups. Through this discourse of submission, the image of the subjugated people emerges. These points played a decisive role in the consolidation of the biblical representation as a parallel to express what happened in New Spain with the Conquest and the meaning that society gave to various outbreaks. This analogy, used by authors to help society understand history and in turn insert New Spain into universal historiography, generated significant symbolic relationships for the consolidation of Creole identity and for the figure of the sick. Although in the early narrative, New Spain was defined as a space where the Devil reigned, this new perception of the

---

[11] "Idolatry in the gentiles of Mexico had its beginning in seven nations, which the Devil brought out of certain remote parts, and far away, which he heard is called New Mexico, and came to populate various places throughout this region, the last one was this one of Mexico, whose signs were the waters (…) Over time the king of the Mexicans took over, subjecting and subjugating all the other kings, founding an imperial monarchy of seven crowns in Mexico".

Conquest as a task of liberation together with the apparitions of the Virgin gave rise to new ways of understanding the discourse in question.

It is not difficult to understand the relationship between the fates of both sites, Tenochtitlan, and Egypt. In the first instance, it is known from the biblical context that both sites suffered several pestilences that culminated in the destruction of their cities. The populations that suffered this violent and tragic end were punished by God as part of a plan to free his chosen people. The large number of patients, who mostly belonged to the indigenous community, as well as the degree of specificity of those who became ill, points towards the punishment of this population. This fact is verified historically by research such as the one carried out by Rodolfo Acuna-Soto et al., whose study determined "there was a clear ethnic preference of the disease, the Spanish population was minimally affected whereas the native population had high mortality rate" (1).

It is interesting to examine the way in which the narrative of the time focuses the blame for the disease not on the figure of the Indian as an individual, but on the land as a nation or group, whose idolatry has provoked the wrath of God. Thus, the figure of evil is focused on the ruler, in this case Moctezuma, represented in some cases by the seven-crowned serpent, and not on the indigenous individual. As Gabriela Rodríguez Sandoval explains, this point is demonstrated through the lexical field chosen by the author: "The punishment of the Indians for their 'idolatry' came through ten plagues that God sent". The relationship of the plagues with anger and the concept of punishment takes us back to the biblical context in which God sent the plagues to punish Pharaoh who refused to listen to His message. This point is developed by Motolinía in his work: *Historia de los indios de la Nueva España*, where he writes:

> Hirió Dios y castigó esta tierra y a los que en ella se hallaron, así naturales como extranjeros, con diez plagas trabajosas. La primera fue de viruelas y comenzó de esta manera. Siendo Capitán y gobernador Hernando Cortés, al tiempo que el capitán Panfilo de Narváez desembarcó en esta tierra, en uno de sus navíos vino un negro herido de viruelas, la cual enfermedad nunca en estas tierras se había visto, y a esta sazón estaba esta Nueva España en estremo muy llena de gente, y como las viruelas se comenzasen a apegar a los indios, fue entre ellos gran enfermedad y pestilencia en toda la tierra (Benavente, *Historia de los indios* 18).[12]

---

[12] "God smote and punished this land and those who were in it, both natives and foreigners, with ten laborious plagues. The first was smallpox and it started like this. Being Captain and Governor Hernando Cortés, at the time that Captain Panfilo de Narváez disembarked in this land, in one of his ships came a black man wounded with smallpox, a disease that had never been seen in these lands, and at that time this New Spain was extremely

As observed in the narration, the diseases that plagued New Spain from early dates during the time of the Conquest are explained from a concept of God's wrath and punishment through epidemics. Even though the epidemic in question began due a slave's illness, the author highlights the way in which this pestilence spread among the indigenous. This ideological framework suggests that the diseases are part of a much larger divine plan to which the Spanish belong and participate. It also shows that they were unleashed on the indigenous people due to their sins, in particular idolatry. This punishment of epidemics or plagues responds to their refusal to pay attention to what God has asked of the people. As Rodríguez Sandoval explains: "Motolinía las expone en su *Historia* y en los *Memoriales* pero es en este último donde trata de relacionarlas una a una con las diez plagas que Dios envió a Egipto por la obstinación del faraón al no liberar a Israel" (33).[13] This reference points to the ten plagues of Egypt that God sent to destroy that nation due to their idolatry, to free the Chosen People (Israelites). This dichotomy generated by the author through symbolic relations, established between the figure of the people condemned by idolatry and the devil's deception and the Spanish, who came to bring the light of Catholicism, thus, places Spain as an instrument of their liberation. In contrast, the narratives regarding the epidemics began to spread the ideology that the epidemics suffered by the indigenous people in the first years of the Conquest were nothing less than the divine punishment that God sent to society, to end their kingdom and to lead this territory to its true destiny. Many writers, thanks to the beliefs set forth by the counter-reformation, saw New Spain as an opportunity to establish the true kingdom of Christ and his church.

This point is developed by several authors including Torquemada, who takes the relationship with the Old Testament a little further and in his work equates Cortés with the figure of David who defeated the giant Goliath. Torquemada's interpretation reintroduces the rhetoric of liberation and a war component. The author seeks to insert, through his narrative, the Mexica empire together with the four great monarchies of universal history. To achieve this end, he argues that like these, Moctezuma's empire went through the cycle of apogee, decline, and finally ruin. Thus, he explains that the final defeat or its fall is revealed as a consequence of divine wrath, for sins of idolatry, immorality, and bloodshed observed in its sacrifices. Within this interpretation, Torquemada further develops the image by making the Spanish nation,

---

crowded with people, and as the smallpox began to attach itself to the Indians, it was a great disease among them and pestilence spread throughout the land".

[13] "Motolinía exposes them in his *Historia* and in the *Memoriales*, but it is in the latter where he tries to relate them one by one with the ten plagues that God sent to Egypt due to Pharaoh's obstinacy in not liberating Israel".

through its representation in the figure of Cortes, emerge as an instrument to punish society for its sins. In this way, Torquemada builds in his work the *Monarquía Indiana* a parallel between the monster that this empire represented and the biblical defeat of the giant that threatened people of Israel. In his narrative, the image of the Spanish empire emerges as an essential instrument to save the indigenous from an even more tragic end. The symbolic networks that the author creates reveal Spain as a nation destined to punish the idolaters of New Spain and its lands.[14] Within this ideology, the sick appear as a collateral damage and as necessary evil to weaken the Mexican Empire and to free them from the clutches of the devil who controlled the territory.

This point is of particular significance as several pandemic texts, including the already referenced article from *El Sol*, form their argumentative foundation around the idea of compounding world crisis and international calamities that serve as indicators that the end of the world may be nearing. The concept of apocalyptic omens, as introduced in the colonial context, still serve a key function in pandemic narrative, and has been used as an ideological bridgeway to link a series of events across the globe. These omens serve as a warning, whether it is for those in the Christian faith or believers in alternative prophecies, that the world is moving toward its end. In some instances, current narrative relates the idea of apocalypse to that of religious restoration, a way of leading those who survive back to Christ before it is too late. In this sense, it can be interpreted that the discourse of liberation set forth in the colonial writings stills is echoed in these ideals as those survivors would be the chosen ones. This rhetoric bares startling resemblance to that of the colonial era narratives whose authors used the destruction of Egypt as a symbolic representation for the plagues that shattered indigenous communities.

Capital Sin and Religious Restauration: Eighteenth Century and Modern Narrative

By the end of the seventeenth century, one can observe a clear displacement and possible attempt to invert this ideology and discourse regarding the condemnation of the people towards the idea that the sufferings were because of the capital or mortal sins of the Spaniards, who brought the diseases. This change in terms of ideology surrounding the epidemics is largely due to the consolidation of a Creole identity, from which a process of questioning the superiority of peninsular Spain was born. It was because of this movement that the authors and intellectuals of the time began to question ideas that their ancestors imposed.

---

[14] This idea was developed by Sonia V. Rose in her text "La revision de la conquista: narración, interpretación y juicio".

Although many authors of the period accept the importance of the role Spaniards played in the successful conversion of the indigenous community, Vetancurt argues that the Conquest was the work of God, who used the Spaniards as an instrument to carry out his divine plan, reducing their role to one of support. In this new perspective of providentialism, the author manages to centre New Spain in a favourable position, no longer projecting it as a space condemned by idolatry. Nonetheless, he does criticize the indigenous people for their sins, explaining that it was because of them that a change in government took place. In part, due to his position as a Creole, Vetancurt exerts a harsh criticism against the actions of the Spaniards in his narrative, citing their role in the arrival of the epidemics. The author highlights the sin of greed, which is a capital sin that the Spanish committed since their arrival. His work narrates an episode in which they did not pay a sailor who had taken them to the Americas. As the priest explains, it was the punishment for greed and other sins that finally led both the Spanish and those who joined with them to their tragic end with the death of many. The exculpation of the indigenous is interesting, particularly because his discourse focuses on highlighting the responsibility of the conquerors and their shortcomings. His account centres on the *Noche Triste* as clear evidence of divine punishment. Vetancurt writes, "Castígalos después [Dios] con sucesos ejemplares, y manifestó su indignación con los tristes fines" (155–166).[15] The author associates these acts of robbery, murder, and the greed they showed with the cruelties they committed and the wrath of God they suffered. Vetancurt seeks to refocus the blame on the Spaniards and free the indigenous people from the previous discourse of condemnation and the total decadence of their ancient society. Such vindication of the indigenous people points us to the foundations of Creole discourse and marks the revaluation of epidemics and their meaning within the narrative produced during this period.

His ideas, although they do not represent a complete break with the previous tradition, were part of a complete transformation of the discourse used to discuss epidemics. These same concepts, a delicate balance religious restoration of the pure and punishment for sin, can be seen reflected in Pandemic narrative today as both assertions of faith and as questioned ideals. The rejection of this belief, as argued by authors in different countries, allows us to better understand the counter argument and what ideologies are in current circulation. A 2020 news article from *El Financiero* titled "Covid-19 es un 'grito de Dios' por la culpa del aborto, eutanasia, y diversidad sexual: Obipso de Cuernavaca"[16], demonstrates

---

[15] "Punishing them later [God] with exemplary events, and he manifested his indignation with their sad ends".
[16] "Covid-19 is cry of God for the guilt of abortion, euthanasia, and sexual diversity: Bishop of Cuernavaca".

the validity of this particular ideological framework in current narrative. The news article reports on the ideas disseminated by Bishop Ramón Castro, highlighting the capital or mortal sins that have led society to its demise (Bacaz). The use of divine punishment as a framework for comprehending reasons the pandemic occurred demonstrates the strong foundation that these early teachings laid for future epidemiological narrative and their continued use as a lens for understanding world events. It also highlights the way in the believers in this ideology classify the sick: if Covid-19 is a punishment those who have it must have done wrong or have bad morals.

The association of those who have fallen ill with the virus and sin, particularly in countries with strong ties to the Catholic Church, generated a wave of responses from those aiming to reduce social stigma as a means of combating the spread of the virus. Publications in public newspapers, online publishing platforms and other websites throughout countries such as Guatemala and Colombia demonstrate the predominance of scientific logic and an adamant rejection of traditional epidemiological narrative, despite the cultural ties that link them to the theological basis for the argument. José María Tojeira, journalist and writer from Guatemala declares, "Ni el Estado ni las Iglesias deben contribuir al aumento del miedo o de los sentimientos de culpa" (Tojeira).[17] These strong words provide affirmation that the authors have seen past the traditional frameworks and reject the imposed ideology of capital sin as it relates to the Pandemic. This rupture with theological lenses is particularly noteworthy as it liberates the public from a source of considerable shame and social isolation and seeks to use a shift in narrative as a way to alter the course for the treatment of individuals or communities affected by the virus.

Conclusion

While the traditional ideological frameworks for the comprehension and literary projection of the pandemic continue to have a strong presence and relevancy, there is an overriding expression of discourse aimed at dispelling these ideals for the modern public, despite the implications of conflict that this may have with religious communities. These writings, generally propagated on virtual platforms, seek to remedy centuries of subjugation and guilt due to perceptions generated by colonial epidemiological narrative. The outpourings of texts seeking to change the trajectory of epidemiological narrative demonstrate a significant rupture with literary tradition and seek to focus the narrative on scientific and research-based knowledge. The cohabitation of these ideals, as well as the rejection of traditional common places, reveal an interesting and

---

[17] "Neither the State nor the churches should contribute to the increase of fear or feelings of guilt".

delicate relationship. Pandemic narrative is still evolving, still being analysed by survivors, and will inevitably continue to seek out cultural references and commonplaces that allow people to relate to their situation and those of others. By better understanding the origins of these expressions we are better equipped to understand the underlying implications and help shape the overall narrative that will in time define the Covid-19 pandemic and how survivors experience it.

Bibliography

Acuna-Soto, Rodofo, et al. "When Half the Population Died: The Epidemic of Hemorrhagic Fevers of 1576 in Mexico". *FEMS Microbiology Letters*, vol. 240, no. 1, 2004, pp. 1–5.

Bacaz, Verónica. "COVID-19 es 'un grito de Dios' por culpa del aborto, eutanasia y diversidad sexual: Obispo de Cuernavaca". *El Financiero*, 22 March, 2020, https://www.elfinanciero.com.mx/nacional/pandemia-del-covid-19-es-un-grito-de-dios-por-temas-como-aborto-eutanasia-y-diversidad-sexual-obispo-de-cuernavaca/

Batalla Cueto, Pablo. "Los Aztecas y nosotros. Presagios del final". *El Cuaderno*, 29 March 2022, elcuadernodigital.com/2022/03/24/los-aztecas-y-nosotros-presagios-del-final/.

Beltrán Moya, José Luis. *Historia de las epidemias en España y sus colonias (1348-1919)*. La Esfera de los libros, 2006.

Benavente, Toribio de. *Memoriales*. Edited by Nancy Joe Dyer, El Colegio de México, 1996.

—. *Historia de los indios de la Nueva España*. Edited by Mercedes Serna and Bernat Castany, Real Academia Española, 2014.

Díaz del Castillo, Bernal. *Historia verdadera de la conquista de la Nueva España*, edited by Carmelo Sáenz de Santa María, Alianza, 1992.

Fabry, Geneviève. "El imaginario apocalíptico en la literatura hispanoamericana: esbozo de una tipología". *Cuadernos LIRICO*, no. 7, 2012, http://journals.openedition.org/lirico/689.

Flores, Enrique "La destrucción de Jerusalén: fantasma, violencia y conquista en un libro de cordel del siglo XVI". *Revista de literaturas populares*, no. 1, 2003, pp. 67–86.

Hernández, Saúl. "Coronavirus: ¿el fin del mundo está cerca?" *El Sol de México*, 3 July 2020, https://www.elsoldemexico.com.mx/mexico/sociedad/coronavirus-el-fin-del-mundo-esta-cerca-covid-19-religiones-apocalipsis-teorias-profesias-5444732.html.

La estigmatización social asociada a la Covid-19: Guía para prevenir y abordar la estigmatización social. UNICEF, February 2020, https://coronavirus.onu.org.mx/wp-content/uploads/2020/03/200633-covid-19-stigma-guide-es.pdf.

Oviedo y Valdés, Gonzalo Fernández de. *Cronica de las indias*, Salamanca, 1851.

Rodríguez Sandoval, Gabriela. "La herencia apocalíptica en Fray Torbio de Benavente, 'Motolinía'". *Estudios de Historia Novohispana*, no. 63, 2020, pp. 33–66.

Roggerone, Santiago Martín. *Apostilla sobre el imaginario apocalíptico.* Consejo Nacional de Investigaciones Científicas y Técnicas, 2020, https://ri.conicet.gov.ar/handle/11336/152378.

Rose, Sonia V. "La revisión de la conquista: narración, interpretación y juicio". *Historia de la literatura Mexicana: la cultura letrada en la nueva España del siglo XVII*, edited by Raquel Chang-Rodríguez, vol. 2, UNAM, 2002, pp. 247–269.

Sánchez, Miguel. *Imagen de la Virgen María, madre de Dios, de Guadalupe milagrosamente aparecida en la ciudad de México: celebrada en su historia, con la profecía del capítulo 12 del Apocalipsis*, Imprenta de LaViuda de Bernardo Calderón, 1648.

Shiller, Robert J. *Narrative Economics: How Stories Go Viral & Drive Major Economic Events.* First Paperback Edition, Princeton University Press, 2020.

Torquemada, Juan de. *Monarquía Indiana.* UNAM, Instituto de Investigaciones Históricas, 1975, https://historicas.unam.mx/publicaciones/publicadigital/monarquia/index.html.

Tojeira, José María. "Coronavirus y religión". *Nómada*, 25 March 2020, https://nomada.gt/blogs/coronavirus-y-religion/.

Vetancurt, Agustín de. *Teatro mexicano: descripción breve de los sucesos ejemplares, históricos, políticos, militares, y religiosos del nuevo mundo Occidental de las Indias*, María de Benavides, Viuda de Juan de Ribera, 1698.

White, Hayden. *El contenido y la forma.* Paidós, 1992.

Chapter 10

Costa Rica Trabaja y Se Cuida[*]

Oral Historical Reflections on Pandemic Inequities

Carmen Coury

Southern Connecticut State University

Abstract

In 2021, ordinary people throughout the world were daily trying to make sense of how Covid-19 was reshaping their lives. This chapter makes use of twelve oral histories to interrogate how ordinary Costa Ricans at this time perceived the pandemic. This chapter locates several narratives that ordinary Costa Ricans were beginning to develop at the time about the pandemic, their government's response, and their role in protecting themselves and their community. Critical in framing the perceptions of interviewees was the vaccination drive that the Costa Rican government was undertaking at the time and misinformation on vaccines, which was hindering vaccination and other public health efforts to control the spread of the virus in the country. Informants discussed their thoughts on vaccines, misinformation, government, and personal responsibilities, but additionally, the ways they saw the pandemic widening existing socioeconomic inequities within Costa Rica and globally.

Keywords: Costa Rica, Vaccinations, Personal Responsibility, Neo-Liberalism, Misinformation

* * *

Introduction

In 2021 the pandemic was an ongoing and evolving global event, which had already cost millions of human lives, shaken economic stability, and had forced people to change how they interacted socially. As the pandemic unfolded ordinary people throughout the world, including in the Central American

---

[*] The phrase "Costa Rica trabaja y se cuida", is a slogan developed by the Costa Rican government in September of 2020. The slogan sought to guide a safe reopening of the nation's economy, after several months of pandemic shutdowns. The phrase might best be translated as: "Costa Rica works and takes care of itself".

Republic of Costa Rica, were daily trying to make sense of how Covid-19 was reshaping their lives. For oral historians, contemporary technology, namely, smartphones and video meeting software, provided a chance to record ordinary people's perspectives and experiences during this pandemic.[1] In March of 2020 historian Jason Kelly organized a global "rapid response" oral history initiative, *The COVID-19 Oral History Project*.[2] In collaboration with this effort, the author of this chapter interviewed twelve Costa Ricans between May and June of 2021 to record how the pandemic was impacting them as well as their broader society.

Oral histories represent a distinctive and valuable narrative resource, deriving their significance from the fundamental notion that individuals are inherently narrative beings who comprehend the world around them by constructing and sharing stories. Oral histories capture both the narratives that ordinary people are fashioning about their lives and the narratives that they are developing about the social, economic, political, and cultural realities in which their personal narrative is embedded. These narratives can serve to humanize the accounts developed by historians and other scholars in relation to past and present events. Nevertheless, it is crucial to acknowledge that oral histories encounter certain limitations, primarily in relation to the impact of time, which can distort and reshape narrators' memories. A rapid response effort was employed, to mitigate this challenge, though this approach introduced additional potential constraints. Since the pandemic was an ongoing event at the time of the interviews, both the narrator and the researcher lacked foresight regarding the future evolution of the conditions they were experiencing. Consequently, the interviews resulting from this rapid response effort offer a series of snapshots, capturing a particular moment within the trajectory of the pandemic.

---

[1] Oral histories have been collected of earlier pandemics, most notably during the Great Depression Federal Writers' Project, which recorded interviews of ordinary US-Americans, including several where narrators reflected on the Spanish Flu pandemic of 1918-1919. Unlike this 1930s project that reflected on an incident that had taken place over a decade ago, the works collected for *The COVID-19 Oral History Project* were recorded as this pandemic unfolded. Ideally this will allow for future scholars to gage perceptions of the pandemic as it was unfolding. Spanish Flu Oral histories can be accessed through US The Library of Congress website: https://www.loc.gov/search/?c=25&q=flu&st=list

[2] In April and May of 2020 in support of this global effort, the author collected fifteen oral histories of Costa Rican adults living in San José and the greater San José metro area, known as the Central Valley. Eight interviewees in this initial effort were women and seven were men. Thirteen were employed and two were retired. In an effort to see how the situation on the ground had shifted during the first year of the pandemic, the author reached out to all fifteen of her initial narrators and invited them to a follow up interview. Two chose not to participate, one sadly, had passed away.

This chapter makes use of this collection of twelve oral histories (Appendix A).[3] These interviews reveal several disparate narratives that ordinary Costa Ricans were beginning to develop in mid-2021, a period in which the country was experiencing its third wave of Covid-19 infections. Narrators expressed their thoughts on how the pandemic was impacting their jobs, the broader economy, their understanding of government responsibility, and their interpersonal relationships. Additionally, narrators assessed their nation's vaccination drive and the role of misinformation in hindering this effort. The first-hand accounts and personal experiences narrators encompass a multitude of pandemic experiences and perspectives, but a salient concern all narrators shared was that Covid-19 was underscoring, if not widening, deep-rooted socio-economic inequities both within Costa Rican society and between the Global North and the Global South.[4]

Shifting State and Individual Responsibilities and Culpabilities

The Costa Rican government was initially very successful in containing the spread of Covid-19, which was first detected in the country in March of 2020 (Esposito and Murillo). In fact, as late as 1 June 2020 the country had only 1,084 confirmed cases and ten fatalities linked to this pathogen ("Costa Rica Coronavirus Cases"). With a national population of just over 5 million, these statistics suggested that for the first months of the pandemic Costa Ricans had a firm handle on the virus.

In March of 2020 the Costa Rican government adopted a series of measures to safeguard public health, including the forced closing of in-dining services at restaurants and bars and vehicular restrictions, which largely succeeded in keeping Costa Ricans home. Additionally, the government created the *Bono Proteger* programme, which provided a small subsidy to the nation's most vulnerable citizens ("Programa Proteger"). While there were issues with this programme's rollout, it provided sufficient monies to allow street venders and other members of the informal economy to largely stay home in the first months of the pandemic (Nuñez Chacón, "240.860 personas").

---

[3] In 2021, seven women and five men whose ages range from twenty-nine to sixty-four years of age were interviewed. All but one interviewee lived and worked in the greater San José metropolitan area. Narrators' occupations included a police officer, a university professor, a social worker, a school counselor, a secondary school teacher, an attorney, an oral surgeon, a shop owner, an adjunct instructor, and a retired agronomist. This small sample is not statistically significant, but instead presents several case studies, which may meaningfully help current and future scholars examining the human impacts of the pandemic on Costa Rican society. Additional information on the interviewees, pandemic interviewing methods, and interview questions can be found in Appendices A, B, and C.
[4] All interviews were uploaded to the *COVID-19 Oral History Project* website. Interviews can be accessed here: https://covid-19archive.org/s/oralhistory/page/welcome.

Arguably the state's actions in the first months of the pandemic put public health concerns above economic interests and encouraged Costa Ricans to see their state as a paternal protector. This idea was embodied in the figure of the nation's Health Minister, Dr Daniel Salas, who provided daily televised briefings on the pandemic for several months in 2020. In late March of 2020, *Diario Extra* would report that memes of Salas as "Superman" and/or "Clark Kent" were widely circulating on social media (Morales). Salas' celebrity arguably reflected a broader desire on the part of the masses for a responsive state that would guide them safely through the pandemic (Kordick Rothe).

Costa Ricans confronted a very different pandemic a year later. By 31 May 2021, a staggering 318,986 individuals had been infected and 4,041 of these individuals had died ("Costa Rica Coronavirus Cases"). Moreover, as interviewees were quick to explain, these numbers were rising daily as the country was facing its third and most deadly wave of infection to date. When asked what had changed in the first year of the pandemic, narrators pointed to a pair of potential causes for the rise in cases: shifting priorities on the part of the government and social exhaustion with public health recommendations.

For attorney Irene Lobo Hernández the government's decision to reopen the nation's beaches in advance of the Easter Week holiday explained at least one of the causes of the recent surge in cases. Lobo noted that the government's decision was moved not by public health concerns, but a desire to alleviate the financial hardship tourist-dependent beach communities were facing. Unfortunately, as Lobo detailed with the reopening of the beaches "people believed…that the government was providing an invitation to return to life as it was [before the pandemic] and so the people did not take care of themselves". More to the point, she explained that the nation's beaches filled up with national tourists and that "none of them respected the public health mandates, none of them respected [social] distancing". Lobo added, "we have to keep taking care of ourselves… we must keep washing our hands and wearing a mask out, but the people forgot".

Lobo's emphasis on self-care is worth highlighting as it reflects the rhetorical success of the government's "Costa Rica trabaja y se cuida", or "Costa Rica works and takes care of itself", policy that started in September of 2020. The adoption of this slogan went hand in hand with the government's decision to slowly reopen the nation's economy ("Costa Rica permitirá mayor apertura"). For Psychology professor, Carmen Caamaño Morua, this policy reflected the government's decision to place the Chamber of Commerce's interests before those of the public good. Moreover, she suggested that in the first months of the pandemic the state had strictly followed the Ministry of Health's recommendations and encouraged its citizens to think of the government as the protector of the public good. Beginning in September, however, the state began requiring its citizens to assume individual responsibility for their health. This new slogan, as Caamaño asserted, liberated the government from the task of keeping the population safe and reflects a more neoliberal ideal of personal responsibility. This rhetorical campaign arguably succeeded. Indeed, each of my twelve narrators, asserted at some point in our conversation that the rise in infection rates was the product of citizens' choosing not to follow public health mandates, rather than of poor state policies.

For Erika Franco Quirós, who works at a night school as a school counsellor in the rural community of Siquirres, the "largest lesson I have learned in this pandemic, is that [your health] … is not the responsibility of the Ministry of Health nor of Doctor Salas, but yours". Franco added that it was everyone's responsibility to follow the public health protocols "for your conscience, for your loved ones, [and] for your society". Franco's reflection not only shows that she had personalized this new governmental policy but had in effect liberated the Minister of Health from the responsibility of keeping Costa Ricans healthy. As the government asked citizens to take increasing responsibility for their health and that of their communities, Salas' celebrity declined. Flory Chacón Roldán, an adjunct professor at the University of Costa Rica, explained Salas was "no longer the face of confidence, people no longer make cakes shaped like Daniel Salas, nor do they send him gifts…" Despite his waning popularity, Chacón stressed that she retained a deep-seated respect for Salas, and his apolitical "passion for public health".

Implicit in the government's "Costa Rica trabaja y se cuida" slogan, is the idea that those who fell ill failed to care for themselves and their family and are thus culpable. This idea is clearly articulated by retired agronomist, Javier Echeverría Hernández, who responded "it's purely one's fault", to the question of who or what might explain the uptick in cases during the first half of 2021. Echeverría added that people were intentionally flouting public health-inspired regulations; as an example, he shared that he had neighbours who "often … have clandestine parties…". Store owner, Rodrigo Hernández Cordero, also brought up the issue of underground parties, which he explained were largely organized by "young people". While Hernández felt these parties had the potential to be super-spreader events, unlike Echeverría, he was not comfortable blaming the partygoers, noting "when I was young … we [partied] … I cannot blame a young person [for] … doing what I would have done".

Some interviewees suggested that while it was true that personal decisions greatly decreased or increased an individual's risk of contracting Covid-19, some people had greater opportunities to ignore social distancing and other public health mandates without scrutiny. This idea was highlighted by Chacón, who "sometimes works weddings" to supplement her income as an adjunct professor. She related that she had recently worked at a "wedding for very wealthy people" and was struck by how little Covid-19 shaped this event. She recalled that 300 people attended the wedding, even though at the time of the wedding, public health mandates limited social gatherings to 75 individuals. She added that she did not feel at risk of contracting Covid-19, however, because the event was outside, she was masked, and all the attendees were required to have proof of a recent negative Covid-19 test to attend. While the wedding's organizers took precautions to safeguard the health of their guests, they broke the law and did so with impunity. Chacón explained "the police came, but they could not enter, because it was a private event…" and they had no warrant. Chacón was quick to contrast what happened at this wedding with what happened to less wealthy people who disobeyed social distancing regulations: "that day the police could not enter, but…the police [regularly] enter working class neighbourhoods to remove folks [gathered] in small houses".

Chacón's socio-economic analysis was echoed in Caamaño's impression of how the media demonized the poor who violate public health protocols. Reflecting on news coverage she had seen, she explained that the media "expose people who have parties in [poor] neighbourhoods like Leon XIII…they put the camera in their faces". Caamaño added that because "the homes of the wealthy have large walls no cameras can enter", when they throw parties. In Caamaño's estimation this inequity was amplified in the nation's judiciary, a claim she illustrated by pointing out that when the courts were asked to issue warrants to search wealthy homes suspected of violating pandemic restrictions "they speak of civil liberties, but there are no civil liberties when the police enter a party in a poor neighbourhood". Importantly, illegal parties were not the only way people were contracting Covid-19 as Caamaño noted, many of the ill "had … been forced to be on the frontline … supermarket [workers] and janitors. These workers have had high infection rates and deaths".

Neo-Liberal Pandemic Priorities and Economic Challenges

The decision to reopen the economy in September of 2020 was arguably spurred by very real economic concerns that might best be understood through the September 2020 announcement by the government that they had secured a 1.75 billion dollars loan package from the International Monetary Fund (IMF) to help cover pandemic related expenses. The IMF loan was contingent upon the freezing of public sector wages and tax reform. These announced austerity measures were met with widespread popular protests. While none of my narrators claimed that they participated in these protests, thousands of small business owners and union members paralyzed traffic in the nation's capital of San José for nearly two months (Cuffe). National economic conditions were dire. In June of 2020, Costa Rica recorded a 24% unemployment rate (Zúñiga). By December of 2020, Costa Rica confronted an 8.7% fiscal deficit (O'Neill).

These circumstances encouraged labour and business leaders to meet with policymakers and broker an agreement that allowed for the Legislative Assembly to pass the IMF loan proposal in January of 2021 (Murillo).

As the IMF conflict and poor financial indicators suggest, the pandemic was largely experienced as an economic rather than a public health crisis for most Costa Ricans in 2020. This was certainly the case for small storeowner Rodrigo Hernández Cordero. The crippling impact of Covid-19 vehicular restrictions, which went into effect in March of 2020 and were not relaxed until February of 2021, had forced Hernández to consider laying off employees, in May of 2020, for the first time in over forty years of business (Kordick Rothe). A year later, in May of 2021, Hernández, asserted that the economic situation remained dismal. This was at least partially due to the reinstatement of vehicular restrictions in March of 2021, in response to the outbreak of this third wave of infection (Gonzalez, et al.). Additionally, however, the virus itself seemed a more concrete threat in 2021 than it had in 2020. Hernández had found "people are not going out much, [because] we have had some large upticks in infections and deaths". Hernández shared his customers' fears of the virus but added "we don't close because there is no money … to stay closed…" Hernández emphasized the economic stress sharing "so many locales are empty, many stores are closed, many of us [shop owners] are just trying to survive, it is not a pretty situation".

Fears of the virus and vehicular restrictions likely kept many potential shoppers at home in 2021, but so too did personal economic circumstances. In May of 2021 Costa Rica had reduced its unemployment rate by a full 7% from the year before, but at 17.4% it remained high (Zúñiga). Similarly, the underemployment rate had contracted by 9%, yet 15.5% of workers remained underemployed. Equally telling, between 2020 and 2021, 138,000 workers joined the informal economy, which supported 875,000 workers (Zúñiga). These numbers show that while the economic reopening had reduced both under and unemployment rates, it had failed to create more labour security.

Although none of my informants reported being unemployed in May of 2021, many of them were struggling financially, including attorney Irene Lobo who explained that in the year since the pandemic began she found herself with: "much less work … many folks have had to close their businesses [so many of my] clients are hurting [economically]… there is much less work for me now, so I only come into the office four days a week". As Lobo was paid only when she completed work for clients, she added "the situation is bad, sincerely, economically things are not good".

Public sector workers were finding they did not have the job security many once believed. This was made clear to Silvia Azofeifa Ramos, who is an adjunct at the University of Costa Rica, after the dismissal of a colleague who she described as "an older gentleman" who had "worked at the university for twenty-nine years". Azofeifa clarified, "he was not fired, but they [university administrators] did not renew his contract, which is almost the same thing". Clearly concerned about her former colleague's welfare she added "We are in a pandemic. What job could a man his age possibly find?". Azofiefa's rhetorical question was one that many workers and their families were forced to ask themselves in 2020 and 2021 as they watched clients, shoppers, patrons, positions, businesses, and contracts dissipate.

Azofeifa's concern for her unemployed colleague mirrored those of many narrators, who worried about the pandemic's long-term impact on the middle class. Police officer Francisco Guzmán Solano opined that "the current [economic] situation has mainly affected the middle-class". He went on to explain that the Costa Rican middle-class was defined by their ability to secure and pay bank loans to finance the purchase of a home and car. Guzmán noted that when middle-class workers lost their jobs it often meant they also lost their home and car. Guzmán suggested that middle-class workers were "the most affected" of the "half a million people without work". Emphasizing the downward mobility middle-class workers had experienced, Guzmán shared that "the poverty [rate] increased 12% from a year and a half ago". Guzmán's work convinced him that "when the unemployment rate is very high…folks rob to eat". Hence, he was not surprised by the "discouraging" increases "in vehicular thefts [and] petty theft" he had seen at work.

The Emotive and Social Costs of the Pandemic

As Covid-19 cases rose through the start of 2021, the pandemic arguably transformed from a potential public health threat into a concrete and immediate one. While none of my narrators knew anyone who had died from Covid-19 in 2020, in 2021, all twelve informants revealed that they had lost a close friend or family member to the virus. Additionally, one interviewee, Danitza Guzmán Solano, shared that she had contracted the virus earlier in 2021.

As the pandemic became increasingly familiar, some narrators began to contemplate how the virus had already reshaped their lives. For social worker José Pablo Enríquez Arcia, the pandemic had "been like an earthquake in my life…what I had before is no longer there". Enríquez clarified that what was gone was a long-term romantic partner. The recent breakup led Enríquez to contemplate the "heavy psychological weight [that comes] from thinking about yourself, as a possible transmitter of something terrible, in this case a disease". Taking this idea further, Enríquez explained that the consequence of recognizing "yourself as a [potential] agent of transmission" had dire consequences for romantic intimacy and broader social intimacy. Enríquez, who lived alone, added "I want to see my family, but I am very frightened of infecting them, and being the cause of their death… it is very difficult, how… do we interact with one another without our bodies, I think this idea weighs on many people".

Enríquez's words likely would have resonated with Franco who shared that the pandemic "led me and my [romantic] partner to break up, because…he is in Panama, and I am here…it's easy to blame Covid. Perhaps, if the border was open, maybe the situation would be different, but it is not. And I must accept that". While Franco, like Enríquez, highlighted the challenges of intimacy in a pandemic, the dissolution of her relationship also places into focus how international travel restrictions spurred by the pandemic had painfully separated couples and families.

Ending a romantic partnership is never easy, but for Franco the pandemic made it more difficult to work through the pain of losing her boyfriend. As she noted, "I have felt this breakup differently, from others I have had [because of the pandemic,] it's been…for me and so many others very difficult the emotional [repercussions]". Franco lived alone and explained "the emotional [pain] builds up… alongside the isolation…the inability to share, perhaps, with your circle of close friends… and feel better…this is what [currently] makes the emotional situation so difficult". Additionally, these same public health protocols made it all but impossible for Franco to consider the possibility of finding a new romantic interest. She reflected: "there is no way, in fact, where I'm going to meet someone, as I do not even go out, and so I am learning to live day-by-day". Enríquez, clearly, had also thought about how the pandemic might limit his romantic prospects: "I have thought about how much time will it be until I receive a hug…and how [in a pandemic] this is a transgressive action [and so too] kissing and many other things".

Enríquez and Franco provide a window into how the pandemic was forcing people to re-evaluate human intimacy and connection. These questions were also front and centre for those who had lost family and friends to Covid-19, like Lobo, whose older sister, Eugenia passed away on 4 April 2021. Lobo explained that pandemic realities had made it difficult for her to find closure. Indeed, she detailed how her "sister was admitted to the hospital and I could not…even see her, we [Lobo's family] could not say our goodbyes…". Reiterating the pain of losing her sister, Lobo shared "it hurts a lot, not even being able to say goodbye, not even being able to be with her for her last moments…". Lobo and her family were not only unable to comfort her sister in her final moments but were forced to mourn her passing alone. As Lobo explains, pandemic protocols meant "we had to hurry to put her in a coffin and bury her… [and] we could not do anything more than bury her". In times of sickness and heartbreak people seek out comfort from others in the form of an embrace or a heartfelt exchange of words. In other circumstances, Lobo's family might have organized a large funeral and wake allowing their extended family to come together and mourn their loss.

Like many others in this pandemic, Lobo and her family, however, were left to mourn in isolation and her sister was forced to spend her final days alone.

The need to socially distance alongside stay-at-home measures unintentionally worsened the situation for countless victims of domestic abuse. Silvia Muñoz Mata, who is a domestic violence activist, observed "an increase in domestic violence", since the pandemic began, despite the fact that "statistics do not show an increase". Muñoz explained this was "because victims...reside with their aggressor and can't denounce the violence, as their aggressor is [often] there with them listening and reading their text messages". Muñoz furthermore suggested that the public health slogan "stay home", had limited her ability and that of NGOs and state agencies to provide workshops, services, and other activities to women and children who lived in abusive conditions.

These concerns about abuse in the home, were shared by educators, like, Danitza Guzmán, a public high school social studies teacher, who noted many students confronted difficult "situations" at home that complicated learning. To highlight this issue, Guzmán mentioned the then-recent "suicides...of a nine-year-old boy and six-year-old". Both cases, which took place within 18-hours of one another, made headlines in papers, like *Diario Extra* (Castro Chávez). For social worker, José Pablo Enríquez, "these child suicides...raise big questions about...young people's mental health..." and underscored "the need, despite [social workers] fears of contracting Covid-19...to provide clinical work". For educators, activists, and social workers, the pandemic had left children and other vulnerable populations without ready access to important mental health and other institutional supports.

Private and Public Educational Divisions

Since the pandemic started, Costa Rican children have also seen their access to public education reduced. Between March and December of 2020, the nation's public schools adopted a fully online educational system. Remote learning, however, highlighted the fact that approximately 325,000 school-aged children did not have consistent access to the internet and/or a tablet or smart phone (Condega). This was particularly the case in rural regions; the Ministry of Education responded to this resource scarcity with photocopied lesson plans, which were distributed throughout the country, for less fortunate students to pursue their learning remotely on their own (Cordero Pérez).

Fears that public school students were falling behind academically, especially those without the digital resources to attend their classes virtually, led the Minister of Education to adopt a "combined" teaching model in January of 2021. In this combined model, students had the option to complete all their coursework remotely or to attend class in small subgroups every several days and complete other schoolwork remotely ("Educación Combinada").

For teachers, like Danitza Guzmán, the combined model greatly increased educators' workload by requiring them to prepare and teach both online and in-person lessons each day to different sections of each class. While teaching exclusively remotely or exclusively face-to-face would have been easier for Guzmán, her primary concern with combined education was that her students were behind. Social distancing requirements in her small classrooms meant she saw each student "just once every fifteen days". On the days between on-ground meetings, students were expected to work through a "study guide" she prepared for them. The students, however, had not advanced at home. This was largely, she believed, because they were asked to "help out at home" when they "need to be in class". When Guzmán and I spoke, she explained that her world history class should have been "starting the Cold War [module] but we have not even started the Russian Revolution". Given how far behind her student were, as most were in their penultimate year of high school, Guzmán struggled to imagine how they would perform on their university qualifying exams. In clear frustration, Guzmán added she feared that her pupils were a "lost generation".

As difficult as the first six months of the 2021 academic year had been for Guzmán and her students, she felt nothing short of defeated by the Ministry of Education's decision to "reprogram" the academic calendar. The schedule shift saw her, and all her students forced to take a "holiday" from May 24th through July 9th. This meant that from 12 July 2021 through 21 January 2022, classes would run with just a one-week break for Christmas and New Year ("MEP oficializa calendario"). The Ministry of Education announced this reprogramming on 17 May 2021, in response to increasing infection rates among teachers ("Ministerio de Educación de Costa Rica").

Importantly, however, the Ministry of Education permitted private schools to retain the traditional academic calendar that allowed their students to complete their courses before the December holiday. As Guzmán explained "my niece who attends a private [school], remains [in classes virtually]…". Since college entrance exams for the University of Costa Rica, the nation's premier university, were scheduled for 11 January 2022, this placed private-school students who were able to attend fully virtual classes arguably at a considerable advantage over their public-school counterparts (Universidad de Costa Rica).

Balancing the Public Health and Public Educational Needs

As worried as Guzmán was about her students' academic work, she was equally concerned about her own safety and that of other educators. Guzmán was not alone. Franco, who works as a school counsellor, explained that "as much as you may want to follow [public health] protocols... many educational institutions... cannot". To make her point, Franco noted "I work with five other people" in a room too small to follow "social distancing recommendations". Making these conditions more dangerous was the fact that few teachers or educational support staff were vaccinated. While medical professionals, firefighters, and police officers were largely vaccinated in January as part of the first phase of the vaccine rollout, teachers were not. Positing as to why the government had not included teachers in phase one of the rollout, given their front-facing work, Guzmán jokingly responded that the government must have believed teachers were "immortal... like the Olympian gods..."

The nation's educational unions responded to educators' concerns on 14 May 2021 delivering an open letter to Costa Rican President Carlos Alvarado Quesada. The *Seminario Universidad*, reported the unions demanded a return to fully remote learning since 150 educational staff had died of Covid-19 (Nuñez Chacón, "Sindicatos"). While President Alvarado made no executive order, the unions' letter likely helped save teachers' lives. Indeed, it almost certainly prompted the Ministry of Education's decision to reshuffle the academic schedule and the Ministry of Health's decision on 18 May 2021 to begin vaccinating teachers ("Autoridades dan seguimiento"). Guzmán's clear discontent with the government, even after both the Ministry of Education and Health seemingly bowed to educator's demands, highlights the multifaceted challenge government officials faced in 2021 as they sought to keep the economy running while also keeping people safe.

The Quest for Vaccines in an Inequitable World

Educators' demands that the government vaccinate them underscores the faith that all but two of my interviewees expressed in vaccines. This idea arguably reflected government officials' early commitment to securing timely access to a vaccine. In March of 2020, President Alvarado, took a leading role in starting a global conversation on how the World Health Organisation might ensure that not just wealthy countries would be able to purchase Covid-19 vaccines once they were made available (Alvarado Quesada and Adhanom Ghebreyesus). These conversations led to the formation of COVAX, in April of 2020, which was established to ensure poorer nations, like Costa Rica, with access to vaccines (Berkley).

On 24 December 2020 the Costa Rican government began its Covid-19 vaccination programme and in mid-January of 2021, the news outlet France 24 would report that Costa Rica, alongside Argentina, Chile, and Mexico, were the only Latin American nations to have begun vaccinating their citizens (Cué Barberena). Critical to this effort was the nation's cherished socialized healthcare system, the *Caja Costarricense de Seguro Social* (CCSS), which purchased all the vaccines the country received through March of 2021 (Macaya). Neighbouring countries that relied exclusively on COVAX to start their vaccine programmes had later starting dates and slower campaigns. In fact, Costa Rica received its first 43,200 COVAX doses in April of 2021 over three months after the CCSS began administering vaccines ("COVAX vaccine roll-out").

First responders, who made up the "First Group" of the vaccine rollout, were largely immunized in the first two months of 2021. On 24 February 2021, the government began vaccinating individuals over the age of 58, who composed the "Second Group" in the vaccination programme ("Costa Rica inicia vacunación"). This second phase was not nearly as fast as the first; indeed, it was still ongoing alongside the third phase, which began on 12 May 2021, which made vaccines available to anyone over the age of sixteen with pre-existing risk factors ("Grupo 3 de vacunación").

Many of my interviewees expressed both pride and frustration with the CCSS's vaccination campaign. Echeverría, for instance, eagerly noted that while Costa Rica had "the third highest vaccination rate in Latin America", the vaccination campaign had "been very slow in my estimation, and I think that is the general impression". Seemingly affirming Echeverría's impressions, several narrators expressed that they wished that the CCSS could more rapidly vaccinate them and/or their loved ones. Yet, none blamed the CCSS for the slow rollout. Moreover, many, like police officer Francisco Guzmán, expressed that they were "grateful to the health personnel" at the CCSS, who had been daily risking their lives to care for Covid-19 patients. For Guzmán, the problem was a question of personnel, namely there were insufficient doctors and nurses to both care for the ill and vaccinate the healthy populace.

While Guzmán focused on a systemic need for more "human infrastructure", others, like Chacón, blamed global socio-economic inequities. Chacón, opined that "vaccines should be here", in the same numbers as they were in wealthier countries. She added that tragically "the same formula [for a successful vaccination campaign] in Israel, where they were able to so rapidly vaccinate themselves" was impossible in Costa Rica, because her nation was not as wealthy as Israel. For Chacón, the fact that Costa Rica could not afford to undertake a vaccination campaign with the same rapidity as wealthier countries was unjust. Moreover, as Chacón noted, it highlighted the global community's failure to answer the World Health Organisation's call in early 2020 for "an equitable and democratic distribution of vaccines".

One of the principal ways that interviewees brought up the inequitable allocation of vaccines was through what Caamaño described as "vaccine tourism", a phenomenon that she explained placed into relief both the fact that "some countries have more vaccines than others" and that "just some" Costa Ricans had the money required to tap into the vaccine surplus of wealthier countries. Echoing Caamaño's critique, Lobo explained "everyone should be able to get vaccinated without need to travel...it is painful to see that some countries have the ability to vaccinate everyone, and some do not". With the costs of a weekend vaccination trip, running between 800 and 1200 dollars, this option was far beyond the means of most Costa Ricans. Indeed, in 2021, the average monthly salary of a Costa Rican worker was just 830 dollars (Stotz). As expensive as vaccine travel was between the months of February and March of 2021, Costa Rica saw 112% increase in travel to the US, which the media attributed to the sale of vaccine travel packages (Garza). By August, 15,000 Costa Ricans had received a vaccine abroad (Rodríguez). While the number of vaccine tourists was arguably statistically insignificant, the fact so many interviewees brought up this phenomenon, points to the importance it played in shaping how Costa Ricans understood the role of wealth in defining access to vaccines. Yet, some vaccine travellers, as Chacón pointed out, were taking on "credit card" debts to secure a vaccine abroad. Although none of my informants had travelled to get vaccinated, several, like Muñoz, shared that "if I had the [financial] ability... I would go immediately".

Falsehoods, Conspiracies, and the Anti-Vaccination Movement

By mid-June 2021 the CCSS reported 740,000 Costa Ricans were fully vaccinated and over two million had received at least their first dose of the vaccine (Rodríguez). By October of 2021, as vaccine availability increased, 64% of the country had received at least one dose of the vaccine (Rodríguez). While these were arguably impressive numbers for a small country, for Dr Roman Macaya Hayes, Executive President of the CCSS, the Covid-19 vaccination rollout had not been nearly as successful as he would have projected. In an October 2021 interview for the Centre for Strategic and International Studies, Macaya explained that the country's previous vaccine campaigns had had "very high acceptance...we quickly reach vaccination rates ... above 95%". As recently as 2019, Macaya noted the CCSS had launched an HPV vaccine campaign that reached a 98% vaccination rate that same year. The Covid-19 campaign had, however, proved "harder, we're reaching diminishing returns". For Macaya the cause was clear: "misinformation...spread" through social media (Macaya).

Supporting Macaya's perceptions, each of my narrators reported that they were aware of several vaccine conspiracy theories circulating on social media. Most, like Francisco Guzmán, laughingly shared how they had heard false claims of how the vaccine implanted "a chip" of some sort. Caamaño noted that she had seen a video claiming the virus and vaccine had both been developed by "Bill Gates", in a profit-driven scheme intended to "earn [him] millions". All my interviewees expressed a combination of amusement and disbelief in the misinformation they had seen circulating on social media. Yet they also all had either a family member, close friend, or work colleague who had expressed anti-vax ideas to them. Echeverría shared that his younger brother had been deeply influenced by misinformation and was not only a "non-believer" in the vaccine but was an adherent to the "infamous" hydroxychloroquine as both a preventative and a cure. Additionally, two of my narrators, Rodrigo Hernández Cordero and his son, Rodrigo Hernández Montero, who were both eligible to receive the vaccine at the time of our interview, had chosen not to be vaccinated.

Hernández Montero, who is an oral surgeon, questioned the scientific process behind the vaccines' approval. Critical for him was the fact that "the FDA… [only] approved [the vaccine] for emergency [use]…" which meant the vaccine, "has not completed the normal phases" of study. Hernández Cordero, like his son, felt "the vaccine is still an experiment" and he did not wish to be a "guinea pig" for science. Both men shared that they felt they were keeping safe by doing their best to social distance, wash their hands frequently, and wear masks. Of course, as an oral surgeon, Hernández Montero consistently interacted with unmasked patients. This is perhaps why he found that people were "often surprised" that he had chosen not to be vaccinated. Hernández Montero noted he was not alone. In fact, he knew several doctors and dentists at his hospital who had also refused the vaccine.

At the time of our interview, none of these workers had faced disciplinary consequences, though Hernández Montero had been asked to justify his refusal to his supervisors. At this meeting he explained "it's not that I do not want to get vaccinated, it's that I still want to see… to [better understand] what I am injecting myself with". His supervisor had promised him a response from the CCSS in a week, but "two months have gone by, and they still have not responded". Today, the FDA has fully approved both the Moderna and Pfizer vaccines. Given that the Pfizer vaccine is available in Costa Rica, it is possible, Hernández Montero, his father, and colleagues have decided to join the ranks of the vaccinated. However, as misinformation continues to circulate, this is far from certain.

Whilst Hernández Cordero and Hernández Montero were both vaccine hesitant in mid-2021, they appear to have been a minority. In fact, the advent of vaccine tourism arguably reveals that thousands of Costa Ricans had no such hesitations. For most of my informants, like Franco, the vaccine was a source of considerable hope, that things might be able to return to normal. At the time interviewees had cause to believe vaccines would provide a reprieve from the challenges the pandemic had unleashed on their lives, communities, and nation. Indeed, as Franco and others noted, they were deeply inspired by the images that were circulating on social media of US-Americans ditching their masks after the CDC lifted the mask requirement in late April for fully vaccinated people (Sun). Shortly after the interviews were completed in 2021, however, the highly contagious Delta variant reshaped the pandemic once again (Anthes).

Conclusion

While the pandemic continues to evolve, these twelve oral histories provide a series of snapshots of Costa Rican society in mid-2021 that reveal divisions not just over the question of vaccination safety, but between socioeconomic classes. Indeed, social restrictions meant to stop the spread of Covid-19 were being flouted with impunity by the wealthiest in Costa Rica, while violations of these same restrictions by members of the poorer classes resulted in public humiliation, fines, and even arrests. Additionally, the economic strains of pandemic-inspired shutdowns were being felt by members of the working and professional classes, who reported an unprecedented reduction in clients and customers.

At the same time, therapists, activists, teachers, social workers, and school councillors worried about the consequences that "stay home" measures were having on the children and women whose wellbeing was their principal concern. They arguably had reason for alarm, as the pandemic was creating conditions that inspired interpersonal divisions and isolation.

Perhaps, however, the most disconcerting divide that the pandemic expanded was that between private- and public-school students. The May 2021 decision to shut public schools for an early "holiday", while allowing private schools to continue remotely, put public school students at a greater disadvantage. Yet, as 325,000 public school students lacked the infrastructure to access an online classroom, fully remote education would arguably have put these poorer students at an even greater disadvantage. The forced recess, however, meant seniors from the nations' public high schools would be required to take their college entrance exams before completing their final year of school. As these exams and the university have long been an avenue by which bright, hardworking, poor children enter the middle class, the pandemic appeared to have closed that option to many of these children.

Vaccines promised to help begin the process of recovery and repair, for many, but Costa Rica (and other poorer nations) proved unable to provide vaccines with the same speed as wealthier nations. The emergence of vaccine tourism in 2021 highlighted deep socio-economic divisions both within Costa Rica and between the Global North and South. Moreover, the rise of this health travel embodied the government's successful neoliberal "Costa Rica trabaja y se cuida" campaign that made individuals responsible for their own health, a responsibility the wealthiest proved most able to take on.

Bibliography

Alvarado Quesada, Carlos, and Tedros Adhanom Ghebreyesus. "Globalizing the Fight Against the Pandemic". *Project Syndicate,* 29 May 2020, https://www.project-syndicate.org/commentary/covid19-access-pool-vaccine-data-ip-sharing-by-carlos-alvarado-quesada-and-tedros-adhanom-ghebreyesus-2020-05.

Anthes, Emily. "The Delta Variant: What Scientists Know". *The New York Times,* 14 October 2021, https://www.nytimes.com/2021/06/22/health/delta-variant-covid.html.

"Autoridades dan seguimiento al Proceso de vacunación de docentes". *Gobierno de Costa Rica,* 2 June 2021, https://presidencia.gobiernocarlosalvarado.cr/comunicados/2021/06/autoridades-dan-seguimiento-al-proceso-de-vacunacion-de-docentes/.

Azofeifa Ramos, Silvia. Interview. Conducted by Carmen Kordick Coury, 19 May 2021. *A Journal of the Plague Year,* https://covid-19archive.org/s/oralhistory/item/56676.

Berkley, Seth. "COVAX Explained". *Gavi the Vaccine Alliance,* 3 September 2020, https://gavi.org/vaccineswork/covax-explained.

Caamaño Morua, Carmen. Interview. Conducted by Carmen Kordick Coury, 11 June 2021. *A Journal of the Plague Year,* https://covid-19archive.org/s/archive/item/56686

Castro Chávez, Josué. "2 niños se ahorcan en menos de 18 horas". *Diario Extra,* 15 May 2021, https://www.diarioextra.com/Noticia/detalle/449843/2-ni-os-se-ahorcan-en-menos-de-18-horas.

Chacón Roldán, Flory. Interview. Conducted by Carmen Kordick Coury, 21 May 2021. *A Journal of the Plague Year,* https://covid-19archive.org/s/oralhistory/item/56691.

Cordero Pérez, Carlos. "De 324.616 estudiantes sin internet in Costa Rica, solo a 14.000 se le brindaría una solución". *El Financiero,* 3 September 2020, https://www.elfinancierocr.com/tecnologia/de-324616-estudiantes-sin-internet-en-costa-ric/ZUEWSP3S6BCY3BLPU3VTAKG7W4/story/.

Condega, Xavier. "Estudiantes sin 'conexión a Internet, prácticamente estuvieron excluidos de la educación', lamenta Villalta". *elmundo.cr,* 26 January 2021, https://www.elmundo.cr/costa-rica/estudiantes-sin-conexion-a-internet-practicamente-estuvieron-excluidos-de-la-educacion-lamenta-villalta/.

"Costa Rica Coronavirus Cases". *Worldometers,* 10 January 2022, https://www.worldometers.info/coronavirus/country/costa-rica/.

"Costa Rica inicia vacunación a mayores de 58 años, segundo grupo prioritario". *Swissinfo.ch,* 24 January 2021, https://www.swissinfo.ch/spa/coronavirus-costa-rica_costa-rica-inicia-vacunaci%C3%B3n-a-mayores-de-58-a%C3%B1os--segundo-grupo-prioritario/46398404.

"Costa Rica permitirá mayor apertura de comercios durante septiembre". *el Dinero,* 26 August 2020, https://eldinero.com.do/118613/costa-rica-permitira-mayor-apertura-de-comercios-durante-septiembre/.

"COVAX vaccine roll-out Costa Rica". *Gavi the Vaccine Alliance,* 7 April 2021, https://www.gavi.org/covax-vaccine-roll-out/costa-rica.

Cué Barberena, Federico. "Vacunación en América Latina: un comienzo irregular y a paso lento". *France 24,* 13 January 2021, https://www.france24.com/es/am

%C3%A9rica-latina/20210112-vacunacion-america-latina-comienzo-irregular-lento.

Cuffe, Sandra. "Costa Rica's 'explosive' debt crisis: All you need to know". *Aljazeera*, 16 January 2021, https://www.aljazeera.com/news/2021/1/16/costa-rica-explosive-debt-crisis-all-you-need-to-know.

Echeverría Hernández, Javier. Interview. Interview. Conducted by Carmen Kordick Coury. 20 May 2021, *A Journal of the Plague Year*, https://covid-19archive.org/s/oralhistory/item/51349.

"Educación Combinada". *Ministerio de Educación Pública*, XX month year, https://www.mep.go.cr/educacion-combinada.

Enríquez Arcia, José Pablo. Interview. Conducted by Carmen Kordick. Coury, 05 May 2021. *A Journal of the Plague Year*, https://covid-19archive.org/s/oralhistory/item/56783.

Esposito, Anthony and Alvaro Murillo. "Costa Rica Confirms First Coronavirus Case in Central America". *US News and World Reports*, 6 March 2020, https://www.usnews.com/news/world/articles/2020-03-06/costa-rica-confirms-first-coronavirus-case-in-central-america.

Franco Quirós, Erika. Interview. Conducted by Carmen Kordick Coury. 21 May 2021, *A Journal of the Plague Year*, https://covid-19archive.org/s/oralhistory/item/56793.

Garza, Jeffry. "Vacunación flexible dispara salida de ticos hacia los Estados Unidos". *La República*, 7 May 2021, https://www.larepublica.net/noticia/vacunacion-flexible-dispara-salida-de-ticos-hacia-los-estados-unidos.

Gonzalez, Elizabeth, et al. "The Coronavirus in Latin America". *Americas Society/Council of the Americas*, 10 February 2021, https://www.as-coa.org/articles/coronavirus-latin-america#costa-rica.

"Grupo 3 de vacunación contra COVID-19 amplía rango de edad: ahora incluye personas de 16 a 58 años con factores de riesgo". *Ministerio de Salud*, 12 May 2021, https://www.ministeriodesalud.go.cr/index.php/prensa/43-noticias-2021/1028-grupo-3-de-vacunacion-contra-covid-19-amplia-rango-de-edad-ahora-incluye-personas-de-16-a-58-anos-con-factores-de-riesgo#:~:text=12%20de%20mayo%20del%202021,enfermar%20gravemente%20de%20COVID%2D19.

Guzmán Solano, Danitza. Interview. Conducted by Carmen Kordick Coury, 23 June 2021. *A Journal of the Plague Year*, https://covid-19archive.org/s/oralhistory/item/56827.

Guzmán Solano, Francisco. Interview. Conducted by Carmen Kordick Coury, 10 June 2021. *A Journal of the Plague Year*, https://covid-19archive.org/s/oralhistory/item/56844.

Hernández Cordero, Rodrigo. Interview. Conducted by Carmen Kordick Coury, 27 June 2021. *A Journal of the Plague Year*, https://covid-19archive.org/s/oralhistory/item/56861.

Hernández Montero, Rodrigo. Interview. Conducted by Carmen Kordick Coury 15 June 2021. *A Journal of the Plague Year*, https://covid-19archive.org/s/oralhistory/item/56866.

Kordick Rothe, Carmen. "Voces pandémicas: Historias orales sobre el impacto del COVID-19 en el Valle Central de Costa Rica". *Mesoamérica*, vol. 59, 2022, pp. 71–94.

Lobo Hernández, Irene. Interview. Conducted by Carmen Kordick Coury, 1 June 2021. *A Journal of the Plague Year*, https://covid-19archive.org/s/oralhistory/item/56875.

Macaya, Roman. "Building a Resilient Health System: Costa Rica's 80 Year Experiment". Interview by Katherine Bliss. *Pandemic Planet/Center for Strategic and International Studies*, 19 October 2021, https://www.csis.org/analysis/building-resilient-health-system-costa-ricas-80-year-experiment.

"MEP oficializa calendario escolar 2022". *Noticias Costa Rica*, 26 December 2021, https://ncrnoticias.com/nacionales/mep-oficializa-calendario-escolar-2022/.

"Ministerio de Educación de Costa Rica suspende las clases a partir del 24 de mayo y reorganiza ciclo lectivo debido a la pandemia". *CNN Newsource*, 17 May 2021, https://kvia.com/news/noticias/2021/05/17/ministerio-de-educacion-de-costa-rica-suspende-las-clases-a-partir-del-24-de-mayo-y-reorganiza-ciclo-lectivo-debido-a-la-pandemia/.

Morales, Laura. "Daniel Salas protagonista en memes creados por costarricenses". *Diario Extra*, 23 March 2020, https://www.diarioextra.com/Noticia/detalle/414253/daniel-salas-protagonista-en-memes-creados-por-costarricenses.

Muñoz Mata, Silvia. Interview. Conducted by Carmen Kordick Coury, 31 May 2021. *A Journal of the Plague Year*, https://covid-19archive.org/s/oralhistory/item/56887.

Murillo, Alvaro. "In final vote, Costa Rican lawmakers approve $1.8 bln IMF loan". *Nasdaq*, 19 July 2021, https://www.nasdaq.com/articles/in-final-vote-costa-rican-lawmakers-approve-%241.8-bln-imf-loan-2021-07-20.

Nuñez Chacón, María. "240.860 personas se quedaron sin Bono Proteger porque se acabó el dinero". *Semanario Universidad*, 3 February 2021, https://semanariouniversidad.com/pais/240-860-personas-se-quedaron-sin-bono-proteger-porque-se-acabo-el-dinero/.

—. "Sindicatos de Educación exigen intervención de Alvarado para volver a clases a distancia". *Semanario Universidad*, 14 May 2021, https://semanariouniversidad.com/pais/sindicatos-de-educacion-exigen-intervencion-del-presidente-alvarado-para-volver-a-la-virtualidad/.

O'Neill, Aaron. "Costa Rica: Unemployment rate from 1999 to 2020". *Statista*, https://www.statista.com/statistics/443317/unemployment-rate-in-costa-rica/.

"Programa Proteger". *Ministerio de Trabajo y Seguridad Social*, 7 December 2021, https://www.mtss.go.cr/elministerio/despacho/covid-19-mtss/plan_proteger/bono_proteger.html#:~:text=El%20Programa%20Proteger%20(Decreto%20No,ingresos%20por%20el%20COVID%2D1.

Rodríguez, Elizabeth. "Costa Rica supera los 2 millones de personas vacunadas contra la Covid-19". *La República*, 15 June 2021, https://www.larepublica.net/noticia/mas-de-dos-millones-de-personas-vacunadas-contra-la-covid-19-en-costa-rica.

Stotz, John. "Average and Minimum Salary in San José, Costa Rica". *Check in Price*, 11 April 2021, https://checkinprice.com/average-minimum-salary-in-san-jose-costa-rica/#:~:text=Costa%20Rica%20has%20a%20rather,in%20the%20country%20are%20nationwide.

Sun, Lena H. "CDC says fully vaccinated Americans can go without masks outdoors, except in crowded settings". *The Washington Post,* 27 April 2021, https://www.washingtonpost.com/health/2021/04/27/cdc-guidance-masks-outdoors/.

Universidad de Costa Rica. "Fechas y trámites finales proceso de admisión UCR 2021-2022". *Universidad de Costa Rica,* 28 February 2021, https://ori.ucr.ac.cr/sites/default/files/archivos/2021/Fechas_tramites_finales_proceso_admision_2021-2022-7DIC.pdf

Zúñiga, Alejandro. "Costa Rica unemployment rate drops to 17.4%". *The Tico Times,* 8 September 2021, https://ticotimes.net/2021/09/08/costa-rica-unemployment-rate-drops-to-17-4#:~:text=Unemployment%20in%20Costa%20Rica%20was,decreased%20by%207.0%20percentage%20points.

Appendices

Appendix A

Demographic Information on all interviewees at the time of their interview.

Name	Sex	Age	Occupation	Interview Date	Home Location
Silvia Alzofeifa Ramos	F	32	Adjunct Professor	19 May 2021	Sabanilla de Montes de Oca, San José
Carmen Caamaño Morua	F	59	Psychology Professor	11 June 2021	Sabanilla de Montes de Oca, San José
Flory Chacón Roldán	F	32	Adjunct Professor	21 May 2021	Sabanilla de Montes de Oca, San José
Javier Echeverría Hernández	M	62	Retired Agronomist	20 May 2021	Curridabat, San José
José Pablo Enríquez Arcia	M	29	Social Worker	20 May 2021	Barrio Luján, San José
Erika Franco Quirós	F	33	School Counsellor	21 May 2021	Santa Lucía de Barva, Heredia
Danitza Guzmán Solano	F	40	High School Teacher	23 June 2021	Barrio Corazón de Jesús, Heredia
Francisco Guzmán Solano	M	43	Police Officer	10 June 2021	Barrio Fátima, Heredia

Rodrigo Hernández Cordero	M	63	Small business owner	27 June 2021	Santa Lucía de Barva, Heredia
Rodrigo Hernández Montero	M	41	Oral Surgeon, CCSS	15 June 2021	San Rafael, Heredia
Irene Lobo Hernández	F	62	Attorney	1 June 2021	Barva, Heredia
Silvia Muñoz Mata	F	46	Domestic Violence Activist	31 May 2021	San Francisco, Heredia

Appendix B

A Note on Pandemic Methods and My Positionality

Power dynamics between the oral historian and narrators significantly influence the collection and interpretation of oral histories. Oral historians inevitably shape the construction of individual narratives through the interview questions they employ and then again through the selection of vignettes they make from individual accounts to craft a synthesized narrative of a historical moment.

In the present study, the Covid-19 pandemic impacted these dynamics in ways that are challenging to quantify. That said, my positionality, as a first-generation US-American and the daughter of a Costa Rican immigrant, provides me with a unique cultural background and set of personal experiences that undoubtedly influenced my approach to interviewing my twelve narrators. My proficiency in Spanish, my maternal language, allowed my interviewees to speak without concern that I would not understand what they were saying, despite my being a foreigner and not being in the country at the time of the interview.

Conducting interviews via Zoom allowed engagement with participants in Costa Rica while being physically located in the United States. This remote interviewing method simplified scheduling, as it only required interviewees to have internet access and a device. Nevertheless, it introduced technological challenges, leading to occasional disruptions due to connectivity issues. Such interruptions necessitated the repetition of questions or answers and temporary pauses to address technical difficulties. These factors affected the researcher's positionality by influencing the level of engagement, communication, and interruptions in the interview process. Another challenge was that as I was not in the country, I was unable to observe or experience many of the situations that my informants were describing. In past oral history work, I have been able to use my own personal observations to shape my questions and to help guide the conversation; this was not possible in these circumstances. Overall, the researcher's positionality, shaped by personal background and the remote nature of the interviews, influenced the study's dynamics and the construction of narratives within the oral history project.

Appendix C

Interview Questions

Each interviewee was asked the questions below. Most of the questions were prepared in 2020 by Jason Kelley, Ph.D. and translated by the author from English into Spanish. Questions with a * at the end were written by the author.

Background Questions

- What is the date and time?
- Where are you now?
- What is your name? Where were you born and on what date?
- Where do you live, and what is it like to live there?
- If you could think back to where you were a year ago, what were your thoughts of the pandemic back then? In particular, what was most impacting you, your family, and community back then? *
- To what extent have your thoughts on the pandemic changed since then? *
- What issues have most concerned you about the COVID-19 pandemic?
- When you first learned about COVID-19, what were your thoughts about it? How have your thoughts changed since then?
- Looking back on. Your daily routine during the pandemic how has it changed? In other words, can you share with me what a "normal" day in your life is like during the pandemic? *

Employment

- What do you do for a living? *
- Has COVID-19 affected your job? In what ways?

- Has COVID-19 changed your employment status? In what ways?
- What concerns do you have about the effects of COVID-19 on your employment and the economy more broadly?
- Has the COVID-19 pandemic affected the employment of people you know? In what ways?

Prevention and Vaccination

- I know that the Caja Costarricense de Seguro Social started vaccinating older adults in January of this year. What do you think of the Caja's vaccination campaign? *
- Have you been vaccinated? Have you received both doses of the vaccine?*
- If not, do you plan on getting vaccinated? *
- Some people doubt the efficacy of vaccines and the intentions of the pharmaceutical companies that developed the vaccines. Do you trust that the vaccines were produced with the goal of saving human lives? *
- Do you know anyone who distrusts the vaccines? Why are they distrustful? What do you think about those who oppose vaccination efforts? *

Family and Household

- Share with me a little about your nuclear family. In other words, please share with me a little information on the people with who you cohabitate. Also, do you have parents, siblings, children, or other close family members with whom you do not reside? *
- How would you describe your daily household activities? To what extent have they changed in the last year? *
- How has COVID-19 affected you and/or your family's day-to-day activities?
- Has the COVID-19 outbreak affected how you associate and communicate with friends and family? In what ways?

- What have been the biggest challenges that you have faced during the COVID-19 outbreak?
- What have you, your family, and friends done for recreation during COVID-19 (feel free to include details about shows, games, books, etc.)?

Community

- How are people around you responding to the COVID-19 pandemic?
- Have you seen the people around you change their opinions, in response to the pandemic?
- Have you seen your day-to-day activities or your relationships with others change in response to the pandemic?
- "Self-isolation" and "flattening the curve" have been two key ideas that have emerged during the pandemic. How have you, your family, friends, and community responded to requests to "self-isolate" and "flatten the curve"?
- When we spoke for the first-time last year, very few people were using facemasks in Costa Rica outside their homes. Has the situation changed? Do you use a facemask now outside the home? *
- When we first spoke a year ago less than 30 people had died. The situation in Costa Rica has changed dramatically since then, thinking about public health and Covid-19, why do you think the situation is so different now? *

Health

- Have you or anybody you know gotten sick during the COVID-19 outbreak?
- What has been your experience in responding to the sickness?
- In what ways do you think that COVID-19 is affecting people's mental and/or physical health?

Information

- What have been your primary sources of news during the pandemic?
- Have your news sources changed during the course of the pandemic?

Government

- How have municipal leaders and government officials in your community responded to the outbreak?
- Do you think they have done the best they could in these circumstances?
- Do you have any thoughts on how local, state, or federal leaders are responding to the crisis differently?

The Future

- Has your pandemic experience transformed how you think about your family, friends, and community? In what ways?
- Knowing what you know now, what do you think that individuals, communities, or governments need to keep in mind for the future?
- Lastly, thinking about the future how do you feel? Are you more optimistic or pessimistic? Why? *

Chapter 11

The Collective Narratives of Covid-19 in Guatemala

The State, The Church, The People

Trudy Mercadal

Independent Researcher

Abstract

Guatemala, the northernmost and least impoverished nation of Central America, suffered low levels of contagion relative to other Latin American countries. Nevertheless, given its historic problems—violence, inequality, poverty, authoritarianism, racism, and corruption—the Covid-19 pandemic proved catastrophic. In the absence of efficient government planning and transparency, the low rate of public trust in the State worsened. In crisis scenarios, the State may use a narrative to control the spread of information; and, for the people, it is a way to make sense of the world. In Guatemala, however, its government became increasingly polarized and neglectful, leading to organized religion and the people to find ways to cope with the crisis. This essay analyzes three types of contending public narratives that prevailed in news media during the Covid-19 crisis: the government, organized Christian leaderships, and community groups.

Keywords: Church, community, Covid-19, government, narrative

***

Introduction

Guatemala is the largest and most stable economy in Central America, as well as one of the most unequal countries in the region. The country reports the sixth highest rate of chronic malnutrition worldwide, 59% of the population is poor and 23% lives in extreme poverty (*World Bank in Guatemala*). Alongside El Salvador and Honduras, it comprises the area known as the Northern Triangle, ranked among the most violent regions in the world. Over 300,000 people leave the Northern Triangle annually, bound for North America to work as undocumented migrants. The situation is so desperate for many that the pandemic did not stem migration flows despite travel restrictions.

On 5 March 2020, the government of Guatemala, led by newly elected president Alejandro Giammattei,[1] declared a State of Calamity and Red Alert, a few days ahead of the World Health Organisation's (WHO) announcement of a worldwide pandemic, which was soon followed by a complete national shutdown. Nevertheless, Guatemala was unprepared for the arrival of the coronavirus pandemic, which added to a stew of pre-existing political and social problems. The information provided by Guatemalan authorities in relation to Covid-19 proved to be constantly disorganised, conflictive, alienating, fragmented and too often, simply absent. There were two main government discourses: first, an authoritarian and self-congratulatory discourse by the Executive branch and, secondly, a mutinous discourse from health institutions and the Vice Presidency.

In 2023, Guatemala reached its third year since the first Covid-19 cases, throughout which it endured an uninterrupted mask mandate and several lockdowns that included closing international borders, businesses, schools, churches, social gatherings, and more. Given its historical problems —violence, inequality, endemic poverty, rampant corruption, among others— the health crisis proved catastrophic for the country, and, in the absence of efficient government planning and transparency, the citizenry's trust in government took a turn for the worse. In crisis scenarios, the state may use narrative to control the spread of information; for the people, however, narrative is a way to make sense of their world. This chapter analyses three public narratives —that of a polarised government, two different types of Church leadership, and two community groups— as they emerged through social and news media to offer a better understanding of the pandemic experience in Guatemala.

Methodology

Collective narratives provide a meaningful framework for making sense of the world and, also, exert an important influence public opinion. In both these scenarios, collective narratives are a crucial part of the political process. Examining the collective narratives that emerged during the first year of the pandemic crisis helps us learn how a dominant narrative may slant perceptions but also, open spaces for the narrative of contesting voices.

Literature available on pandemic discourses and narratives mostly stems from the medical field. In 1999, Greenhalgh and Hurwitz, spear headers in the field of narrative-based medicine, argue that "narrative provides meaning, context,

---

[1] A former penitentiary director running on a conservative ticket, Alejandro Giammattei was elected president of Guatemala on 11 August 2019 and began serving in January 2020.

perspective for the patient's predicament (...) a possibility of understanding which cannot be arrived at by any other means" (318). Furthermore, in 2009, Kalitzkus and Matthiessen distinguished between narrative-based medicine and evidence-based medicine, stressing the focus on the patients' narrative as well on its functions as a qualitative research tool. They propose that when the goal is to understand how people make meaning of discourses during a pandemic, the importance of opening up the theoretical praxis for subjectivities beyond the medical field lays in that "medicine has no respective theory or methods of analysis of meaning. It draws on the knowledge of interpretive sciences" (83).

More recently, scholars have used a variety of narrative theory approaches to analyse discourses of the coronavirus pandemic. In 2022, for example, Jessica Howell drew on fiction literature and oral history as approaches to examine the narratives and discourses of long-Covid-19 survivors; and Persson et al. employed critical discourse analysis to examine the main discursive frames that characterised medical populism during the pandemic in Brazil and its impact on public health policy. These are of particular interest, as Howell develops an analysis based on orality and storytelling, and Persson et al. rely on a linguistics-based interdisciplinary approach to examine the political discourse and public policy strategies developed by the former Brazilian president Jair Bolsonaro.

In 2021, Reuben Ng et al. conducted a transnational study of news media narratives of Covid-19 using a selection of ten target keywords to analyse the pandemic's impact on social perceptions. These scholars synthesise the aims of pandemic narratives in the public arena when they state that "news media narratives matter because they shape societal perceptions and influence the core tent poles of our society" (1).

While the contributions of narrative-based medicine to the practice of meaning analysis in the context of health care and catastrophic events are undeniable, it limits the narrative to the arena of medicine and public health. On the other hand, the more recent theoretical approaches from other disciplines, as cited above, have expanded the methodological toolbox of medical-based narrative in order to engage in discourse analyses of the Covid-19 pandemic.

For James McNamara, content analysis is a primary method "to study a broad range of 'texts', from transcripts of interviews and discussions in clinical and social research to the narrative and forms of films, TV programmes, and the editorial and advertising content of newspapers and magazines" (1). It is important to clarify that, while content analysis is often conceived as quantitative method, this paper follows the idea, established by Berger and Luckmann in the 1960s, and recently espoused by McNamara, that "media texts are open to varied interpretations", the social impact of which cannot be objectively quantified (2). In fact, as the previously mentioned scholars have noted, qualitative analysis methods have been successfully incorporated into the framework of media content analysis.

Other theoretical frameworks support the importance of discourses in mass media. Such is cultivation theory —developed by George Gerbner et al. in 1969— which posits that extended exposure to media shapes how the audience perceives the world around them. For instance, cultivation theorists, such as L.J. Shrum, James Shanahan and Michael Morgan, highlight the importance of understanding that cultivation theory does not look at the effect of programming on its viewership, as much as looking at television —and today, other contemporary forms of mass media— in their narrative role.

Related to cultivation theory is mainstreaming theory. Mainstreaming holds that news media homogenises issues in order to disseminate shared meanings among the viewership. These may serve to distract the public from social problems and disadvantages and direct attention to a more positive regard of those institutions that create inequalities. Therefore, mainstreaming certain discourses reifies their importance in the perception of media consumers and works towards a homogenised narrative. As Gerbner et al. argued in 2002, the practice of mainstreaming obscures social nuances such as inequality and the power relationships that underlie them.

For the purposes of my research, then, I used the approaches of orality and language analysis to set the guidelines for methodological implementation. Being that this chapter examines the discourse of different demographics and seeks to engage in a holistic narrative analysis, I realised it would be necessary to adopt a variety of analytical approaches. The main method used for the analysis was media content analysis, developed in the 1920s and, which according to Kimberly Neuendorf, it is still "the primary message-centered methodology" (9).

A wide variety of concepts, such as safety, public health, and vaccination may change in relation to human experiences and social context, such as racism, economic inequality, religious beliefs, gender, and so on. As Gubrium and Gubrium posit in their analysis of Covid-19 narratives, a signifier or specific concept —that is, from the language of the medical field— "may change in relation to intersectional lived experiences", such as systemic racism, gender and economic inequality, and others (2244). This chapter strives to follow in that direction, examining social phenomena —in this case pandemic narratives— from an intersectional standpoint illuminates how power and identities cut across layers of class, ethnicity, and religious affiliation.

To keep track of Covid-19 narratives in Guatemala, I conducted a content analysis of Covid-19 reporting in news media outlets —both in print and digital platforms— from the inception of the pandemic in March 2020 until the end of 2021. I focused on articles in the popular public domain more likely to reach the news consuming public, specifically the most popular print and online news media — Agencia Ocote, La Hora, No-ficción, Plaza Pública, Prensa Comunitaria and Prensa Libre, among others. I also looked at specific texts on Twitter and Facebook. Following the model offered by Ng et al., I focused on a series of related keywords, such as "coronavirus", "Covid-19", "government", "pandemic" and "vaccines". Finally, for the purposes of organising the main public narratives in this essay during the pandemic, these were divided into Government, Church, and Community.

This chapter aims to contribute to the literature of pandemic narratives as an analysis built from social perceptions of public discourses and the ways in which these narratives shift in time. The global impact of the pandemic and its enduring effects justify studying its media representation in countries which fall outside the global stage occupied by high-income nations. Hopefully, this framework may prove useful to other researchers as it lays out the legwork of evaluating political narratives from various groups around a public interest issue of national concern.

The Government

In Guatemala, still recovering from a 36-year civil war and beset by a long series of corrupt governments, the state is generally viewed by the public with mistrust. Nevertheless, at the beginning of his administration in January 2020, the public appeared to grant President Giammattei the benefit of the doubt. The inception of his administration coincided with the arrival of the pandemic, which led to an initial perception that, as a physician, he would be the ideal president to lead the country during the pandemic. Soon, however, public perception shifted. The public began to perceive that the new government was inept and that it sought to appease popular discontent by manipulating public health data. Early on, the official Covid-19 information was suspected to be tainted by political expediency.

On 11 March 2020, Giammattei imposed a travel ban for people arriving from abroad and curfews were imposed (Menchú, "Guatemala Bans Entry"). Nonessential businesses were shut down and masks became mandatory in all public places (López). The pandemic worsened the economic hardship of Guatemala and its neighbouring countries, since a sizeable part of the national economy depends on agricultural exports to its neighbours. Imports and exports halted when Central American governments, hoping to prevent the spread of Covid-19, closed their borders. Severe food and medical supplies shortages followed. The pre-pandemic economic downturn that affected the region worsened with the disruption of economic activity (*Social Panorama of Latin America*).

Internal travel was also restricted, except for essential workers. The export bans led to waste in undelivered crops, greatly affecting small producers. Reports appeared in news and social media showing farmers donating their food crops to hungry Guatemalans rather than letting it go to waste. In one, published by La República in May 2020, a Maya farming couple is shown in traditional attire under the headline "Guatemala: campesinos donan sus cosechas a familias afectadas por la cuarentena".[2]

The press —especially the independent rural news— made sure to highlight the narratives of solidarity, specifically from the most downtrodden group in the nation, set in stark contrast to the indifference and ineffectuality shown by the state. And these were shared widely through social media. On the other hand, the Ministry of Agriculture (MAGA) published on its official portals its distribution of seeds to farmers affected by the pandemic, albeit the seeds were donated by the UN World Food Programme with the Ministry playing a middleman role ("MAGA recibe donación de semillas").

Peak conflict was reached in September 2020, amply reflected in diverse news media. For instance, a digital news outlet —No-ficción— began a coronavirus report by stating "En realidad, el déficit de pruebas indicaría una realidad diferente y que debe ser escondida para que suceda una reapertura total [del transporte]" ("El espectáculo").[3] Thus, No-ficción was accusing the government of fudging the data to keep numbers low. The goal, according to the outlet, was to reopen air travel, which remained shut down and was the cause of growing pressure from the business sector. The article added that the significantly fewer positive cases of Covid-19 reported in the country in a short lapse could be related to the lack of testing, as there was fewer testing being done than in previous months.

University-based media outlets also reported on the pandemic from a standpoint of mistrust. In September 2020, the hybrid medium Plaza Pública —sponsored by the Jesuit university in Guatemala— also suggested that the government was manipulating coronavirus testing in order to keep numbers low and cited a physician and former Minister of Public Planning of Guatemala, Karin Slowing, who highlighted the lack of transparency by the state, as she declared "no sabemos cuán diseminada está la infección en las comunidades" (Estrada).[4]

The September 2020 edition of the journal *Revista Análisis de la Realidad Nacional*, issued and distributed by the State University of San Carlos, accused the president of representing the ineptitude, cronyism, and structural and institutional failures of the state, adding "en menos de ocho meses, Giammattei pasó de un alto

---

[2] "Guatemala: Farmers Donate Crops to Quarantine-affected Families".
[3] "In reality, the deficit of testing suggests a different reality, which must be hidden for the complete reopenning of transportation".
[4] "We don't know the extent of the spread of the infection in the communities".

respaldo ciudadano (...) a una drástica caída de su credibilidad" ("La crisis recargada" 23).[5] The article included surveys that supported these statements.

The following year, in May 2021, the online news media Diálogos explained that, at the beginning of the pandemic, the Ministry of Public Health had been strongly criticised for lack of transparency in their publications of data. It also suggested that the government had failed to tabulate over 1,600 deaths by Covid-19, by categorising them plainly as "natural deaths" to obscure the true cause of death (Mendoza). Finally, international organisations, including Human Rights Watch, intervened, accusing the Giammattei administration of hindering journalists' access to public information ("Guatemala: Ataques").

Disorganisation and obfuscation indeed appeared to affect the data collection efforts of government agencies, from testing and contagion rates to crime statistics. According to a 2016 US Agency for International Development (USAID) report on crime in Guatemala, the reasons for faulty data collection include discoordination among bureaucracies, repetitive data collection, lack of proficiency of administration platforms and systems, lack of understanding about data collection and classification, deficient training and technology, and prioritisation of politically important information over accuracy or usefulness (Dudley). The importance of being able to collect data in times of crisis cannot be stressed enough; as the UN Economic Commission for Latin America and the Caribbean determined in their 2021 report *Covid-19 Mortality: Evidence and Scenarios* that "countries that have been able to compile and rapidly process high-quality information have had more resources at their disposal for developing Covid-19 Action Plans" (27).

None of these problems were acknowledged by executive branch representatives. In fact, they sought to obscure with discursive tactics that swung between trite bureaucratic speech and authoritarian defensiveness, which heralded the rising authoritarianism that would become rampant in the last years of the Giammattei administration and post-Covid Latin America in general (Miguez Canchaya). It was not uncommon, for instance, for Giammattei to refuse to take questions during press conferences; moreover, he has a history of accusing the press of operating with "a political agenda" (Najarro, "Según Giammattei"). In public appearances, Giammattei's speeches could fall into pathos and include calls for unity, as well as self-pitying statements about facing difficult decisions in loneliness and heroic pronouncements on saving the nation and defeating the disease ("La crisis recargada" 22).

Meanwhile, open conflicts became frequent between government institutions, in particular the Executive and the Ministry of Public Health. Take,

---

[5] "In less than eight months, Giammattei shifted from a high citizenry support … to a drastic fall in credibility".

for example, the problem of the public health system proving unable of covering large areas of the country in their health care and data-gathering effort. In August 2020, the Minister of Public Health, Amelia Flores, acknowledged that her office relied for their data collection on the 441 doctors and medics from the International Cuban Brigades working in Guatemala. Moreover, given the Guatemalan government's inability to provide pandemic care in highland areas such as Huehuetenango and Alta Verapaz, the state relied on the Cuban Brigades for medical service in the region.[6] In a following press conference, Flores stressed the importance of the Cuban Health Brigades in the pandemic effort, right after President Giammattei and his Minister of Foreign Relations, under pressure from right-wing groups, declared their intent to cancel the Cuban brigades mission.[7] The contradictory declarations appeared as an open spat between the president and Health Minister, with the president finally flipping his stance. In the end, the Cuban Brigades remained in the country, mainly because the overburdened public health system would have been unable to function without them ("Polémica en Guatemala").

The polarisation between high government executives persisted. On 20 November 2020, the Vice President of Guatemala, Guillermo Castillo, demanded from President Giammattei his resignation "for the good of the nation" (Castillo 00:03:23–04:40). Castillo also offered to resign his post, proposing that both of them resign jointly, but the presidential press office declined to comment ("El vicepresidente"). These public disagreements evidenced the cracks in the official narrative and delegitimised the government's constant calls for national unity. The executive branch persisted in refusing to address the accusations directly, relying instead on a strategy of authoritarian statements, insults towards opponents who "sought to sow conflict", and grandiose posturing with battle ready phrases, such as the hashtag #JuntosSaldremosAdelante (made viral by the government) and ending every speech with his signature "¡Dios bendiga a Guatemala!" (Giammattei).[8]

At the time, Giammattei was very active in constructing a heroic narrative. In one notable instance, he claimed to have declined the Covid-19 vaccine despite his health preconditions, with the dramatic phrase "si Dios permite que esa vacuna que estaba destinada para mí, sirva para alguien más y salve una vida. Yo estoy tranquilo conmigo mismo",[9] but factcheckers soon uncovered that

---

[6] Two of the most densely populated departments of Guatemala.
[7] In the end, the Cuban and Guatemalan governments renegotiated the agreement and the Cuban Brigades remained. Of the 441 doctors and medics, 154 were fully dedicated to coronavirus care in the country.
[8] "#TogetherWeWillGetAhead" and "God Bless Guatemala".
[9] "If God allows, let the vaccine that was destined for me be given to someone else to save a life. I am at peace with myself".

when President Giammattei made that statement, he had already been vaccinated, and accused him of playing a politics of lies ("Guatemala: La receta"). Giammattei, however, continued to adhere to a strategy of ignoring most factchecking findings and accusations, by not addressing the issue.

A different narrative flooded news and social media: the coverage —not only by media, but also by activist nurses and doctors and even patients—of overrun public hospitals and clinics which, lacking beds and supplies, and staffed by overwhelmed medics, were unable to serve the throngs of ill people in need of care. In some cases, people died outside the hospitals while waiting for a bed to clear, a horror widely spread in social media by news media and common citizens, who shared photos and videos taken by smartphones. As the virus spread, and entire families fell ill with Covid-19, reports of high rates of casualties spread a sense of alarm and doom.

One of the contributors to the disaster is, it bears repeating, the high rates of corruption. In January 2020, Guatemala was ranked as fourth by Transparency International in their list of the most corrupt countries in the world (*Corruption Perceptions Index*). A year later, the organisation released a report revealing that the persistent corruption of these nations undermined Covid-19 health care efforts and contributed to a regression of democracy, underlining that "corruption and emergencies feed off each other, creating a vicious cycle of mismanagement and deeper crisis" (Vrushi and Martínez).

On the other hand, despite the high rates of corruption and the barrage of negative publicity against the government in news and social media, Guatemala maintained a relatively low rate of contagion compared to other Latin American nations (*Guatemala: Coronavirus Pandemic*). This fact was often used by government spokespeople and institutions to bolster the president's efforts. Another fact used in his defence was that President Giammattei had been barely sworn into office when the Covid-19 pandemic hit. At first, he promised effective measures, including a 3,000-bed state-of-the-art public hospital dedicated to Covid-19 in Guatemala City (España). To achieve this, his administration fought for congressional approval of an international loan, which was hugely unpopular with the public. In a Presidential Message, he defended the move and called for national unity again ("Mensaje del presidente"). The loans became even more unpopular when the loan funds' administration was handled in secrecy, which spread speculation and discontent among public, fuelled by relentless media coverage. Very soon, the hashtags #dondeestaeldinero ("where is the money?") and #renunciagiammattei ("Giammattei resign") became viral in Twitter (Gamboa). This scenario lays bare the role of social media in the narrative and counternarrative of contemporary political dialectics.

At the other end of the spectrum lay the televised media. The giant broadcaster Albavision[10] remained solidly loyal to the official party, and mostly declined to cover the health workers' protests and any news focused on the lack of transparency of public funds management. Much of the coverage was done by alternative or independent news outlets and shared via social media. It was probably due to the fragmentation of channels by which the citizenry could access information, that it was very difficult for the official discourse to be able to —as per cultivation theory tenets— have a significant effect on the perceptions of the public at large.

The situation of health workers was crucial. As was the case worldwide during the lockdown, essential personnel —especially in the medical field— were at the frontline of the pandemic. By May 2020, public healthcare workers detonated the social media protest campaign in the Covid-19 hospital announced with great fanfare by President Giammattei as the "state-of-the-art" Hospital Parque de la Industria, which ended up as another public relations fiasco. Health workers explained they were not supplied with basic protective gear, medical supplies or medication, the food was of poor quality and, in many cases, their wages were months in arrears ("Guatemala: médicos protestan"). The higher echelons of public health authorities responded by calling for unity, yet while admitting there was some scarcity of supplies in hospitals, they also insisted that there were enough basic supplies to function and suggested that the health workers were exaggerating the situation ("Autoridades se pronuncian").

The Guatemalan College of Pharmacists and Chemists filed a formal complaint with the Human Rights Ombudsman in representation of the healthcare workers, demanding an inspection of the conditions in which they had to work ("Guatemala: médicos protestan"). Amnesty International accused the Guatemalan government of turning its back on health workers and of placing them at great risk ("Las personas trabajadoras"). A year later, physicians of public Hospital Roosevelt, filed a legal suit against President Giammattei and Minister Flores, for mismanagement of the pandemic (Roman and Kestler). The protests continued into the first quarter of 2022.

As the crisis extended in time, President Giammattei and other authorities became increasingly authoritarian against protesters and the press. Government authorities sought to censor medical personnel by shaming and threats. As virus continued to spread, Giammattei blamed the high rates of contagion on the public's lack of responsibility, especially during contagion peaks (Escobar, "Giammattei afirma"). The executive branch remained in defensive position

---

[10] The owner of Albavisión, Remigio Ángel González, was sued in 2019 for fraud and scamming. His wife, Alba Elvira Lorenzana, is a fugitive from justice since 2016, with an international warrant for her arrest. Lorenzana is accused of illicit campaign funding.

while public health workers, who enjoyed great popular support, persisted in demanding better conditions. Giammattei explained discontent as "un arma que están utilizando quienes ya sabemos que se dedican no a la construcción sino de [sic] la destrucción" (M. García).[11]

Unemployment spread and reports of severe food insecurity among the middle class increased. Guatemalans were used to witnessing high rates of poverty, but the middle classes had always felt relatively safe from precarity. During the pandemic, however, growing numbers of people appeared on city streets and highways waving white flags, begging for food and work (Olmstead). The images flooded social media and all kind of news outlets, adding to the government's public relations nightmare. In April 2020, Giammattei announced a national monthly family stipend of Q.1,000 (127 dollars) for the needy and requested a budget increase from Congress to provide bonuses to 800,000 Guatemalan families as well as 200,000 boxes of food ("Presidente Giammattei anuncia"). The news was disseminated in government media and all other news outlets.

Rife with red tape and accusations of corruption and fraud, the measure failed to reach those who needed it most and was quietly cancelled after Giammattei admitted there were problems: "tenemos un problema y es un problema de números" (O. García).[12] Government efforts at food distribution had similar results, leading to accusations of ineptitude, theft, and cronyism. Unemployment and hunger continued to spread, and the narrative of the political elites as inept shifted to politicians as actively evil. When in April 2020, in the wake of a breakdown in the Covax supply channel and a widespread scarcity of vaccines, President Giammattei —a physician— broadcasted a nationwide speech to promote the use of Ivermectin —an antiparasitic drug— as a better substitute for Covid-19 vaccines (Mazariegos Rivas), the public moved from referring to him as a man who did not care about the people, to one actively capable of promoting harmful ideas for political reasons.

By the time in September 2020 when things came to a head, the Presidential Commission on Covid, headed by Edwin Asturias, had been unable to keep most promises. The Commission reported steady falls in Covid-19 contagion rates, yet news media uncovered that data manipulation accounted for the decreasing rates. One case was particularly egregious. The coastal department of Escuintla showed some of the highest rates for Covid-19. On 3 August 2020, however, the Commission reported that Escuintla positive rates had dropped dramatically, but fact-checkers proved the opposite was true ("Aumentan los casos"). The Commission had promised a baseline of 5,000 Covid-19 tests per

---

[11] "A weapon used by those we already know are dedicated not to building but to destruction".
[12] "We have a problem, a numbers problem".

day (Estrada), a goal it claimed to have reached. Journalists found that not only the government could not show to have reached the goal, but that the reason rates had fallen in Escuintla, was that Covid-19 testing was drastically cut down in public clinics.

A pattern was established, in which bright results claimed in the official story were persistently questioned or proven false by the media and civil society, useless to hide the endless string of failures.[13] By then, the main function of the press had become to counter the official narrative, reduced to ineffectually mainstreaming official cant. While at first the executive branch used to rebate every accusation, it soon stopped responding and turned to a strategy of victimisation: claiming to the target of malicious misinformation tactics, it ignored factchecking results. Indeed, the president disappeared, making few public appearances and avoiding unscripted questions. In the press, he began to be called as "the president who does not speak to the press" (Najarro, "Giammattei, el presidente que no habla"). The sense among the public was of a leadership vacuum. Undaunted by the exposure of inaccuracies, the Giammattei administration persisted in its bureaucratic discourse, taking credit for declining positive rates, claiming it as the result of its efficient management of the pandemic. And this set the tone for their future communication strategies ("Evolución del coronavirus").

The discursive strategy combined a contemptuous and authoritarian tone and avoidant behaviour, as well as lack of transparency, to cover for the consequences of ineptitude and corruption. It was also accompanied by armies of bots repeating political slogans in favour of the government on social media such as Twitter, to combat the surges of citizen indignation expressed therein.

The Church

In June 2020, the rates of Covid-19 were so high in the department of Escuintla, site of the largest seaport in the country, that the Catholic Diocese, concerned by health and economic hardship of its poorest residents, published an open letter of protest and an itemised list of recommendations. The Diocese claimed that public hospitals and clinics were overrun, and people unable to get care for themselves and their families. The Bishop of Escuintla demanded that the government address the suffering endured by the people of the area. In another case of bad public press for the Giammattei administration, the issue transcended Guatemala, and was picked up by the official news outlet of the Vatican, Vatican News (Tufani).

---

[13] It is important to note that the few factchecking agencies in Guatemala are part of civil society.

The importance of this act cannot be overstated. The Catholic Church is an influential political actor in Guatemala: approximately 50% of the population is Catholic (Office of International Religious Freedom). Since the beginning of the pandemic, the Church stood solidly on the conservative side of prevention, including cancelling for two years in a row the traditional Holy Week processions attended by millions of Guatemalans, closing churches and, in time, opening some but placing strict safe spacing and masking measures (Escobar, "Coronavirus: Qué acciones"). By 2021, the Archdiocese continued to recommend the faithful to watch the televised Mass at home.

The Protestant Pentecostal churches hold the second largest affiliation in the country (Office of International Religious Freedom). As established by Virginia Garrard in her historical study on the Pentecostal religion in Guatemala, the country is the "most Protestant nation in Latin America", and most Guatemalan Protestants are Pentecostals, making them hold a significant amount of political power (63). Many of the churches were defiant of the shutdown and maintained their worship meetings. Others stated they would be mindful of Public Health recommendations, and most insistently pressured Congress during lockdowns to allow religious services. There were frequent protests from Pentecostal and other protest denominations of Covid-19 restrictions and lobbying at Congress to allow worship and establish clear protocols ("Solicitan que se analice protocolo"). In some cases, evangelical pastors urged their followers to disobey government sanitary regulations and attend religious events. These, in turn, frequently became sources of mass contagion (Escobar, "Coronavirus: Qué acciones").

It is important to note, however, that while the Catholic Church is a single institution able to establish a coherent and unitary position, the Protestant Church encompasses various groups that do not follow a single leadership. Also, many Protestant churches and pastors are financed by donations given by the faithful during services, so persistent lockdowns threatened the survival of many. Moreover, as noted by Garrard and others, the strongest protestant churches are branches of Evangelical churches established in the United States and follow the dogma and narrative lines of the latter (Morales).

In November 2020, the official bloc in the Guatemalan Congress, emboldened by the impunity it had managed to gain, approved the largest budget in the history of the country. Its lack of transparency was protested by opposition congressmembers and civil society and led to a surge in public discontent followed by massive nationwide protests, despite sanitary regulations against public assembling ("Protestas en Guatemala"). The media showed how the largest protests were noted for their participants maintaining safe spacing and masks, despite its large scope. In one case, during a confusing event, protesters were accused of trying to set fire to Congress (Vera and Álvarez). Among the issues protested was the neglect towards public hospitals, which showed the impact of the protests via social media by medical personnel ("Protestas en Guatemala"). Present at the protests were groups of Catholic nuns and friars, representing their orders and showcasing a visible Catholic presence.[14]

As vaccines became available worldwide, Guatemalan media reported that the neighbour countries of Mexico and El Salvador were months ahead of Guatemala in vaccination rates. As the weeks passed, health authorities remained unable to provide an arrival date for vaccinations and at some points, hounded by the press, blamed the World Health Organisation's distribution system.[15] To be fair, there is some truth to this accusation. However, as organisations such as the Global Health Institute pointed out in 2020, in a report on global purchasing agreements for the new vaccines, "many of these countries will be able to vaccinate their entire populations —and some will do so many times over— before billions of people are vaccinated in low-income countries" ("Will Low-Income Countries").

In early 2021, Guatemalan news media published detailed reportage about how thousands of dollars in funds for medical supplies were unaccounted (Guatemala Leaks). It bears repeating that press and social media reported that frontline medical personnel were side-lined for the vaccine, with preferential treatment for government officials and cronies, contributing to public ire.

The official organ of the Catholic Church in Guatemala, Conferencia Episcopal, following a formal Vatican declaration remained at the forefront of demanding equality in the administration of the Covid-19 vaccination and that the state act responsibly towards fostering a more just and caring society (Comisión Vaticana Covid-19). In fact, the Catholic Church insisted from a variety of platforms on the state's duties in ensuring access to pandemic care and alleviation of economic hardship. At the same time, the main narrative of the Evangelical Church was —with some exceptions— persistent in highlighting the importance in faith and prayer, above science and public health methods.

It could be argued, then, that the religious narrative for each church was largely representative of its dogma, although care would have to be taken into assuming that there were no singularities or differences. The Catholic church showed a more unified narrative that managed to both support the government's incentives of sanitation and vaccination, while at the same time, using its prophetic tradition of speaking truth to power. Thus, it coherently adhered to a pastoral vision of caring and speaking for the faithful from a standpoint of leadership and religious hierarchy, as this standpoint was a

---

[14] Personal observation at the protests.
[15] As of March 2022, Guatemala had yet to surpass providing two (out of three) vaccines to the population.

unified narrative supported and promoted by the Vatican itself (Comisión Vaticana Covid-19). This was not atypical. As established by scholars Philip Berryman in 1987 and Eric Morales-Franceschini in 2018, since the inception of Second Vatican Council in the 1960s, the progressive branch of the Catholic Church in Latin America has engaged in a tradition of speaking in a prophetic voice —that is, speaking truth to power— to authoritarian governments of Latin America.

The Protestant churches, on the other hand, remained in general faithful to beliefs more aligned to a neoliberal and individual-cantered framework, with little trust in government and its perception of state intervention in matters of faith. As Garrard has explained, many protestant churches are ambivalent about getting involved with secular forms of power. Moreover, the Evangelical churches —less unified— were yet oriented by their leadership, who promoted a path to health and salvation through faith. In this view, this placed them in opposition to health policies viewed as state interference.

In the case of both religious narratives, however, while most news media outlet persisted in uncovering government corruption and larceny, most religious leaders largely refrained from directly addressing issues of corruption and fraud. It is important to highlight the singularities, however, such as the members of religious orders of nuns and friars, who attended anti-corruption protests, as well as some Christian religious leaders of both denominations who have preached against corruption from the pulpit, such as Cardinal Álvaro Ramazzini, Bishop of Huehuetenango, popularly regarded as an influential leader in the fight against corruption ("Guatemala: Cardenal encabeza").

Community Groups

It is at the community level where the narratives take a most storied form. In the cases examined below, the stories are framed not only to help make sense of a pandemic that is tearing apart the fabric of quotidian life familiar to collective groups, but also enables agency and resistance to government systemic violence and neglect that makes people feel more dignified, even though they find that there is little they can do to stop government corruption.

At the beginning of the pandemic, there was widespread coverage by news media and social media of community responses to the pandemic. Among these were the cases mentioned above of farmers who shared their crops with the less fortunate (Seed Change). Much less covered by the media was the prevalence of rural communities that sealed themselves against outsiders, threatening potential incomers with violence, even in the case of returning migrants from their communities, recently deported from the United States during the pandemic. These measures may have worked to some extent, as contagion rates remained relatively low in the most isolated rural areas.

However, as vaccination campaigns spread to some rural areas, villagers refused to allow public health workers to bring in vaccination programmes, so that many remained unvaccinated (García and Montenegro). This was caused not only by decades of neglect and even abuse by the state, but also due to the absence of proper information campaigns. Vaccination campaigns and other health initiatives were not published or broadcast in Maya languages, leaving large segments of the population uninformed (García and Montenegro).

Most rural communities in Guatemala are indigenous Maya, the poorest demographic in the nation. Maya peoples bore the brunt of inequality, exploitation, and state violence for almost four decades of civil war in the late twentieth century. The life experiences and historic memory in many rural communities sustain the belief that they have little to expect from the state. This is compounded by the fact that the state, for its part, consistently neglects to provide services to rural communities, who are left to fend for themselves. And while the adverse side of this is that many live in underserved conditions, it has also led to the survival of ancestral systems of social organisation and a narrative of collective self-reliance. In fact, according to international organisations, "the Covid-19 crisis raised the poverty incidence to 59 per cent in 2020" (*World Bank in Guatemala*).

In a travel to isolated K'ekchi' hamlets in the Department of Petén, I participated in formal and informal interviews with several residents and was able to perceive a pervasive mistrust of Covid-19 vaccination. A young mother expressed timidly that she would like to get vaccinated, for which she would have to undergo a trip of over an hour to the nearest clinic, but her grandmother, a village elder, had admonished the family against the vaccine. In traditional communities, it is common for grandmothers to be decisionmakers in matters of family health. One of the main reasons espoused against vaccination was "it is said one could die [from the vaccine]"; another community elder told me, "We take care of our own. We have always taken care of our own. We have our herbs that we use for cures, those are better for us".[16] This narrative of community selfcare in the face of neglect, adversity, and outside threat, is rooted in an ancestral historic memory and has sustained Maya communities through countless ordeals. However, while one must be careful not to essentialise and generalise indigenous community narratives, a majority of rural villages are beset with malnutrition, unemployment or underemployment, lack of educational opportunities, dire housing conditions

---

[16] Interviews in San Francisco, Petén, Guatemala, 2022.

and, given that many generations of extended families share single unit households, the risk of disease contagion is very high (*World Bank in Guatemala*).

In some hamlets, villagers insisted that no one they know has sickened or died of Covid-19 in their community. However, upon closer questioning some admitted that many have died in some of the neighbouring towns.[17] This seems to correlate with newscast interviews during the first year of the pandemic, in which rural community members said that there have been no Covid-19 deaths in their village, because they take care of each other and were closed to strangers. The numbers from public health reports, however, told a different story.[18]

The information that feeds this narrative does not come from conventional news media, nor from government discourse, but from within the community and its local organisations. Among these, community radio networks —most of which operate unlicensed— are of crucial importance. In many villages, as in large rural areas, the antivaccination influence of Pentecostal Evangelical churches is perceivable, as many follow the dogmatic line disseminated by US-headquartered Pentecostal churches (Dias and Graham). In short, the anti-vaccination stance, compounded by faulty government outreach, the alienation of people from the state, as well as mistrust of nonindigenous medicine, led to low rates of vaccination.

Another community response frequently showcased by the press and social media, were *ollas comunitarias*, "community pots". The community pot movement, born in poor barrios of Colombia as a movement of collective solidarity, reciprocity, and resistance, was vital in Guatemala during the pandemic (Dorado). As the lockdown ensued, informal economy workers —which comprise about 70% of the labour force (*Economic Growth*)— were effectively cut from their sources of income, and hunger soon began to spread as thousands of Guatemalans were unable to earn money.

The first pandemic *olla comunitaria* in Guatemala began at a small downtown bar, Rayuela, owned by two young activists, Byron Vásquez and Emilio Molina (García Escobar). Vásquez and Molina announced that hot meals would be served twice daily to anybody who needed it. The endeavour became an extraordinary success, with hundreds of citizens making long queues each day to get a meal. At its peak, according to reports, the *olla comunitaria* served about 2,000 daily meals (Prensa Comunitaria Km169). The kitchen effort was so popular, it never lacked for food donations and

---

[17] Interviews in San Francisco, Petén, Guatemala. 2022.
[18] Health reports suggest that the rural communities' strategy of enclosing and barring entry to outsiders did, in effect, slow down the spread of Covid-19 significantly. However, when the country opened again, the lack of vaccination posed a greater risk, as did the high levels of malnutrition and exposure to opportunistic diseases.

volunteers, with the media and social media covering the effort day after day in very positive ways (Prensa Comunitaria). The young people were soon raised to the status of local heroes and their efforts replicated citywide.

The media contrasted images of the enthusiastic volunteers cooking and serving meals to thousands of citizens, with the government's failures, the neglect and abandonment. In one case that became viral in social media, an establishment politician, seeking to take advantage of the *olla comunitaria* to gain some publicity, arrived at Rayuela with boxes of food, followed by his cameramen. What the cameras filmed, however, was the young owners rushing out to reject the donation forcefully, while the crowds cheered happily when the shamed politician left with his undelivered supplies (García Escobar). The visual and textual narrative followed a David and Goliath theme, that is, the little people giving a black eye to the corrupt political "establishment" that operates with impunity.

As with the footage of protesting public health workers, videos of *olla comunitaria* volunteers and users, disseminated via social media, overtook conventional media, and contributed to the creation of local heroes by common citizens. These fragmented images and sound bites crafted a narrative collage of the collective pandemic experience that seemed much more authentic, than the authoritarian and patently false discourse promoted by state authorities and their official channels ever could. It is important to highlight, however, that the coverage of the public health workers protests and the *olla comunitaria* movement reflected an urban experience that shows marked differences with the isolated rural communities' narratives and how the pandemic has been experienced across rural and urban settings, and a majority of non-indigenous versus mostly indigenous populations.

The *olla comunitaria* was considered a source of anti-government sentiment and soon became a target of harassment by city authorities, including forced closures in the midst of meal serving, food confiscations, intimidation of the queueing people, and other forms of bullying aimed at closing it down, all of it documented and shared online by locals (García Escobar). The popularity of the *olla comunitaria* was such, however, that the city aggressiveness fuelled the "us versus them" narrative. Through its social media account and citing the hashtag #GuatemalaTieneHambre (Guatemala is hungry), the Olla Comunitaria informed it would close on 15 September 2020, due to a mood of hostility and intimidations against them: "La Olla Comunitaria Cierra en medio de un ambiente hostil, intimidaciones y en una 'nueva normalidad' que solo acentúa nuestra permanente crisis" (Hernández).

On 12 December 2020, Rayuela, headquarters of the Olla Comunitaria, burned down after closing time. Although the culprits were never found, given the rancour shown by the city government, the public blamed government forces. The Olla Comunitaria organisation's social media presence published inspirational quotes, such as "Our home has been consumed by fire. Today we have lost everything except the will and heart to go on" (García et al.).[19] However, the *olla comunitaria* movement had inspired similar groups that operated for a while, not only in Guatemala City, but also in Quetzaltenango, Sololá, Quiché, and others ("Olla Comunitaria responsabiliza"). The narrative that stemmed from this movement, altogether with that of solidary farmers and public health workers, each forming a story of heroism and personal sacrifice, stood in stark contrast to that of a callous government administration fed by its empty discourse and absent political leadership.

Finally, several protests occurred throughout the first year of the pandemic. Although most took place at emblematic seats of government —the main plaza facing the Palacio de la Cultura[20], as well as at Congress, the Supreme Court, and the Electoral College— other protests included main road blockages throughout the country. Soon into the pandemic a protest slogan emerged: "Where is the money?", which spread as a social media campaign (Alvarenga).[21]

The slogan points to all the instances of funds mismanaged by the Giammattei administration during the pandemic, became embedded in popular culture and has been splashed across the media, in memes, on signs, graffiti, chanted during protests, and asked during government press conferences. It is important to highlight that the slogan was created by Giammattei himself during his presidential campaign and that it was the discovery of government graft and theft that led to the massive protests that ousted President Otto Pérez Molina and Vice President Roxana Baldetti in 2015 (Lohmuller). However, because of its urban setting and main cause —mismanagement of taxpayer's money— the nugget of the 2015 protests was largely considered a middle-class issue.

The protest and ire were similar this time around, and some drew thousands of participants. But the presidential administration seemed more solidly set in its power because the multilateral anti-corruption organisation, CICIG, that had previously led the prosecutions of government corruption, was expelled from Guatemala in 2019 by President Jimmy Morales ("Guatemala expels"). Moreover, the pandemic had empowered the government —strongly backed by the military— and weakened the people. Although Guatemala was not as hard

---

[19] Olla Comunitaria, through Rayuela's kitchen, served over 150,000 meals during the first wave of Covid-19, as well as for refugees of the Eta and Iota hurricanes.
[20] The building, used mainly for ceremonial purposes, is the symbolic seat of the presidency.
[21] The "Where is the money?" campaign was also used in the nation of Honduras around the same time and similarly appeared on graffiti murals, social media memes, protest signs, and others.

hit as other Latin American nations, the pandemic impoverished, sickened, and decimated the population making it harder to rally for protests.[22]

The corollary to the community narratives has been the narratives of mourning. During the first months of the pandemic, entire families fell ill, and as individuals were hospitalised, they often lost contact with their families. Thousands were buried in mass graves without accompaniment. People lost the support that always came with the traditional wakes and interment ceremonies. What has remained, then, is a widespread arrested development of mourning, as reflected in the headline of No-ficción: "Nadie puede llorar a las víctimas de la pandemia", which began by stressing the absence of the state at this time of most need for a helpless citizenry: "Los fallecidos por Covid-19 en Guatemala se cuentan por millares. Son enterrados como equis equis en los cementerios nacionales. Nadie puede acercarse cuando son depositados en sus tumbas, dejados caer a su suerte, sin supervisión de las autoridades (…) Sin flores, sin luto, sin familiares que los recuerden" (Menchú, "Nadie puede llorar").[23]

Conclusion

A narrative cannot tell a whole truth —nor is there such a thing as a whole truth— of what occurred in a nation and experienced by the people in a catastrophe. At most, as I endeavoured to portray, it allows snapshots of the voices that emerged, evolved, and intersected in time among specific groups during this period. In that context, it portrays the realities of a plurality of people which, more often than not, belied the official discourse. What was possible to glean from exploring these narratives of the pandemic's first year, show, firstly, an official narrative moulded by higher echelons of government, which sought to work as a smokescreen for its evident failures and alleged malfeasance. The official narrative failed as counter stories emerged from other government entities such as the public health leader and staff. As the latter was embraced by the news media, social media, and the public, the state's failure to make effective their narrative led to an overall perception of absent leadership.

Secondly, church leadership also crafted public narratives. Catholic leadership, on one hand, demanded greater involvement and accountability from the state, with a prophetic voice that stressed the deep suffering of the people, while on the other it urged its parishioners to keep to the sanitary measures recommended

---

[22] According to WHO calculations by April 2021, Guatemala had suffered 228,684 cases confirmed and 7,558 casualties (Mendoza).

[23] "The dead for Covid-19 in Guatemala number thousands. They are buried as XX [unknown] in public cemeteries. No one may approach as they are lowered into their graves without supervision by authorities, placed in some hard-to-find space (…) Without flowers, without mourning, without relatives to remember them".

by the government. Evangelical Christian leadership, on the other hand, mostly demanded from the government an easing of sanitary measures and the ban on public gatherings. In some instances, it also maintained an active antivaccine position as an act of faith. In both cases, the narrative was crafted from above, in a paternalistic and hierarchical mode.

Finally, the most horizontal narratives emerged from the people, both in urban and rural settings. In rural areas, there was a sense of circling of wagons while keeping to a narrative of collective resistance and historic memory that has long served as a system of survival. In urban areas, however, the narrative took on a heroic shape, of the common people watching out for each other and disparaging the government —as the establishment— for its failures and corruption.[24]

It is not within the scope of this essay to cover all the complexities of Covid-19 in Guatemala. Further research would be desirable on the narratives that emerged in other crucial fields, such as families, civil society, the arts, and education, and across gender, age, and class. It is my hope that this "slice of life" is helpful to understanding how different narratives can emerge within a society, the ways in which these may be both facilitated and positioned by the media and social media, and how they may give voice to the collective experiences in any given society.

Bibliography

Alvarenga, Jacqueline. "Guatemaltecos se unen a campaña: ¿Dónde está el dinero?" *NB*, 18 August 2020, https://notibomba.com/guatemaltecos-se-unen-a-campana-donde-esta-el-dinero/.

Associated Press. "Guatemala: Cardenal encabeza la lucha contra la corrupción". *Voz de América*, 3 October 2022, https://www.vozdeamerica.com/a/guatemala-obispo-encabeza-frente--lucha-corrupcion/6774279.html.

"Aumentan los casos de Covid-19 en la provincia de Guatemala". *Forbes Centro América*, 19 August 2020, https://forbescentroamerica.com/2020/08/19/aumentan-los-casos-de-covid-19-en-la-provincia-de-guatemala.

"Autoridades se pronuncian ante protestas de médicos en Hospital Parque de la Industria". *TN23*, 12 May 2020, https://www.tn23.tv/autoridades-se-pronuncian-ante-protestas-de-medicos-en-hospital-de-parque-de-la-industria/.

Berger, Peter L., and Thomas Luckmann. *The Social Construction of Reality*. Penguin Books, 1966.

Berryman, Phillip. *Liberation Theology: The Essential Facts about The Revolutionary Movement in Latin America and Beyond*. Pantheon, 1987.

---

[24] Three years after Covid-19 was first detected, less than 50% of Guatemalans had received the first dose of the vaccine and less than 35% were fully vaccinated (*Live COVID-19 Vaccination Tracker*).

Castillo, Guillermo. "Conferencia de Prensa de la República de Guatemala". *Facebook*, uploaded by Vicepresidencia de Guatemala, 20 November 2020, https://www.facebook.com/watch/?v=400275001164926.

Comisión Vaticana Covid-19. "Vacuna para todos. 20 puntos para un mundo justo y sano". *Vatican*, 2020, https://www.vatican.va/roman_curia/pontifical_academies/acdlife/documents/rc_pont-acd_life_doc_20201229_covid19-vaccinopertuttti_sp.html.

Corruption Perceptions Index. Transparency International, 2020, https://www.transparency.org/en/cpi/2020.

Covid-19 Mortality: Evidence and Scenarios. Economic Commission for Latin America and the Caribbean, 2021, https://repositorio.cepal.org/server/api/core/bitstreams/ce326be4-9dd9-4720-8763-001784002b9b/content.

Dias, Elizabeth, and Ruth Graham. "Política, fe y vacunación: el rechazo de los evangélicos blancos a las vacunas podría prolongar la pandemia". *New York Times*, 5 April 2021, https://www.nytimes.com/es/2021/04/05/espanol/vacunas-religion.html.

Dorado, Fernando. "La Olla Comunitaria". *El Comején*, 10 July 2020, https://elcomejen.com/2020/07/10/la-olla-comunitaria/.

Dudley, Steven. *Homicides in Guatemala: The Challenge and Lessons of Disaggregating Gang-Related and Drug Trafficking-Related Murders*. USAID, 2016, https://insightcrime.org/wp-content/uploads/2023/08/Gang-and-DTO-Homicides-in-Guatemala-Final-Report_CARSI-USAID-InSight-Crime.pdf.

Economic Growth. Guatemala. USAID, 2023, https://www.usaid.gov/guatemala/our-work/economic-growth.

"El espectáculo debe continuar: semana del 21 al 27 de septiembre". *No-ficcion*, 29 September 2020, https://www.no-ficcion.com/projects/covid-guatemala-semana-21-27-septiembre.

"El vicepresidente de Guatemala pide públicamente a Giammattei la renuncia de ambos". *Voz de América*, 20 November 2020, https://www.vozdeamerica.com/a/centroamerica_vicepresidente-de-guatemala-pide-renuncia-presidente-giammattei/6069592.html.

Escobar, Irving. "Giammattei afirma que ahora el coronavirus en Guatemala 'ya es problema de la gente'". *Prensa Libre*, 6 August 2020, https://www.prensalibre.com/guatemala/politica/giammattei-afirma-que-ahora-el-coronavirus-en-guatemala-ya-es-problema-de-la-gente-breaking/.

—. "Coronavirus: Qué acciones están adoptando las iglesias de Guatemala". *Prensa Libre*, 13 March 2020, https://www.prensalibre.com/ciudades/guatemala-ciudades/coronavirus-que-acciones-estan-adoptando-las-iglesias-de-guatemala-por-covid-19-ultima-hora/ .

España, Mariajosé. "La realidad de las 3 mil camas y el millón de vacunas semanales que Giammattei prometió". *Prensa Libre*, 6 June 2023, https://www.prensalibre.com/guatemala/politica/la-realidad-de-las-3-mil-camas-y-el-millon-de-vacunas-semanales-que-giammattei-prometio/.

Estrada, Saundi. "Con pocas pruebas los departamentos desconocen su situación real". *Plaza Pública*, 6 September 2020, https://www.plazapublica.com.gt/content/con-pocas-pruebas-los-departamentos-desconocen-su-situacion-real.

"Evolución del coronavirus en Guatemala". *No-ficción*, January 2021, https://www.no-ficcion.com/project/evolucion-coronavirus-guatemala_Accessed 22 March 2021.

Gamboa, Verónica. "Renuncia Giammattei, la petición en redes sociales por la crisis de Covid-19 en el país". *Soy 502*, 2 July 2021, https://www.soy502.com/articulo/renuncia-giammattei-peticion-redes-sociales-50172.

García Escobar, Alejandro. "Un año de hambre y fuego: Las crónicas de Rayuela". *Agencia Ocote*, 20 April 2021, https://www.agenciaocote.com/blog/2021/04/20/episodio-45-un-ano-de-hambre-y-fuego-las-cronicas-de-rayuela/.

García, Manuel. "Giammattei justifica dificultades para comprar vacunas por 'el buen manejo de la pandemia'". *La Hora*, 5 May 2021, https://lahora.gt/nacionales/mgarcia/2021/05/05/giammattei-justifica-dificultades-para-comprar-vacunas-por-el-buen-manejo-de-la-pandemia/.

García, Oscar, and Henry Montenegro. "Salud dice que rechazo a la vacuna contra el covid-19 se da en varios departamentos porque 'mucha gente tiene miedo'". *Prensa Libre*, 11 October 2021, https://www.prensalibre.com/guatemala/comunitario/salud-dice-que-rechazo-a-vacuna-contra-el-covid-19-se-da-en-varios-departamentos-porque-mucha-gente-tiene-miedo-breaking/.

García, Óscar, et al. "Incendio consume local donde funciona la Olla Comunitaria de Rayuela y este domingo sería la reapertura". *Prensa Libre*, 12 December 2020, https://www.prensalibre.com/ciudades/guatemala-ciudades/incendio-consume-local-donde-funciona-la-olla-comunitaria-de-rayuela-breaking/.

García, Oscar. "Coronavirus: Alejandro Giammattei afirma que readecuan fondos por el aumento de 800 mil beneficiados en el Bono Familia". *Prensa Libre*, 7 August 2020, https://www.prensalibre.com/guatemala/comunitario/coronavirus-alejandro-giammattei-afirma-que-readecuan-fondos-por-el-aumento-de-800-mil-beneficiados-en-el-bono-familia/.

Garrard, Virginia. "Pentecostalism and Power in Guatemala". *Current History*, vol. 122, no. 841, 2023, pp. 63–68.

Gerbner, George, et al. "Growing Up With Television: Cultivation Processes". *Media Effects: Advances in Theory and Research*, edited by Bryant Jennings and Dolf Zillmann. Lawrence Erlbaum, 2002, pp. 43–68.

Giammattei, Alejandro [@DrGiammmattei]. "Le pido a todos que guardemos la calma. Es momento de unirnos porque juntos saldremos de esta emergencia. Hemos estado trabajando sin descanso y lo continuaremos haciendo, la salud de los guatemaltecos es nuestra prioridad. ¡Que Dios bendiga a Guatemala!" *Twitter*, 14 March 2020, https://twitter.com/drgiammattei/status/1239001922759163905.

Greenhalgh, Trisha, and Brian Hurwitz. "Narrative-Based Medicine. Why Study Narrative?". *BMJ*, vol. 318, no. 7175, 1999, pp. 48–50.

"Guatemala: Ataques a la libertad de prensa". *Human Rights Watch*, 18 February 2021, https://www.hrw.org/es/news/2021/02/18/guatemala-ataques-la-libertad-de-prensa

Guatemala Leaks. "El gobierno de Guatemala oculta datos de los beneficiarios de los fondos de rescate". *Ojoconmipisto*, 12 November 2020, https://www.ojoconmipisto.com/el-gobierno-de-guatemala-oculta-datos-de-los-beneficiarios-de-los-fondos-de-rescate/

Guatemala: Coronavirus Pandemic Country Profile. Our World in Data, 2023, https://www.transparency.org/en/news/cpi-2020-research-analysis-why-fighting-corruption-matters-in-times-of-covid-19

"Guatemala: campesinos donan sus cosechas a familias afectadas por la cuarentena". *La República*, 24 May 2020, https://larepublica.pe/mundo/2020/05/24/coronavirus-en-guatemala-pareja-de-ancianos-campesinos-donan-sus-cosechas-a-familias-afectadas-por-la-cuarentena-rddr/

"Guatemala expels UN-backed anti-corruption commission". *BBC*, 8 January 2019, https://www.bbc.com/news/world-latin-america-46789931

"Guatemala: La receta de Giammattei para tapar un año de fracasos con la compra de Sputnik V". *Plaza Pública*, 2 March 2022, https://www.plazapublica.com.gt/content/la-receta-de-giammattei-para-tapar-un-ano-de-fracasos-con-la-compra-de-sputnik-v

"Guatemala: médicos protestan por falta de insumos y pago". *Nodal*, 13 May 2020, https://www.nodal.am/2020/05/guatemala-medicos-protestan-por-falta-de-insumos-y-pagos/

Gubrium, Aline, and Erika Gubrium. "Narrative Complexity in the time of Covid-19". *The Lancet*, vol. 297, no. 10291, 2021, pp. 2244–2243.

Hernández, Fredy. "La Olla Comunitaria y Rayuela cerrarán el comedor solidario". *Soy 502*, 9 September 2020, https://www.soy502.com/articulo/olla-comunitaria-anuncia-cierre-comedor-solidario-24039

Howell, Jessica. "Covid-19 Narratives and Layered Temporalities". *Medical Humanities*, no. 48, 2022, pp. 211–220.

Kalitzkus, Vera, and Peter F. Matthiessen. "Narrative-Based Medicine: Potential, Pitfalls, and Practice". *The Permanente Journal*, vol. 13, no.1, 2009, pp. 80–86.

"La crisis recargada". *Revista de Análisis de la Realidad Nacional*, vol. 9, no. 32, 2020, pp. 21–23.

"Las personas trabajadoras de salud de Guatemala corren peligro a causa de Covid-19, pero también a causa de su gobierno". *Amnistía Internacional*, 3 July 2020, https://www.amnesty.org/es/latest/news/2020/07/trabajadoras-salud-guatemala-corren-peligro-covid19/

Live COVID-19 Vaccination Tracker. Covidvax Live, https://Covidvax.live/location/gtm Accessed 14 May 2022.

Lohmuller, Michael. "Guatemala's Government Corruption Scandals Explained". *Insight Crime*, 21 June 2016, https://insightcrime.org/news/analysis/guatemala-s-government-corruption-scandals-explained/

López, Yuri. "Gobierno decreta toque de queda, para aislar la pandemia". *Diario de Centro América*, 22 March 2020, https://dca.gob.gt/noticias-guatemala-diario-centro-america/gobierno-decreta-toque-de-queda-para-aislar-pandemia/

"MAGA recibe donación de semillas para apoyar a personas agricultroes ante la emergencia de la Covid-19". *Ministerio de Agricultura, Ganadería y Alimentación*, Gobierno de Guatemala, 5 June 2020, https://www.maga.gob.gt/maga-recibe-donacion-de-semillas-para-apoyar-a-personas-agricultoras-ante-la-emergencia-de-la-covid-19

Mazariegos Rivas, Ángel. "Por qué la Ivermectina no sustituye a la vacuna, como aseguró Giammattei". *Agencia Ocote*, 23 April 2023, https://www.agenci

aocote.com/blog/2021/04/23/por-que-la-ivermectina-no-sustituye-a-la-vacuna-como-aseguro-giammattei/

McNamara, James R. "Media Content Analysis: Its Uses, Benefits and Best Practice Methodology". *Asia Pacific Public Relations Journal*, vol. 6, no. 1, 2005, pp. 1–34.

Menchú, Sofía. "Guatemala Bans Entry of Europeans, Chinese, and Others to Keep Out Coronavirus". *Reuters*, 11 March 2020, https://www.reuters.com/article/us-health-coronavirus-guatemala-idUSKBN20Y2XF

—. "Nadie puede llorar a las víctimas de la pandemia". *No-ficcion.*, 1 June 2022, https://www.no-ficcion.com/project/olvidados-fallecidos-covid19

Mendoza, Carlos. "La pandemia en Guatemala: mortalidad y vacunas. ¿Cómo vamos?" *Diálogos*, 5 May 2021, https://www.dialogos.org.gt/blog/la-pandemia-en-guatemala-mortalidad-y-vacunas-como-vamos

"Mensaje del presidente Giammattei". *Ministerio de Gobernación*, Gobierno de Guatemala, 26 March 2020, https://mingob.gob.gt/mensaje-del-presidente-giammattei/

Minguez Canchaya, Lucia. "The Role of Covid-19 in Latin America's Democratic Erosion". *Democratic Erosion*, 13 January 2023, https://www.democratic-erosion.com/2023/01/12/the-role-of-covid-19-in-latin-americas-democratic-erosion/

Morales-Fransceschini, Eric. "Latin American Liberation Theology". *Global South Studies*, 9 May 2018, https://globalsouthstudies.as.virginia.edu/key-thinkers/latin-american-liberation-theology

Morales, Sergio. "Evangélicos ganan terreno en el país". *Prensa Libre*, 22 April 2014, https://www.prensalibre.com/guatemala/comunitario/evangelicos-ganan-terreno-pais-0-1124887528/

Najarro, Fátima. "Según Giammattei, los medios manipulan para imponer 'su agenda'". *La Hora*, 8 September 2022, https://lahora.gt/nacionales/fatima/2022/09/08/segun-giammattei-los-medios-manipulan-para-imponer-su-agenda/

—. "Giammattei, el presidente que no habla con la prensa". *La Hora*, 7 September 2022, https://lahora.gt/nacionales/fatima/2022/09/07/giammattei-el-presidente-que-no-habla-con-la-prensa/

Neuendorf, Kimberly A. *The Content Analysis Guidebook*. Sage, 2002.

Ng, Reuben, et al. "News Media Narratives of Covid-19 Across 20 Countries: Early Global Convergence and Later Regional Divergence". *PLoS ONE*, vol. 16, no. 9, 2021, pp. 1–12.

Office of International Religious Freedom. "2021 Report on International Freedom: Guatemala". *U.S. Department of State*, 2 June 2022, https://www.state.gov/reports/2021-report-on-international-religious-freedom/guatemala/

"Olla Comunitaria responsabiliza a Giammatte sobre los efectors que pueda caudar las nuevas restricciones". *Crónica*, 15 May 2020, https://cronica.com.gt/olla-comunitaria-responsabiliza-a-giammattei-sobre-los-efectos-que-pueda-caudar-los-nuevas-restricciones/

Olmstead, Gladys. "Banderas blancas: el nuevo código del hambre". *No-ficción*, 20 May 2020, https://www.no-ficcion.com/projects/banderas-blancas-codigo-de-hambre

Persson, Erik, et al. "'This is Just a Little Flu': Analysing Populist Discourses on the Covid-19 Pandemic in Brazil". *Public Policy Administration*, 30 November 2022, pp. 1–32.

"Polémica en Guatemala por eventual salida de médicos cubanos en medio de la pandemia". *France 24*, 28 August 2020, https://www.france24.com/es/20 200828-pol%C3%A9mica-en-guatemala-por-eventual-salida-de-m%C3%A9 dicos-cubanos-en-medio-de-pandemia.

Prensa Comunitaria Km169 [@PrensaComunitar]. "En apoyo a la Olla Comunitaria, un movimiento que está alimentando aproximadamente a 2000 personas diariamente en distintos lugares de Guatemala y El Salvador". *Twitter*, 29 June 2020, https://twitter.com/prensacomunitar/status/1277658324029317122.

Prensa Comunitaria. "Concierto en vivo en apoyo a la Olla Comunitaria". *Facebook*, 29 June 2020, https://www.facebook.com/Comunitaria.Prensa /posts/3113052182145933

"Presidente Giammattei anuncia más ayuda a hogares y empresas". *Diario de Centro América*, 13 April 2020, https://dca.gob.gt/noticias-guatemala-diario-centro-america/presidente-giammattei-anuncia-mas-ayuda-a-hogares-y-a-empresas/

"Protestas en Guatemala. 3 claves para entender las movilizaciones que acabaron con el Congreso en llamas". *BBC Mundo*, 23 November 2020, https://www.bbc.com/mundo/noticias-america-latina-55051500

Roman, Julio, and Carlos Kestler. "Médicos del Hospital Roosevelt presentan amparo contra Giammattei y la ministra Flores, por mal manejo de la pandemia y lanzan propuesta". *Prensa Libre*, 10 September 2021, https://ww w.prensalibre.com/guatemala/comunitario/medicos-del-hospital-roosevelt -presentan-amparo-contra-giammattei-y-la-ministra-flores-por-mal-manej o-de-la-pandemia-y-lanza-propuesta-breaking/

Seed Change. "Farming to keep her loved ones safe from hunger during the pandemic in Guatemala". *We Seed Change*, 9 November 2020, https://wesee dchange.org/farming-to-keep-her-loved-ones-safe-from-hunger-during-the -pandemic-in-guatemala/

Shanahan, James, and Michael Morgan. *Television and its Viewers: Cultivation Theory and Research*. Cambridge University Press, 2009.

Shrum, L.J. "Cultivation Theory: Effects and Underlying Processes". *The International Encyclopedia of Media Effects*, edited by Patrick Rossler, Wiley & Sons, 2017.

Social Panorama of Latin America 2018. Economic Commission for Latin America and the Caribbean, February 2019, https://www.cepal.org/en /publications/44396-social-panorama-latin-america-2018.

"Solicitan que se analice protocolo sanitario previo a abrir iglesias". *Congreso de la República*, 17 July 2020, https://www.congreso.gob.gt/noticias_congres o/4561/2020/2

Tufani, Alina. "Covid-19. Guatemala: La diócesis de Escuintla alerta el aumento de casos". *Vatican News*, 6 July 2020, https://www.vaticannews.va/es/iglesia /news/2020-07/covid-19-guatemala-llamado-diocesis-escuintla-nuevos-cas os.html

Vera, Asier, and Peter Álvarez. "Manifestantes queman el Congreso de Guatemala en una protesta contra la corrupción que exige que renuncie el presidente". *El*

Mundo, 22 November 2020, https://www.elmundo.es/internacional/2020/11/21/5fb98674fdddff46428b4676.html

Vrushi, Jon, and Roberto Martínez. "Why Fighting Corruption Matters in Times of Covid-19". *Transparency International*, 28 January 2021, https://www.transparency.org/en/news/cpi-2020-research-analysis-why-fighting-corruption-matters-in-times-of-covid-19

"Will Low-Income Countries Be Left Behind When Covid-19 Vaccines Arrive?" *Duke Global Health Institute*, 9 November 2020, https://globalhealth.duke.edu/news/will-low-income-countries-be-left-behind-when-Covid-19-vaccines-arrive.

World Bank in Guatemala: Overview. The World Bank, September 2020, https://www.worldbank.org/en/country/guatemala/overview Accessed 4 April 2023

Index

A

Abortion
  ILE, 92, 99
  IVE, xiv, xxx, 78, 92, 93, 94, 95, 96, 97, 98, 99, 100, 101, 102, 103, 104, 105, 106, 107, 108, 164, 186
Affect Theory, xx
  Affect, xx, xxi, xxxii, 2, 3, 7, 14, 15, 93, 101, 223
  Affective turn, 3
Allende, Salvador, 3, 4, 10, 11, 28, 38
Anti-vax, 205
Apocalypse, 175, 176
Argentina, xiv, xv, xxvii, xxviii, xxx, 92, 93, 94, 95, 107, 108, 109, 176, 202

B

Biomedicine, 112
Bolsonaro, Jair, xix, xxviii, 41, 43, 49, 52, 55, 62, 67, 219
Brazil, xiii, xix, xxvi, xxvii, xxxii, xxxiii, 20, 36, 41, 47, 48, 49, 50, 51, 52, 53, 54, 56, 57, 58, 59, 60, 61, 64, 70, 107, 219, 242
Buchui Plaza, Kakín, 125

C

Carrasco, Eduardo, 10, 11, 12
Chile, xii, xxvii, xxviii, xxx, xxxii, 1, 3, 4, 5, 6, 7, 8, 10, 11, 13, 14, 15, 16, 17, 18, 21, 22, 23, 24, 26, 27, 28, 30, 31, 32, 33, 34, 35, 36, 37, 38, 39, 112, 115, 125, 127, 129, 130, 202
Chilean New Song, xxviii, 3, 4, 5, 8, 9, 10, 11, 12, 13, 14
#Chiledespertó, 7
Chloroquine, 42, 48, 53, 54
Collective narratives, 218
Colombia, xiv, 36, 115, 172, 187, 233
Conquest, 174, 177, 178, 179, 180, 181, 182, 184, 186
Contreras, Gabriela, 128
Costa Rica, xxvii, xxx, 44, 68, 191, 192, 193, 194, 195, 196, 197, 201, 202, 203, 204, 205, 206, 207, 208, 209, 210, 211, 214
Covax, 22, 227
Covid-19 poetry, 112, 131
Critical discourse analysis
  CDA, 219

D

Dictatorship, xxviii, 1, 4, 7, 9, 10, 13, 14, 42
  Pinochet, Augusto, 4

E

Ecuador, xi, xii, xvii, xx, xxiii, xxvi, xxvii, xxix, xxxii, xxxiii, 155, 156, 157, 158, 159, 162, 163, 165, 166, 167
Emotional framing, 3, 5, 14, 15
Epidemiological narrative, 174, 176
Escobar, Pablo, 10
Exile, xiv, 4, 5, 10, 136

F

Fake news, 49, 51, 84
Feminicide, 85
Feminist activist, xiv, 92, 93, 96, 105, 107

G

Gardeneira, Diana, 156, 159
Gatica, Gustavo, 7, 11
Gender-based violence, ix, xxviii, 73, 76, 86, 113, 156, 162, 163, 164, 165
Giammattei, Alejandro, 218, 221, 222, 223, 224, 225, 226, 227, 228, 235, 238, 239, 240, 241, 242
Guatemala, xv, xxvii, xxx, 187, 217, 218, 220, 221, 222, 223, 224, 225, 228, 229, 230, 231, 232, 233, 234, 235, 236, 237, 238, 239, 240, 241, 242, 243
Guillermo Castillo, 224

H

Human rights, xiii, xv, 42, 44, 45, 46, 47, 49, 50, 115
Hydroxychloroquine, 46, 48, 53, 205

I

Illapu, 2, 3, 4, 5, 8, 9, 10, 11, 13, 14, 16
Inti-Illimani, 2, 10, 11, 16
Ivermectin, 48

J

Jara, Víctor, 4, 9, 11
Jimmy Morales, 235

L

López Obrador, Manuel, 46
Lula da Silva, Luiz Inácio, 42, 61

M

Mental health, xxiv, 200
Mexico, xiv, xv, xxvii, 36, 75, 146, 179, 180, 182, 188, 202, 230
Misinformation, xviii, xxxiii, 51, 193, 204, 205, 228
Misoprostol, 94, 98
Moreno, Lenin, 160, 161, 166

N

Neoliberalism, 56, 114
New normal, xxix, 156, 157, 158, 159, 164, 165
New Spain, xv, 171, 173, 175, 176, 177, 179, 181, 182, 183, 184, 185, 186

O

Obstetric violence, 93, 163, 164
olla comunitaria, 233, 234, 235

P

Pablo Chill-E, 2, 3, 10, 11, 12, 14, 16
Pandemic narrative, 169, 171, 172, 173, 174, 178, 185
Paris, Enrique, 25, 28
Parra, Violeta. *See* New Chilean Song
Peru, xiv, xx, xxvii, xxviii, xxx, 73, 74, 75, 76, 77, 78, 80, 81, 86, 88, 89, 111, 112, 115
Piñera, Sebastián, 2, 37
Populism, 20, 43, 54, 66, 219

Public health, xxiv, xxviii, xxxiii, 18, 19, 20, 21, 23, 24, 27, 28, 30, 31, 33, 34, 46, 51, 60, 94, 112, 114, 115, 116, 122, 123, 127, 157, 162, 193, 194, 195, 196, 197, 198, 199, 200, 202, 214, 219, 220, 221, 224, 226, 227, 230, 232, 233, 234, 235, 236

Q

Quilapayún, 2, 10, 11, 12, 13, 16

R

Regimes of subjectivity, 159
Román Marroquín, Valeria, 116

S

Salas, Daniel, 194, 195, 209
Sanitary citizenship, 113, 114, 115, 116, 117, 121, 123, 124, 127, 130, 131
SenRed, 92, 93, 96, 97, 98, 99, 100, 101, 102, 103, 104, 105, 106
Sepúlveda, Jesús, 130
Sexual violence, 73, 75, 77, 78, 79, 82, 163
Siches, Izkia, 26, 29, 38
Social isolation, 56, 138, 139, 141, 172, 187
Social media, xvii, xviii, xix, 46, 75, 136, 156, 169, 175, 194, 204, 205, 222, 225, 226, 227, 228, 230, 231, 233, 234, 235, 236, 237
Structural violence, 161, 162

U

Utopia, 124, 125, 128, 129, 130, 142

V

Vaccine, xxviii, 18, 19, 20, 22, 23, 24, 26, 27, 28, 30, 31, 32, 33, 34, 48, 51, 52, 122, 136, 202, 203, 204, 205, 206, 207, 213, 224, 230, 232, 237
  AstraZeneca, 22
  Moderna, 205
  Pfizer, 22, 24, 27, 29, 30, 31, 35, 37, 38, 47, 48, 53, 69, 205
  Sinovac, 22, 23, 24, 27, 29, 30, 31, 34, 35, 36
Vaccine tourism, 26, 203, 205, 206
Venezuela, xiv, xxvii, xxix, 46, 136, 137, 138, 139, 140, 144, 145, 146, 148, 149, 150, 152

W

Women's writing, 135, 136, 137
World Health Organisation
  WHO, x, xviii, 157, 165

Y

Yonofui, 113, 114, 133

Z

Zoriano Arias
  El Monstruo de Chontalí, 81, 82, 84

www.ingramcontent.com/pod-product-compliance
Ingram Content Group UK Ltd.
Pitfield, Milton Keynes, MK11 3LW, UK
UKHW032212171224
452513UK00010B/617